EARLY MUSIC HISTORY 10

EDITORIAL BOARD

EARLY MUSIC HISTORY 10

STUDIES IN MEDIEVAL
AND
EARLY MODERN MUSIC

Edited by

IAIN FENLON
Fellow of King's College, Cambridge

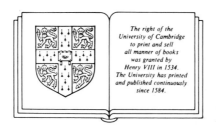

The right of the
University of Cambridge
to print and sell
all manner of books
was granted by
Henry VIII in 1534.
The University has printed
and published continuously
since 1584.

CAMBRIDGE UNIVERSITY PRESS

Cambridge

New York *Port Chester* *Melbourne* *Sydney*

Published by the Press Syndicate of the University of Cambridge
The Pitt Building, Trumpington Street, Cambridge CB2 1RP
40 West 20th Street, New York, NY 10011–4211, USA
10 Stamford Road, Oakleigh, Melbourne 3166, Australia

First published 1991

Phototypeset in Baskerville by Wyvern Typesetting Ltd, Bristol
Music examples originated by The Stingray Office, Oxford
Printed in Great Britain at the University Press, Cambridge

ISSN 0261–1279

ISBN 0 521 40354 5

SUBSCRIPTIONS The subscription price to volume 10, which includes postage, is
£39.00 (US $75.00 in USA and Canada) for institutions, £25.00 (US $42.00 in
USA and Canada) for individuals ordering direct from the Press and certifying
that the annual is for their personal use. Airmail (orders to Cambridge only) £8.00
extra. Copies of the annual for subscribers in the USA and Canada are sent by air
to New York to arrive with minimum delay. Orders, which must be accompanied
by payment, may be sent to a bookseller, subscription agent or direct to the
publishers: Cambridge University Press, The Edinburgh Building, Shaftesbury
Road, Cambridge CB2 2RU. Payment may be made by any of the following
methods: cheque (payable to Cambridge University Press), UK postal order,
bank draft, Post Office Giro (account no. 571 6055 GB Bootle – advise CUP of
payment), international money order, UNESCO coupons, or any credit card
bearing the Interbank symbol. Orders from the USA and Canada should be sent
to Cambridge University Press, 40 West 20th Street, New York, NY 10011–4211.

BACK VOLUMES Volumes 1–9 are available from the publisher at £34.00 ($75.00
in USA and Canada).

NOTE Each volume of *Early Music History* is now published in the year in which it is
subscribed. Volume 10 is therefore published in 1991. Readers should be aware,
however, that some earlier volumes have been subscribed in the year *after* the
copyright and publication date given on this imprints page. Thus volume 8, the
volume received by 1989 subscribers, is dated 1988 on the imprints page.

CONTENTS

v

REVIEW

NOTES FOR CONTRIBUTORS

PRESENTATION

Contributors should write in English, or be willing to have their articles translated. All typescripts must be double spaced *throughout*, including footnotes, bibliographies, annotated lists of manuscripts, appendixes, tables and displayed quotations. Margins should be at least 2.5 cm (1″). The 'top' (ribbon) copy of the typescript must be supplied. Scripts submitted for consideration will not normally be returned unless specifically requested.

Artwork for graphs, diagrams and music examples should be, wherever possible, submitted in a form suitable for direct reproduction, bearing in mind the maximum dimensions of the printed version: 17.5 × 11 cm (7″ × 4.5″). Photographs should be in the form of glossy black and white prints, measuring about 20.3 × 15.2 cm (8″ × 6″).

All illustrations should be on separate sheets from the text of the article and should be clearly identified with the contributor's name and the figure/example number. Their approximate position in the text should be indicated by a marginal note in the typescript. Captions should be separately typed, double spaced.

Tables should also be supplied on separate sheets, with the title typed above the body of the table.

SPELLING

English spelling, idiom and terminology should be used, e.g. bar (not measure), note (not tone), quaver (not eighth note). Where there is an option, '-ise' endings should be preferred to '-ize'.

PUNCTUATION

English punctuation practice should be followed: (1) single quotation marks, except for 'a "quote" within a quote'; (2) punctuation outside quotation marks, unless a complete sentence is quoted; (3) no comma before 'and' in a series; (4) footnote indicators follow punctuation; (5) square brackets [ ] only for interpolation in quoted matter; (6) no stop after contractions that include the last letter of a word, e.g. Dr, St, edn (but vol. and vols.).

BIBLIOGRAPHICAL REFERENCES

Authors' and editors' forenames should not be given, only initials; where possible, editors should be given for Festschriften, conference proceedings, symposia, etc. In titles, all important words in English should be capitalised; all other languages should follow prose-style capitalisation, except for journal and series titles which should follow English capitalisation. Titles of series should be included, in roman, where relevant. Journal and series volume numbers should be given in arabic, volumes of a set in roman ('vol.' will not be used). Places and dates of publication should be included but not publishers' names. Dissertation titles should be given in roman and enclosed in quotation marks. Page numbers should be preceded by 'p.' or 'pp.' in all contexts. The first citation of a bibliographical reference should include full details; subsequent citations may use the author's surname, short title and relevant page numbers only. *Ibid.* may be used, but not *op. cit.* or *loc. cit.*

ABBREVIATIONS

Abbreviations for manuscript citations, libraries, periodicals, series, etc. should not be used without explanation; after the first full citation an abbreviation may be used throughout text and notes. Standard abbreviations may be used without explanation. In the text, 'Example', 'Figure' and 'bars' should be used (not 'Ex.', 'Fig.', 'bb.'). In references to manuscripts, 'fols.' should be used (not 'ff.') and 'v' (verso) and 'r' (recto) should be typed superscript. The word for 'saint' should be spelled out or abbreviated according to language, e.g. San Andrea, S. Maria, SS. Pietro e Paolo, St Paul, St Agnes, St Denis, Ste Clothilde.

NOTE NAMES

Flats, sharps and naturals should be indicated by the conventional signs, not words. Note names should be roman and capitalised where general, e.g. C major, but should be italic and follow the Helmholtz code where specific ($C_{,,}$ $C,$ $C\,c\,c'$ c'' c'''; c' = middle C). A simpler system may be used in discussions of repertories (e.g. chant) where different conventions are followed.

QUOTATIONS

A quotation of no more than 60 words of prose or one line of verse should be continuous within the text and enclosed in single quotation marks. Longer quotations should be displayed and quotation marks should not be used. For quotations from foreign languages, an English translation must be given in addition to the foreign-language original.

NUMBERS

Numbers below 100 should be spelled out, except page, bar, folio numbers etc., sums of money and specific quantities, e.g. 20 ducats, 45 mm. Pairs of numbers should be elided as follows: 190–1, 198–9, 198–201, 212–13. Dates should be given in the following forms: 10 January 1983, the 1980s, sixteenth century (16th century in tables and lists), sixteenth-century polyphony.

CAPITALISATION

Incipits in all language (motets, songs, etc.), and titles except in English, should be capitalised as in running prose; titles in English should have all important words capitalised, e.g. *The Pavin of Delight*. Most offices should have a lower-case initial except in official titles, e.g. 'the Lord Chancellor entered the cathedral', 'the Bishop of Salford entered the cathedral' (but 'the bishop entered the cathedral'). Names of institutions should have full (not prose-style) capitalisation, e.g. Liceo Musicale.

ITALICS

Titles and incipits of musical works in italic, but not genre titles or sections of the Mass/English Service, e.g. Kyrie, Magnificat. Italics for foreign words should be kept to a minimum; in general they should be used only for unusual words or if a word might be mistaken for English if not italicised. Titles of manuscripts should be roman in quotes, e.g. 'Rules How to Compose'. Names of institutions should be roman.

AUTHORS' CORRECTIONS

It is assumed that typescripts received for publication are in their final form. There may be an opportunity to make minor emendations at the copy-editing stage, but corrections in proof *must* be restricted to printer's and publisher's errors. Any departure from this practice will be at the discretion of the editor and the publisher, and authors may be subject to charge.

Early Music History (1991) Volume 10

KEVIN BROWNLEE

MACHAUT'S MOTET 15 AND THE *ROMAN DE LA ROSE*: THE LITERARY CONTEXT OF *AMOURS QUI A LE POUOIR/FAUS SAMBLANT M'A DECEÜ/VIDI DOMINUM*

Guillaume de Machaut's motet no. 15 is structured, from a literary point of view, around an opposition fundamental to the late medieval courtly tradition: that between two key personification characters, Amours and Faux Semblant. This opposition is introduced as the first words of the triplum ('Amours qui a le pouoir') are sung against those of the motetus ('Faus Samblant m'a deceü').

In the present essay I propose, first and foremost, to consider the broader literary context provided for the Amours–Faux Semblant opposition in motet 15 by the *Roman de la rose*, the French vernacular literary work that served as the point of departure for virtually all late medieval courtly poetry. I shall then turn to a second kind of context for the words of the motet, that provided by the text of the tenor. The more general literary phenomenon to be investigated, therefore, involves the ways in which the meaning of a particular lyric, or lyrico-musical, composition is in part determined, 'conditioned' by a variety of narrative contexts which constitute the tradition in which it is situated, against which it is meant to be read.[1]

---

* An earlier version of this essay was given at a colloquium on 'The Gothic Motet: Politics, Words and Music in the Fourteenth Century', held at Princeton University on 22 October 1989. I should like to thank Margaret Bent for having invited me to participate in the colloquium and for her subsequent helpful critical comments.

[1] In the case of the *Rose*, therefore, I am not positing a precise intertextual dependence of motet 15 on the Amours–Faux Semblant sequence in Jean de Meun's poem. I am, rather, viewing this sequence as a central determining factor for the way in which the subsequent mainstream tradition of courtly poetry in late medieval France conceived of

1

Before proceeding to the motet's context, I shall first undertake a brief structural analysis. The full text of the motet is as follows:[2]

Triplum

Amours qui a le pouoir
De moy faire recevoir
  Joie ou mort obscure,
Ne fait par sa grace avoir
5 A ma dame tel voloir
  Qu'elle m'ait en cure.
Durer ne puis longuement,
Car pour amer loiaument
Ne pour servir liement,
10 Sans penser laidure,
Ne pour celer sagement
N'ay confort n'aligement
  De ma dolour dure;
Einsois com plus humblement
15 La sueffre et endure,
De tant est plus durement
Traitiés mes cuers, que briefment
Morray dolereusement
  De dueil et d'ardure,
20 Et tant sui plus eslongiés
De merci et estraingiés
  De ma dame pure.
Mais aveuc tous ces meschiés
Sueffre Amours, qui est mes chiés,
25 Que Raison, Droiture,
Douçour, Debonnaireté,
Franchise, Grace et Pité
N'ont pouoir à Cruauté,
  Ensois regne et dure
30 En corps d'umblece paré
Cuers qui est pleins de durté
  Et de couverture,
Refus qui d'espoir osté
  M'a la norriture,

Motetus

Faus Samblant m'a deceü
Et tenu en esperance
  De joie merci avoir;
Et je l'ay com fols creü
5 Et mis toute ma fiance
  En li d'amoureus vouloir.
Las! or m'a descongneü,
Quant de moy faire aligence
  Ha heü temps et pooir;
10 N'en riens n'a recongneü
Ma dolour ne ma grevance,
  Eins m'a mis en nonchaloir.

Tenor

Vidi dominum facie ad faciem
[et salva facta est anima mea.]

---

the Amours–Faux Semblant relationship in terms of linguistic and behavioural conventions. The *Rose*'s unique position of literary dominance vis-à-vis that tradition in general and Machaut's courtly œuvre in particular amply justify this view. See D. Poirion, *Le poète et le prince: L'évolution du lyrisme courtois de Guillaume de Machaut à Charles d'Orléans* (Paris, 1965); P.-Y. Badel, *Le 'Roman de la rose' au XIVe siècle: Etude de la réception de l'œuvre* (Geneva, 1980); K. Brownlee, *Poetic Identity in Guillaume de Machaut* (Madison, 1984).

[2] Quoted from V. Chichmaref, ed., *Guillaume de Machaut: poésies lyriques*, 2 vols. (Paris, 1909), modified by F. Ludwig, ed., *Guillaume de Machaut: Musikalische Werke*, 4 vols. (Leipzig, 1926–54). Translations are mine.

35 Et Dangiers qui despité
    M'a sans cause et si grevé
    Qu'il m'a par desdaing mené
      A desconfiture.

Triplum: 'Amours qui a . . .' (vv. 1–38): Love, who has the power to make
me receive either joy or dark death, does not, through his grace, give my
lady the desire to care for me (vv. 1–6). I cannot last for long, because
neither from loyal loving, nor from gracious serving (without an ugly
thought), nor from discreet concealing, do I have comfort or relief from
my harsh pain (vv. 7–13). Rather, the more humbly I suffer and endure it,
the more harshly is my heart treated, so that I shall shortly die of grief and
burning desire, and the farther I am removed from favour and the more I
am distanced from my pure lady (vv. 14–22). But with all these mis-
fortunes, Love (who is my lord) allows Reason, Equity, Sweetness, Good
Nature, Openness, Grace and Pity to have no power against Cruelty (vv.
23–8); Instead, there reigns continuously in a body adorned with humility
a Heart which is completely hard and closed, Refusal who has taken the
food of hope away from me, and Resistance who has spurned me without
cause and has so injured me that he has led me, through disdain, to my
ruin (vv. 29–38).

Motetus: 'Faus Samblant m'a . . .' (vv. 1–12): False Seeming has deceived
me and has held out the joyful hope of my obtaining favour. And I like a
fool believed him, and put all the trust of my loving desire in him. Alas!
now he has undeceived me, after having had the time and the power to
win my allegiance; In no way has he rewarded my pain and my suffering,
rather he has treated me badly.

Tenor: 'Vidi dominum': I have seen the Lord face to face; and my life is
preserved.

The triplum and the motetus involve contrasting self-presentations of the speaking subject, who is, in both cases, a standard
male courtly lyric *je*, articulating a conventional complaint against
the object of his desire, i.e. that she remains unmoved by him in
spite of the intense suffering his love for her causes him. In neither
case does he address his lady directly, however. Rather, he tells two
different stories, or two different versions of the same story, of his
unrequited love, each involving a different self-presentation. In the
triplum, the speaking subject presents himself as a loyal servant of
Amours 'who is my lord' ('qui est mes chiés', v. 24). Love has the
power to reward his servant by moving the lady in his favour, but
he has, so far, refrained from doing so. In the motetus, there is a
contrastive self-presentation of the speaking subject as an unwitting

victim of Faux Semblant, who has purposefully and successfully deceived him (by means of his lady's appearance), before openly revealing this deception. To sum up: the lyric *je* of the triplum has been moved by Love, who does not act upon the 'inside' of the Lady; the lyric *je* of the motetus has been deceived by False Seeming, who has acted by means of the 'outside' of the Lady.[3] The opposition between these two contrasting self-presentations is a 'dialogic' one in the Bakhtinian sense of the term, i.e. the two apparently contradictory terms are mutually defining, at the same time as they seem to be mutually exclusive.[4] The generic form of the motet is, of course, particularly appropriate to this kind of dialogic opposition, and thus, as we shall see, to the Amours/Faux Semblant interrelationship as figured in the *Roman de la rose*.

In this context, I should like to mention Sylvia Huot's recent literary study of thirteenth-century French motets (from the Montpellier codex) from the standpoint of 'multi-voicedness'. Huot explores how the thirteenth-century motet as a literary genre exploited its formal features (especially 'simultaneity', as discussed by Margaret Bent[5]) in favour of dialogism, in particular, to dramatise the oppositions between the various registers (including generic conventions) for articulating desire in the thirteenth-century French literary system.[6]

Before turning to the *Rose* in the context of motet 15, I want to stress the extraordinary degree to which Machaut's literary œuvre as a whole is informed by this work: not only does he utilise the *Rose*

---

[3] For an analysis of the semantic and formal interplay between the voices in another of Machaut's motets, see L. Wright, 'Verbal Counterpoint in Machaut's Motet *Trop plus est belle – Biaute paree de valour – Je ne sui mie*', *Romance Studies*, 7 (1985–6), pp. 1–11.

[4] See the lucid presentation by T. Todorov in his *Mikhail Bakhtin: The Dialogical Principle*, trans. W. Godzich (Minneapolis, 1984), especially ch. 4, 'Theory of the Utterance', pp. 41–59. See also M. M. Bakhtin, 'Discourse in the Novel', *The Dialogic Imagination: Four Essays*, trans. C. Emerson and M. Holquist (Austin, 1981), pp. 259–422; and D. Carroll, 'The Alterity of Discourse: Form, History, and the Question of the Political in M. M. Bakhtin', *Diacritics*, 13/2 (1983), pp. 65–83. It should be added that Bakhtin's own views of literary history led him in large part to neglect medieval literature, which in fact provides a particularly fertile field for interpretative analysis from a Bakhtinian viewpoint. An excellent recent example is C. Segre, 'What Bakhtin Left Unsaid: The Case for the Medieval Romance', *Romance: Generic Transformation from Chrétien de Troyes to Cervantes*, ed. K. Brownlee and M. S. Brownlee (Hanover, NH, and London, 1985), pp. 23–46.

[5] See M. Bent, 'The Late-Medieval Motet', *The Everyman Companion to Medieval and Renaissance Music*, ed. D. Fallows and T. Knighton (forthcoming).

[6] See 'Polyphonic Poetry: The Old French Motet and its Literary Context', *French Forum*, 14 (1989), pp. 261–78, where Huot analyses the role of generic and codicological context for the literary interpretation of thirteenth-century French motets.

as a source of poetic constructs at every level; he also situates his œuvre as a whole in relation to the *Rose*, which thus provides a very important kind of authorisation for Machaut's entire literary enterprise. The *Prologue* is, of course, particularly important in this respect.[7]

The centre of the *Roman de la rose* is, in several significant ways, structured around the opposition between Amours and Faux Semblant – an opposition that is also 'dialogic' in that it involves contrary but mutually defining terms which end by 'contaminating' each other. This takes place at a variety of levels. At the level of plot, the characters Amours and Faux Semblant engage in an extended dialogue, which ends with Faux Semblant being accepted into the army of the god of love. At the level of language, Amours embodies courtly discourse, which is meant to be both elegant and sincere, while Faux Semblant's discourse is largely clerkly – even theological – as well as fundamentally deceptive. In terms of mode and authority Amours stands for, and explains, lyric, while Faux Semblant introduces (contemporary) history into the plot line of the poem for the first time. Let us consider this sequence in some detail.

Near the midpoint of the conjoined *Rose* text, the Dieus d'Amours appears to Amant and reproaches him with having been too changeable ('muables', v. 10325)[8] in the service of Love, with having desired to leave this service on account of the hardships suffered in his thus far unsuccessful love of the Rose. Amant confesses and repents of his fault, begging pardon and readmittance to Love's service, which Amours grants after making Amant repeat the 'ten commandments of love', the essential code of courtly speech and behaviour (vv. 10403–12). Having affirmed that Amant now serves him very loyally ('leiaument', v. 10433), Amours promises to help him win the Rose, and summons his troops in order to lay siege to the castle which prevents Amant from reaching his beloved.

It is in answer to this summons that Faux Semblant[9] the charac-

---

[7] See Brownlee, *Poetic Identity*, pp. 16–20.
[8] Citations are from E. Langlois, ed., *Le Roman de la rose par Guillaume de Lorris et Jean de Meun*, 5 vols. (Paris, 1914–24).
[9] For a detailed consideration, see K. Brownlee, 'The Problem of Faux Semblant: Language, History and Truth in the *Roman de la rose*', *The New Medievalism*, ed. K. Brownlee, M. S. Brownlee and S. Nichols (Baltimore, forthcoming).

5

ter appears in the *Rose* for the first time, provoking a quite compre-hensible shock and surprise on behalf of Amours, for the courtly linguistic and behavioural system which he embodies excludes, by definition, False Seeming. The implications of this contradiction are temporarily set aside as Amours first addresses his 'legitimate' assembled barons in the famous speech (vv. 10495–678) in which the god of love authorises Jean de Meun's continuation of Guil-laume de Lorris's poem in terms of the first-person lyric mode and the poetic tradition of courtly discourse.[10] Love ends his speech with a double request of his barons: that Guillaume qua lover-protagonist be helped in his quest to win the rose and that Jean qua poet-narrator be helped in *his* 'quest' to *write* the romance. In their affirmative reply, his barons beg the god of love to give over his anger against Faux Semblant and to consider him as one of their number (their 'baronie', v. 10925). It is this request and Amours's immediate agreement that introduce Faux Semblant into the poem directly, speaking in his own voice.

Faux Semblant's long speech (vv. 10931–12014; 1084 lines) is actually an extended dialogue with the god of love. The dialogic structure of Faux Semblant's self-presentation constitutes an essen-tial and unique part of his identity. None of the other major 'discur-sive' characters in the poem (Raison, Ami, La Vieille, Nature, Genius) involves this kind (or this degree) of dialogue. In a very real sense, Faux Semblant is presented as a 'function' of his inter-locutor: the god of love himself. This has important implications for both characters. Two dialogic models are simultaneously at issue: (1) the scholastic examination and (2) the personal confession. Two discursive modes are thus simultaneously – and paradoxically – operative: (1) the new dialectic mode of late thirteenth-century philosophical debate, associated with the Dominicans, and (2) the new self-revelatory mode of late thirteenth-century spiritual narra-tive, associated with the Franciscans.

The dialogue between Love and Faux Semblant involves a series of seven questions posed by Love, who thus plays the role of examiner-confessor. Faux Semblant's seven answers constitute, on

---

[10] On the god of love's speech, see K. D. Uitti, 'From *Clerc* to *Poète*: The Relevance of the *Romance of the Rose* to Machaut's World', *Machaut's World: Science and Art in the Fourteenth Century*, ed. M. P. Cosman and B. Chandler, *Annals of the New York Academy of Sciences*, 314 (1978), pp. 209–16.

the one hand, a penetrating and polemical discussion of certain doctrinal matters in the context of contemporary practices and abuses, in particular poverty, abstinence and mendicancy. On the other hand, Faux Semblant's answers involve an extended self-definition as character and as language. As character, Faux Semblant is a kind of archetypal religious hypocrite whose disguise is the role of a mendicant friar. As language, he embodies a radical detachment of sign from referent, a systematically duplicitous discourse which is ungrounded in, unguaranteed by, any extra-linguistic or transcendent 'truth'.

Let us now turn to a brief schematic consideration of the dialogue between Love and False Seeming in structural and in thematic terms. As will be seen, an overall pattern of shifting is involved in the relations between questions and answers, as well as in the identities of the two interlocutors. This is because the status of the 'truth' that emerges from the dialogue is a function of the evolving speech situation, which is dramatised as such. In linguistic terms, there is a continual shifting of appropriateness conditions; the cooperative principle is repeatedly 'redefined' in order for the dialogue to continue.[11]

Love's first set of questions (vv. 10943–51) is posed on behalf of the assembled host and involves the issue of semiotic recognition: by what signs can Faux Semblant be known and in what places can he be found? Faux Semblant's answer (vv. 10952–83) involves a systematic evasion: He has 'mansions diverses' (v. 10952) which he cannot reveal in detail because of his fear of his companions who want their whereabouts to be kept a secret.

Love's second set of questions (vv. 10984–98) repeats and elaborates the first set, stressing that Faux Semblant must now tell the truth because he is one of Love's barons. The emphasis is on revelation, on the uncovering of what is normally hidden. Love demands that Faux Semblant name his various 'mansions' and that he explain his mode of life. Faux Semblant's reply (vv. 10999–11082) introduces the motif of clothing as disguise in a context in

---

[11] For an extremely useful treatment of appropriateness conditions and of the cooperative principle in the context of literary analysis see M. L. Pratt, *Toward a Speech Act Theory of Literary Discourse* (Bloomington, 1977), pp. 81–91, 125–32, 214–23. See also H. P. Grice, 'Logic and Conversation', *Syntax and Semantics*, III: *Speech Acts*, ed. P. Cole and J. L. Morgan (New York, 1975), pp. 41–58.

which seeming and being are radically separated. Clothing as sign is presented as fundamentally unreliable in a religious context. Both Faux Semblant's clothes and his words deceive qua signs.

Love's third question (vv. 11083–90) involves the reverse side of the sign/referent dichotomy in the context of religious clothing. Love asks if one can find true religious faith in secular clothes. Faux Semblant's reply (vv. 11091–222) begins by affirming that clothing as sign is not reliable in this direction either. He then goes on to characterise his own identity as an infinitely expandable series of disguises which involves the effective nullification of social, age and gender distinctions, through the manipulation both of language (vv. 11194–5) and of clothing, most especially in the context of religion.[12]

Love's fourth question (vv. 11223–37) is an elaboration: 'Di nous plus especiaument/Coment tu serz desleiaument' (vv. 11227–9; 'tell us more especially in what way you serve disloyally'). Appearance and reality, word and deed, sign and referent are contrasted in three related ways. Then, having once again affirmed the disjunction between sign and referent in terms of his purely external devotion to poverty, Faux Semblant launches into an extended discussion of the Bible's treatment of the subject of mendicancy.[13] It is important to note that here Faux Semblant speaks the 'truth'. His biblical interpretations are valid.

Love's fifth set of questions (vv. 11407–13) involves an important elaboration of these theological and exegetical concerns as he asks when a sincere religious vocation can legitimately include begging. Significantly, Love's questions here presuppose a truthful interlocutor, and Faux Semblant's fifth answer (vv. 11414–524) is in accord with this presupposition. In a significant shift of position Faux Semblant himself bears witness to theological truth, then

---

[12]   Faux Semblant concludes with a somewhat paradoxical self-revelation (vv. 11219–22):
      . . . En tele guise
      Come il me plaist je me desguise.
      Mout est en mei muez li vers,
      Mout sont li fait aus diz divers.
  ('I disguise myself in whatever way pleases me. I'm not what I seem to be; my acts are very different from my words.')

[13]   The primary focus is on the Gospels and St Paul (Luke 18: 20; 1 Cor. 11: 29; 2 Cor. 8: 9; and 1 Thess. 4: 11–12) as Faux Semblant interprets the New Testament to mean that begging was systematically prohibited for Christ and the Apostles.

shifts back 'into character' as he describes the threats posed by this truth to his own way of life as a hypocritical mendicant.

There is a corresponding shift in Amours's position as interlocutor when he poses his sixth set of questions, for he reacts only to what Faux Semblant has turned back into, expressing shock at the latter's 'granz desleiautez apertes' (v. 11527; 'great and open disloyalty') and asking: 'Don ne crains tu pas Deu?' (v. 11528; 'Don't you fear God, then?') Faux Semblant's sixth answer (vv. 11528–618) begins with an extensive self-revelation, in which his activities as deceiver and hypocrite are described in detail. Next, Faux Semblant again shifts perspective, as he turns to a discussion of how these deceiving criminals ('felons', v. 11599) can be recognised ('aperceivre', v. 11599). What is at issue is once again the status of signs and the question of how to 'read', how to interpret them correctly. It is thus highly significant that Faux Semblant's response is to turn to the one text whose signs never deceive: the Bible. For he launches into a detailed paraphrase and gloss of Matthew 23: 2–4, the *locus classicus* for the subject of hypocrisy.

It is in the midst of this sequence of biblical exegesis that Love asks his seventh and final question (v. 11619), a brief and specific query about the meaning of Matthew 23: 4. At this point in their dialogue, Love plays the role of student to Faux Semblant as master exegete. Once again, the shifting appropriateness conditions operative in this sequence of the *Rose*'s diegetic speech situation implicitly present Faux Semblant as a locus of truthful discourse. Faux Semblant's seventh answer' (vv. 11619–976) begins by confirming this status, as he finishes the gloss on Matthew 23: 4–8 with exemplary Christian exegetical insight. What follows is another abrupt shift in perspective, as Faux Semblant resumes his 'mendacious identity' in order to make further disclosures concerning his deceitful activities as a religious hypocrite whose words and dress belie his true nature. It is important to note that repeated shifts in perspective occur quite frequently throughout this section, as Faux Semblant alternately praises and condemns the code of hypocrisy, adopting in turn the viewpoint of Antichrist and the viewpoint of God. Faux Semblant ends with an explicit articulation of the inherently ambiguous nature of his discursive practice. There is by definition no external guarantee for the truth of what he says. And

Kevin Brownlee

the problem of credibility is placed entirely with the receiver of his discourse.[14]

This problematic is, as it were, dramatised in the scene immediately following, as the god of love 'officially' takes Faux Semblant into his service, now that their interrogation cum dialogue is over. In response to Love's question: 'Me tendras tu ma couvenance?' (v. 11985; 'Will you keep your agreement with me?'), Faux Semblant gives an emphatically affirmative answer, but because of his nature as speaking subject, all of his words are by definition untrustworthy. Love is thus obliged to question the validity of the very words he most desires to hear. Faux Semblant responds by saying, in effect, that no extra-linguistic guarantee is possible for his discourse.[15] Yet this is not tantamount to characterising it as consistently mendacious. Rather, Faux Semblant's discursive practice is fundamentally and radically ambiguous with regard to 'truth', for if on the one hand it is self-defined as a string of empty signifiers detached from any referent, it is also capable of articulating historical and religious truths of the greatest import, as his dialogue with Amours has shown. Love is thus obliged to accept Faux Semblant into his army on the only terms possible: 'Or seit, je t'en crei senz plevir' (v. 12010; 'So be it, I believe you without guarantee').

By this point in the text, the figure of Faux Semblant has emerged as a kind of emblem of multi-voicedness. At the most obvious level, this ostensibly unified speaking subject involves a

[14] In light of this kind of repeated interpretative 'instability' that is built into Faux Semblant's discourse at every level, it is fitting that he conclude by focusing explicitly on the truth status of his discourse in the context of this specific speech situation (vv. 11969–76):

> Mais a vous n'ose je mentir;
> Mais se je peüsse sentir
> Que vous ne l'aperceüssiez,
> La mençonge ou poing eüssiez;
> Certainement je vous boulasse,
> Ja pour pechié ne le laissasse;
> Si vous pourrai je bien faillir
> S'ous m'en deviez mal baillir.

('But to you I dare not lie. However, if I could feel that you would not recognise it, you would have a lie in hand. Certainly I would have tricked you, and I would never have held back on account of any sin. And I will indeed betray you even if you treat me badly for it.')

[15] Faux Semblant's precise words to the god of love at this juncture are particularly suggestive: 'Metez vous en en aventure, / car, se pleges en requerez, / ja plus asseür n'en serez, / non veir se j'en baillie ostages, / ou letres, ou tesmoinz, ou gages' (vv. 11990–4); 'Take your chances on it, for if you demand pledges, you will never be more sure, in fact, not even if I gave hostages, letters, witnesses, or security').

10

series of conflicting voices which are repeatedly played off against each other.[16] Furthermore, Faux Semblant's polyphonic discourse cannot be effectively interpreted (or judged) from an internal point of view. This is perhaps most obvious with regard to the complex question of the 'truth content' of what Faux Semblant says as related to the constantly shifting voices and perspectives that constitute his speech. In terms of discourse analysis, the 'truth' of Faux Semblant's language is a function of context, of the (diegetic) speech situation, which is itself also changing constantly. For the relationship between Faux Semblant and Amours as interlocutors is profoundly dialogic. Multiple viewpoints are built into both speaker and addressee, in such a way as to give an inescapable 'doubleness' to their individual utterances in relation to a temporally evolving speech situation which alone confers meaning upon the characters' discourse.[17]

The net result of all this is that both the narrative context in which Faux Semblant appears and the dialogic structure of his extended speech link him to the god of love. In addition, a number of suggestive parallels are established between the discourse of Amours and that of Faux Semblant. Furthermore, within the plot line of the *Roman de la rose*, the help of the character Faux Semblant is essential to the successful storming of Jealousy's castle (vv. 12033–533), and thus to the taking of the Rose, i.e. to the ultimate success of Amours's endeavour to help Amant.[18]

---

[16] The voice of the hypocritical friar (linked to the generic discourse of the *fabliau* and the *Roman de Renart*); the voice of the biblical exegete and moralising social critic (linked to the persona of Guillaume de Saint-Amour and, to a somewhat lesser degree, to the anti-courtly sub-genre of trouvère political satire as exemplified by Rutebeuf); the voice of the radical Joachite prophet (linked most specifically to the *Evangile pardurable*).

[17] In order to account for this kind of complexity in a literary context which foregrounds and thematises the speech situation as such, a powerful interpretative tool is provided by Oswald Ducrot's revisionist 'theatrical' model of a fundamentally 'polyphonic' speech act, as described in 'Esquisse d'une théorie polyphonique de l'énonciation', *Le dire et le dit* (Paris, 1984), pp. 171–233.

[18] Furthermore, when Amant finally enters the castle under the guidance of La Vieille, he finds Amours together with Faux Semblant and goes so far as to pray for the latter out of gratitude for his help in advancing Amant's love suit. False Seeming has been his essential ally (vv. 14748–52):

> Si pri pour aus, vaille que vaille.
> Seigneur, qui veaut traïtres estre,
> Face de Faus Semblant son maistre,
> E Contrainte Astenance preigne:
> Doubles seit e simple se feigne.

('Therefore I pray for them [=False Seeming and his consort Constrained Abstinence], for whatever that is worth. My lords, he who wants to be a traitor should make False

All of this is relevant in terms of the narrative context for Machaut's motet 15. What is suggested by the motet and reinforced by this narrative context is that the language of Amours and the language of Faux Semblant, though superficially different, are part of the same system: the fallen linguistic world of appearances, of seeming, in which courtly discourse – the language of erotic love – is 'ungrounded', as it were, by definition. That is, its truth value remains elusive, and detached from its beauty or its rhetorical power. 'Sincerity' is impossible to determine on the basis of courtly discourse, which takes place in a context in which language is deceptive, in which there is a gap between linguistic seeming and being.

This problematic of courtly discourse (of the language of desire) is a recurrent theme in Machaut's lyrico-narrative *dits amoureux*, in particular the *Voir-dit* and the *Remede de Fortune*. Both of these first-person love stories conclude by casting doubt upon the truth or 'sincerity' of the courtly *dame*'s language: her declaration of love and her denial of infidelity.[19]

On the one hand, it should be emphasised that Machaut's treat-

Seeming his master and take Constrained Abstinence. He may then practise duplicity and pretend simplicity.')

It should also be noted, however, that Nature explicitly disapproves of Faux Semblant (vv. 19345–54), and excludes him (vv. 19355–9) from taking part in her 'saluance' (salvation v. 19357), her solution to Amant's problem, which is the mission on which she sends Genius. Nature's condemnation of Faux Semblant involves, nevertheless, an ambiguous affirmation of his close link to Amours (vv. 19360–8):

> Bien les deüst Amours bouter
> Hors de son ost, s'il li pleüst,
> Se certainement ne seüst
> Qu'il li fussent si necessaire
> Qu'il ne peüst senz aus riens faire;
> Mais s'il sont avocat pour eus
> En la cause aus fins amoureus,
> Don leur mal seient alegié,
> Cet barat leur pardone gié.

('If Love had not known certainly that they [=False Seeming and Constrained Abstinence] were so necessary to him that he could do nothing without them, he should have shoved them out of his army if it pleased him. But if there are advocates to lessen their wickedness in the case for pure lovers, I pardon them their fraud.')

At the moment of Genius's arrival on the scene before the castle, we learn that Faux Semblant 'partiz s'en iert plus que le pas / des lors que la vieille fu prise / qui m'ouvri l'uis de la pourprise / . . . Il n'i vost onques plus atendre, / ainz s'en foï senz congié prendre' (vv. 19446–8, 19451–2; 'had left in a hurry as soon as the Old Woman was captured, the one who opened the door of the enclosure for me . . . He had not wanted to wait any longer, but had fled without asking leave').

19 See Brownlee, *Poetic Identity*, pp. 54–63, 141–56.

ment of this theme, both in the *dits* and here in motet 15, has an important element of playfulness (and of verbal cleverness) which is reflected in the very terms in which the theme is articulated, as well as in the late medieval aesthetic which appreciated linguistic patterning and paradox for its own sake. On the other hand, as the recent work of Jacqueline Cerquiglini has shown,[20] this dominant theme in Machaut's courtly poetry is symptomatic of a more generalised 'crisis of language' – of signification – characteristic of late medieval French literature. Indeed, much of the anti-courtly thrust of Christine de Pizan's polemical attacks against the *Roman de la rose* and its literary progeny can be seen as a strong reaction against this 'crisis', against the notion that language – and, in particular, literary language – is a sign system without firm 'grounding' in an ethical referentiality.[21]

By way of conclusion, I should like to suggest that Machaut's motet 15 implicitly opposes this fallen linguistic world – the world of *both* Amours and Faux Semblant – to God's transcendent Word, to God as the ultimate guarantor of the Word, as well as to the experience of God unmediated by fallen human language. This opposition is suggested by the 'context' of the motet's tenor, that is, by the Latin text associated with the tenor, and its biblical and liturgical setting.[22] The kind of evocation of words by music that I am here assuming strikes me as operative in certain other motets of Machaut, of which at least three merit special mention.[23] First, motet 4 (*De Bon Espoir/Puis qu'en la douce/Speravi*), where the tenor comes from the Introitus *Domine, in tua misericordia speravi*. Gilbert Reaney comments that the text of the tenor 'fits very well with the idea of the lover's hope in the French texts of the upper parts'.[24] I feel, rather, that the key in this motet is the *opposition* between the amorous, courtly hope explicitly articulated in the triplum and

---

[20] See *'Un engin si soutil': Guillaume de Machaut et l'écriture au xive siècle* (Paris, 1985), especially part 3: 'Un monde en éclats ou la crise généralisée des signes', pp. 157–200.

[21] For Christine as critical reader of the *Rose*, see K. Brownlee, 'Discourses of the Self: Christine de Pizan and the *Romance of the Rose*', *Romanic Review*, 79 (1988), pp. 199–221.

[22] For an interesting consideration of the liturgical/biblical context of another of Machaut's motets (*Fons totius superbie/O livoris feritas/Fera pessima*), see H. H. Eggebrecht, 'Machauts Motette Nr. 9', *Archiv für Musikwissenschaft*, 19–20 (1962–3), pp. 173–95, 281–93.

[23] For the more general aspect of this phenomenon in motet composition, see Bent, who begins her discussion with the remark 'Art further consisted in devising clever (and often cleverly concealed) symbolic relationships (both verbally allusive and numerically musical) between the tenor and the parts added to it.'

[24] See G. Reaney, *Guillaume de Machaut* (London, 1971), p. 51.

motetus, and the Christian, spiritual hope evoked by the tenor. Secondly, there is motet 8 (*Qui es promesses de Fortune/Ha! Fortune/Et non est qui adjuvat*), where the opposition is between Fortune and Providence. Again, a secular perspective established in the French upper parts is contrasted with a spiritual perspective implicit in the tenor. Thirdly, there is motet 23 (*Felix virgo mater/Inviolata genetrix/Ad te suspiramus*), where the tenor is from the antiphon *Salve regina*. This motet utilises the text of the tenor in a somewhat different way – to reinforce, to underwrite the semantic content of the texts of the upper voices. Of particular importance in this context are the citations from the *Salve regina* at the end of the motetus (vv. 54, 56).

The text of the tenor for Machaut's motet 15 comes from the third nocturn at Matins on the second Sunday of Lent. Its biblical provenance is Genesis 32: 30. Here Jacob, after having wrestled with the angel and received both a new name (Israel) and a divine blessing, exclaims: 'Vidi dominum facie ad faciem; et salva facta est anima mea'[25] (I have seen the Lord face to face; and my life is preserved). This direct and truthful relationship with the divine is re-evoked by St Paul in 1 Corinthians 13: 12, in the context of his famous discussion of *caritas*: 'Videmus nunc per speculum in aenigmate: tunc autem facie ad faciem' (Now we see in a mirror dimly; but then face to face).

In the last analysis, then, Machaut's motet 15 is structured around two different oppositions: the first, between Amours and Faux Semblant, in fact turns out to be a false opposition, for the two seemingly contrary terms are implicitly presented as two sides of the same, problematic, coin. The second is a true opposition, between the world of human seeming and the world of divine being. The import of both oppositions results from 'context'. In each case, the full meaning of the words of the motet depends upon the evocation of other texts which inform the motet's 'reception', the way in which it is understood.

University of Pennsylvania

---

[25] Citations are from *Biblia sacra iuxta Vulgatam Clementinam*, ed. A. Colunga and L. Turrado, 4th edn (Madrid, 1965).

Early Music History (1991) Volume 10

MARGARET BENT

DECEPTION, EXEGESIS AND SOUNDING NUMBER IN MACHAUT'S MOTET 15

Kevin Brownlee's essay is a welcome addition to current studies that apply literary, textual and historical insights to fourteenth-century motets. The opportunity to comment on his paper before publication stimulated these observations; he graciously agreed that I should offer them as a coda.

The motet is given here in an annotated copy of Schrade's edition, and with a suggested emendation at the end (Example 1).[1] It is 120 breves long. The tenor consists of one *color* (melodic statement) disposed in four equal *taleae* (rhythmic statements) each of ten perfect longs, numbered I, II, III, IV, in the transcription. 10 longs × 3 = 30 breves; 4 *taleae* × 30 = 120. Peter's threefold denial and the thirty pieces of silver paid for Judas's betrayal have associations of deceit; the choice of these numbers for a motet about deceit may be far from accidental.[2] The tenor has forty notes, ten in each *talea*, twenty in each half. The tens of the tenor, whether

---

[1] Polyphonic Music of the Fourteenth Century 2 (Monaco, 1956). One of the striking features of this motet as printed by Ludwig and Schrade is the dissonant appoggiatura at the end of the triplum. Although confirmed by all sources, it is very hard to swallow, even as a deliberate piece of word-painting (of 'desconfiture' and 'nonchaloir', the final triplum and duplum words), when we can point to so few uses of dissonance that bypass grammatical sense in the service of depiction. It can be emended out by making the last triplum notes minim, minim, semibreve, long instead of semibreve, breve, long. This small violation of the isorhythmic correspondence imposes a choice between musical sense and formal congruence, but the final corresponding of the upper-voice isorhythm is truncated anyway. It respects the *-ure* feminine rhyme and matches the corresponding point at the cadential arrival.

[2] For another use of 30 see the exemplary study by Wulf Arlt, ' "Triginta denariis" – Musik und Text in einer Motette des *Roman de Fauvel* über dem Tenor *Victimae paschali laudes*, *Pax et sapientia: Studies in Text and Music of Liturgical Tropes and Sequences, in Memory of Gordon Anderson*, Acta Universitatis Stockholmensis: Studia Latina Stockholmensis 29 (1986), pp. 97–113.

Example 1. Guillaume de Machaut, *Amours qui a le pouoir/Faus Samblant m'a deceü/Vidi dominum*

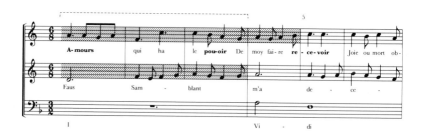

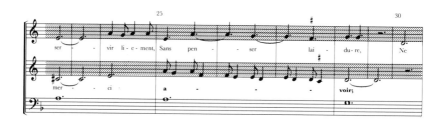

III

18

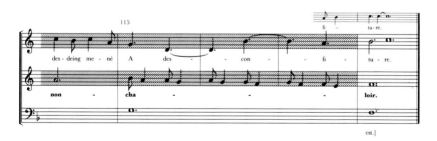

counted as notes or breves, when multiplied by twelve (the number, *inter alia*, of the tribes of Israel) produce 120.

The music of triplum and motetus (or duplum) is disposed in two rhythmically identical *taleae* each of sixty breves, each spanning two thirty-breve tenor *taleae* (i + ii = iii + iv); the motet falls into two rhythmically identical halves. The midpoints of those halves are marked by the second and fourth tenor *taleae* (ii, iv) and also by the four divisions of the motetus text. But viewed another way, triplum and motetus can both be divided into four varied *taleae* (i = iii, ii = iv) coinciding with those of the tenor. In each of these four thirty-breve *taleae* the first three breves (actually four in the triplum), and the last fifteen (the entire second half), are rhythmically identical. (These passages are shaded in Example 1.) Thus a total of just over eighteen bars out of each thirty are rhythmically the same; the golden section of 30 falls at 18.54. These large and systematic deviations within otherwise identical sections may be considered part of the deceptive programme of the motet.

The texts (Table 1) differ hierarchically in length, as triplum and motetus normally do, and each is differently patterned. They are distinct as are their subjects, Amours and Faux Semblant, which Brownlee shows to be presented in an apparent opposition that is in fact false.

Table 1 *Text of Machaut's motet 15 (for translations see above, p. 3)*

Triplum	Rhyme	Syllables	Words
Amours qui a le **pouoir**	a	7	5
De moy faire **recevoir**	a	7	4
Joie ou mort obscure,	b	6	4
Ne fait par sa grace **Avoir**	a	7	6
5 **A** ma dame tel **voloir**	a	7	5
Qu'elle m'ait en cure.	b	6	6
Durer ne puis longuement,	c	7	4
Car pour amer loiaument	c	7	4
Ne pour servir liement,	c	7	4
10 Sans penser laidure,	b	6	3
Ne pour celer sagement	c	7	4
N'ay confort n'aligement	c	7	5
De ma dolour dure;	b	6	4
Einsois com plus humblement	c	7	4
15 La sueffre et endure,	b	6	4
De tant est plus durement	c	7	5

Table 1 *continued*

Triplum	Rhyme	Syllables	Words	
Traitiés mes cuers, que briefment	c	7	5	
Morray dolereusement	c	7	2	
De dueil et d'ardure,	b	6	5	/83
20 Et tant sui plus eslongiés	d	7	5	
De merci et estraingiés	d	7	4	
De ma dame pure.	b	6	4	
Mais aveuc tous ces **meschiés**	d	7	5	
Sueffre **Amours** qui est **mes chiés,**	d	7	6	Amours:
25 Que **Raison**, Droiture,	b	6	3	word 103
Douçour, Debonnaireté	e	7	2	
Franchise, Grace et Pité	e	7	4	
N'ont pouoir à Cruauté,	e	7	5	
Ensois regne et dure	b	6	4	
30 En corps d'umblece paré	e	7	5	
Cuers qui est pleins de durté	e	7	6	
Et de couverture,	b	6	3	
Refus qui d'espoir osté	e	7	5	
M'a la morriture,	b	6	4	
35 Et Dangiers qui despité	e	7	4	
M'a sans cause et si grevé	e	7	7	
Qu'il m'a par desdaing mené	e	7	7	
A desconfiture.	b	6	2	/85
Motetus				
1 Faus Samblant m'a deceü	a	7	5	
Et tenu en esperance	b	8	4	
De joie merci **avoir**;	c	7	4	
Et je l'ay com fols creü	a	7	7	
5 Et mis toute ma fiance	b	8	5	
En li d'amoureus **vouloir**.	c	7	5	/30
Las! or m'a descongneü	a	7	5	
Quant de **moy** faire aligence	b	8	5	
Ha heü temps et **pooir**;	c	7	5	
10 N'en riens n'a recongneü	a	7	6	
Ma dolour ne ma grevance,	b	8	5	
Eins m'a mis en **nonchaloir**.	c	7	6	/32

The triplum text's thirty-eight lines divide by line count, metrical and rhyme scheme only at the middle, its 19 + 19 lines matching the two musical *taleae* of both upper parts. Each half follows the same rhyme scheme but with only the 'b' rhyme (*-ure*) maintained throughout both halves. The twelve b-lines each have six syllables, all other lines seven.

aab aa b cccb ccb cb cccb |
ddb dd b eeeb eeb eb eeeb |

The parallel duplication makes regularity out of these two irregular forms. Similarly irregular but paired stanzas in Machaut's lais are also subjected to a similar rhyme discipline.

The motetus text has twelve lines, arranged in four groups of three lines, each of which has abc rhyme and seven–eight–seven syllables. The four three-line groups correspond to the four *taleae* of the tenor; they thus encourage an interpretation of the upper parts as four *taleae* with deviations, whereas the textual structure of the triplum favours a division into only two strictly repeating halves. Just as false-seeming may go in either of two directions, so the 'Faus Samblant' motetus could have adapted its structure either to the four equal musical *taleae* of the two-faced ('facie ad faciem') tenor or to the two parallel textual halves of the triplum. In fact, the music of both upper parts does both; they can be interpreted either as two strict or as four varied *taleae*. The composer's duplicitous and ambivalent strategy is reflected in our analysis.

Counting elided words as two,[3] the triplum's 83 + 85 words are so arranged that the 'Et' that begins line 20 precedes the musical midpoint; the triplum thus has eighty-four words in each musical half of the piece. The coincidence of the midpoint of the music with the midpoint of the triplum word count makes possible a strict correspondence between word and note in the rhythmic repetitions. Musical overlapping of structural joins is often found in motets; here we find textual construction following the same procedure by a slight dislocation of line count and word count.

In similar fashion, and by word count, the first half of the motetus text has thirty words and the second half thirty-two. The thirty-first word is 'Las!', and there are thirty-one words after it,

---

[3] The triplum has 268 notes, 38 lines and 168 words (counting elided words, transcribed with apostrophes, as two words). The duplum has 188 notes, 12 lines and 62 words.

In the following, $x + y$ means: x is the number of words counting elided words, transcribed with apostrophes, as single words; y is the number of words with apostrophes; $x + y$ is the word count reckoning 'M'a' as two words:

triplum, 78 + 5, 78 + 7 in the two halves (83, 85)
duplum, 27 + 3, 28 + 4 (30, 32)

starting with the parallel to line 1. This may be heard as an 'Hélas' spanning the musical midpoint, with the triplum's 'Et' that starts line 20, word 84, preceding and aurally linked to 'Las' in the motetus. The midpoint by word count in both triplum and motetus falls after the first word of the second half of the text as defined by lines and syllables, again at the musical middle, and coinciding in both texts.

The words of the tenor are not supplied in the manuscripts but can be reinstated to the slightly varied chant. The final 'anima mea' is left off, leaving unstated what is saved. Nine syllables fall in each half of the motet, with one of the two 'faces' mirrored in each half around the midpoint, the second ('faciem') following the musical golden section:

> Vidi dominum facie ad
> faciem [et] salva facta est . . .

As we have pointed out, triplum and motetus divide musically at the middle into two rhythmically identical arcs (breves 1–60 = 61–120), each of which encompasses two tenor *taleae*. This structure perfectly accommodates the triplum text, which is suited only to a division at the middle, and is compatible with the motetus text which divides into quarters. We have also pointed out an alternative interpretation of triplum and motetus as constituting four *taleae* with deviation between breves 4 and 15. Not only are the opening rhythms of both triplum and motetus repeated at the beginnings of the second and fourth tenor *taleae* (bars 31, 91, marked II and IV in the score) as well as the first and third (I, 1; III, 61); in addition, at II (31–3) both triplum and motetus strikingly maintain identical pitches for three breves' duration, so that bars 1–3 are, quite exceptionally, fully identical with 31–3, an added false-seeming, since not even rhythmic identity is maintained between the fourth and fifteenth breves. The listener is thereby deceived into expecting that the triplum and motetus are going to have not two but four regular *taleae*, corresponding to the four of the tenor. The deceit is further signalled here (at tenor *talea* II) by the triplum words 'pour celer saigement', and the motetus's 'et je l'ay com fols creu'. Indeed, all four tenor *taleae* are initiated with words of deceit in the motetus, the voice of Faux Semblant: in addition to these words at II, *talea* I starts with 'deceu', III with 'descongneu', IV with 'recongneu'. At III, the beginning of the more concealed 'real' repeat, it is least conspicuous, indeed, 'wisely concealed', and lasting only one breve. Thus, in the motetus, the two parallel halves of the music open with the very close textual parallel 'Faux Semblant has deceived', 'he has undeceived'. The 'deceitful' musical repetition occurred in the first half (we were deceived at II); it is not maintained (hence undeceived, 'descongneu') at III, the true repeat; the revelation to Jacob (tenor 'faciem') is also linked to this. At *talea* IV (bar 91), the second 'deceptive' repeat, Faux Semblant fails to reward ('n'a recongneu'); here, moreover, the triplum figure of the opening (a' $a'g'a'$) appears a fifth lower (d' $d'c'd'$), changing places with the motetus as Jacob had with Esau, a further false-seeming that abases itself in a downward transposition to the words 'corps d'umblece'. This inverts a formal device of Machaut's lais, where the twelfth stanza climactically duplicates the first a fifth higher. The middles of the middles (*taleae* II and IV, bars 31 and 91) thus become nodes of deception or ambiguity.

In sense, too, the true middle of the piece is signalled by the selfconscious measuring of time and distance. 'Briefment morray dolereusement de dueil et d'ardure' brings us to the middle of the triplum, while the second half starts off by measuring his distance, 'Et tant sui plus eslongiés'. One recalls Gurnemanz's midday exposition to Parsifal in the middle of Act 1: 'Zum Raum wird hier die Zeit'.

The four motetus groups end respectively with the words 'avoir', 'voloir', 'pooir', 'nonchaloir'. Three out of these four words are shared in the -oir rhyme of the triplum (lines 1, 2, 4, 5): 'pouoir', 'recevoir', 'avoir', 'voloir'; all these triplum words are heard within the first half of *talea* I, and are then heard, with the order of the pairs reversed, to end each of the four *taleae*, thus underscoring, through the only shared rhymes between the texts, the rhythmic identity of the four musical endings.

The first five lines of the triplum form an acrostic ADINA.[4] David Howlett has reminded me (as he has taught me so much else) that Leah's youngest daughter was named Dinah (Genesis 30: 21). The first note of the triplum is A, sung to a word beginning with A; the phrase for the last A of Adina begins and ends on A and

---

[4] Although the motet is full of betrayed faith, I hesitate to make too much of the acrostic FEDE that begins the motetus.

the whole five-line passage is set off by a rest after the first rhyme, 'voloir', perhaps confirming that the b-rhyme of line 6 belongs in structure, if not in sense, with what follows, as is more clearly the case after the corresponding line 24. All other major rests in the triplum follow the b-rhymes of lines 6, 10, 15 and 19 and fall correspondingly in the second half of the motet. So the acrostic lines are isolated; their somewhat special treatment might encourage belief that the acrostic is intentional rather than accidental. Concealment of various kinds may be signalled by the prominent long note given near the beginning to 'obscure' (triplum, line 3; bars 7–9), as well as by the hiding of structural joins by musical and textual overlapping.

The final lines of the paired poems, in which the speaker bemoans his ruin (triplum) and bad treatment (motetus) are opposed to Jacob's wrestling with the angel that lead to his blessing and re-naming as Israel, after which he says 'I have seen the Lord face to face; and my soul is preserved' (Genesis 32: 30). Just as the ambiguities of the upper-voice texts are presented as two faces or facets of the same tenor foundation, so are they reconciled in disparity both musically, and with respect to textual form. This supports Brownlee's claim that his first opposition, between Amours and Faux Semblant, is indeed only apparent.

As to the second, 'true' opposition, that between 'the world of human seeming and the world of divine being', I suggest that the choice of Jacob's words for the tenor is less straightforward than 'divine being' implies. The biblical Jacob who utters the tenor words 'Vidi Dominum facie ad faciem, et salva facta est anima mea' is the musical and symbolic foundation of the motet. The tenor's 'facie ad faciem', face to face, advertises itself (to the initiated) as a two-faced seeing; the words follow Jacob's re-naming as Israel – two names. Jacob is yoked to its false seeming by his own earlier 'two-faced' deception of his father Isaac (by cheating his older twin brother Esau both of his birthright and of his father's blessing), as he was in turn deceived by Laban when he served seven years for Rachel and was then given her sister Leah. The first deception was promoted by his mother Rebekah, the second by her brother Laban, another sibling relationship in this complex of sibling pairs. Jacob's twinned relationship to deceit, as both a perpetrator and a victim, is implicit in the choice of his words; his

25

two-faced history is now resolved in his face-to-face encounter with his God. The motet's startling alignment of the God of Jacob and the god of love is highlighted in the triplum text by the false-seeming pun on mischief, 'meschies', and my lord (Lord?), 'mes chies'. The tenor is here being recruited to underscore a double meaning, in both its biblical and liturgical setting; it opposes the god of love (who has deceived the lover) to the God of Jacob, and it parallels, by simultaneous presentation, the deceptions of which Jacob was perpetrator and victim with those of Amours and Faux Semblant. Faux Semblant is 'accepted into the army of the god of love'; the treacherous Jacob is accepted, re-named Israel, and sees his God after combat with the angel.

The opening triplum word, 'Amours', makes one other appearance in that text, in line 23. The thirty-eight lines divide by golden section at 23.48 and 14.52. The twenty-fourth line is 'Sueffre Amours qui es mes chies' (with its critical pun on mischief and 'my lord', the god of love). This line just precedes bar 74; the 120 breves of music divide by golden section at 74.16 (i.e. early in bar 75) and 45.84. 'Amours' is here preceded by 'mischief' and followed by 'my lord'; this key word is thus flanked by the two punned appearances of mischief in lines 23 and 24. (Machaut's motet 10 also includes the line 'Amours qui est mes chies', and precedes 'Amours' symmetrically with 'meschies'.) The golden section of the triplum's 168 words falls at 103.8; the 103rd word is 'Amours'. Line 24, in turn, directly precedes the musical golden section at bar 75, a turning-point that is preceded by bad things and followed by the list of seven virtues (in lines 25–7, and with the rhythmic recurrence).[5] The tenor word at this same point is, appropriately, 'faciem'. The opening word 'Amours' is also the golden section word; 'Amours' is not only situated between the bad and good faces of the mischief pun, but functions as both the herald and the pivot of the entire triplum text to separate bad and good things in general. That the golden section of triplum text by lines and words just anticipates the musical golden section gives structural weight to a turning-point of textual sense. The motetus words 'moy faire aligence' span the mischief pun in the triplum, tying the motetus text to the music

---

[5] The seven virtues immediately following the musical golden section are headed by 'raison'; Jeffrey Dean points out that this also meant a mathematical relation, from 'ratio', in which sense it is used in Boethius' *De institutione arithmetica*.

at this point; the golden section word itself is 'moy', the thirty-eighth of sixty-two.

The 'je' of each of the upper parts is paralleled by the first person of the tenor, 'Vidi', in the voice of Jacob; he has seen the face of God, has loved, deceived and been deceived. Brownlee shows that the 'je' of the triplum has been moved by love while the 'je' of the motetus has been deceived by Faux Semblant. The two 'contrasting self-presentations' are here made simultaneous, two-faced. Faux Semblant speaks in his own voice in the *Roman de la rose*; he is introduced into the poem by the god of love. We might add that Jacob in the tenor speaks in his own voice, setting up a simultaneous presentation of the 'Dominus' he saw, in the tenor, with the god of love, 'Amours qui est mes chies', in the triplum. In the motetus Brownlee finds 'a contrastive self-presentation of the speaking subject as an unwitting victim of Faux Semblant, who has purposefully and successfully deceived him (by means of his lady's appearance) before openly revealing his deception'. The clothing of the lady deceives; the clothing of the music deceives. 'Faux Semblant's clothes and his words deceive qua signs.' Faux Semblant wants to conceal his whereabouts. False-seeming is, after all, exactly what Jacob had earlier undertaken in deceiving Isaac and stealing Esau's birthright, even to the extent of changing his exterior by wearing Esau's clothes and feigning hairiness with the kid skins that were the by-product of his mother Rebekah's fake venison.

The tenor not only opposes the divine being, represented by liturgical chant, to the human loving of the upper parts; it itself embodies many layers of duplicity. As well as being presented simultaneously, the music and text of tenor, triplum and motetus are in completely parallel symmetry, face to face. Of the two 'faces' in the tenor, one falls in each half of the motet. The two faces of the tenor are matched, feigned or avoided, and matches in turn are made, feigned or avoided with the upper parts in matters of metrical and musical structure. Many other promising aspects, such as phonic coordination of vowel and consonant sounds between the triplum and motetus, and the full extent of verbal reference between their texts, have not been explored here. This richly suggestive counterpoint of musical and textual structures and symbolism invites a parallel examination of other Machaut motets.

Princeton University

27

BOJAN BUJIĆ

'FIGURA POETICA MOLTO VAGA': STRUCTURE AND MEANING IN RINUCCINI'S *EURIDICE*

Early Italian opera with its diverse roots, stretching into the history of music, Classical and Renaissance literature, and the culture of the late Cinquecento, continues to attract historians of culture and musicologists. If one only glances over the work done in this area during the last twenty-five or so years one cannot fail to be impressed by the important writings on early opera by Nino Pirrotta, on the Florentine Camerata by Claude Palisca, on the Classical literary tradition in the early librettos by F. W. Sternfeld and on early Mantuan opera by Iain Fenlon.[1] We also owe a detailed account of the first performance of Peri's and Caccini's *Euridice* to Claude Palisca, and a study of Peri's *Euridice* to Tim Carter.[2] In the

---

[1] N. Pirrotta, 'Early Opera and Aria', *New Looks at Italian Opera*, ed. W. W. Austin (Ithaca, NY, 1968), pp. 39–107; Italian version in N. Pirrotta and E. Povoledo, *Li due Orfei* (Turin, 1969; 2nd edn, 1975), pp. 276–333; Eng. trans., revised, as *Music and Theatre from Poliziano to Monteverdi* (Cambridge, 1982), pp. 237–80. Other relevant papers are collected in *Music and Culture in Italy from the Middle Ages to the Baroque* (Cambridge, MA, and London, 1984).

C. Palisca, *Girolamo Mei: Letters on Ancient and Modern Music to Vincenzo Galilei and Giovanni Bardi*, Musicological Studies and Documents 3 (American Institute of Musicology, 1960). 'Musical Asides in the Diplomatic Correspondence of Emilio de' Cavalieri', *The Musical Quarterly*, 49 (1963), pp. 339–55. 'The *Camerata fiorentina*: A Reappraisal', *Studi Musicali*, 1 (1972), pp. 203–34.

F. W. Sternfeld, 'The Birth of Opera: Ovid, Poliziano and the *Lieto fine*', *Analecta Musicologica*, 19 (1979), pp. 30–51. 'Intermedi and the Birth of Opera', *The Florentine Intermedi of 1589*, ed. I. Fenlon (London, 1979), pp. 10–16. 'The Orpheus Myth and the Libretto of *Orfeo*', *Claudio Monteverdi: Orfeo*, ed. J. Whenham (Cambridge, 1986) [henceforth *WhenO*], pp. 20–34. 'Orpheus, Ovid and Opera', *Journal of the Royal Musical Association*, 113 (1988), pp. 172–202.

I. Fenlon, 'The Mantuan Stage Works', *The New Monteverdi Companion*, ed. D. Arnold and N. Fortune (London, 1985), pp. 251–87. 'The Mantuan Orfeo', *WhenO*, pp. 1–19.

[2] C. Palisca, 'The First Performance of "Euridice"', *Queens College Department of Music Twenty-Fifth Anniversary Festschrift*, ed. A. Mell (New York, 1964), pp. 1–23. T. Carter, 'Jacopo Peri's *Euridice* (1600): A Contextual Study', *The Music Review*, 43 (1982), pp. 83–103.

latter two studies the stress was on the final result of the collaboration between Ottavio Rinuccini, Jacopo Peri and Giulio Caccini. It
seems, however, that a detailed look at one of the components,
Rinuccini's dramatic poem *Euridice*, may offer some valuable
insights into the very foundation of Peri's and Caccini's completed
artistic effort and also throw new light on some aspects of Striggio's
Orfeo.

Ottavio Rinuccini has become famous by association. Were it
not for his poetry set to music by Peri, Caccini and, particularly,
Claudio Monteverdi, he would have remained a minor Florentine
poet of the late Cinquecento unlikely to be known outside a circle of
specialists among historians of Italian literature. As it is, the fact
that he provided texts for the first Florentine attempts in the new
genre of opera ensures him a worthy place in the history of music,
though in the historical accounts of the early opera he still tends to
remain in the shadow of the composers who set his verse. The very
title of Barbara Russano Hanning's essay 'Apologia pro Ottavio
Rinuccini' suggests that the prime mover in her scholarly effort was
a sense of injustice towards Rinuccini,[3] although in reality her
discussion proceeded almost too strongly in the direction of general
theories of tragedy that might have inspired Rinuccini, rather than
dealing with the structure and merits of his poetry. Hanning's
argument was challenged by Gary Tomlinson, who objected to
several details of her presentation without attempting to change its
general course.[4] It was left to Nino Pirrotta to deal with this,
somewhat obliquely, in a footnote added to the Italian version of
his essay 'Early Opera and Aria', where he voiced his doubt that
Rinuccini is to be evaluated primarily for his adherence to the
Classical theory of tragedy.[5] In the same essay he praised Rinuccini's ability to recognise the emotional power and tragic pathos
generated by the episodes of Euridice's death and Orfeo's despair,[6]

---

[3] B. Russano Hanning, 'Apologia pro Ottavio Rinuccini', *Journal of the American Musicologi-
    cal Society*, 26 (1973), pp. 240–62. The paper is a reworked chapter from Hanning's
    doctoral dissertation. The dissertation was published as *Of Poetry and Music's Power:
    Humanism and the Creation of Opera* (Ann Arbor, MI, 1980).

[4] G. Tomlinson, 'Ancora su Ottavio Rinuccini', *Journal of the American Musicological Society*,
    28 (1975), pp. 351–6.

[5] Pirrotta, *Li due Orfei*, p. 329, Eng. trans., p. 264.

[6] *Ibid.*, p. 282, Eng. trans., p. 243. Throughout the present study the forms 'Orpheus',
    'Venus' etc. refer to the characters from Greek mythology, whereas 'Orfeo', 'Venere' etc.
    refer to Rinuccini's characters.

leaving it thus open for future interpreters to seek the proof of the literary merit of the verse in the manner of its invention.

In this paper I shall argue that the real importance of *Euridice* lies in an extraordinarily strong sense of overall form, and that the form is, in turn, the result of skilful use of artifice, literary reference and allusion, and of juxtaposition of contrasts. These devices point up the qualities of contrivance which art historians, such as John Shearman, like to see as manifestations of mannerism working through deliberately sought *difficultà*.[7] This 'difficulty' is usually manifested through complexity which stands in the way of immediate and easy comprehension of a work of art and is thus designed to draw the spectator into a close examination of the details of construction. Among the details of construction that form the basis of the mannerist aesthetics of the late Cinquecento Shearman singles out the *contrapposto*, the device which consists of joining together verbal opposites, and the one that turns up with some considerable frequency in Guarini's *Il pastor fido*.[8] Having put the words 'un vivace morire' into Mirtillo's mouth, Guarini feels obliged to explain that by bringing together these opposing concepts he was able to achieve a most pleasing poetic figure: 'Accoppia insieme questi due contrapposti e di morte e di vita, con figura poetica molto vaga volendo esprimere l'eccessivo dolore della partita.'[9] Although in our examination of the literary models which served Rinuccini for *Euridice* we shall inevitably have to look at the Classical sources of the story of Orpheus, it is as well to bear in mind that as a pastoral *Euridice* must number *Il pastor fido* among its progenitors.[10]

---

[7] J. Shearman, *Mannerism* (Harmondsworth, 1967), pp. 21 and 41.

[8] *Ibid.*, pp. 91–6.

[9] Battista Guarini, *Il pastor fido*, ed. E. Bonora (Milan, 1977), Act 3, scene 3, line 503, and Guarini's commentary on the line. Discussing the poetry of the same period, though using for it the term 'Baroque', Gérard Genette points out the importance of verbal contrasts: '*Diviser* (partager) *pour unir*, c'est la formule de l'ordre baroque.' G. Genette, ' "L'or tombe sous le fer" ', *Figures I* (Paris, 1966), p. 38.

[10] Florentine interest in Guarini and in *Il pastor fido* goes back to the mid-1580s. Responding to a request from Guarini, Lionardo Salviati undertook to 'improve' the language of his pastoral play and then upheld the example of Guarini's language as an argument in his attack on Tasso. On Salviati's recommendation Guarini was admitted to the Accademia Fiorentina in 1587 and to the Accademia della Crusca in 1588. On the latter occasion Guarini went to Florence with the manuscript of *Il pastor fido* knowing of the Grand Duke Ferdinando's interest in having the play performed; the performance did not in fact take place. Guarini was in Florence again in 1599–1601 and contributed a dialogue of Juno and Minerva to the wedding celebrations for which Rinuccini wrote his *Euridice*. For

I

It is perhaps not too fanciful to propose that the whole plan of the dramatic intention in *Euridice* is suggested in the first three stanzas of Tragedia's Prologue: no longer eager to cause the faces of spectators to turn pale while witnessing suffering and shedding of blood, no longer singing on a sorrowful stage filled with tears, she is going to drive funereal images away from under the royal roof, change the mournful buskins and invoke sweet emotions. I am here reiterating the points made by Barbara Russano Hanning and deliberately repeating them since her insistence on the importance of the opening stanzas must remain an inevitable starting-point for any investigation of the meaning of the Prologue.[11] However, I hope to take the discussion in a different direction in order to reveal Rinuccini's ingenuity in building his argument from the very beginning of the work in accordance with his own clearly formulated plan. In any case, Tragedia's refusal to accept her conventional role and her announcement that she wishes to sing of joy instead of sorrow are in themselves subversions of tragic conventions.

The opening stanzas of the Prologue have a twofold function: they inform those familiar with the story of Orpheus that the gruesome ending will be changed into a *lieto fine*, and also that in the course of the play potentially tragic events will change their nature. The second point, though less explicit, is ultimately the more important: the Prologue is not a statement of a static fact, but sums up the development and flow of the story which is to be enacted. In the process of the story sorrow is to be dispersed and replaced by final happiness, the realisation of which ultimately depends on the portrayal of its opposition, gloom and despair. It is perhaps unimportant that the reference in the text to the 'royal roof' has to be interpreted somewhat loosely. As is only too well known, *Euridice* was first performed in the Pitti Palace as a part of the festivities to mark the wedding of Maria de' Medici and Henri IV of Navarre, and its roof is royal only by inference, since Maria, though not yet married to the king, was at the time normally referred to as the queen.[12] The palace itself was, of course, acquired for the Medici

details of Guarini's literary links with Florence see V. Rossi, *Battista Guarini ed 'Il pastor fido'* (Turin, 1886), and P. M. Brown, *Lionardo Salviati* (Oxford, 1974).

[11] Hanning, 'Apologia', pp. 244–6.

[12] 'Royal roof', in the original 'regi tetti': Luigi Fassò (see below, note 14) interprets this to mean 'la reggia di Francia' (p. 24), but there is no reason not to see in 'regi tetti' a

family by Cosimo I, the bride's grandfather, with the money provided by his Spanish wife Eleonora of Toledo. Far from irrelevant, though, is the realisation that the seemingly mere polite references to royal persons foreshadow other veiled allusions to the recent Medicean political past which are found later in the play. The full significance of this will be dealt with later; suffice it to say now only that the reading of the Prologue as an integral part of the play, adumbrating the nature of the course the action is about to take, must be considered essential.

Neither the early prints of *Euridice* nor the printed scores of Peri's and Caccini's versions of the opera present consistent clear divisions into scenes or acts. There are, of course, two points at which the descent into the underworld and the return to the full light of day are indicated. After line 397 (end of scene 3) Rinuccini has 'Qui il Coro parte, e la scena si tramuta', and after line 583 (end of scene 4) 'Si rivolge la scena, e torna come prima'.[13] Nevertheless, some more points of division are clearly implied by the structure of the text and, in the scores, by typographical means such as ornamented initials. Following partly these indications, partly his own feelings, the first modern editor of the text, Angelo Solerti, divided it into six scenes, and the later editions, by Andrea della Corte and Luigi Fassò, took over Solerti's division without challenging it.[14] Howard Mayer Brown's modern edition of Peri's opera rightly divides it into five acts (or scenes).[15] Nevertheless, Solerti

---

[13] reference to the premises of the performance. The two words are, after all, of respectable Ovidian lineage: 'cum facibus regalia tecta cremaro' (*Metamorphoses*, VI, 614, the story of Philomela, Procne and Tereus), although the context is, of course, different.

[13] The numbering of lines is after Solerti and Della Corte (see note 14).

[14] A. Solerti, *Gli albori del melodramma* (Milan, etc., 1904–5; repr. Hildesheim, 1969), II, pp. 107–42; A. Della Corte, ed., *Drammi per musica*, Collezione di Classici Italiani 50 (Turin, 1926), pp. 289–326; Della Corte, ed., *Drammi per musica dal Rinuccini allo Zeno* (Turin, 1958), I, pp. 69–106; L. Fassò, ed., *Teatro del Seicento*, La Letteratura Italiana: Storia e Testi 39 (Milan and Naples, 1956), pp. 23–49. Neither Solerti nor Della Corte provided any commentaries and therefore Fassò's edition, containing ample annotations and textual commentaries, is superior to those of his predecessors. Fassò's numbering of lines also distinguishes his edition from the two preceding ones. They number 790 lines, whereas Fassò's edition numbers 814 lines. The difference of twenty four lines arose from the fact that Fassò wrote out in full the repetitions of the ritornello 'Al canto, al ballo' in the finale of scene 1. In spite of the logical preference for Fassò's text I have followed Solerti's and Della Corte's numbering not only because most music historians are familiar with these editions, but also because their layout of the passage in question corresponds closely to the layout of the first printed edition (*L'Euridice*, Florence: Giunti, 1600). The two methods of numbering do not alter significantly the balance between the sections discussed later.

[15] Jacopo Peri, *Euridice*, ed. H. M. Brown, Recent Researches in the Music of the Baroque Era 36–7 (Madison, WI, 1981). The edition does not number the lines, but it provides a

Table 1 *Division of text in Rinuccini's 'Euridice'*

Section	Line nos.	No. of lines	
Prologue	1–28	28	
Scene 1	29–100	72	397 lines
Scene 2	101–292	192	
Scene 3	293–397	105	
Scene 4	398–583	186	393 lines
Scene 5	584–790	207	

[Solerti: scene 5, 100 lines; scene 6, 107 lines]

had a point in dividing the text into six scenes: by recognising the change in the nature of dramatic action to be found halfway through scene 5, where Orfeo and Euridice reappear, he succeeded in dividing the longest scene into two shorter ones. This in turn resulted in a neat division into three scenes at either side of Orfeo's monologue at the gates of hell which occurs roughly halfway through the poem. Solerti's is a conjectural division, and although in upholding a historical principle of division into five units we do not have to adhere to it, it does usefully point out a certain feeling of central symmetry of structure which is far from fortuitous.

Euridice contains 790 lines of text divided as shown in Table 1. Tragedia's Prologue explains the basic emotional content of the play, the course of the change from tragic mood to happy one. Needless to say, before we witness the despair of tragedy we have to experience happiness and rejoicing as a starting-point. The whole of scene 1 is therefore devoted to a representation of pastoral rejoicing. Scene 2 continues in the same manner, but Dafne reports the death of Euridice and the mood darkens considerably, with Orfeo hinting that he wishes to join her in death. Scene 3 opens with Arcetro's report that Orfeo, having found the spot at which Euridice died, did not kill himself but was taken away by Venere.

parallel English translation. Brown's notes list discrepancies in wording between the printed libretto and Peri's published score. Brown's decision to divide the opera into five scenes rather than six rests on a conviction that this would conform to the theatrical practice of the time. This is borne out by the fact that Paskoj Primović, the author of the near-contemporary Croat translation (*Euridice*, Venice: Salis, 1617) divided his translation into five acts at identical points. I have discussed this translation in 'An Early Croat Translation of Rinuccini's "Euridice" ', *Muzikološki Zbornik* (University of Ljubljana), 12 (1976), pp. 16–29.

The chorus sings about the inevitability of change: neither the good nor the sorrow is eternal ('Non è il ben, nè 'l pianto eterno'), thus taking up the theme of change suggested in the Prologue. Counting the number of lines we are now at the midpoint of the dramatic poem: the Prologue and the first three scenes amount to 397 lines, the remaining two to 393 (or in Fassò's edition to 421 + 393 lines). The opening of scene 4 shows the gates of hell, to which Venere has led Orfeo. Preparing to enter it Orfeo gives a description of the infernal landscape, of the horrible fields deprived of light and echoing to the sad sounds of his lament. In terms of the hero's psychological state as well as the imagery employed this is a complete contrast to the gaiety and optimism of scene 1. It is the lowest point since the physical descent into hell is also the *katabasis*, or psychological descent into sorrow and despair. But it is also the turning-point. Orfeo pulls himself together and, encouraged by Venere, summons the strength to plead with Pluto; Euridice is restored to him and the gloom of the underworld is illuminated by a ray of hope. There is therefore a roughly symmetrical pattern to the whole scene, where the hope voiced by Venere at the outset only as a possibility is confirmed by action at the end of the scene. Scene 5 does not continue this development in a straight line. Initially the mood is still that of anguish until Aminta brings the news that Orfeo has been seen, which inevitably produces a feeling of relief and gratitude among the pastoral throng. Halfway through the scene Orfeo and Euridice reappear. This (line 684) is the beginning of Solerti's sixth scene. We do not have to accept that division, but it is as well to be aware that the second half of scene 5 corresponds in mood and function to the first scene of the opera: happiness has been fully regained and is now shared by all.

To be sure, there is something almost too neat in this ordering of scenes round a central point, though this must not be taken as negative criticism. Rinuccini knew that he was writing poetry which would be presented through singing. The novelty of presentation may in itself be sufficient to sustain the interest of the spectators, but it also contains the danger that, prolonged through singing, the text would become diffuse. It therefore requires neat ordering, and, recognising the basic alteration of moods within the triad of happiness–sorrow–happiness, Rinuccini was led towards a symmetrical pattern. This pattern is made explicit through a num-

35

ber of pointers such as literary references and allusions that seem to have the role of pillars on which the whole construction rests.

As the first of these pillars we may mention the often referred-to quotation from Petrarch in line 53: 'Non vede un simil par d'amanti 'l sole.' It provided both Peri and Caccini with a suitable point for concluding a portion of the scene with an ensemble. It is repeated several times by those participating in the scene and the spectators would have had time to recognise it and reflect on its literary source, Petrarch's pastorally intoned sonnet *Due rose fresche, et colte in paradiso*.[16]

As has been mentioned, pastoral rejoicing continues into he second scene, until line 162, when Dafne appears, obviously distraught, and prepares herself to report the death of Euridice. The preparation itself is prolonged for theatrical effect and occupies a significant stretch of the poem, lines 162–89.[17] A small but interesting discrepancy between Rinuccini's original and Peri's setting appears early in this stretch. After Rinuccini's original line 172 Dafne is given a single new line: 'O giorno pien d'angoscia e pien di guai' (line 172a) which stands as a solitary interjection between Arcetro's and Orfeo's lines. One may speculate on the authorship of this line. It and another addition, to be discussed later, do not appear in Caccini's setting of Rinuccini's text and at this stage it would be difficult to ascribe them either to Rinuccini or to Peri with any certainty, though an assumption could be made that they are Rinuccini's. The choice of words for line 172a betrays intimacy with the meaning and implication of the Petrarch quotation in scene 1, line 53: the sonnet from which it comes ends with the words 'o felice eloquentia, o lieto giorno!' The new line in scene 2 is thus a reversal of these words, which, although unstated, are implied by the reference to Petrarch, so obviously highlighted by the ensemble repetition in both Peri's and Caccini's settings.[18] Indeed, the addition also forms a link with line 175, spoken by

---

[16] No. 245 in the *Canzoniere*. All quotations in the main text are from G. Contini, ed., *Francesco Petrarca: Canzoniere* (Turin, 1964). For the sake of historical consistency the text of a late sixteenth-century edition is reproduced in Appendix 1.

[17] The treatment of this portion of Rinuccini's text in Peri's setting and a comparison of it with the relevant section of Monteverdi's *Orfeo* is discussed by G. Tomlinson, 'Madrigal, Monody, and Monteverdi's "via naturale alla imitatione" ', *Journal of the American Musicological Society*, 34 (1981), pp. 62–6.

[18] I discussed the importance of these additions in 'An Early Croat Translation'.

Orfeo: 'In questo allegro dì, gentil donzella?'[19] There is thus first a feeling of a *contrapposto* achieved locally, since the two opposites, happiness and sorrow, are brought into close proximity. Then, on a different structural level, a *contrapposto* is also achieved between scenes 1 and 2 as larger units. With Dafne's additional line what was merely implied becomes explicit and binds the process and transformation of moods and feelings into a strong and well-ordered structure. The summing up is then provided by the final ensemble of scene 2 (lines 265–92), where the poetic diction abounds with examples of opposites: a face filled with the freshness of flowers, then deprived of its resemblance to lilies and roses; snowy Apennines and the warmth of April; the fierce lion subdued. Some of these are clearly distant echoes of the description of Orpheus' powers, others are simply a literary device helping to underline the theme of change. In a way, they are also further elaborations of the unity of opposites found in the penultimate line of Petrarch's *Due rose fresche*: 'onde 'l cor lasso anchor s'allegra et teme'.

Compared to the long second scene of 192 lines, the third one, containing only 105 lines, is far more condensed. Its central portion is occupied by Arcetro's monologue (lines 338–67, in which he reports having seen a female deity descend on a chariot pulled by two doves to take with her Orfeo who was grieving on the spot at which Euridice met her death. Rinuccini avoids mentioning the name of the goddess, though the chariot pulled by doves instantly reveals her as Venus to anybody versed in the symbols associated with pagan deities. The spectators are thus aware of her identity before the shepherds, since Rinuccini scrupulously follows the convention in pastoral poetry of representing shepherds as ignorant of the deeper meanings of mythology and symbolism:

> A te, qual tu ti sia de gli alti Numi,
> Ch'al nobile pastor recasti aita,
> Mentre avran queste membra e spirto e vita,
> Canterem lodi ogn'or tra incensi e fumi.
> (*Euridice*, 368–71)

Rinuccini then drives home the point of flux, providing in the choral finale yet another statement that everything changes, that

[19]   In Peri's score the words are changed to 'In così lieto dì'. See Peri, *Euridice*, ed. Brown, p. xxi.

each day can be sad as well as joyful, thus tying together in condensed form the sentiment expressed at disjunct points throughout scenes 1 and 2:

> Al rotar del ciel superno
> Non pur l'aer e 'l foco intorno,
> Ma si volve il tutto in giro:
> Non è il ben nè 'l pianto eterno;
> Come or sorge, or cade il giorno,
> Regna qui gioia o martiro.
> *(Euridice, 384–9)*

The mention of rotation is adroitly placed here, for it is only a few lines later, at the end of scene 3, that, counting the number of lines, we reach the approximate middle of the poem.

The change is again obvious on two levels: in terms of the story the loss of Euridice is now about to be transformed into the process of her redemption, and in terms of the literary background of the narrative and its details we are leaving the pastoral setting of Virgil's *Georgics* and Ovid's *Metamorphoses* and turning in the direction of Virgil's *Aeneid*.

Arcetro's description of Venere's descent from the heavens and the way Orfeo is drawn to her with signs of recognition of the magnificence of the moment (lines 349–65) is perhaps Rinuccini's transformation of lines 190–8 of the *Aeneid*, book VI:[20]

> vix ea fatus erat geminae cum forte columbae
> ipsa sub ora viri caelo venere volantes,
> et viridi sedere solo. tum maximus heros
> maternas agnoscit avis laetusque precatur:
> 'este duces, o, si qua via est, cursumque per auras
> derigite in lucos ubi pinguem dives opacat
> ramus humum. tuque, o, dubiis ne defice rebus,
> diva parens.' sic effatus vestigia pressit
> observans quae signa ferant, quo tendere pergant.

('Scarcely had he said it when a pair of doves chanced to come flying from the sky directly before his very eyes, and settled on the green turf. Then did Aeneas, great hero, recognize his own mother's birds, and with joy he prayed: "O you, be my guides if there is indeed some way! Direct your course through the air to the glade where the bough of blessings shadows a rich soil below. And, Mother Divine, fail me not at this critical time!" So

---

[20] This and all subsequent quotations of Virgil in the original Latin follow the 'old' Oxford text: *P. Vergili Maronis opera*, ed. F. A. Hirtzel (Oxford, 1900 and subsequent reprints).

he spoke, and then checked his steps, watching to see what message the birds might send and where they would next decide to go.')[21]

Indeed in Rinuccini's reworking of his sources images and characters are confused, are transformed one into another and fleetingly pass through the reader's or spectator's consciousness. In Virgil only the doves of Venus appear but not Aeneas' mother herself, while it is the Sibyl who takes him into the gloom of the subterranean Dis:

> Ibant obscuri sola sub nocte per umbram
> perque domos Ditis vacuas et inania regna;
> (*Aen.* vi, 268–9)

('They were walking in the darkness, with the shadows round them and night's loneliness above them, through Pluto's substanceless Empire.')[22]

Here, according to Virgil, everything is silence and night, absence of sound and of anything stirring, until they reach the weeping and the commotion of Acheron. Rinuccini spares us this second, more intense and gripping scene of Virgil's underworld and dwells on the description of the still and empty landscape to which Venere has led Orfeo. She leaves him now, remarking that just as she, the daughter of heaven, was moved by his singing, the underworld too might yield to his lament:

> Forse avverrà che quel soave pianto
> Che mosso ha il Ciel, pieghi l'Inferno ancora.
> (*Euridice*, 416–17)

The second of these two lines is significant, for it is surely more than a coincidence that it recalls Luigi Tansillo's words 'Se non si piega il Ciel, muover l'inferno', the last line of his sonnet *Valli nemiche al Sol*.[23] Tansillo's sonnet, occasioned by a real event, a volcanic erruption at Campi Flegrei on 29 September 1538, paints a terrifying picture of desolation, stillness, darkness and fumes, as if the underworld itself has been exposed to human eyes. After the last line of Tansillo's sonnet has been transformed by Venere, Rinuccini continues what must be a conscious paraphrase of the same source, since the opening lines of Tansillo:

> Valli nemiche al Sol, superbe rupi,
> Che minacciate al Ciel, profonde grotte,
> D'onde non parton mai silentio, e notte,

---

[21] Virgil, *The Aeneid*, trans. W. F. Jackson Knight (Harmondsworth, 1958), p. 153.
[22] *Ibid.*, p. 155.   [23] For the full text see Appendix 2.

39

can easily be recognised as the inspiration behind Orfeo's

> Funeste piagge, ombrosi orridi campi,
> Che di stelle, o di Sole
> Non vedeste giammai scintill'e lampi,
> (*Euridice*, 418–20)

and lines 9–12 of Tansillo's sonnet describe Euridice's and even Orfeo's predicament admirably:

> Erme campagne, abbandonati lidi,
> Ove mai voce d'huom l'aria non fiede,
> Spirto son'io dannato in pianto eterno.

Even if Rinuccini's direct source is Tansillo, Virgil is here still discreetly in the background, since Tansillo's 'Se non si piega il Ciel, muover l'inferno' is commonly accepted to be modelled on Virgil's 'flectere si nequeo superos, Acheronta movebo' (*Aen.* vii, 312), and the Virgilian inspiration behind scene 4 as a whole is strongly maintained.[24]

At this juncture Rinuccini dispenses with Charon, who will become prominent in Striggio's later libretto for Monteverdi, and brings Orfeo and Plutone together with little ceremony. Orfeo addresses him thus:

> O de gli orridi, e neri
> Campi d'Inferno, o de l'altera Dite
> Eccleso Re, che a le nud'ombre imperi,
> (*Euridice*, 451–53)

and these words conveniently reflect back to the imagery of Tansillo's sonnet while owing something to Virgil's description of Orpheus' entrance to the underworld as given in *Georgics*, book iv:

> Taenarias etiam fauces, alta ostia Ditis,
> et caligantem nigra formidine lucum
> ingressus, manisque adiit regemque tremendum
> nesciaque humanis precibus mansuescere corda.
> (*Georgicon*, iv, 467–70)

---

[24] Virgil's line was widely known and achieved the status of a proverb after having been used by Pope Innocent viii and King Ferdinand of Aragon. See L. Tansillo, *Poesie liriche*, ed. F. Fiorentino (Naples, 1882), p. 228. In modern times it was given a new lease of life by Sigmund Freud, who took it as the motto of his *The Interpretation of Dreams*.

It should be pointed out that in addition to the reference to Tansillo, there is some considerable affinity between Venere's words in *Euridice*, lines 416–17, and two lines in Poliziano's *La favola di Orfeo*, spoken by Orfeo before his descent into the underworld: 'Forse che diverrà pietosa morte / Chè già cantando abbiam mosso una pietra'. See A. Poliziano, *Tutte le poesie italiane*, ed. G. R. Ceriello (Milan, 1952), p. 66.

('Even the jaws of Taenarum he braved, / Those lofty portals of the Underworld / And entering the gloomy grove of terror / Approached the shades and their tremendous king, / Hard hearts no human prayer can hope to soften.')[25]

At the same time, it is possible to see that Rinuccini is equally aware of the words spoken by Orpheus in Ovid's *Metamorphoses*, book x, lines 29–30: 'per ego haec loca plena timoris, / per Chaos hoc ingens vastique silentia regni' ('Now by these regions filled with fear, / By this huge chaos, these vast silent realms').[26]

The story now has to depart from the most widely known Classical version as Rinuccini has no intention of depriving Orfeo of Euridice again. Pluto is finally persuaded to release her, just as Venere had foretold, though Rinuccini seems to be reluctant to leave Virgil. Thus, when at the conclusion of the scene the two choirs come together singing:

> Scender al centro oscuro
> Forse fia facil opra;
> Ma quanto, ahi! quanto è duro
> Indi poggiar poi sopra.
> Sol lice a le grand'alme
> Tentar sì dubbie palme.
>
> (*Euridice*, 578–83)

Rinuccini paraphrases and condenses the Sibyl's words to Aeneas in the sixth book of the *Aeneid*:

> . . . 'sate sanguine divum,
> Tros Anchisiade, facilis descensus Averno:
> noctes atque dies patet atri ianua Ditis;
> sed revocare gradum superasque evadere ad auras,
> hoc opus, hic labor est. pauci, quos aequus amavit
> Iuppiter aut ardens evexit ad aethera virtus,
> dis geniti potuere. . . .'
>
> (*Aen.* vi, 125–31)

(' "Seed of the Blood Divine, man of Troy, Anchises' son, the descent of Avernus is not hard. Throughout every night and every day black Pluto's door stands wide open. But to retrace the steps and escape back to the upper airs, that is the task and that is the toil. Some few, sons of gods, have been given the power because either they were loved by Jupiter in fair favour or were exalted by their own brilliant heroism above the world of men." ').[27]

---

[25] Virgil, *Georgics*, trans. L. P. Wilkinson (Harmondsworth, 1982), p. 140.
[26] W. S. Anderson, ed., *P. Ovidii Nasonis Metamorphoses* (Leipzig, 1985); Ovid, *Metamorphoses*, trans. A. D. Melville (Oxford, 1986), p. 225.
[27] Virgil, *The Aeneid*, trans. Jackson Knight, p. 151.

To Virgil Rinuccini of course owes the entire topic and some of the wording, but Dante's presence is felt too. In Rinuccini's 'Ma quanto, ahi! quanto è duro' there is an echo of Dante's 'Ah quanto a dir qual era è cosa dura' (*Inferno*, I, 4).[28] Even Virgil's significant phrase 'hoc opus, hic labor est' strengthens the Dantean link: it had already served Dante as a model which he paraphrases in *De vulgari eloquentia*, II, iv, with a clear reference to the sixth book of the *Aeneid*:

Sed cautionem atque discretionem hanc accipere, sicut decet, hic opus et labor est, quoniam nunquam sine strenuitate ingenii et artis assiduitate scientiarumque habitu fieri potest. Et hii sunt quos Poeta Eneidorum sexto Dei dilectos et ab ardente virtute sublimatos ad ethera deorumque filios vocat, quanquam figurate loquatur.[29]

('But to exercise the appropriate caution and discretion, that is the task and that is the toil, for the proper result can never be achieved without the effort of invention and constant application of the full range of knowledge. And it is those whom the Poet in the sixth book of the *Aeneid* describes as beloved of God and raised to the sky by glowing virtue, and as sons of gods, though he is speaking figuratively.')

It so happens that in the course of this section of *De vulgari eloquentia*, devoted to an explanation of the types of poetic style, Dante also offers his definition of poetry as 'fictio rethorica musicaque poita' ('invention established through rhetoric and music'). As Dante's treatise became available in 1577 in its original Latin version, it is reasonable to assume that this section in particular must have attracted the attention of the members of both Bardi's and Corsi's circles.[30] Nino Pirrotta's contention is that Rinuccini was too young to participate in the discussions at Bardi's Camerata, whereas Tim

28 I owe this point to Dr Z. G. Barański.
29 Dante, *De vulgari eloquentia*, book II, chapter iv, §10. The quotation follows the edition by P. V. Mengaldo as reproduced in Dante, *De vulgari eloquentia*, ed. S. Cecchin (Milan, 1988), p. 108.
30 During the best part of the sixteenth century the treatise was known only in an Italian translation by Giovanni Giorgio Trissino. It became available in its original Latin in 1577 when Jacopo Corbinelli, a Florentine exile living in Paris, obtained from Florence a manuscript in Latin and published it. See 'De vulgari eloquentia', *Enciclopedia Dantesca*, 4 vols. (Rome, 1970–3, suppl. 1978; 2nd, revised edn, 1984), II, pp. 406–7. In the phrase quoted here the manuscripts of Dante's Latin version transmit both 'posita' and 'poita'. 'Poita' is a latinisation of the Greek verb *poiein* which suggests 'making' or 'inventing', whereas 'posita' suggests 'set to'. Trissino translated it from the original which had the latter version, as 'fizione rettorica, e posta in musica'. See Dante, *De la volgare eloquenzia ... di M. Giovanni Giorgio Trissino* (Ferrara, 1583), fol. 26. The phrase 'posta in musica' would have particularly endeared this passage of Dante's to the members of the Bardi and Corsi circles.

Carter stresses the more practical bent of Corsi's circle.[31] Though these assertions may be perfectly true, we must not deny Rinuccini either the knowledge of Classical and humanist sources or the skill to transform them to suit his literary purpose.[32]

The long final scene of *Euridice* opens in a mood of uncertainty and expectation: Orfeo has not returned, although Arcetro and the chorus know that he is under the protection of a goddess. This uncertainty is soon dispelled by Aminta who first refers inconclusively to the happy news about the lucky lovers, then in a short monologue (lines 605–13) instructs the shepherdesses not to lament and eventually tells them of Orfeo's successful return. At the beginning of Aminta's monologue Peri's setting brings the second deviation from Rinuccini's original by inserting this time five new lines:

> Se de' tranquilli petti
> Il seren perturbò nuntia dolente,
> Messagiero ridente,
> La torbida tempesta e i fosch' orrori
> Ecco disgombro e rassereno i cori.
> (Euridice, 604a–e)

Since the insert blends so well with the poetic language that surrounds it, we may be on somewhat safer ground in attributing it to Rinuccini, though whether the idea was his or Peri's has to remain undecided. Whoever was the instigator of the additions must have been strongly aware of their structural significance. Indeed, it could be argued that lines 604a–e play a small role in terms of the narrative, but an extremely important one as a structural indicator by bringing out the opposing symmetry of Rinuccini's poem. Just as in the second scene Dafne was the bearer of sad news, and this was reinforced by the first insert, now, at the point structurally corresponding to it, Aminta reverses her role and

---

[31] Pirrotta, 'Rinuccini', *Enciclopedia dello spettacolo*, 9 vols. (Rome, 1954–62), VIII, cols. 1003–4; Carter, 'Jacopo Peri's *Euridice*', p. 85. See also C. Palisca, *The Florentine Camerata: Documentary Studies and Translations* (New Haven, CT, and London, 1989), p. 8.

[32] A careful scrutiny of *Euridice* which reveals the extent of Rinuccini's knowledge of various literary sources seems to undermine the validity of Gabriello Chiabrera's often cited comment that Rinuccini 'non studiò scienza nessuna, ed anco della lingua latina poco fu esperto', quoted in F. Raccamadoro-Ramelli, *Ottavio Rinuccini: Studio biografico-critico* (Fabriano, 1900), p. 35. The habit of slighting one's colleagues and rivals was, as much as the inclination towards excessive praise, a persistent manner in the writings of the time. Even if Chiabrera's invective was partly true and Rinuccini did have difficulties in following Virgil's original Latin, the *Aeneid* would have been accessible to him in Annibale Caro's Italian translation.

appears as a messenger of joy. We are not left to infer this for ourselves: the insert is here in order to highlight this structural relationship.

The mood of the remainder of the scene is now, predictably, one of joy. This is underlined by Aminta's and Arcetro's words (lines 657–83) and then further reinforced by Orfeo's and Euridice's reappearance which opens the second half of scene 5 (Solerti's scene 6). Orfeo tells of his descent, but with no details of the horror of the underworld since this would inevitably contaminate and disrupt the optimistic mood of the scene. If anything, there is a self-congratulatory tone in Orfeo's verses as he praises not only his good luck, but also the quality and hence the power of his singing. It is, however, Aminta who has the last word in the scene, before the choral finale removes any distinction between the characters. Aminta's concluding monologue could at first glance be characterised as predictable and in a sense traditional. Traditional since it starts by mentioning the sun in its celestial path, thus alluding to astrological imagery, which was popular in the Florentine *intermedi*, and predictable since it refers yet again to Orfeo's power to calm rivers and torrents with his lyre. His very last line: 'Mover gli Dei del Ciel, piegar l'Inferno' (1. 742) is a different version of Tansillo's line, first heard at the end of Venere's monologue at the entrance to the underworld, and it is given added weight by this reference to a previous point in the drama.[33]

The repeat of Tansillo's line serves as a very good reminder of the fact that the entire poem is finely balanced around the central point, Orfeo's entrance into the underworld. If we briefly recapitulate the plot of the scenes at either side of that point, a symmetrical pattern clearly emerges (Table 2).

There are indeed two structural levels of symmetry within the poem. One could be seen in operation within each half, and the other extends over the whole length. The symmetry within the first half, concluding with scene 3, is represented through the following important points: (a) the mention of the change from suffering to joy in the Prologue is balanced by the renewed reference to the

---

[33] It is interesting that in Peri's as well as Caccini's setting the wording of this line is altered to 'Mover gli dei del ciel, placar l'Inferno' (see H. M. Brown's edition, p. xxxvi). I am prepared to conjecture that the change was introduced by Peri on his own initiative or even at Caccini's instigation to increase the variety of vowel colours in the line: in Rinuccini's version there is a single *a* in this line, and the altered version softens the effect of an overwhelming presence of the vowel *e*.

Table 2 *Symmetrical structure of Rinuccini's 'Euridice'*

Prologue	Announcement of the representation of progress from tragedy to joy.
Scene 1	Pastoral rejoicing. Petrarch quoted. Invitation to Venere to assist in pastoral rejoicing.
Scene 2	Orfeo's happiness, refers to Venus and light (l. 117, cf. scene 5, 1st part, l. 611). Dafne (first insert) reports the death of Euridice. The mood darkens.
Scene 3	Arcetro reports on Orfeo led away by Venere. The choir sings of the exchange of joy and suffering.
Scene 4	Scene changed to the underworld. Venere leads Orfeo to the entrance to Hades, Tansillo paraphrased. Plutone releases Euridice.
Scene 5 (1st part)	Scene changed back. Arcetro's gloom, refers to an absence of light (l. 611, cf. scene 2, l. 117). Aminta announces good news (second insert). The mood lightens and leads to rejoicing.
Scene 5 (2nd part)	Orfeo and Euridice reappear, pastoral rejoicing. Second paraphrase of Tansillo.

fluctuation of the two emotional states at the end of scene 3; (b) an invitation to Venere to assist in the rejoicing is balanced by her appearance at the moment of acute need. Balance is less prominently mapped out in the second half, but is nevertheless maintained by the two appearances of the Tansillo paraphrase.

The second level, which embraces the whole text (assuming a division after scene 3) rests on several points:

(a) the wedding allusion of the Petrarch quotation in scene 1 is balanced by the laudatory allusion to Orfeo represented by the paraphrase of Tansillo in scene 5, 2nd part;

(b) Orfeo's reference to a change from night to day (scene 2, ll. 117–19) is balanced by Arcetro's reference to declining daylight (scene 5, 1st part, ll. 584–9):

> *Orfeo*: Bella Madre d'Amor, da l'onde fôra
> Sorgi, e la nott'ombrosa
> Di vaga luce scintillando indora.
>
> (*Euridice*, 117–19)

Arcetro: Già del bel carro ardente
Rotan tepidi i rai nel ciel sereno,
E già per l'oriente
Sorge l'ombrosa notte e 'l dì vien meno,
(*Euridice*, 584–9)

The line 'Come or sorge, or cade il giorno' (388) in the closing section of scene 3 appears then as the pivot around which the two quoted passages are balanced, though both are at some distance from it.

(c) Dafne's arrival with bad news is balanced by Aminta's arrival with good news, both points being reinforced by additional lines after the completion and publication of Rinuccini's poem.

(d) Characteristic turns of phrase, though an inevitable ingredient of poetic style, may also assume structural relevance:

Ninfe: Raddoppia e fiamme e lumi
Al memorabil giorno,
Febo, ch'il carro d'or rivolgi intorno.
(*Euridice*, 42–4)
Orfeo: Raddoppia foco a l'alme e luce al giorno,
E fa servi d'Amor la terra e 'l cielo.
(*Euridice*, 689–90)

The complete structure, when viewed in this manner, reveals the existence of an extraordinarily fastidious plan which relies on small, strategically placed details that ensure that the shape, resembling a giant arch with two sub-arches, is firmly held in place.[34] We can now extend this engineering image further: it is not at all surprising, once the first version of the poem was published, that both Rinuccini and Peri had time and opportunity to reflect on the details of construction and realised that it needed a little strengthening in two strategic places; to this end the additional lines were inserted. One may muse further: if the realisation was Rinuccini's then we can see that he worked more closely with his Florentine friend Peri than with the Roman Caccini, with whom he

---

[34] The elaborate structure of contrasts and parallels may be extended beyond the elements in Table 2, but I did not do this, for fear of overburdening it with graphic signs. The parallelisms may be taken as supporting evidence for Roman Jakobson's theory that all poetry relies strongly on an elaborate structure of 'striking symmetries and antisymmetries, balanced structure, efficient accumulation of equivalent forms and salient contrasts'. See R. Jakobson, 'Poetry of Grammar and Grammar of Poetry', *Lingua*, 21 (1968), p. 603. I am grateful to Professor Giulio Lepschy for drawing my attention to the affinity between my analysis and Jakobson's theory.

probably did not discuss the finer points of his poem; if the instigator was Peri, then this is proof enough that the symmetry and
balance as presented above are not imposed on the poem by an
over-zealous scholar in search of a clear pattern, but were
recognised by a contemporary.

In the symmetrical pattern the quotation from Petrarch remains
without an exact counterbalance since its sentiment is not exactly
repeated by the latter Tansillo paraphrase. Indeed, we can see that
the undertone of the dramatic poem changes from that of an innocent portrayal of wedding bliss at the very beginning to a praise of
Orfeo's powers at the end. Moreover, by turning twice to Tansillo
Rinuccini creates a kind of verbal Leitmotiv which makes explicit
the theme of contrast, opposition and final reconciliation. Its
repeated use in the libretto (albeit with variations in wording) and
its position at two structurally important points give it a special
prominence, and a search for an explanation of the reasons which
led Rinuccini to use this particular literary reference may cast more
light on the hidden allegorical significance of the libretto as a
whole.

II

The occasion for which the opera was written was, of course, a
sumptuous Medici wedding, one in a line of several such occasions
throughout the sixteenth century signifying the increasing international success and dynastic links of the Medici rulers of Florence.
The works of art which played a part in celebrating this success
may therefore be seen as closely linked with the political life of the
times as well as with the personal fortunes of members of the
Medici family. This political context of some Medicean musical
works of art has already been explored by Anna Teicher and Iain
Fenlon with special reference to the performance of the intermedi in
1589, and by Barbara Russano Hanning in connection with Rinuccini's *Dafne*.[35] In what follows I shall take a similar path.[36]

[35] A. Teicher, 'The Spectacle of Politics', *The Florentine Intermedi*, pp. 17–21. B. Russano
Hanning, 'Glorious Apollo: Poetic and Political Themes in the First Opera', *The Renaissance Quarterly*, 32 (1979), pp. 485–513. I. Fenlon, 'Preparations for a Princess: Florence
1588–89', *In cantu et in sermone: for Nino Pirrotta on his 80th Birthday*, ed. F. Della Seta and F.
Piperno (Florence and Perth, 1989), pp. 259–81.

[36] I have relied mainly on R. Galluzzi, *Istoria del granducato di Toscana* (Florence, 1781),
revised edn, *Storia del granducato di Toscana*, 10 vols. (Florence, 1822) [henceforth *GS*; all
references are to the 1822 edition]; and F. Diaz, *Il granducato di Toscana*, Storia d'Italia,
ed. G. Galasso, xiii/1 (Turin, 1976).

47

Although the Medici had been inextricably involved in the financial and political affairs of Florence since the fourteenth century, their elevation to a hereditary position was a sixteenth-century affair dating from 1532, when Alessandro Medici became the first Duke of Florence as a result of a power game involving the Medici Pope Clement VII and the Emperor Charles V. Charles added to Alessandro's status by approving the union in marriage between his daughter Margaret, then aged only fifteen, and the young duke. In January 1537 Alessandro was assassinated by his distant relation Lorenzino who, as a descendant of Lorenzo il Vecchio, was a member of the junior branch of the Medici family. It is to this junior branch that the hereditary rule now passed when the Senators of Florence approved as the new duke Cosimo the son of the condottiere Giovanni delle Bande Nere.

Cosimo was seen by the Senators as an inexperienced youth, showing little interest in politics and therefore unlikely to intervene too strongly in the affairs of government. They were, of course, wrong, since he turned out to be passionately interested and very successful in exercising his control over Florence and Tuscany, as well as extremely ambitious in his attempts to advance the standing of the Medici among the princely houses of Italy. It was clear to him that one way of succeeding in this ambition was through prudent marriage. Unsuccessful in obtaining as his wife the widow of his predecessor Alessandro, he accepted Charles's suggestion and in 1539 married Eleonora, daughter of Don Pedro of Toledo, the Viceroy of Naples. In the politics of power he cautiously supported the Habsburgs both in order to check any French aspirations in Italy and to use the goodwill of the Habsburgs in order to increase his influence on the territories close to Florence. His success in the war with Siena only increased his ambition, and the peace of Le Cateau in Cambrésis in 1559 left him in actual control of Tuscany. In theory, though, as a duke he was a vassal of the Holy Roman Emperor, and he now started making plans for a change in status which would lift him above the level of other dukes in Italy, particularly the Este. He had no hope of fulfilling his ambition to become a king, and elevation to the status of an archduke was in the emperor's gift – something Ferdinand I, who succeeded Charles V, was not prepared to consider.[37] Maximilian II

[37] The possibility of Cosimo being given the status of a king by the pope arose in 1560 in

seemed rather more inclined to humour Cosimo, whose son and heir Francesco married the emperor's sister the Archduchess Joanna in 1565, but the plan was opposed by Philip II of Spain as well as by the Austrian archdukes, Maximilian's brothers. One of Maximilian's learned counsellors, Johann Ulrich Zasius, suggested as a compromise the title of 'grand duke', unlikely to cause offence since it was not used either by the Habsburgs or in Italy.[38] With this Cosimo got no further since Maximilian was reluctant to commit himself to a move which would offend, among others, the Este, whom in terms of diplomatic precedence he favoured above the Medici. Cosimo now turned to the pope in the hope that the elevation would come from him. The pontiff, Giovanni Angelo Medici, reigning as Pius IV, though not a member of the Florentine family liked to pass himself off as a relation; he was well inclined to oblige Cosimo, although it was his successor, Pius V, who carried out the plan, conferring the title of grand duke on Cosimo by a decree of 27 April 1569 and thus putting into practice the suggestion formulated by Zasius. Cosimo was crowned by the pope on 5 March 1570, thereby provoking the indignation of the emperor. It was later left to the skill of Pius's successor Gregory XIII to influence Philip II to persuade Maximilian to recognise the title. This he did by the decree of Regensburg of 2 November 1575, conferring the title not on Cosimo but on Francesco I, who had succeeded his father the previous year. Indeed, the emperor's powers went a little further than the pope's, since the pope had been able to make only Cosimo a grand duke, whereas now in addition the emperor could declare the whole of Tuscany a grand duchy.

Despite all the fluctuations in cordiality between the emperors and the two grand dukes, both Cosimo and Francesco remained essentially loyal to the emperor on the one hand and to Spain on the other, convinced that by playing the Habsburg card right they were ensuring the stability of Tuscany. In the case of Francesco this overall diplomatic consideration was stronger than his personal feelings towards his Habsburg wife Joanna, since his real affection was reserved for his mistress, later his second wife, Bianca Cap-

conjunction with the attempt to secure the hand of Princess Maria of Portugal for his son and heir Francesco. See *GS*, II, p. 276, and Diaz, *Il granducato*, p. 187.

[38] See *GS*, III, pp. 55–6. On Zasius see *Allgemeine deutsche Biographie*, 55 vols. (Leipzig, 1875–1910), XLIV, pp. 706–8.

pello. The pro-Spanish policy of Cosimo and Francesco irritated Caterina de' Medici and accounted for a great deal of the tension between Tuscany and France. That, of course, changed when Ferdinando succeeded his brother as grand duke in 1587. Generally opposed to his brother's pro-Spanish sentiments, skilled in diplomacy and used to the intrigues of the papal court at which he served as a cardinal before his succession (having been created a cardinal at the age of fourteen), Ferdinando was able to see that, just as the earlier Medici benefited from playing off the pope against the emperor, the future stability of Tuscany was likely to rest on his ability to keep in balance the forces of Spain and France. Unlike Francesco he remained on good terms with Caterina de' Medici, and his increasingly French sympathies were confirmed when in 1589 he married Caterina's granddaughter Christine of Lorraine.[39]

Ferdinando inherited from his father not only the ambition to achieve stable government of Tuscany, but also the ambition to see the house of Medici well connected through marriage. Cosimo did succeed in obtaining for Francesco a sister of the emperor, but the emperor's other sister was married to an Este, and it was now only the superior title of grand duke that put the Medici above the Este. Ferdinando must have been strongly aware of this when in the early 1590s he started looking for a suitable match for his niece, Francesco's daughter Maria, then some eighteen years of age. If Ferdinando's ambitions were to be sustained, the marriage had to be of such a kind as to elevate the Medici above the aristocratic and political levels achieved so far. It was with this in mind that Ferdinando rejected the suggestions of Philip II and later of Philip III of Spain that Maria should be married to the Duke of Braganza.[40] A suitor did appear in the early 1590s in the person of Henri of Navarre, a leading French Protestant then married to Margaret, daughter of Henri II Valois and Caterina de' Medici. It was clear to Ferdinando that if, after the death of Henri III in 1589, Henri of Navarre was to be successful in his bid for the French throne, he had to renounce Protestantism and become a Catholic.

[39] In the long run the French connection remained of little value, and the close relations with Austria in the seventeenth century proved to be of greater importance for the development of Florentine politics. See *GS*, VI and VII, *passim*, and Teicher, 'The Spectacle', p. 21.

[40] See *GS*, V, pp. 63 and 218.

Henri, already heavily in Ferdinando's financial debt, expressed in 1592 his readiness to embrace Catholicism, obtain an annulment of his marriage to Margaret and marry Maria.[41] But the political situation in France was still extremely unstable, and Henri's real affection was reserved for his mistress, Gabrielle d'Estrées. Another possible match for Maria, that with Ranuccio, Duke of Parma, did not have the approval of Philip II and did not fit Ferdinando's schemes.[42] The Emperor Rudolf II appeared in 1593 as yet another marriage broker offering to find a suitable match for Maria, but it was not until 1597 that he declared that he wanted her for himself, though not before he had achieved peace in his campaign against the Turks.[43] Maria was by then getting old by the standards of Medici brides, and Ferdinando was understandably becoming impatient. The match with Henri became again a more serious concern at the news of the death of Gabrielle d'Estrées: he had to be secured for Maria before he fell for yet another French mistress. But the obstacle was the sum of 1,000,000 scudi which Henri, already heavily in debt to Ferdinando, now brazenly demanded as Maria's dowry. The wish to see Maria married was apparently so strong among the leading Florentines that Rinuccini's friend and patron Jacopo Corsi petitioned Ferdinando to allow that the sum be raised by a public subscription.[44] The sum paid by Ferdinando was eventually settled at 600,000 scudi, though not before another political storm appeared to threaten the marriage. Relations with Spain, somewhat tense since as far back as 1591, when the Florentines occupied the castle of If near Marseilles, worsened further. The Spanish did not like the possibility of a close union between Tuscany and France and, exploiting a disagreement between Tuscany and the Papal State over some Tuscan irrigation plans, the Duke of Sessa managed to gain a good deal of sympathy for the Spanish position at the papal court in Rome.[45] In addition, the papal nuncio in Paris also worked against the marriage. It would be interesting to know, too, whether the Florentine secret service was aware that in October 1599, when pressed by François de

---

[41] *Ibid.*, pp. 125–7 and 223–6.

[42] *Ibid.*, p. 222.

[43] *Ibid.*, p. 223, and R. J. W. Evans, *Rudolf II and his World: A Study in Intellectual History 1576–1612* (Oxford, 1973), p. 57.

[44] *GS*, v, p. 227.

[45] *Ibid.*, p. 228.

Balzac, Henri signed a promise to marry his most recent mistress, Balzac's daughter Henriette d'Entraygues.[46] Henri obviously did not take this promise seriously and, undeterred by the Spanish-inspired opposition in Rome and Paris, remained resolute, most probably because he needed the dowry money. The last obstacle, that of papal consent, was finally overcome, and the proclamation of the impending marriage was made in Florence on 30 April 1600.[47]

It is important to note that the union celebrated by the performance of the opera was achieved after a protracted series of negotiations during which designs on a European scale, as well as setbacks, were most prominent. In political and dynastic terms the marriage was a triumph for Ferdinando. He carried out his resolve to have Maria marry above the ducal status into which she was born and in the process achieved a symbolic union between the Habsburgs and the Valois-Bourbon. This, of course, was not the first time that these families had been united through marriage: François I married Eleanor Habsburg, the sister of Charles V, and later his grandson Charles IX of France, the son of Henri II and Caterina de' Medici, married Elisabeth of Austria, the daughter of Maximilian II, but viewed from Florence in the late 1590s the marriages would have had less symbolic significance. The former was by now a part of distant history, and the latter involved Caterina de' Medici who, after all, distanced herself from the Florentine and Medici concerns. The Medici did not play a central role in arranging either of the marriages, whereas now Ferdinando could be seen as a mastermind behind the whole operation. Indeed, Scipione Ammirato in the preface to his *Istorie fiorentine*, dated 1 June 1600, sees in characteristically sycophantic fashion the forthcoming marriage not only as an event eagerly welcomed by the whole of Christendom, but also as an act which in its significance stands as the pinnacle of Ferdinando's achievements.[48] Ferdinando

---

[46] J. Garrisson, *Henry IV* (Paris, 1984), p. 247.

[47] *GS*, VI, p. 5. The date of the proclamation makes the Petrarch sonnet from which Rinuccini quotes in *Euridice* particularly appropriate, as it begins with the lines 'Due rose fresche, e colte in paradiso / l'altrier nascendo il dì primo di maggio.' Pietro Bembo's often reprinted commentary suggests that the 'amante antiquo, e saggio' stands for King Robert of Naples, and the image of a monarch extending his benevolence to young lovers would not have been lost on cultured Florentines in 1600. See Appendix 1.

[48] 'Io stimava di por fine a questa istoria con la vita del gran Duca Francesco; ma essendo stato confortato da molti a tirarla avanti infino a quest'anno fortunato del 1600. per esser

had, after all, realised in the only way practicably open to him the ambition of his father of becoming a king; and if Cosimo had to settle for the title of grand duke then at least the elevation of his granddaughter to the royal throne of France through the agency of his son, the reigning grand duke, could be seen as a superb achievement. References to the 'royal roof' and the royal glory that we find in the Prologue to *Euridice* must therefore be seen as having a deep significance, not only in referring to the King of France but also in flattering the royal aspirations of the Medici which extend back to the 1550s. The theme of union and reconciliation of opposites, found in the outline of the story of the opera as well as in so many details of the imagery and wording of the text, are not only typical features of mannerist style but also directly symbolic of the union of a half-Habsburg Medici bride and a Valois-Bourbon groom, coming as it did at the end of a whole century of struggle in Europe in which the two major dynasties played such prominent roles. The Medici, first supporting the Habsburg side and now cautiously inclining towards France, could therefore be represented as the wise and triumphant mediators, and the marriage, celebrated two years after the peace at Vervins, as a fitting confirmation of that treaty.

I have allowed myself to explore in some detail two aspects of historical development that precede the performance of *Euridice*: the protracted negotiations over Maria's marriage, and the dynastic aspirations of the Medici. Both of these seem to throw a particularly interesting light on the line with which Venere sends Orfeo into the underworld: 'Che mosso ha il ciel, pieghi l'Inferno ancora' (*Euridice*, 417). The line acquires added significance since, as we have seen, it appears slightly transformed as the concluding solo line of the entire opera, before the triumphant choral finale: 'Mover gli Dei del Ciel, piegar l'Inferno' (742). I have already mentioned that Tansillo's line, on which this one has been modelled, derives in turn from Virgil's 'flectere si nequeo superos, Acheronta movebo' (*Aen.* VII, 312). In Virgil the words are spoken in anger by Juno,

---

anno di remissione & di perdono, sono anche indotto a farlo, se così a Dio piacerà, per haver in esso l'Altezza vostra congiunto in matrimonio la sua nipote col Cristianissimo Re di Francia: dal qual congiungimento se seguiranno que beni, che tutta la Cristianità va augurando, & vostra Altezza havrà con una magnanima azione illustrato grandemente tutte l'altre opere sue'; Scipione Ammirato, *Dell'istorie fiorentine . . . libri venti* (Florence, 1600), preface, unpaginated.

who is summoning all the help she can get in order to delay, and if possible even to prevent, the wedding of Aeneas and Lavinia. Her basic motive is revenge, since Aeneas is the son of Anchises and Venus, and Juno considers herself wronged in the judgement of Paris, who gave the golden apple to Venus. Note that the internal opposition is the essence of Virgil's line: Hades will presumably do what the gods refuse to do on Juno's behalf. This is weakened in Tansillo's version and, in Rinuccini's rewording of Tansillo, changed yet again so that it becomes a statement within the narrow bounds of a *contrapposto* rather than the wrenching opposition achieved by Virgil. By putting the paraphrased words of Juno, who originally tries to disrupt a marriage, into the mouth of her opponent Venus, Rinuccini reverses their meaning, implying first the wish that the marriage should succeed against the odds and then, at the end of his libretto, confirming this to have been the case. It is too tempting to see in this a veiled reference to the protracted negotiations over Maria's wedding and an expression of joy at the knowledge of all the obstacles overcome. In addition, Rinuccini shows himself to be a sensitive and prudent courtier: quoting Virgil at one remove, as it were, through Tansillo, he managed to retain some of the allegorical significance of the line while removing the possibility of any direct identification of France, Spain or Austria, Valois-Bourbon or Habsburg, with any of the opposing elements of the Virgilian line.

In the political climate in which Rinuccini wrote *Euridice* this circumspection was undoubtedly wise, but it is also conceivable that this detachment served a double purpose. Since much of the allegory may refer to the symbolic union of the Habsburgs with the Valois-Bourbon through the mediation of the Medici, it could also have referred to Ferdinando as the power behind the union, for, if we recall Ammirato's words, the marriage was seen as his supreme achievement. Maria was therefore only the object around which the festivities were arranged, but the real inspirer of the event who won glory for himself was Ferdinando. The line from Virgil via Tansillo, first exhorting Orfeo and then triumphantly confirming his achievement of bringing opposites together, could therefore have further significance by referring not only to the dynastic union but also to the agent of the union. It is, after all, to be expected that, if a courtier writes a dramatic poem to be used for the celebration of a state wedding, the poem will include an element of flattery. It is here hidden below the surface as a result of an elegant artifice rather than because of any apparent political causes.

It is perhaps something of a puzzle why Rinuccini called his work *Euridice* and not *Orfeo*. Throughout the poem Euridice remains very much in the background, and to her Rinuccini assigned only 27 lines of text compared to Orfeo's 159. That Euridice was meant to represent Maria must remain a conjecture – one, moreover, which is based on little tangible evidence. Another conjecture, that there was a link between Ferdinando and Orfeo, at least appears to be a little better supported by circumstantial evidence.

Virgil's line as interpreted by Rinuccini concerns not only the unity of opposites but more precisely Orfeo's powers, which as a theme becomes more and more prominent as the libretto progresses. A link between Orpheus and the attainment of wisdom, which guarantees peaceful existence based on law and order, dates back to Horace's *Ars poetica*. Horace is precise in his description of Orpheus as a bard who becomes law-giver:

While men still roamed the forests, they were restrained from bloodshed and a bestial way of life by Orpheus, the sacred prophet and interpreter of the divine will – that is why he is said to have tamed tigers and savage lions. . . At one time this was the way of the wise man: to distinguish between public and personal rights and between things sacred and profane, to discourage indiscriminate sexual union and make rules for married life, to build towns, and to inscribe laws on tablets of wood. For this reason honour and fame were heaped upon the bards, as divinely inspired beings, and upon their songs.[49]

That the implications of this fragment of Horace were well understood in sixteenth-century Florence is shown by the allegorical portrait of Cosimo I as Orpheus by Bronzino, dating from the 1540s.[50] We must also bear in mind that an allusion relying heavily on Classical literature and wisdom is particularly appropriate in the case of Ferdinando. During his time as a cardinal in Rome he developed a passionate interest in Classical art and became one of the most important collectors of Greek and Roman sculpture. And

---

[49] Horace, *On the Art of Poetry*, 391–401, in Aristotle, Horace, Longinus, *Classical Literary Criticism*, trans. T. S. Dorsch (Harmondsworth, 1965), pp. 92–3.

[50] Now in the Philadelphia Museum of Art. On Cosimo as Orpheus see K. Langedijk, 'Baccio Bandinelli's Orpheus: A Political Message', *Mitteilungen des Kunsthistorischen*

Bojan Bujić

it is again in the spirit of flattery that Rinuccini may have conveniently overlooked the fact that in spite of his zeal as a collector Ferdinando was less interested in Classical scholarship and literature on which the message of *Euridice* relies so heavily. The very basis for using the allegory of Orpheus had already been established in the Medicean tradition, and Rinuccini used it skilfully. In the case of Bronzino's Cosimo I as Orpheus, flattery was in a sense an emptier gesture since it rested on wishful thinking rather than on Cosimo's achievement, still lacking in the early 1540s, whereas in a possible reference to his son Ferdinando as Orpheus the recent political history of Florence would have given flattery a more tangible foundation.

Magdalen College, Oxford

POSTSCRIPT

By way of a postscript it would be useful to re-examine once again the relationship of Striggio's text for Monteverdi's *Orfeo* to Rinuccini's *Euridice* in the light of the details that have emerged so far.[1] We may be fairly certain that Striggio and Monteverdi knew Peri's opera, and the existence in print of the libretto and of the two settings have made it possible to subject them to close and repeated scrutiny. Indeed, in their investigation of the relationship between the two librettos, both Nino Pirrotta and F. W. Sternfeld make precise references to the details that Striggio must have fashioned in response to Rinuccini's verse.[2] We may now go a little further.

Institutes in Florenz, 20 (1976), p. 48, and *The Portraits of the Medici, 15th–18th Centuries*, I (Florence, 1981), p. 117. Hanning in *Of Poetry and Music's Power* draws attention to Langedijk's 1976 paper and to 'the possible influence of the weight of Medici tradition upon Rinuccini' (pp. 52 and 218, n. 43) without attempting to link this tradition with any particular features of *Euridice*.

[1] The existence of two versions of text for Act 5 of Monteverdi's *Orfeo*, to be discussed below, makes it difficult to refer to an authoritative edition of the whole libretto. In *Gli albori del melodramma*, III, pp. 270–2, Solerti placed the text set by Monteverdi in a footnote and did not number the lines. Della Corte's edition in *Drammi per musica*, I, pp. 187–93, presents a curiously conflated version of both texts that corresponds neither to the printed libretto nor to Monteverdi's score. The two texts are presented separately by Hanning, *Of Poetry and Music's Power*, pp. 322–9, and I shall here adopt her numeration which assigns numbers with prime to the lines of the Monteverdi version. Whenham prints the original Striggio version with a parallel English translation in *WhenO*, pp. 35–41.

[2] N. Pirrotta, 'Monteverdi and the Problems of Opera', *Music and Culture in Italy*, pp. 236–45, and F. W. Sternfeld, 'The Orpheus Myth and the Libretto of "Orfeo" ', *WhenO*, pp. 27–8. See also G. Tomlinson, 'Madrigal, Monody', p. 60.

Structure and meaning in Rinuccini's *Euridice*

1. The parallel that is most readily noticeable is that between Rinuccini's quotation of Petrarch in scene 1, 53, and Striggio's quotation of Dante ('Lasciate ogni speranza voi ch'entrate', *Inf.* III, 9) in *Orfeo*, Act 3, 339.[3] The parallel is obvious only because in each case an easily recognisable model is involved, but there the similarity stops, since the contexts in which they are placed and the sentiments expressed are very different. A parallel does, indeed, exist, but is to be found between Rinuccini's paraphrase of Tansillo and Striggio's quotation from Dante: they appear at identical places in the development of the plot and have a certain, albeit tenuous, connection through the person of Virgil.

It is also interesting to compare the implications of the two situations. By bringing a goddess associated with the upper world into the underworld Rinuccini creates an immediate, visual, *contrapposto*, since by a convention going back to Classical antiquity deities of the upper world do not appear in Hades. Venere's appearance at the entrance to Hades at the point when the first change of scene takes place creates a powerful visual effect for all those able to interpret the meaning of the situation against the background of the literary convention. Ovid's *Metamorphoses* is here again a good source. Juno had to be overcome by quite exceptional rage and blinding desire for revenge in order to force herself to enter Hades (*Met.* IV, 447, the story of Athamas and Ino); similarly, Minerva is prevented from entering the cave of Envy (*Met.* II, 765, the story of Aglauros' envy) and is able only to knock at the door with her spear. Dante, too, is strongly aware of this procedure. When Beatrice appears in Limbo to summon Virgil to Dante's aid, Virgil expresses his surprise at seeing her in the surroundings to which she does not belong:

> Ma dimmi la cagion che non ti guardi
> de lo scender qua giuso in questo centro
> de l'ampio loco ove tornar tu ardi.
> (*Inf.* II, 82–4)

By placing Venere at the entrance to Hades Rinuccini strongly hints at this convention and creates a sense of tension resulting from wonder – however briefly sustained – at the possibility that the convention might be broken. This also helps him to continue with his method of underlining structural points: this *contrapposto* which occurs halfway through the poem provides a counterbalance for the one with which the poem started. There, at the beginning of the Prologue, Tragedia creates tension by

---

[3] See Hanning, *Of Poetry and Music's Power*, p. 52; see also Pirrotta in his discussion appended to A. M. Monterosso Vachelli, 'Elementi stilistici nell'*Euridice* di Jacopo Peri in rapporto all'*Orfeo* di Monteverdi', *Congresso internazionale sul tema Claudio Monteverdi e il suo tempo*, ed. R. Monterosso (Verona, 1969), p. 127.

denying that she will perform a tragic role. The reason for bringing Tragedia on might have had its root in a desire to honour the royal bride with the personification of an exalted literary genre, but, this having been done, Rinuccini was able to use the detail as a part of an overall structural plan. Moreover, the topos of Venus in the underworld is recognised by Rinuccini as a valuable and strong theatrical device and he returned to it some eight years later at the opening of *Il ballo delle ingrate*.

Striggio, on the other hand, does not create a situation which points to anything beyond the actual theatrical appearance. By calling his character Speranza he failed to give her any goddess-like qualities and removed the possibility of a secondary reference. The impact of Speranza abandoning Orfeo at the gate of hell and the appearance of the word 'speranza' in the quotation from Dante are undoubtedly powerful and immediate as theatrical devices but do not have the additional, second, layer of meaning available to Rinuccini.

2. It is debatable whether the same or similar rhyming schemes or an occasional correspondence of related phrases witness to Striggio's reliance on Rinuccini, or whether they are the inevitable appearances of the poet's stock-in-trade.

There is only a weak link, but a link nonetheless, between Striggio's Caronte:

> Ma lunge, ah lunge sia da questo petto
> pietà, di mio valor non degno affetto.
> (*Orfeo*, Act 3, 387–8)

and Rinuccini's Tragedia:

> Lungi via, lungi pur da' regi tetti
> [simolacri funesti, ombre d'affanni:
> ecco i mesti coturni e i foschi panni]
> cangio, e desto ne i cor piu dolci affetti.
> (*Euridice*, 9–12)

The relationship of *petto/affetto* and *tetti/affetti* is, of course, one of sound and not of meaning, but the two rhymed hendecasyllables in Striggio have a little more in common with the lines spoken by Rinuccini's Tragedia. In the latter case the mention is of a state of mind being changed, while in the former, as if bearing in mind Tragedia's words, Caronte refuses to be moved by Orfeo's singing. A slightly stronger proof of Striggio's awareness of his predecessor is to be found in Orfeo's 'dimmi, vedesti mai / alcun di me più fortunato amante?' (Act 1, 79–80), the real parallel with Rinuccini's quotation from Petrarch.

In addition, we can see that Striggio's words 'così grazia in ciel impetra / chi qua giù provò l'Inferno' in the final chorus of Act 5 (653'–4') hint at the second Tansillo paraphrase appearing similarly placed towards the end of the closing scene of *Euridice*.[4] John Whenham has drawn attention to the biblical inspiration of the lines immediately following in Striggio's libretto ('e chi semina fra doglie / d'ogni grazia il frutto coglie').[5] This Christian moralising sentiment with its slightly doleful tinge may indicate Striggio's willingness to accept some sentiments pervading the poetry of the Counter-Reformation. With a historian's hindsight it is now gratifying to appreciate that a libretto written towards the end of the first decade of the seventeenth century should contain side by side lines deriving from the literary tradition of the Cinquecento and the new spirit of religious feeling.

3. One of the most difficult critical issues to be raised by the Striggio–Monteverdi collaboration is that of the opera's two endings. The printed libretto follows Ovid and Poliziano and closes with the confrontation of Orfeo and the Bacchantes, whereas the printed score has the fifth act set to a substituted text in which Apollo consoles Orfeo and lifts him up to the celestial spheres. The latter version is generally considered dramatically weak. It provided Monteverdi with only a short text, so that the resulting setting appears unconvincing, too abrupt and short when compared with the preceding four acts. Joseph Kerman went as far as to say that 'this Platonic apotheosis is musically and intellectually blank',[6] and that is perfectly true if one views the work with the detached critical attitude of a modern scholar. Dangerous though it is to try to discover in a work of art submerged or half-realised intentions, it may be possible to account for the unsatisfactory nature of Striggio's text by comparing it with Rinuccini's. Iain Fenlon has attempted to reconstruct the concatenation of events which might have led to the substitution of the qualified happy ending for the original unhappy one.[7] To this could now be added an attempt to explain why the ending seems so unsatisfactory, something the knowledge of the circumstances on its own cannot explain.

In the hasty and short Act 5 of *Orfeo* very little happens, and the central point in terms of the action is, of course, the appearance of Apollo as a *deus ex machina*. His descent follows Orfeo's echo lament, the musical central point of the act. Whatever weight is to be attached to the part of the act following Apollo's appearance, it must come out of the meaning of the poetic text. Apollo promises Orfeo that from now on he will for ever be seeing a semblance of Euridice among the sun and the stars. As Fenlon suggests, the idea for this may have come from Hyginus' *Astronomia*,[8] but we still have to account for the role of these words in the context of the

---

4 See main text, p. 42.
5 Whenham, 'Five Acts: One Action', *WhenO*, pp. 75–6.
6 J. Kerman, *Opera as Drama* (New York, 1956), p. 37. The portion concerning *Orfeo* is reprinted in *WhenO*, pp. 126–37.
7 Fenlon, 'The Mantuan *Orfeo*', *WhenO*.
8 *WhenO*, p. 4

libretto. Of course, Gary Tomlinson's suggestion, endorsed by Fenlon, that the text of Act 5 as set by Monteverdi may not be by Striggio should also be borne in mind.[9]

Striggio's libretto, like Rinuccini's, began by describing pastoral rejoicing. The tragic news of Euridice's death brought the feeling of despair, the despair that took Orfeo to the subterranean world from which he started emerging with Euridice back into the light, before she was finally denied him. Orfeo's echo lament, the only portion of text shared by both versions of the libretto, is shortened by four lines in Monteverdi's setting. This may have been done in an effort to lessen the importance of the passage in which Orfeo pours scorn on love and laments his undoing brought about by Amor. Symbolically he is still tied to Euridice, since even Apollo's offer of immortal bliss ('Dunque se goder brami immortal vita, / vientene meco al ciel ch'a se t'invita', *Orfeo*, Act 5, 633'–4') only causes him to ask anxiously whether this means that he would no longer see her dear eyes. Apollo's Neoplatonic explanation, signalling his translation to the celestial spheres, is thus in itself a *contrapposto* since Orfeo, having once emerged from the underworld and still tied to it by his love of Euridice, is going to be linked, more strongly and lastingly, to the celestial world above. This unity of opposites is then confirmed by the final chorus, whose voices urge him to proceed on the path of happiness, something he now so manifestly deserves: he who braved hell will attain grace in heaven ('così grazia in ciel impetra / chi qua giù provò l'Inferno', *Orfeo*, Act 5, 653'–4'). As we have already shown, the lines may well come from Striggio's conscious emulation of Rinuccini's second Tansillo paraphrase. Might this suggest that Striggio was aware of the whole concept of symmetry and the repeated instances of the unity of opposites that are so carefully deployed in Rinuccini's poem? If so, we may assume one of two possibilities: either that he was aware of the structure of *Euridice* at the beginning of his work on *Orfeo*, or that he began to understand it only at the time he embarked on the second version of Act 5. Although quite early in *Orfeo* there are hints of Striggio's familiarity with Rinuccini, I am inclined to favour the latter assumption.

It goes without saying that in a story which traces the progress from joy to sorrow it is inevitable that there will be contrasts and that the force of poetic diction will demand the occurrence of similar words in contrasting contexts. This would account for some similarities between Rinuccini's and Striggio's version as well as for some references and reminiscences common to both. In addition there are in Striggio's text, as in Rinuccini's, points where the focus is sharpened. Thus at the very beginning of Act 1 a shepherd sings the words 'In questo lieto e fortunato giorno' (*Orfeo*, Act 1, 21) which then reappear in the duet of shepherds, suitably changed into

[9] *Ibid.*, pp. 16 and 188, n. 29.

'in questo mesto giorno' in the closing ensemble of Act 2 (276) after the news of Euridice's death. The words therefore function as a *contrapposto* spread over a large tract of the opera and highlighting the contrast between the two acts in a manner which recalls Rinuccini's large-scale structuring. But where Rinuccini seems confident in his manipulation of verbal opposites, Striggio, as if concerned lest the relationship of the two phrases be missed, follows the second one with an instant summing up, at the peril of an uncomfortably close reiteration: 'quanto più lieto già, tant'or più mesto?' (Act 2, 277). The return to joy, if there is such a process in Act 5, is then expressed in a manner, rather than in the actual words, related to the earlier change. The chorus encourages Orfeo: 'Vanne, Orfeo, felice a pieno / a goder celeste onore' (Act 5, 645'–6'), thus producing the effect of contrived rather than easily achieved symmetry. The symmetry may be aided a little by the connection that exists between Apollo's 'Saliam cantando al cielo' in Act 5 (641') and the shepherd's 'cantiam pastori, / con sì soavi accenti' in Act 1 (34–5). There is also some correspondence between Orfeo's invocation of Apollo in Act 1:

> Rosa del ciel, gemma del giorno, e degna
> prole di lui che l'universo affrena,
> sol ch'il tutto circondi e 'l tutto miri'
>   (*Orfeo*, 75–7)

and the god's actual appearance at the point of complete contrast in Act 5:

> Padre cortese, al maggior uopo arrivi,
> ch'a disperato fine
> con estremo dolore
> m'avean condotto già sdegno et amore.
>   (*Orfeo*, 622'–5')

Condensed and brief as it is, the text used by Monteverdi in Act 5 appears to be an afterthought rather than a logical follow-up to the preceding four acts. As much as Rinuccini seems to have been guided by a large-scale unifying scheme, Striggio's main achievement in Acts 1–4 was to provide sets of dramatic situations which, once moulded by Monteverdi, revealed to the full their hidden potential. The sense of structure was generated by Striggio through a succession of episodes and did not have to depend on an arch structure spanning the entire work. Symmetry, when it does appear, seems to work through a series of adjacent 'numbers', in the manner proposed for the first act by Donald Grout, Silke Leopold and Iain Fenlon,[10] and ultimately depends on Monteverdi's ingenuity as much as on Striggio's sense of form. Striggio's original Act 5

---

[10] I. Fenlon, 'The Mantuan Stage Works', pp. 272–3 (see note 1). Fenlon adapts the scheme first outlined by D. J. Grout, *A Short History of Opera* (2nd edn, New York, 1965), p. 52. See also S. Leopold, *Claudio Monteverdi und seine Zeit* (Laaber, 1982), p. 115.

does not attempt to create any sense of arch-shaped symmetry in relation to the preceding ones, it simply provides another succession of poignant dramatic moments. The text of Monteverdi's ending, on the other hand, reflects a desire for overall symmetry. The textual details discussed above seem to point towards such a wish, as if its author, aware of the symmetry achieved by Rinuccini, were endeavouring to tie up some of the loose ends that he discerned in the existing text of Striggio's Acts 1–4. The urge towards symmetry seems to have been stronger in the author's mind than the consideration of how it might be achieved. It was as if any logical development leading to such a goal was sacrificed to the means, no matter how ungainly, of attaining it, which would account for the brevity and haste of Monteverdi's Act 5. This speaks in support of the assumption that Striggio wrote Monteverdi's Act 5 in an attempt to emulate Rinuccini's procedure, having understood it only after his original version was already complete. This argument may also be applied in order to add weight to the Tomlinson–Fenlon hypothesis that someone other than Striggio, possibly Ferdinando Gonzaga, was the author of the new Act 5. That hypothesis was based on the quality of the verse, and to this may now be added that the author of the verse, as if uncertain how to proceed unaided, may have recognised some of the possible parallels with Rinuccini and then exploited them to the full by imposing on Striggio elements of Rinuccini's solution. The result is not wholly satisfactory because the symmetry was grafted on instead of being allowed to develop from within Striggio's text.

This notwithstanding, Kerman's harsh judgement that the Neoplatonic apotheosis in Act 5 is 'intellectually blank' may be softened a little if we bear in mind that it results from an attempt to mould the libretto on the example of a recent predecessor which, in its careful handling of opposing symmetries, establishes a strong link with the mannerist artistic sensibility of the late Cinquecento. Guarini was well aware that a *contrapposto* functions best if its contrasting elements are placed closely together. With the dash of a virtuoso Rinuccini disregarded that principle, dotted them over a large time-span and laid out the entire story of Orpheus against the background of this 'figura poetica molto vaga'. In attempting a comparable achievement Striggio appears to have been rather less successful.

APPENDIX I

Petrarch

Due rose fresche, e colte in paradiso
    Laltr'hier nascendo il dì primo di maggio.
    Bel dono, e d'un amante antiquo, e saggio,
    Tra duo minori egualmente diuiso:
Con si dolce parlar, e con un riso
    Da far innamorar un huom seluaggio,
    Di sfauillante, & amoroso raggio
    E l'uno, e l altro fe cangiare il uiso.
Non uede un simil par d'amanti il sole,
    Dicea ridendo, e sospirando insieme;
    E stringendo ambedue, uolgeasi attorno.
Cosi partia le rose, e le parole:
    Onde 'l cor lasso ancor s'allegra, e teme.
    O felice eloquentia; o lieto giorno.

Annotatione: Essendo il Re Roberto di Napoli (come dicemmo di sopra) in Auignone: & ritrouandosi un giorno in un giardino ou'erano anche il Petrarca, & M.[adonna] L.[aura] pigliando l'vno, e l'altro per mano, diede loro due rose, la qual cosa egli ha uoluto descriuere in questo Sonetto, oue dice, Due rose fresche colte in *Paradiso*, cio è in un lieto, & ameno giardino. *Cangiar'il uiso*, mutar di colore: d'honesto, & uergognoso rossore tignendolo. *Volgeasi attorno*, quando al Poeta, & quando à M.[adonna] L. [aura].
Source: *Il Petrarca con nvove spositioni, et insieme alcune molto utili, & belle Annotationi* . . . (Venice: Giorgio Angelieri, 1586), pp. 319–20.

APPENDIX 2

Luigi Tansillo

Valli nemiche al Sol, superbe rupi,
    Che minacciate al Ciel, profonde grotte,
    D'onde non parton mai silentio, e notte,
    Aer, che gl'occhi d'atra nebbia occupi,
Precipitosi sassi, alti dirupi,
    Ossa insepolte, herbose mura, e rotte
    D'huomini albergo, & hora à tal condotte
    Che temono ir fra voi Serpenti, e Lupi.

Erme campagne, abbandonati lidi,
  Oue mai voce d'huom l'aria non fiede,
  Spirto son'io dannato in pianto eterno,
Che fra voi vengo à deplorar mia fede,
  E spero al fin con dolorosi stridi,
  Se non si piega il Ciel, muouer l'inferno.

Source: [Cristoforo Zabata], *Della scelta di rime di diversi eccelenti autori . . . Parte prima* (Genoa: A. Roccatagliata, 1582), p. 3. The text reproduced here is likely to have been the one accessible to Rinuccini since it appeared twice in near-contemporary anthologies: in the one quoted here and an earlier one, also edited by Zabata (Genoa, 1573). A different reading was established in 1926 by Erasmo Pèrcopo in his edition of L. Tansillo, *Il canzoniere edito ed inedito* (Naples, 1926), I (the only one published), pp. liii and 23–4. Pèrcopo's contention is that alterations to the above version contained in a manuscript now in Madrid are by Tansillo himself, though little evidence is offered in support of the claim.

Early Music History (1991) Volume 10

ANTHONY M. CUMMINGS

GIULIO DE' MEDICI'S MUSIC BOOKS*

For Nino Pirrotta

David S. Chambers's provocative study of the cardinalate in the late fifteenth and early sixteenth centuries is rich in implications for music historians. A document of December 1509 suggests that at that time a cardinal's household averaged 144 *familiares*, and the 1526 census revealed similar figures. Moreover, the corporate income of the College of Cardinals had been regulated since 1289 by a Bull of that year that decreed that a half of certain items of papal revenue was to be divided among cardinals resident in Rome, although the actual amounts that individual cardinals received fluctuated in response to changes in the size of the college. There were other sources of income: Roman residents were entitled to the revenue of their 'title' church, and those few who held office in the Roman bureaucracy commanded extraordinary salaries.[1] For cardinals with musical interests, the institutional and economic conditions necessary to sustain a musical establishment therefore existed, and despite the relative absence of information on such

* I welcome the opportunity to express my gratitude to Ms Sheryl Reiss, the author of a Princeton University doctoral dissertation on Cardinal Giulio de' Medici as a patron of art, for generously and graciously sharing the results of her research with me and for reading a draft of this paper and suggesting a number of improvements; and to Professors Janet Cox-Rearick of Hunter College of the City University of New York and John Shearman of Harvard University and Dr Julian Kliemann of Villa I Tatti, The Harvard University Center for Italian Renaissance Studies in Florence, for answering questions about iconographic devices in Medici art. Some of the research for this paper and all of the writing of it were undertaken during the academic years 1988–9 and 1989–90, when I was first a Fulbright Scholar in Florence and then National Endowment for the Humanities and Robert Lehman Foundation Fellow at Villa I Tatti. I am grateful to the Commissione per gli Scambi Culturali fra l'Italia e gli Stati Uniti and to the Academic Advisory Committee of Villa I Tatti for affording me the opportunity to spend two such professionally profitable and personally satisfying years in Florence.

[1] D. S. Chambers, 'The Economic Predicament of Renaissance Cardinals', *Studies in Medieval and Renaissance History*, 3 (1966), pp. 287–313, especially pp. 293, 295, 297–9.

Anthony M. Cummings

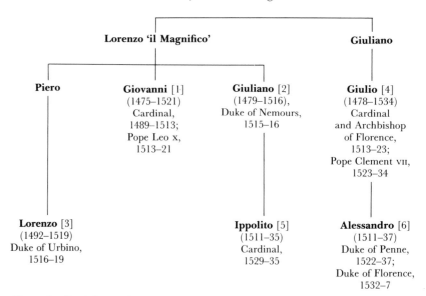

Figure 1   Partial genealogy of the Medici family. The numbers indicate the order in which its members succeeded one another as the family's principal representative in Florence in the years 1512–37.

establishments, we may assume that there were singers and instrumentalists among the *familiares* of many cardinals' households.

Among the cardinals of the time who would have been unusually well positioned to participate in Roman musical life was Giulio de' Medici. As a member of the most famous of Florentine families, he had been witness to an extraordinary tradition of artistic patronage; and as a cardinal resident in Rome during the papacy of his first cousin, Leo x (Giovanni de' Medici), he was witness to the patronage practices of one of the greatest patrons of music in European history.

Giulio was the illegitimate son of Giuliano, the younger brother of Lorenzo 'il Magnifico', and a woman named Fioretta.[2] He was born on 26 May 1478 only weeks after his father had been assassinated in the Cathedral of Florence at the time of the so-called Pazzi Conspiracy; his uncle Lorenzo, who himself narrowly escaped

[2]   My biography of Giulio is based largely on A. Prosperi, 'Clemente vii', *Dizionario biografico degli italiani*, 32 vols. (Rome, 1960–), xxvi, pp. 237–59.

66

death at the hands of the Pazzi and their co-conspirators, undertook responsibility for his nephew. When Lorenzo's sons were exiled from Florence in 1494 Giulio accompanied them into exile, and when they were restored in 1512 Giulio returned with them. From the very first days of the restoration Giulio played a central role in the city's governance, in great part because of his relationship to his cousin Cardinal Giovanni, Lorenzo il Magnifico's eldest surviving son and at that time the family's senior member. Within weeks of Giovanni's election to the papacy, he appointed Giulio Archbishop of Florence (9 May 1513); later that year (20 and 29 September) he legitimised him and named him cardinal. Other important appointments followed: on 1 September 1514 Giulio was made Legate to Bologna, and on 9 March 1517 he became Papal Vice-Chancellor and as such held the most important position in the Roman bureaucracy. It was also one of the most lucrative: Giulio's accounts for 1521–2 contain the entry: 'Cancelleria di Roma facendo el solito d[ucati] 6000'.[3] Giulio had a room in the papal palace and thus enjoyed the special access to the pope of a Palatine Cardinal.[4] After the death of his cousin Lorenzo II, Duke of Urbino, who had been the family's principal representative in Florence in the years after 1513, Giulio assumed Lorenzo's role, and, presumably in order to enhance his authority further still, Leo named him Legate to Tuscany, a position he himself had earlier held. After having installed Cardinal Silvio Passerini of Cortona as his agent in Florence, Giulio returned to Rome in October 1519, but his presence in Florence was demanded repeatedly because of the regime's instability; he was there within a month of his departure in 1519, again in February 1520 and, later that year, from the end of July until the beginning of September; he left for Florence again in January 1521, returned to Rome at the end of April that year, and was again in Florence from late 1522 until the end of March 1523. Within a few months of his Roman *entrata* of April 1523, which John Shearman has rightly characterised as politically important,[5] he was elected pope.

[3] Chambers, p. 299 n. 52. On Chambers' source, see also the important note by M. Bullard, *Filippo Strozzi and the Medici* (Cambridge, 1980), p. 140, n. 75; I am grateful to Sheryl Reiss for bringing this note to my attention.

[4] *Ibid.*, p. 292 and n. 15.

[5] J. Shearman, 'A Functional Interpretation of Villa Madama', *Römisches Jahrbuch für Kunstgeschichte*, 20 (1983), pp. 315–27, especially p. 324.

Anthony M. Cummings

What do we know of Giulio's musical interests? It is not my objective to review the documentation pertaining to his musical patronage as Pope Clement VII, since it is abundant and difficult enough to assess comprehensively, scattered as it is among several publications.[6] Giulio's papal patronage, moreover, is not our principal concern here and is relevant only for what it may tell us generally about his personal musical interests. What does seem clear from even a brief review of the documentation from his time as pope is that the reference in the diaries of Marino Sanuto to the effect that 'he doesn't want jesters or musicians, he doesn't go hunting, nor [does he have] other amusements, as the other popes did'[7] seems not to be substantiated by other evidence, some of it contained elsewhere in Sanuto's own diaries: a reference for April 1528 specifies that during the pope's absence from Rome after the Sack 'His Holiness has taken singers and others with him and he is reassembling the court and hopes to have the *rocca* of Viterbo, where he wishes to go',[8] and an entry for 17 August 1533 reads: 'after lunch the pope was in bed, and there was music by three lutenists'.[9] Sanuto's diaries also provide evidence of Clement's own

[6] In addition to those published here, the principal texts pertaining to Clement's patronage that are at present available may be found in the following: R. Sherr, 'New Archival Data concerning the Chapel of Clement VII', *Journal of the American Musicological Society*, 29 (1976), pp. 472–8, *passim*; H.-W. Frey, 'Regesten zur päpstlichen Kapelle unter Leo X. und zu seiner Privatkapelle', *Die Musikforschung*, 8 (1955), pp. 58–73, 178–99 and 412–37, and 9 (1956), pp. 46–57, 139–56 and 411–19, especially 8, pp. 180 n. 47 and 197, and 9, pp. 49, 144–5 and 152; A.-M. Bragard, 'Détails nouveaux sur les musiciens de la cour du Pape Clément VII', *Revue Belge de Musicologie*, 12 (1985), pp. 5–18, *passim*; Frey, 'Klemens VII. und der Prior der päpstlichen Kapelle Nicholo de Pitti', *Die Musikforschung*, 4 (1951), pp. 175–84, *passim*; Frey, 'Michelagniolo und die Komponisten seiner Madrigale', *Acta Musicologica*, 24 (1952), pp. 147–97, especially pp. 163 n. 67, 164 n. 68, 170–1 and n. 108 and 172; F. X. Haberl, 'Die römische "schola cantorum" und die päpstlichen Kapellsänger bis zur Mitte des 16. Jahrhunderts', *Bausteine für Musikgeschichte*, III (Leipzig, 1888, repr. 1971), pp. 71–5; A. Ducrot, 'Histoire de la Cappella Giulia au XVIe siècle depuis sa fondation par Jules II (1513) jusqu'à sa restauration par Grégoire XIII (1578)', *Mélanges d'Archéologie et d'Histoire*, 75 (1963), pp. 179–240 and 467–559, especially pp. 191 and n. 2, 192 and n. 1, 498 and n. 1, 500 and n. 3, 532 n. 2 and 536–7; E. Plon, *Benvenuto Cellini, orfèvre, médailleur, sculpteur* (Paris, 1883), pp. 10–11 n. 1; A. Cametti, 'I musici di Campidoglio', *Archivio della Società Romana di Storia Patria*, 48 (1925), pp. 25ff.

[7] 'no vol bufoni, non musichi, non va a caza, ne altri piaceri, come feva li altri Pontefici'; *I diarii di Marino Sanuto*, 59 vols. (Venice, 1879–1903), XLI, col. 283. Unless otherwise noted, translations of sixteenth-century texts are my own.

[8] 'Soa Santità ha tolto cantori et altri, et rinova la corte e spera haver la roca di Viterbo dove vol andar'; *ibid.*, XLVII, col. 270.

[9] 'da poi pranso [il] Pontefice . . . era in leto . . . et si havea una musica di tre lauti'; *ibid.*, LVIII, col. 610.

musicianship; a chronicler described the coronation ceremony for the Emperor Charles V in February 1530: 'After the Secret was finished, the pope said the Preface, and very well, having a good voice and being a perfect musician.'[10] And Antonio Soriano, a Venetian envoy in Rome during Clement's papacy, wrote similarly: and certainly one sees no one more favoured and holding and performing religious observances more devoutly than His Holiness; serving him greatly in this is music, an art quintessentially his, such that the pope – it is said – is among the good musicians at present in Italy'.[11] (Colin Slim has interpreted a reference in the horoscope cast by Lucas Guarico for the harpsichordist and organist Vincenzo da Modena as evidence that Giulio may have received instruction on the organ, a reference that may thus provide further witness still to his musicianship.)[12] Other sources testify to musical activities at Clement's court; in a dispatch of 1525 Francesco Gonzaga described a dinner 'at the pope's property [the Villa Madama on the Monte Mario], where the most beautiful accommodation is under construction with some rooms already finished, as sumptuous and magnificent as can be, done during his time as cardinal. The dinner was most estimable and amply supplied with foods, and throughout there was musical entertainment of various kinds.'[13] In 1526 Gonzaga wrote:

The cavalier Franceschino [Cibo] took Her Ladyship [Isabella d'Este] into the room where Our Lord ordinarily eats, and having prepared there a beautiful meal of confections, fruits and other things, [the pope] then had come Francesco da Milano, most excellent player of the lute, as perhaps Your Excellency [Federico Gonzaga] knows, who with two companions played music with two lutes and a viol.[14]

[10] 'Finito che fu le secrete il papa disse el prefatio et molto bene, per haver bona voce, et esser perfeto musico.' *Ibid.*, LII, col. 648.

[11] 'e certo niun altro si vede più graziata e devotamente celebrare ed eseguire alcune ecclesiastiche osservanze, di quello che fa Sua Santità; servendola in questo anche molto la musica, arte a lui molto propria; di sorte che è fama, il papa essere delli buoni musici che ora siano in Italia'; see E. Alberi, ed., *Relazioni degli ambasciatori veneti al Senato*, 2nd series, III (Florence, 1846), p. 278.

[12] See H. C. Slim, 'The Keyboard Ricercar and Fantasia in Italy, *c.* 1500–1550' (Ph.D. dissertation, Harvard University, 1960), pp. 161–3.

[13] 'alla vegna de S. S.ᵗᵃ [the Villa Madame], dove è un principio de un bellissimo alloggiamento cum qualche stantie finite, sumptuose et magnifiche al possibile, fatte nel tempo che era Cardinale. La cena fu molto honorevole et copiosa assai de vivande et sempre fin che si stette li, . . . si ebbe intertenimenti de musica de varie sorte.' A. Luzio, 'Isabella d'Este e il sacco di Roma', *Archivio Storico Lombardo*, 4th series, 35/x (1908), pp. 5–107, 361–425, especially pp. 14–15.

[14] 'Il cavagliero Franceschino [Cibo] condusse Sua Signoria [Isabella d'Este] in la stantia

Anthony M. Cummings

Edward Lowinsky recounted other incidents related in Cellini's autobiography and Cosimo Bartoli's *Ragionamenti* that reflect on the place of music at Clement's court.[15] Moreover, there are a great many entries in the papal account books from Clement's time that record payments to musicians and a great many letters, Bulls and documents of other kinds that served to confer various favours on papal musicians.[16] The members of Clement's musical establishment included, among many other singers, Bernardo Pisano, Charles d'Argentille, Costanzo Festa, Eustachio de Monte Regali Gallus, Ivo Barry, Jean Beausseron, Jean Conseil, Niccolò de Pitti (whose correspondence with Clement includes an interesting letter of 1528 in which Pitti described his recent compositional activity)[17] and Vincent Misonne, and, among the instrumentalists, Gian Maria Giudeo, Francesco da Milano and Lorenzo da Gaeta. Of Clement's singers, Conseil seems to have played an unusually important role: in 1528, after the Sack, he was sent on a recruiting trip in order to identify prospective singers for the Cappella Sistina; we can chart his progress on the basis of a series of interesting letters between Giovanni Salviati, Papal Legate in France, and his father Jacopo, the pope's secretary.[18]

The available documentation for Giulio's musical interests as cardinal is much less extensive and therefore easier to review and interpret. As a member of the Compagnia del Diamante, which was under the direction of his cousin Giuliano, Lorenzo il Magnifico's youngest son, Giulio, may have helped to organise the 1513 carnival festivities, the first since his family's restoration to Florence.[19] Among the carnival activities arranged by the Compagnie del Diamante and del Broncone, which was under Lorenzo II's direc-

dove Nostro Signore manza hora ordinariamente, et havendo preparata li una bella colatione de confetti di zucharo, frutti et altre diverse cose, fece doppoi venire Francesco de Milano, excellentissimo sonatore de liuto, come forsi deve sapere Vostra Excellentia [Federico Gonzaga], con dui compagni che fecero musica con dui liuti et uno violone.'
W. F. Prizer, 'Lutenists at the Court of Mantua in the Late Fifteenth and Early Sixteenth Centuries', *Journal of the Lute Society of America*, 13 (1980), pp. 5–35, especially p. 34. (The translation is Prizer's.)

15   E. E. Lowinsky, ed., *The Medici Codex of 1518*, 3 vols., Monuments of Renaissance Music 3–5 (Chicago, 1968), I, pp. 64–5.
16   See the texts published in the studies cited above (note 6).
17   Frey, 'Klemens VII.' (see note 6), pp. 180–1.
18   Haberl (see note 6), especially pp. 72–3 n. 3.
19   Prosperi (see note 2), p. 238, and H. Butters, *Governors and Government in Early Sixteenth-Century Florence, 1502–1519* (Oxford, 1985), p. 208 and n. 110.

tion, were performances of *canti carnascialeschi* whose texts and music have come down to us; their texts reveal that the Medici were aware that the occasion possessed considerable 'propaganda' potential that they exploited to their advantage: the various elements of the carnival's activities, the *canti* among them, so effectively created the illusion of the return of a golden age that one chronicler wrote: 'al popolo pareva che fussino tornati i tempi di Lorenzo Vecchio'.[20]

That Giulio quickly established himself as Leo x's trusted agent emerges as clearly from his correspondence concerning musical matters as from other correspondence, and, indeed, it is in that role that we first see unequivocal evidence in the documents of his musical interests as cardinal. Within a year of Leo's election Giulio corresponded with Lorenzo II concerning Lorenzo's attempts on behalf of the Signoria of Florence to secure the services of instrumentalists, and he did not hesitate to challenge Lorenzo implicitly to maintain a certain qualitative standard in his practices as a patron of music: 'I understand the Signoria's desire to have *pifferi* and trombonists from Cesena . . .; and because I do not believe it to be an excellent thing, I judge that there what is called good music is that which costs little, and it appears to me that Your Magnificence does not delight in it as the pope does'.[21] In 1515 Giulio wrote to Lorenzo on behalf of the musician Alessandro Coppini, who wished to be elected Provincial of the Servite Order in the Province of Tuscany, and the fullness of his recommendation, as well as the specificity of its language, suggests that, in this instance, Giulio's advocacy was in no sense perfunctory.[22] Giulio accompanied the pope to Florence in November 1515 on the occasion of Leo's famous Florentine *entrata* and played a role in the musical performances that were so important a part of the activities

---

[20] The 1513 carnival is discussed at length in my study *Music and Political Experience in Medici Florence, 1512–1537* (Princeton, forthcoming).

[21] 'ho inteso el desiderio che quella ha di havere e pifferi et tromboni di Cesena . . .; e perchè non credo vi sia cosa eccellente, judico che costi si chiami buona musica quella che costa poco, et parmi che la M. V. non se ne dilecti come fe el papa'; R. Sherr, 'Lorenzo de' Medici, Duke of Urbino, as a Patron of Music', *Renaissance Studies in Honor of Craig Hugh Smyth*, 2 vols. (Florence, 1985), I, pp. 628–38, especially p. 634 n. 11. For the texts of other letters between Lorenzo and Cardinal Giulio concerning the *pifferi*, see pp. 634 n. 8 and 635 nn. 12 and 14.

[22] R. Sherr, 'Verdelot in Florence, Coppini in Rome, and the Singer "La Fiore" ', *Journal of the American Musicological Society*, 37 (1984), pp. 402–11, especially p. 409.

organised in Florence at the time.[23] In 1518, Giulio wrote to Bernardo Dovizi da Bibbiena, Leo's legate in France at the court of Francis I, that

His Holiness wishes that Your Most Reverend Eminence arrange with the master of the king's chapel to have three *putti cantori* of the age and voice [type] that you may determine by way of the enclosed memorandum that Carpentras drafted for me. And should it be necessary to speak to His Majesty about it, perform the service how and when it seems best to you, in His Holiness's name.[24]

The 'putti' are the subject of a letter of Dovizi's to Giulio: 'the king's mother has taken responsibility for finding and sending three *putti musici* to His Holiness, in accordance with Carpentras's note'.[25] After Lorenzo II died and Giulio assumed responsibility for the Florentine government, there are further traces of his patronage; a document of April 1521 suggests that the tenure of two singers at the Annunziata depended upon 'la volontà del nostro Reverendissimo Messieur Cardinale de' Medici',[26] and in May that year Niccolò de' Pitti, the Prior of the Papal Chapel, wrote to Giulio concerning Verdelot, the most important of the earliest madrigalists, who was in Florence at that time and in some way associated with Giulio.[27] We might argue that the famous lutenist Gian Maria Giudeo, for many years an intimate of various members of the Medici family, was also associated with Giulio during the years between Leo's death and Giulio's election, given that Giulio and his agent, Angelo Marzi, wrote four letters in 1522 on Gian Maria's

---

23 Cummings, *Music and Political Experience*.
24 'N. S. desidera che V. S. Reverendissima facci opera col Maestro di Capella del Cristianissimo di havere tre putti cantori de la età et voce che la vedrà, per un memoriale che sarà in questa che mi ha fatto Carpentrasse. Et quando bisognasse parlarne a Sua Maestà, fate l'offitio come et quando meglio vi parerà, pure in nome di sua Beatitudine.' C. Guasti, 'I manoscritti Torrigiani donati al R. Archivio centrale di stato', *Archivio Storico Italiano*, 3rd series, 24 (1976), p. 10.
25 'Madama ha preso l'assunto di trovare et di mandare a Nostro Signore i tre putti musici, seconda la nota di Carpentrasse'; G. L. Moncallero, *Epistolario de Bernardo Dovizi da Bibbiena*, 2 vols., Biblioteca dell''Archivum Romanicum' 44, 81 (Florence, 1955, 1965), II, p. 127. I can offer no explanation as to why Giulio's letter to Dovizi, which is given here first, is dated 4 September 1518, *after* Dovizi's letter to Giulio, which is dated 18 July 1518, when the content of Giulio's suggests that it must have preceded Dovizi's; I have not seen the original documents, and it may be that one of the editors reported mistakenly on the date.
26 F. A. d'Accone, 'The Musical Chapels at the Florentine Cathedral and Baptistry during the First Half of the 16th Century', *Journal of the American Musicological Society*, 24 (1971), pp. 1–50, especially p. 41.
27 Sherr (see note 22), especially p. 409.

behalf to various prospective benefactors; since Conseil is documented as a member of Giulio's household in Rome in 1517, 1520 and 1521, it may reasonably be suggested that among Giulio's intimates were three of the more famous musicians of the early sixteenth century.[28] Testimony of a different sort to Giulio's artistic and musical interests is provided by Pietro Alcionio's *Medices legatus de exsilio* of 1522, and although the reference must be interpreted in the context of the literary tradition the text exemplifies, it is not inconsistent with the documentary evidence for Giulio's artistic interests; he is depicted as engaged in a discussion with Lorenzo II:

Certainly, Lorenzo, I neglected no genre of ancient letters and I enjoyed them, because I felt letters to be the principal ornament of life; I also endeavoured to learn music and painting thoroughly, because they are of the greatest help in perfecting the body; they keep us engaged in a noble occupation, to the great pleasure of the soul, if we want to master them.[29]

---

[28] On Gian Maria, see A. M. Cummings, 'Gian Maria Giudeo, Sonatore del Liuto, and the Medici' *Fontes Artis Musicae* 38 (1991); on Conseil as a member of Giulio's household, see the texts of documents dated 4 March 1517, 11 January 1520 and 9 April 1521 in Frey, 'Regesten' (see note 6), pp. 180–1. Richard Sherr graciously informed me of the existence of another reference of 1517 (Rome, Archivio Segreto Vaticano, Registri delle suppliche, 1598, fol. 218ᵛ) that similarly documents Conseil as a member of Giulio's *famiglia*; I am grateful to Professor Sherr for providing me with a copy of the document in question.

Two other references suggest that Cardinal Giulio may have taken an interest in the musical education of his protégés or associates; an account book in Rome, Archivio di Stato (Camerale I, Appendice 6), that lists expenses incurred by Giulio's page (fol. 26ʳ, 'MDXXI A presso nota dipiù spese fatte p[er] Stefano di m[esser] Mario Crece[n]tio paggio d[e]l R[everendissi]mo Car[dina]le d[e]' medici incominciate addi 6 di novembre 1520') contains the following item: 'E am[aestr]o Ber[nard]o sonatore diliuto p[er] havere insegnato ad[e]c[t]o Stefano dua mesi.' And in his autobiography, Benvenuto Cellini recorded that Cardinal Giulio offered to assist the young artist and provide letters of recommendation for him should he choose to go to Bologna to study music with a renowned master named Antonio; in this instance, however, I should note that, according to Cellini, Giulio failed to fulfil the terms of his offer, which in any event was made not on Giulio's own initiative but in response to a suggestion from a certain Pierino, a pupil of Cellini's father; see *The Life of Benvenuto Cellini*, trans. J. A. Symonds (London, 1920), pp. 12–15.

[29] 'IUL: Prorsus Laurenti: nullum enim genus antiquarum literarum omisi, quod non attingerem, quia suspiciebar, praecipua vitae ornamenta esse literas, incenaque etiam sum maximo studio perdiscendi Musicam et Picturam quoniam haec ad perfectionem corporum notitiam adiumento affert maximum, illa, quod faciat, nos otium honeste & cum magna animi voluptate tenere, si modo illud complecti velimus.' For assistance with the translation, and for help on many other matters given with characteristic generosity, I am grateful to Dott. Gino Corti of Villa I Tatti. I am grateful for the reference to Alcionio, and for the transcription, to Sheryl Reiss, who also suggested that the narrative content of the scene depicted in Giulio's official seal may be indirect evidence of his musical interests: it is a Nativity scene in which musicians are present, and since

Anthony M. Cummings

There is evidence, too, that Giulio, as Leo's close associate, was present on occasions in Rome when music was performed; documentation of his musical interests therefore consists not solely of references that pertain to Florentine musical developments, which Giulio was evidently asked to monitor on Leo's behalf, but to specifically Roman musical life as well. On two occasions, correspondents reported on musical performances; in July 1513 the Mantuan representative wrote to Francesco Gonzaga: 'Yesterday I went to His Holiness, whom I found at the Belvedere with the Archbishop of Florence. In the antechamber was the Most Reverend Cardinal of Ferrara and the Cardinal of Ancona. I visited His Holiness and then Gian Maria Giudeo made music with viols',[30] and in June 1516 Beltrando Costabili reported to Ippolito d'Este that 'Adriano, Auns, Sauli, Cornaro and Medici ate there [the site of the future Villa Madama] with His Holiness, and Signor Antonio Maria and Frate Mariano and "il Proto", with his music, was present'.[31]

Giulio also possessed two books of polyphonic music which were evidently prepared for him during his time as cardinal, and one can argue accordingly that he is a figure of considerable music-historical importance, since, to my knowledge, there is no other cardinal of the time with whom two such sources can be associated. It is to an examination of these manuscripts that I should now like to turn. Before doing so, however, I might comment briefly on a third manuscript, VatP 1982,[32] sometimes said to have been Giulio's on

musicians are by no means indispensable to the narrative, their presence may suggest that the artist who designed the seal was responding to Giulio's interests.
30 'Heri andai dal Nostro Santità, qual ritrovai a Belvedere . . . cum . . . l'Arcevescovo di Fiorenza. In l'anticamera era el Reverendissimo Cardinale de Ferrara et Monsignore Cardinale de Ancona v[i]site el Nostro Santità et poi la musica di violini che fece Zoanne Maria Judeo.' Prizer (see note 14), especially p. 33. (The translation is Prizer's.)
31 'Et mangioli [the site of the future Villa Madama] cum Sua San.^tà Adriano, Auns, Sauli, Cornaro, et Medici, et el S. Ant.º M.ª et Frate Mariano, et il Protho ge intraveneno cum la sua musica'; J. Shearman, 'A Note on the Chronology of Villa Madama', The Burlington Magazine, 129 (1987), pp. 179–81; for this reference I am grateful to Sheryl Reiss. The pope was not the only host who included Cardinal Giulio among his guests on occasions when music was performed; on 7 May 1518, Pompeo Colonna hosted a convivio on which Cornelius de Fine reported in his diary (Rome, Biblioteca Apostolica Vaticana, Ottob. Lat. 2137): 'plebis autem innumerabilis multitudo, Sonorum, et omnis generis musicorum infinitus numerus: . . .'. For this reference, and for providing me with a copy of the relevant page from the diary, I am again grateful to Sheryl Reiss.
32 Manuscript sigla used in this article are those found in the Census-Catalogue of Manuscript Sources of Polyphonic Music 1400–1550, 5 vols., Renaissance Manuscript Studies 1 (Neuhausen-Stuttgart, 1979–88); on VatP 1982, see vol. IV, p. 25.

74

the basis of its binding, which shows the Medici coat of arms, the familiar shield with a central ball positioned at the top centre and five others arranged in the shape of a V.[33] In my view, however, there is no particular warrant for identifying this manuscript with Giulio, or indeed with any one specific member of the family, since there is nothing about the version of the coat of arms that appears on the binding that serves to distinguish it as one individual's device. In this discussion, therefore, it will not be considered as one of Cardinal Giulio's manuscripts; also excluded from consideration here are the Cappella Sistina sources dating from Giulio's time as Pope Clement VII.[34]

THE MANUSCRIPT VATP 1980-1

Physical characteristics
MS 1980

Binding: MS VatP 1980 is the tenor partbook of what was presumably a four-volume set. It is bound in tooled brown leather, and the word 'TENOR' is stamped at the top centre of the front cover.

Evidence of ownership: Towards the top of the spine is a blue printed sticker with the words 'BIBL. AP. VATICANA Pal. lat. 1980'; towards the

---

[33] See I. Schunke, *Die Einbände der Palatina in der Vatikanischen Bibliothek*, 2 vols., Studi e Testi 216–18 (Vatican City, 1962), I, p. 176, Tafel CXXXIII, and II, p. 902.

[34] On the Cappella Sistina manuscripts, see now J. Dean, 'The Scribes of the Sistine Chapel, 1501–1527' (PhD dissertation, University of Chicago, 1984). Giulio was also Cardinal Protector of the French king, and in that role had a relationship to the church of San Luigi dei Francesi in Rome, as Sheryl Reiss reminded me. Although the relationship was largely ceremonial, I would observe, first of all, that the musical repertory of the church in the early sixteenth century bore some relationship to the Cappella Sistina repertory and, second, that the 'Johannes Heritier' listed among the members of Leo's *famiglia* in 1514 may be identical with the well-known composer Jean Lhéritier, who was one of the early *maestri di cappella* at San Luigi. I would not necessarily argue that the early sixteenth-century music manuscripts from San Luigi should therefore be considered products of Giulio's patronage; however, might not members of the musical establishment at the church have asked Cardinal Giulio to intercede on their behalf in order to secure Lhéritier's appointment and to procure pieces from the Sistine Chapel repertory? On the choirmasters, see H.-W. Frey, 'Die Kapellmeister an der französischen Nationalkirche San Luigi dei Francesi in Rom im 16. Jahrhundert. Teil I: 1514–1577, Teil II: 1577–1608', *Archiv für Musikwissenschaft*, 22 (1965), pp. 272–93, especially 274–6, and 23 (1966), pp. 32–60; on the 'Johannes Heritier' in Leo's household, see Frey, 'Michelagniolo' (note 6), p. 162 n. 63; on the musical repertory of the church, see L. L. Perkins, 'Notes bibliographiques au sujet de l'ancien fond musical de l'Église de Saint Louis des Français à Rome', *Fontes Artis Musicae*, 16 (1969), pp. 57–71, M. Staehelin, 'Zum Schicksal des alten Musikalien-Fonds von San Luigi dei Francesi in Rom', *Fontes Artis Musicae*, 17 (1970), pp. 120–7 (especially pp. 125–6 n. 23, on MS BerlS 40091), and (also on BerlS 40091) Staehelin, review of Lowinsky, *The Medici Codex* (see note 15), *Journal of the American Musicological Society*, 33 (1980), pp. 575–87, especially p. 578 and n. 6.

bottom is a sticker with the pencil inscription '1980'. At the upper left corner of the paper guard sheet that is glued to the inside front cover is a blue sticker identical with that which appears on the spine. Three additional paper guard sheets, foliated I, II and III, precede the manuscript proper; with the sheet that is glued to the inside cover, they form two bifolia: a bifolium consisting of the inside front cover and fol. III, and bifolium I/II. On fol. I^r is written 'Pal. 1980' in blue crayon; fol. III^r contains the index and a stamp 'BIBLIOTHECA APOSTOLICA VATICANA'.

Collation: The manuscript proper consists of eighty-six sheets of gilt-edged paper in oblong quarto; the edges are stamped with designs. Each folio measures *c*. 212 mm long×132 mm high. Gathering I (fols. 1–6) consists of three double sheets; the remaining ten gatherings consist of four double sheets each. At the end is a bifolium, fols. [LXXXVII^r]–[LXXXVIII] (my foliation); fol. [LXXXVIII] is glued to the inside back cover.

Paper types: Although the paper is principally of one type, as the *Census-Catalogue*[35] published by the American Institute of Musicology correctly reported, in addition to the anchor-in-circle watermark that the entry for VatP 1980–1 describes, bifolium 9/12 contains a different mark, two crossed arrows.[36]

MS 1981

Evidence of ownership: VatP 1981's physical characteristics are almost identical with those of VatP 1980, except that its front cover is stamped 'BASSVS', the stickers on the spine read '1981', and fol. I^r contains the inscription 'Bassus' in brown ink above the inscription 'Pal. 1981'. The index on fol. III^r is essentially identical with that of VatP 1980, except for some minor differences in the spellings of the text incipits and the fact that the first two pieces contain the only composer attributions in the manuscript: 'fevi[n]' and '[La] rue'.

Collation: The manuscript consists of ninety-four paper sheets, of which

[35] See the entry for VatP 1980–1 in *Census-Catalogue* (note 32); the paper type specified there, Briquet 491 (see C. M. Briquet, *Les filigranes*, ed. A. Stevenson, 4 vols. [Amsterdam, 1968]), is documented in Florence in 1519, but one version or another of this extremely common mark is found in many parts of Italy, and great care should therefore be exercised in assessing its significance; see V. Mošin, *Anchor Watermarks* (Amsterdam, 1973), *passim*.

[36] See, for example, Briquet 6267–8 and 6280–2. Because the manuscript is in oblong quarto, the watermarks appear at the fold of the page and never appear in their entirety; rather, each appearance is of half of the mark. For these reasons, and because I was unable to arrange for photographs of the marks – and thus cannot offer documentation for any assertion I might make – I am reluctant to attempt to specify more precisely which of Briquet's exemplars most closely resemble the marks in VatP 1980 (though I have *excluded* some exemplars). Further study may serve to identify the marks precisely. As Iain Fenlon reminds me, however, in any analysis of watermarks one has to be aware of the existence of and differences between 'twin' marks; see especially A. Stevenson, 'Watermarks are Twins', *Studies in Bibliography*, 4 (1951–2), pp. 57–91.

fols. [86]–[94] are unfoliated. At the end is a bifolium, fols. [xcv^r]–[xcvi] (my foliation); fol. [xcvi] is glued to the inside back cover. Gathering I (fols. 1–6) consists of three double sheets, gatherings II (fols. 7–14), III (fols. 15–22), IV (fols. 23–30), VI (fols. 35–42), VII (fols. 43–50), VIII (fols. 51–8), IX (fols. 59–66), X (fols. 67–74), XII (fols. 79–[86]) and XIII (fols. [87]–[94]) of four, and V (fols. 31–4) and XI (fols. 75–8) of two.

Paper types: Again, the paper is almost exclusively of the type reported in the *Census-Catalogue*[37] with the exception of guard sheet II, which at the centre shows a different mark, a cardinal's (?) hat with tie-strings, upside down.[38]

Evidence of provenance and date. I have reported on the physical characteristics of the manuscript in such detail because, apart from the illumination that appears at the bottom centre of fol. 1^r, they are the only external evidence for its origin. Nothing about them is inconsistent with the evidence of the illumination: a gold shield, with five red balls arranged in a v-shape and a single blue ball at the top centre with three gold fleurs-de-lis, surmounted by a gold crucifix and a red cardinal's hat and ornamented on either side by red tassels and green laurel (?) branches.[39] Lowinsky observed more than twenty years ago that the illumination almost certainly serves to identify the manuscript's intended recipient as Cardinal Giulio. Its repertory is too late for the manuscript to have been intended for Cardinal Giovanni, who in March 1513 became Pope Leo X, and too early for it to have been intended for Cardinal Ippolito, who became cardinal in January 1529. We now know more about the biographies of several of the composers whose

---

[37] See note 35.

[38] See, for example, Briquet, nos. 3369–70, 3373, 3384–5, 3387–94; but see also the reservation expressed in note 36. In any further study of VatP 1980–1, attempts should be made to procure beta radiographs of the watermarks so that careful comparisons with Briquet's exemplars can be made and the relevance of the evidence of the paper types to a proper interpretation of the manuscript can be determined. Analyses of the readings of the works in the repertory should also be undertaken in order to determine VatP 1980–1's 'textual' relationship to its concordant sources. Both kinds of analysis were beyond the scope of this paper, but I am fully aware of their relevance to a more complete assessment of the manuscript. From the information currently available concerning the evidence both of paper types and of 'textual' traditions represented in the manuscript, I would at least be prepared to say that neither type of evidence is inconsistent with the thesis advanced here concerning MS VatP 1980–1.

[39] See the plate in Lowinsky (note 15), p. 64. The presence of Josquin's chanson *Se conge prans* may be *internal* evidence for a Medici provenance; on its Medicean associations, see M. Brauner, 'The Manuscript Verona, Accademia Filarmonica, *B* 218 and its Political Motets', *Studi Musicali*, 16 (1987), pp. 3–12, especially pp. 6–10.

works are contained in the manuscript than we did when Lowinsky first advanced his thesis, and what more we know only serves to substantiate it. In particular, that Mouton's and Richafort's relationship to Leo x[40] (and Mouton's to another Italian patron)[41] is now clearer, and that Willaert was present in Italy earlier than had been supposed,[42] obviates the need to account for the presence of their works in a Medici manuscript dating from between 1513 and 1523, since a Medici patron could easily have had access to their music in those years. In addition, the manuscript contains one piece by Andrea de Silva, who was in Leo's service,[43] and one by Févin, who, as a member of the French court chapel, represented a musical tradition that Leo especially favoured; it is not difficult to imagine how a piece by Févin might have found its way into a Medici manuscript.[44] Finally, as a survey of concordances makes clear, VatP 1980–1 has a large number of works in common with other Medici sources, or sources that seem to bear some relationship to Medici patronage. Of the twenty-one works in the manuscript, five are also found in FlorL 666, the famous Medici Codex of 1518; as Lowinsky observed, four of the five occur as a group in VatP 1980–1 and their readings are very similar to those in FlorL 666. Four of the twenty-one are found in VatP 1982, a Medici manuscript whoever its specific intended recipient, and three (nos. 15, 16 and 21, which are also found in FlorL 666) occur in the print 1521[6], which shows evidence of a relationship to Medici musical

[40] R. Sherr, 'The Membership of the Chapels of Louis xii and Anne de Bretagne in the Years Preceding their Deaths', *The Journal of Musicology*, 6 (1988), pp. 60–82, especially pp. 71 n. 49 and 78 n. 83.

[41] L. Lockwood, 'Jean Mouton and Jean Michel: New Light on French Music and Musicians in Italy, 1505–1520', *Journal of the American Musicological Society*, 32 (1979), pp. 191–246.

[42] L. Lockwood, 'Adrian Willaert and Cardinal Ippolito i d'Este: New Light on Willaert's Early Career in Italy, 1515–1521', *Early Music History*, 5 (1985), pp. 85–112. In my forthcoming study *Music and Political Experience in Medici Florence*, I present the texts of three documents that demonstrate that Cardinal d'Este was present on the occasion of three different performances of music in Medici Rome, and I speculate that the documents may suggest a personal relationship between Leo and Ippolito that was based in part on a common interest in music and that may help to explain Ferrarese–papal musical connections.

[43] See Frey, 'Regesten' (note 6), 8, p. 61.

[44] See H. M. Brown, 'Févin, Antoine de', *The New Grove Dictionary of Music and Musicians*, ed. S. Sadie, 20 vols. (London, 1980), vi, pp. 515–17; for sixteenth-century testimony to Leo's regard for Mouton, see the dedication to Adrien le Roy's and Robert Ballard's collection of Mouton's motets printed in 1555, as published in F. Lesure, 'Un document sur la jeunesse de Jean Mouton', *Revue Belge de Musicologie*, 5 (1951), pp. 177–8.

circles.[45] The survey of concordances also suggests that Lowinsky's thesis about the manuscript's date is correct: three of the five principal concordant sources date from Giulio's time as cardinal, not from Giovanni's or Ippolito's: BolC Q19 (5 concordances),[46] FlorL 666 (5 concordances) and VatP 1982 (4 concordances).

In sum, the manuscript's physical characteristics, the heraldic device it contains, its repertory and its relationship to concordant sources all serve to substantiate an interpretation that argues for a Medici provenance in the decade between 1513 and 1523. Further discussion of MS VatP 1980–1 is deferred pending a consideration of Giulio's other music book.

THE MANUSCRIPT CORBC 95–6/PARISBNN 1817

Manuscripts 95 and 96 of the Biblioteca Comunale in Cortona and manuscript Nouvelles acquisitions françaises 1817 of the Bibliothèque Nationale, Paris, are the altus, superius and tenor part-books of a four-volume set; the bassus book is missing, although it is rumoured to be housed in a library in Madrid.[47] Since the publication of the article by Gustave Gröber[48] which first established that the Cortona and Paris books belong to the same set, the manuscript has been identified, not as Giulio's, but as his cousin Giuliano's. I believe the evidence suggests that it was more likely to have been prepared for Giulio, and I shall now examine the evidence for its provenance and date in some detail.

Physical characteristics
MS 96

Binding: MS 96 (superius) is bound in tooled brown leather stamped with gold designs.

Evidence of ownership: On the spine is a worn label that bears the inscription '96 Memb'. In the upper left corner of the parchment sheet that is glued to the inside front cover is written '96'; beneath it is the word '*SOPRANO*'

---

[45] I argue thus largely on the basis of the print's repertory (see I. Fenlon and J. Haar, *The Italian Madrigal in the Early Sixteenth Century* [Cambridge, 1988], pp. 205–7), its provenance and date (Rome, 1520) and its relationship to concordant sources (it is most densely concordant with such sources as FlorBN II. I. 232, FlorL 666 and 1521[3], among others).

[46] See Lockwood (note 41), especially pp. 234–41.

[47] A. Atlas, *The Cappella Giulia Chansonnier*, 2 vols. (Brooklyn, NY, 1975), I, p. 241.

[48] G. Gröber, 'Zu den Liederbüchern von Cortona', *Zeitschrift für romanische Philologie*, 11 (1887), pp. 371–404.

and to its right, in purple ink, is 'Supremus'; the centre of the page bears the library stamp: 'CORTONA . ACCADEMIA ETRUSCA (FONDATA NEL 1727) . OBSCVRA DE RE LVCIDA PANGO'. There follows a single modern parchment guard sheet and a parchment bifolium that contains the index.

Collation: The manuscript proper consists of eighty-seven gilt-edged parchment sheets, each measuring *c.* 176 cm long×127 cm high, and collated as follows: gatherings I (fols. 1–10), II (fols. 11–20), III (fols. 21–30), IV (fols. 31–40), V (fols. 41–50), VII (fols. 60–9) and IX (fols. 78–87) are quinterns; gathering VI (fols. 51–9) is a quartern (fols. 52–9) to the back of which is glued a single sheet, fol. 51; and gathering VIII (fols. 70–7) is a quartern. The collation is therefore in quinterns, with the exception of two gatherings, and is thus typically Florentine.[49] Following the manuscript proper are a single parchment guard sheet, which is stitched to the binding behind the last gathering, and a parchment sheet which is glued to the inside back cover and bears the library stamp.

MS 95

Evidence of ownership: MS 95 (altus) is similarly bound and bears a label on its spine which reads '95 [C]od. memb. 95'. The parchment sheet glued to its inside front cover is similarly inscribed and stamped: under the designation '95' that appears in the upper left-hand corner the word '*CONTRALTO*' is written in pencil and in the centre of the page is a parchment label with the word 'alt[us]'. A single parchment guard sheet whose verso is inscribed 'altus' in its upper left-hand corner is followed by the parchment bifolium that contains the index.

Collation: The ninety folios that make up the manuscript proper are bound in nine regular quinterns and are followed by a single guard sheet and a guard sheet bearing the library stamp that is glued to the inside back cover.

MS 1817

Evidence of ownership: MS 1817 is bound in tooled brown leather; its spine bears a label that reads 'FR. nouv. acq. 1817'. Towards the lower left-hand corner of the parchment sheet glued to its inside front cover is the word 'Tenor' written upside down in ink. In the centre of the page is a paper label with what appears to be representations of the obverse and reverse of a coin. One face shows the inscription 'LVG DVN', its two halves surrounding a depiction of a lion; the other shows the inscription 'YEMENIZ'; between the two coin faces is written the numeral '658' in pencil. MS 1817 had previously been in the collection of Nicholas

---

[49] As has been observed (Fenlon and Haar [note 45], pp. 119–20), collation in quinterns is not unequivocal evidence of Florentine origin. Nonetheless, many Florentine manuscripts are so collated; see Atlas (note 47), I, p. 24 n. 4.

Yemeniz and is listed as entry number 658 in the *Catalogue de la Bibliothèque de M. N. Yemeniz* (Paris, 1867); it was bought by the Bibliothèque Nationale in 1866.[50] To the right of the label bearing Yemeniz's name is another, identical with the one on the spine. Glued to the stub of the guard sheet that is the inside front cover is a parchment sheet, blank except for its foliation (3). Stitched to the binding through the stub is the bifolium (fols. 1–2) that contains the index. In the upper right corner of fol. 1, below the foliation, is the inscription 'Acq. nouv. fr. No. 1817', and to the centre left of the page BIBLIOTHÈQUE IMPÉRIALE MSS.' is stamped in red ink; in the lower left-hand corner is the inscription in ink 'R. C. 6032'.

Collation: The manuscript proper consists of eighty-one parchment sheets (fols. 4–84): fols. 4–83 are regular quinterns (although fols. 56/61, 57/60 and 58/59 are not true bifolia: fols. 59, 60 and 61 are single sheets glued to the stubs of fols. 58, 57 and 56); fol. 84 is glued to the stub of the blank sheet glued to the inside back cover.

Heraldic devices and ornamentation. That the manuscript was prepared for a member of the Medici family there can be no doubt. It is the only source to contain three pieces by Heinrich Isaac with specifically Medicean associations: his two elegies for Lorenzo il Magnifico[51] and his instrumental work based on the Medici motto 'Palle, palle', which refers to the balls in the family shield. More important, the shield itself ornaments the pages of the manuscript that contain *Palle, palle*. On fol. 38[r] of the superius and altus books, it is enclosed within the initial 'P' of the text incipit, and on fol. 41[r] of the tenor occurs a considerably more elaborate version (see Figure 2): surmounting the familiar coat of arms itself is a gold crucifix and a cardinal's hat, from either side of which hangs a cord with six tassels; to the right and left sides of the shield are green, leafless laurel (?) branches from which hang black discs with the inscription 'GLO VI S' in gold lettering. There is evidence throughout the manuscript of other attempts to distinguish it as a Medici manuscript: several works whose texts (or second or third parts) begin with the letter 'L' have illuminated initials that incorporate a design reminiscent of the feather that accompanies

---

[50] M. Redmond, 'A Set of Part-Books for Giuliano de' Medici: Cortona, Biblioteca Comunale, MSS. 95, 96 and Paris, Bibliothèque Nationale, Nouvelle acquisition 1817' (M.M. thesis, University of Illinois, 1970), p. 3; K. Jeppesen, *La frottola*, 3 vols. (Copenhagen, 1968–70), II, pp. 17–18. I wish to thank Professor Lawrence Earp of the University of Wisconsin at Madison for examining the manuscript and reporting on some of its physical characteristics.

[51] See my article 'A Florentine Sacred Repertory from the Medici Restoration', *Acta Musicologica*, 55 (1983), pp. 267–332, especially p. 280 and n. 38.

Anthony M. Cummings

Figure 2   Paris, Bibliothèque Nationale, MS Nouv. acq. fr. 1817, fol. 41ʳ.

the diamond ring and motto 'SEMPER' in Lorenzo il Magnifico's personal device.[52] How is the device on fol. 41ʳ of the tenor book to be interpreted? Its imagery is richer than one might at first suppose. As Allan Atlas observed, Isaac modelled the melodic shape of the tenor part on the forms of the Medici coat of arms: the first five longae of the tenor are reminiscent of the arrangement of the five red balls, and the following three longae are reminiscent of the arrangement of the gold fleurs-de-lis that adorn the central blue ball.[53] Moreover, the

[52] A plate of the illuminated initial 'P' as it appears in the superius and altus books may be found in E. Levi, *La lirica italiana nel cinquecento e nel seicento fino all'Arcadia* (Florence, 1909), p. 258bis. For an instance of the feather design, see, for example, the 'L' of 'Laurus impertu fulminus . . .' that forms part of the text of Isaac's *Quis dabit capiti* (fols. 48ᵛ–50ʳ [superius partbook]); for a representation of Lorenzo il Magnifico's device, see J. Cox-Rearick, *Dynasty and Destiny in Medici Art* (Princeton, NJ, 1984), plate 1. In *A Gift of Madrigals and Motets*, 2 vols. (Chicago, 1972), i, p. 36, Colin Slim suggested that the illuminator of CorBC 95–6/ParisBNN 1817 may have been Giovanni Boccardi, on the basis of the illuminations' similarities to those in Chicago, Newberry Library, Case MS.-VM 1578.M91, which he had earlier identified as Boccardi's (pp. 29–36). I find Slim's suggestion plausible. Compare, for example, the illuminated initial 'P' in Figure 2 with the initials 'Q' illustrated in the colour plate facing the title page of vol. i of Slim's study.

[53] A. Atlas, 'Heinrich Isaac's *Palle, palle*: A New Interpretation', *Studien zur italienisch-deutschen Musikgeschichte*, 9, Analecta Musicologica, 14 (1974), pp. 17–25.

82

letters 'GLO VI S' are themselves arranged so as to reflect the arrangement of the balls, as are the red tassels of the cardinal's hat. Janet Cox-Rearick's recent book on imagery in Medici art offers many examples of the kind of 'triangular' arrangement of images that are found in MS CorBC 95–6/ParisBNN 1817.[54] The manuscript's compiler and illuminator chose to illuminate the tenor book in this way, therefore, precisely because it is the *tenor* part that recalls the Medici imagery and thus would have afforded an illuminator the opportunity to include several images that refer simultaneously to one another.

Gustav Gröber cited an example of a medallion with the name 'IVLIANVS . MEDICES . DVX . NEMORII' on one face and the inscription 'GLO VI S' on the other as evidence that the motto was Giuliano's.[55] On the basis of Gröber's citation, CorBC 95–6/Paris BNN 1817 has been considered ever since to have been compiled for Giuliano and to date from between 1514 (the date of the event, the death of Anne of Brittany, that occasioned the writing of no. 51, Mouton's *Quis dabit oculis*) and 1516, the date of Giuliano's death. The anomaly of the motto's appearance in conjunction with a cardinal's hat has not been addressed. However, the medallion that Gröber cited is an eighteenth-century piece, the work of the medallist Antonio Selvi.[56] It is also catalogued in George Francis Hill's classic work on Italian medals of the Renaissance in a section entitled 'Later Restitutions', where it and others in the same series are described as 'iconographically mischievous'.[57] There are other sources chronologically proximate to Giuliano, however, that also attribute the GLOVIS motto to him. Paolo Giovio, for example, wrote in his *Ragionamento . . . sopra i motti e disegni d'arme e d'amore* that Giuliano,

having taken as his wife the aunt of the King of France and being made *Gonfaloniere* of the Church, in order to show that fortune, which had been against him for many years, was beginning to turn to his favour, had a motto invented, without an image, in a triangular shield, namely a six-letter word that said GLOVIS, reading in reverse SI VOLG'.[58]

[54] For example, see Cox-Rearick (note 52), p. 82.
[55] Gröber (see note 48), p. 372 n. 3.
[56] A. Armand, *Les médailleurs italiens des quinzième et seizième siècles*, 3 vols. (Paris, 1883–7), III, p. 191.
[57] G. F. Hill, *A Corpus of Italian Medals of the Renaissance before Cellini*, 2 vols. (London, 1930), I, pp. 284–5.
[58] 'avendo presa per moglie la zia del Re di Francia, . . . et essendo fatto Confalonier della Chiesa, per mostrare che le Fortuna, la quale gli era stata contraria per tanti anni, si

Giovio was sufficiently well positioned that we may accept his testimony as authoritative: he entered Leo's service in 1513, received the Bishopric of Nocera dei Pagani from Clement, and died in 1552, while in the service of Cosimo I de' Medici, Duke of Florence.[59] And MS 2122 of the Biblioteca Riccardiana in Florence contains a famous letter of 1565 written by Vincenzo Borghini (a letter described by Francis Ames-Lewis as a paraphrase of Giovio)[60] in which Borghini, the prior of the Ospedale degli Innocenti and one of Duke Cosimo's trusted advisers, described 'Imprese di Casa Medici'; his entry for Giuliano reads: 'Il Duca Giuliano in uno

GLO

scudo triangolare a questo modo con VI sei lettere GLOVIS'.

S

Different kinds of evidence bear on a proper interpretation of such devices, however, as Ames-Lewis suggested,[61] and the relevant sources are often inconsistent among themselves. Indeed, one occasionally has the sense that late or posthumous sources, whether they be 'theoretical' like Giovio's treatise or Borghini's letter, or 'practical' like Selvi's medals, aim to associate a particular device uniquely with one patron, whether or not the device was uniquely his, in a sense to attempt to clarify an unclear situation or impose an order where, in fact, there was none. This is the view expressed by Albinia de la Mare, who has written that a difficulty in studying the manuscripts of Giovanni and Giuliano di Lorenzo il Magnifico is to distinguish which were made for which member of the family. In her view Medici devices and mottoes cannot yet be assigned with certainty, and perhaps it will never be possible to do so, since they were, to some extent, interchangeable.[62] Despite the fact that Giovio and Borghini unequivocally associate the GLOVIS

cominciava a rivolgere in favor suo, fece fare un'anima senza corpo in uno scudo triangolare, cioè una parola di sei lettere, che diceva GLOVIS, e leggendola a lo rovescio, SI VOLG'; see the edition of the relevant portion of Giovio's treatise in A. Zenatti, 'Andrea Antico da Montona: nuovi appunti', *Archivio Storico per Trieste, l'Istria e il Trentino*, 3 (1884), especially p. 260.

59 M. Perry, ' "Candor Illaesvs": The "Impresa" of Clement VII and Other Medici Devices in the Vatican Stanze', *The Burlington Magazine*, 119 (1977), pp. 676–86, especially p. 679.

60 F. Ames-Lewis, 'Early Medici Devices', *Journal of the Warburg and Courtauld Institutes*, 42 (1979), pp. 122–43, especially p. 122.

61 *Ibid.*

62 A. de la Mare, 'New Research on Humanistic Hands in Florence', *Miniatura fiorentina del Rinascimento*, ed. A. Garzelli, 2 vols. (Florence, 1985), I, pp. 393–600, especially pp. 468–9.

device exclusively with Giuliano, there are numerous examples of its use by Lorenzo il Magnifico and his son Giovanni, and, I believe, at least one instance of its use by Cardinal Giulio. The seeming anomaly of the appearance of what was putatively Giuliano's device in conjunction with a cardinal's hat may therefore be no anomaly at all, since it may well be that the device was as much Giulio's as Lorenzo il Magnifico's, Giovanni's and Giuliano's.

Among the principal *practical* sources, closer in date to Giovanni's, Giuliano's and Giulio's own time, that bear on the question are the following:

GIOVANNI: (1) MS Ashburnham 1075 of the Biblioteca Medicea-Laurenziana, Florence, a beautifully written and illuminated parchment manuscript, replete with Medici devices, which contains an *Officium mortuorum* and the *Septem psalmi penitenti*; on fols. 51^v–52^r, it contains the inscription 'Demandato S. D. N. D. Leonis Divina Provid. Papae. x. Genesius de la Barrera Hispanus Ortus Carmona Hispalen. Dioc Famulatus. S. Suae Pro:fessor Scripsit. Rome Pontific. Prelibati D. N. Ann. viii.' to which a second hand has added '1520'; because the manuscript thus dates from after Giuliano's death (1516), the GLOVIS device

that appears on fol. 30^v, arranged thus,
$$\begin{array}{c} \text{G} \\ \text{LO} \\ \text{V} \\ \text{IS} \end{array}$$
, presumably cannot refer to him; (2) Antico's *Liber quindecim missarum* of 1516 which, on the first page of each mass, contains a representation of a lion holding a globe on which the device is inscribed; Catherine Weeks Chapman remarked on the use of the device in conjunction with the image of a lion, symbolic of Leo;[63] (3) MS Landau Finaly 183 of the Biblioteca Nazionale Centrale, Florence, 'Scritti e Canzoni in lode di Papa Leone x' by Guglielmo de' Nobili; that the GLOVIS motto occurs there (fol. 2^v) in conjunction with Leo's personal device, the

---

[63] C. W. Chapman, 'Andrea Antico' (Ph.D. dissertation, Harvard University, 1964), pp. 63–4. The motto appears in the same form as in MS Ashburnham 1075 of the Biblioteca Medicea-Laurenziana; see the plate of a page of the Antico print in S. Boorman, 'Early Music Printing: An Indirect Contact with the Raphael Circle', *Renaissance Studies in Honor of Craig Hugh Smyth* (see note 21), ii, pp. 533–54, especially p. 553, plate 4.

Anthony M. Cummings

yoke, again demonstrates, and more convincingly still, that the device was not exclusively Giuliano's; (4) the Sala del Papa in the Church of S. Maria Novella in Florence, which was decorated by Ridolfo Ghirlandaio and Jacopo Pontormo on the occasion of Leo's visit to Florence in 1515 and contains the device in a number of places;[64] (5) Giuliano da San Gallo's sketch (Florence, Galleria degli Uffizi, Gabinetto dei Disegni, UA 7949) for the renovation of the Medici palace in Rome (now the seat of the Italian Senate), which contains the following inscription on the reverse: '1513 adi p[rimo] djluglio / disegnj delpalazo delpapa lione j[n]navona djroma Palazo demedjci j[n]navona Di Giuliano da S. Gallo GLO / VI / S'; (6) Jacopo Pontormo's lunette in the Salone in the Medici villa at Poggio a Caiano, whose execution was begun before Leo's death and which contains the device; (7) finally, and perhaps most important, the floor of what is now called (after Vasari) the Stanza della Segnatura in the Vatican apartments, which contains the motto.[65]

GIULIANO: MS Palat. 206 of the Biblioteca Nazionale Centrale, Florence, which contains three sonnets whose texts are preceded by the motto; they are anonymous in MS Palat. 206 but in concordant sources are attributed to Giuliano: *Non è viltà, né da viltà procede* (fol. 152ᵛ) is also found in Biblioteca Medicea-

[64] I am grateful to Dottoressa Giovanna Lazzi of the Sala di Manoscritti of the Biblioteca Nazionale Centrale in Florence for bringing the example of MS Landau Finaly 183 to my attention (Dottoressa Lazzi is preparing a catalogue of the Landau Finaly collection). On the decoration of S. Maria Novella on the occasion of Leo's visit, see J. Shearman, 'The Florentine *Entrata* of Leo x', *Journal of the Warburg and Courtauld Institutes*, 38 (1975), pp. 136–54, esp. p. 148 n. 36. A plate showing the GLOVIS motto in S. Maria Novella may be found in C. and G. Thiem, 'Andrea di Cosimo Feltrini und die Groteskendekoration der Florentiner Hochrenaissance', *Zeitschrift für Kunstgeschichte*, 24 (1961), pp. 1–39, p. 15, plate 16.

[65] I am grateful to Sheryl Reiss for reminding me that Pontormo's lunette at Poggio contains the device and for signalling its particular importance in this context. More so than in some of the other instances of its use cited thus far, in this case it may refer to the family more generally, rather than to Leo specifically. A plate of the lunette at Poggio may be found in Cox-Rearick (see note 52), colour plate 2. A representation of the floor of the Stanza della Segnatura may be found in J. Shearman, 'The Vatican Stanze: Functions and Decoration', *Proceedings of the British Academy*, 57 (1971), pp. 369–424 and plates xxvii–xxxi, especially plate xxxi. For still other 'Leonine' uses of GLOVIS, see the manuscript Vatican City, Biblioteca Apostolica Vaticana, Cappella Sistina, x, fol. lxxi (for this reference I am grateful to Sheryl Reiss) and X. B. de Montault, 'Inventaire de la Chapelle papale', *Bulletin Monumental*, 5th series, 45/7 (1879), p. 267: 'Un messal grande, dove è una messa ad longum dei SS. Pietro e Paolo, coperto di broccato in filo rosso, con 4 scudi d'argento indorato, dove son rilievi et intagli, cioè quattro teste di leone con 4 diamanti con lettere Suave gloviis con 4 fibbie d'argento indorate'.

Laurenziana, MS Pluteus XLI.25, in a section of the manuscript (fols. 254ʳ–273ᵛ) labelled 'Del Magnifico Juliano suo [i.e. Lorenzo il Magnifico's] figliuolo', and in Bologna, Biblioteca dell'Università, MS 2618, fol. 83ʳ, where it is ascribed to 'Juliani Medices'; *Perché hai Seraphin, morte, offeso tanto?* (fol. 153ᵛ) also occurs in MS Palat. 210 of the Biblioteca Nazionale Centrale, the principal source of Giuliano's poetry; and *Se i vostr'ochi ove e mia son sempre involti* (fol. 154ʳ) is also found in Biblioteca Nazionale Centrale, MS II.I.60, fols. 42ʳ–44ᵛ, under the rubric 'Sonetti del S.r Mag.co Juliano Medici', and in MS Pluteus XLI.25 of the Laurenziana, in the section of the manuscript that contains *Non è viltà, né da viltà procede.*[66]

GIULIO: (1) MS Vat. Lat. 5803 of the Biblioteca Apostolica Vaticana, which is dedicated to Cardinal Giulio and contains the motto on fol. 1ᵛ; but since it also contains Leo's devices, its evidence is not entirely unequivocal;[67] (2) Oxford, Bodleian Library, MS Don. F. 408, a printed book (the Third Decade of Livy) with manuscript additions; the opening of each section is illuminated with miniatures and fol. 1ʳ is extensively illuminated (see Figure 3): at the top centre is the GLOVIS device, arranged in the now familiar triangular shape, and at the bottom centre is the Medici shield surmounted by a cardinal's hat; at the right centre is a laurel branch whose left side only shows new growth; the print's colophon, 'Florentiae per haeredes Philippi Iuntae Anno ... M. D. XXII.', serves to demonstrate that in this instance the GLOVIS device can refer neither to Giuliano, who died in 1516, nor to Leo, who died in 1521.

Can it refer to anyone other than Cardinal Giulio? The authors of a catalogue of manuscripts in the Bodleian Library, J. J. G. Alexander and Otto Pächt, describe the device as Cardinal Ippolito

---

[66] See Giuliano de' Medici, *Poesie*, ed. G. Fatini (Florence, 1939), pp. CVI n. 1, CVIII, CXIV and CXVII.

[67] I am grateful to Sheryl Reiss for bringing this example to my attention and sending me a photograph of the relevant folio. I am also grateful to her for informing me of another instance of the device's use: P. M. Giles and F. Wormald, *A Descriptive Catalogue of the Additional Illuminated Manuscripts in the Fitzwilliam Museum*, 2 vols. (Cambridge, 1982), I, pp. 118–19, make reference to a manuscript, Marlay Cutting It 33 b, a vertical border from a liturgical manuscript (possibly a missal) executed for Clement VII, that contains a tablet at the top inscribed 'CLEM. VII. PON. MA', a yoke with the inscription 'Suave' and a tablet at the bottom with the inscription 'GLO VI S'. The device is thus used in a Giulian context, but since it appears in conjunction with Leonine devices (the yoke and the motto 'Suave') it may be that in this instance it should be interpreted as generically Medicean rather than specifically Giulian.

Figure 3   Oxford, Bodleian Library, MS Don F. 408, fol. 1ʳ.

de' Medici's,[68] and, indeed, the book, though printed in 1522, might not have been illuminated until 1529, when Ippolito, who was Giuliano's illegitimate son, was named cardinal. It is possible, however, that Alexander and Pächt may have identified the devices as Ippolito's because they assumed that GLOVIS had been uniquely his father's, and, indeed, inside the front cover of the Bodleian book is a loose sheet of paper with the note: '*Illumination.* (Livius, Liber Primus Florence, 1522). The first page and the initials magnificently decorated for Ippolito de' Medici (afterwards cardinal). See the Medici arms and

GLO

symbols and the famous device VI which was adopted by

S

Giuliano de Medici, the father of Ippolito'.

The argument that the device is Cardinal Ippolito's is not extravagant; the appearance of a motto traditionally associated with Giuliano in conjunction with a cardinal's hat leads one inevitably to posit that such a combination suggests his son. There is, however, independent testimony concerning the book's owner: on the verso of the second of the guard sheets that precede the book proper, faded almost to illegibility, is the inscription 'Clement VII' in the upper left-hand corner. While the devices on fol. 1[r], therefore, may be Ippolito's, the fact that the motto that plays so important a role in the illumination's interpretation was not exclusively his father's, coupled with the date of the print and the inscription on guard sheet [II[v]], suggests that Cardinal Giulio is just as likely to have been the owner; the significance of the Bodleian print for an interpretation of CorBC95–6/ParisBNN 1817 is obvious: if the devices in the Bodleian book can have been Giulio's, those in ParisBNN 1817 can have been as well. For these reasons, therefore, I disagree with Nino Pirrotta's thesis that CorBC 95–6/ParisBNN 1817 may have been Ippolito's.[69] Pirrotta's thesis, too, may have been based on the assumption that the GLOVIS device was orig-

---

[68] O. Pächt and J. J. G. Alexander, *Illuminated Manuscripts in the Bodleian Library*, 3 vols. (Oxford, 1966–), II, p. 109. Iain Fenlon suggested that Boccardi may have illuminated the Bodleian print. The style of the illuminations is not dissimilar to that of CorBC 95–6/ParisBNN 1817, and given that Colin Slim attributed the illuminations in CorBC 95–6/ParisBNN 1817 to Boccardi (see note 52 above), Dr Fenlon's suggested identification, arrived at independently, is plausible. I am grateful to him for making it.

[69] N. Pirrotta, 'Istituzioni musicali nella Firenze dei Medici', *Firenze e la Toscana dei Medici nell'Europa del '500*, 3 vols. (Florence, 1983), I, pp. 37–54, especially p. 43 n. 25.

inally Giuliano's; moreover, the survey of concordances makes clear that many of CorBC 95–6/ParisBNN 1817's most closely related sources date from Giulio's time as cardinal (or before), not from Ippolito's: FlorBN Magl. 164–7 (17 concordances, *c.* 1520),[70] FlorBN II.I.232 (16 concordances, *c.* 1516–21),[71] BolC Q17 and the Medici manuscript VatG XIII.27 (10 concordances each, late fifteenth century),[72] FlorC 2442 and RISM 1504³ (7 concordances each, FlorC 2442 from after 1507/8),[73] FlorBN Magl. 107bis and FlorBN Magl. 178 (6 concordances each, FlorBN Magl. 107bis from before 1513, FlorBN Magl. 178 from 1492–4).[74]

The fact that the device was used interchangeably is consistent with an interpretation of its significance. Cox-Rearick's book makes very clear that, in Medici art, themes of dynastic continuity, rebirth, regeneration and return were central.[75] Concerned as the Medici were with the fragility of their regime, given the many challenges to its very survival, they favoured imagery that celebrated its continuity and evoked the past. And by 1520 the regime was seriously imperilled: Giuliano had died prematurely in 1516, Lorenzo in 1519; the surviving members of the family who were old enough to participate effectively in the governance of Florence (Pope Leo and Cardinal Giulio) were both clerics and, therefore, officially unable to father children (though Giulio was widely rumoured to have been the father of Alessandro de' Medici, later the first Duke of Florence). It is not surprising that the family's works of art are thus replete with images of laurel branches (which, depending on the particular historical circumstances of the moment, either do or do not show new growth) and of wheels (Fortune's wheel, whose turns served to change the conditions affecting the regime) and contain references to spring and the

[70] J. Rifkin, 'Scribal Concordances for some Renaissance Manuscripts in Florentine Libraries', *Journal of the American Musicological Society*, 26 (1973), pp. 305–26, especially p. 313 n. 30.

[71] Cummings, 'A Florentine Sacred Repertory' (see note 51), *passim*.

[72] Atlas (see note 47), *passim* (on VatG XIII.27), and (on BolC Q17) C. Wright, 'Antoine Brumel and Patronage at Paris', *Music in Medieval and Early Modern Europe*, ed. I. Fenlon (Cambridge, 1981), pp. 37–60, especially p. 52 n. 38.

[73] On the date and provenance of FlorC 2442, see, most recently, L. Bernstein, 'Notes on the Origin of the Parisian Chanson', *The Journal of Musicology*, 1 (1982), pp. 275–326, especially pp. 286–7, n. 28.

[74] On FlorBN Magl. 107bis, Rifkin (see note 70), especially p. 312 n. 25; on FlorBN Magl. 178, Atlas (see note 47), I, p. 247.

[75] Cox-Rearick (see note 52), *passim*.

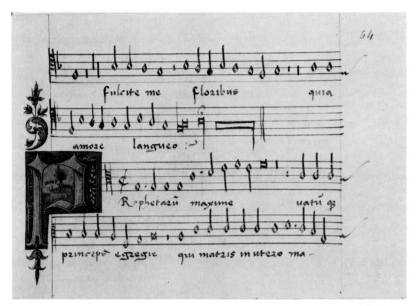

Figure 4   Paris, Bibliothèque Nationale, MS Nouv. acq. fr. 1817, fol. 64ʳ.

return of a golden age. In this context, Giovio's explanation of the GLOVIS device ('[Giuliano] had a motto invented, without an image . . ., that said GLOVIS, reading in reverse SI VOLG'; . . . in order to show that fortune, which had been against him for many years, was beginning to turn to his favour') evokes a constellation of related themes.[76]

On fols. 60ʳ, 62ʳ and 64ʳ of the superius, altus and tenor books appears another illumination that may be similarly interpreted (see Figure 4): enclosed within the initial letter 'P' of Isaac's *Prophetarum maxime* is a white dog tied to a tree, which is encircled by a banner bearing the inscription 'COST ANE' (in the case of the superius and altus books) or 'COST ANTE' (in the case of the tenor book).

---

[76] 'fece fare un'anima senza corpo . . ., che diceva GLOVIS, e leggendola a lo rovescio, SI VOLG; . . . per mostrare che la Fortuna, la quale gli era stata contraria per tanti anni, si cominciava a rivolgere in favor suo'. On the changes in the status of the regime around 1520, see J. R. Hale, *Florence and the Medici: The Pattern of Control* (London, 1977), pp. 95–108. On Fortune's wheel as a Medicean (and specifically Giulian) device, see also R. Eisler, 'The Frontispiece to Sigismondo Fanti's *Triompho di Fortuna*', *Journal of the Warburg and Courtauld Institutes*, 10 (1947), pp. 155–9, especially pp. 156–7 and plate 41b. For this reference, I am grateful to Iain Fenlon.

'COSTANTE' has been interpreted as an Italian translation of Lorenzo il Magnifico's motto 'SEMPER',[77] but I believe it has a different meaning. The fact that the illumination ornaments Isaac's piece is telling, since *Prophetarum maxime* is a piece for the feast of San Giovanni, the patron saint of Florence. Isaac's piece combines a text from the liturgy for the day with an apparently freely composed, non-liturgical text,[78] and no text in the manuscript refers more evocatively to Florence than Isaac's.

The dog may also have been one of the family's symbols. Alessandro Segni's 1685 treatise on Medici emblems exists in at least three drafts; the earliest (MS 1185f of the Biblioteca Riccardiana, fol. 3^v) states that one of the devices of Averardo detto Bicci, Cosimo il Vecchio's grandfather, combined the family shield and the image of a dog. MS Ashb. 660 of the Biblioteca Laurenziana, which contains another draft of Segni's treatise, similarly describes Averardo's device. Averardo's commemorative medallion of *c.* 1720 bears no device but does bear the motto 'FIDE CONSTANTI'.[79] We thus have explicit testimony that both elements of the illumination, the dog and the motto, may have been included in Averardo's impresa. Having questioned the validity of evidence that dates from the eighteenth century in the case of the GLOVIS device, however, I can hardly argue that the testimony of a seventeenth-century treatise and an eighteenth-century medallion is necessarily more valid in this instance, tempting though it may be to do so: given the Medici family's concern for the continuity of their regime in the early sixteenth century, they could not have substantiated claims about their family's importance to the history of Florence more effectively than by invoking the memory of their fourteenth-century ancestor, Averardo detto Bicci, and by illuminating the initial of a piece in honour of Florence's patron saint with Averardo's devices.

It it not necessary to rely on seventeenth- and eighteenth-century evidence to offer an interpretation of the illumination, however. The image of a dog has, since classical times, served as a symbol of

---

[77] Gröber (see note 48), p. 372.
[78] C. Marbach, *Carmina scriptuarum* (Hildesheim, 1963), pp. 318 and 392; M. Just, 'Studien zu Heinrich Isaacs Motetten', 2 vols. (Ph.D. dissertation, Eberhard-Karls Universität, Tübingen, 1960), II, Werkverzeichnis, 'Motetten'.
[79] On MS 660, see Cox-Rearick (note 52), p. 108. On Selvi's medallion, see Ames-Lewis (note 60), especially p. 126, and Hill (note 57), I, p. 284.

fidelity,[80] and in the case of MS CorBC 95–6/ParisBNN 1817 the addition of the motto 'COSTANTE' clarifies the meaning of the reference, whether or not it was intended to allude specifically to Averardo de' Medici: the Medici had served their native city faithfully.

Based on the foregoing, therefore, I offer the following observations about MS CorBC 95–6/ParisBNN 1817: (1) that it was copied, not for Giuliano, but for Cardinal Giulio; (2) that its illuminations evoke traditional Medici themes that reflect the family's concerns about the survival of their regime; (3) that, further, the manuscript may date from the time (1519–23) when Giulio was *de facto* head of the Florentine government, and that the GLOVIS device and the leafless branches of the laurel tree (Lorenzo II's personal emblem, which he had assumed in order to make reference to his grandfather Il Magnifico and which afforded allusion to his own name) signify the regime's continuity, notwithstanding Lorenzo II's death: the leafless laurel, in my interpretation, would represent the dead Lorenzo, and the GLOVIS device would signify the turn of Fortune's wheel that resulted in the regency of Giulio, represented by the cardinal's hat; the fact that Pontormo's lunette at Poggio a Caiano was executed at about the same time and contains the GLOVIS device is suggestive, given that it, too, has been interpreted as reflecting concern about the regime's continuity: it depicts the god Vertumnus, whose aid is invoked in Ariosto's poem of 1519, *Ne la stagion*, written at the time of Lorenzo II's final illness; and, finally, (4) that the imagery of the Bodleian book, similar as it is to that of CorBC 95–6/ParisBNN 1817, is further testimony that themes of renewal were current around 1520 in works of art associated specifically with Cardinal Giulio.

Finally, I would like to discuss Liliana Pannella's thesis that CorBC 95–6/ParisBNN 1817 was written in stages, that the section that contains *Palle, palle* dates from before 1513 and that the car-

---

[80] J. Gelli, *Divise motti imprese di famiglie e personaggi italiani* (Milan, 1916), pp. 238, 450. On the dog as a Medici device, see also Cox-Rearick (note 52), pp. 108 and 142. On the ascription of the attribute of constancy to Leo x in an ephemeral work of art executed on the occasion of his visit to Florence in 1515, see Shearman (note 64), esp. pp. 141 and 145; in my view, however, the use of the inscription 'COSTANTE' in the Cortona–Paris manuscript is likelier to sustain the more general interpretation offered here than a specific interpretation.

dinal's hat thus refers to Cardinal Giovanni before his election to the papacy.[81] Pannella's thesis is based in part on an assessment of the character of the manuscript's repertory. In her view, it is unlikely that the two Isaac laments for Lorenzo il Magnifico would have been copied into a manuscript dating from after 1514; moreover, she cited a change in handwriting after no. 42, the Isaac elegy *Quis dabit capiti meo aquam*, as evidence that the manuscript was written in stages, and that the two Isaac laments and the GLOVIS device appear in an earlier section. As is suggested by the material presented above, however, the appearance of the Isaac pieces in a manuscript of the second decade of the sixteenth century or later is not necessarily an anachronism, concerned as the Medici were with the theme of the return of a golden age. Cox-Rearick has remarked on the retrospective, neo-Laurentian character of restoration art,[82] on its highly selfconscious evocation of an idealised past, and in the context of the political sentiment of the time, the copying of the Isaac pieces does not need to be justified. Moreover, the change in handwriting that Pannella cites is to be explained differently, in my view. The changes in text hand correspond to changes in the *language* of the text. They signal, not disparate stages in the manuscript's history, therefore, but different scribes' varying levels of conversance with the languages of the texts they were responsible for entering. The text hands are difficult enough to distinguish, and even now, having spent many hours examining the manuscript, I am not convinced that I have completely succeeded in doing so. However, as evidence for my assertion, I would point out that, when the language of the text changes, there are often textless or partially texted pieces, as if the scribe responsible for the previous section was insufficiently conversant with the language of the texts in the new section of the manuscript to enter them. For example, nos. 19 and 20 are on Italian texts, nos. 21–7 on French texts; in manuscripts 95 and 96, no. 21 is untexted beyond the incipit. Similarly, after the three Latin works nos. 29–31, nos. 32–4, which are on French texts, are untexted beyond the incipits in MS 95. The change in handwriting after no. 42 that Pannella noted, therefore, may be explainable by

---

[81]   L. Pannella, 'Le composizioni profane di una raccolta fiorentina del cinquecento', *Rivista Italiana di Musicologia*, 3 (1968), pp. 3–47, especially pp. 6–7 n. 3.
[82]   Cox-Rearick (see note 52), pp. 220–3, for example.

virtue of the fact that there is a change in language: no. 42 is on a Latin text, no. 43 on a French text. Moreover, there is at least one instance of the occurrence of the text hand in the putatively 'later' section of the manuscript in the 'earlier' section: the hand of nos. 44–53 contributed to no. 34. The hands alternate throughout the manuscript, therefore, and, in my view, one cannot conclude from them that the section that contains the illumination dates from earlier than 1514.

How did the superius and altus books come to be housed in Cortona? Giulio's principal representative in Florence during the time he spent in Rome in the years between 1519 and 1523 and after his election to the papacy was Silvio Passerini, Cardinal of Cortona, who had been one of his family's most loyal agents. In 1527, after the Sack of Rome, Passerini and Alessandro and Ippolito de' Medici, the two principal members of the family then in Florence, were exiled from the city, and it may be that the manuscript was taken to Cortona at that time. As for the presence of the tenor book in Paris, I can offer no explanation at this time; might we seek one in the many associations between the Medici and the French royal family?

THE REPERTORIES OF CORBC 95–6/PARISBNN 1817 AND VATP 1980–1 AND IMPLICATIONS FOR DATING

If manuscripts CorBC 95–6/ParisBNN 1817 and VatP 1980–1 were indeed prepared for the same patron, it might be argued that their repertories are anomalous in that they are so different. They have a single piece in common, Mouton's *Gaude Barbara beata*, and Stanley Boorman has suggested that the readings that the two manuscripts contain differ to the extent that we cannot posit a common model.[83] Further, CorBC 95–6/ParisBNN 1817 is rich in works by composers with Florentine associations (Agricola, 1 work, and Isaac, 9 works)[84] or whose works are transmitted largely in Florentine sources (Ninot, 4 works); VatP 1980–1's repertory, on the

---

[83] 'Petrucci at Fossombrone' (Ph.D. dissertation, University of London, 1976), pp. 226 and 228.

[84] For biographical information, see the relevant entries in *The New Grove Dictionary* (note 44).

contrary, comprises works ascribed to composers known to have been active in Leonine Rome or at the French Royal Chapel, whose musical traditions Leo x favoured: Brumel, De Silva, Févin, Lhéritier, Moulu, Mouton, Richafort and Willaert;[85] (the nature of the contents of CorBC 95–6/ParisBNN 1817 would be misrepresented, however, if one failed to take note of the fact that it, too, contains works by Mouton, as well as the two surviving motets by Michele Pesenti; Pesenti was in Leo's service in 1520 and 1521,[86] and the presence of his music in CorBC 95–6/ParisBNN 1817 may be further evidence for a dating in the years between 1519 and 1523, since it may be his relationship to a Medici patron that accounts for the inclusion of his music in a Medici manuscript). Finally, the contexts formed by each manuscript's concordant sources are entirely different: as we have seen, CorBC 95–6/ParisBNN 1817 shares its repertory most extensively with Florentine manuscripts from the late fifteenth and early sixteenth centuries; VatP 1980–1, on the other hand, shares its repertory most extensively with the two Medici manuscripts FlorL 666 and VatP 1982, with the north Italian manuscript BolC Q19, and with the manuscripts SGallS 463 and 464.

The repertories may reflect different phases of Cardinal Giulio's career. The 'Roman' phase (1513–19) is reflected in the repertory of VatP 1980–1, the 'Florentine' phase (1519–23) in the repertory of CorBC 95–6/ParisBNN 1817. One should bear sharply in mind, however, that political and diplomatic connections between centres of patronage were never closer in early modern Italy than they were between Florence and Rome between 1513 and 1534. There is archival evidence of exchanges of music between the two cities[87] and there were ample opportunities for other such exchanges that are not attested by documentary references. Moreover, the various phases of Giulio's career cannot be distinguished so neatly, as a review of his biography makes clear. Nonetheless, the two repertories are interesting in their differences. Giovanna Lazzi of

---

[85] *Ibid.*, and Sherr's study cited in note 40. On Lhéritier among the members of Leo's *famiglia*, see note 34, above.

[86] Frey, 'Regesten' (see note 6), 9, pp. 140 and n. 94, 141 and 142 n. 7.

[87] Some texts may be found in A. M. Cummings, 'Medici Musical Patronage in the Early Sixteenth Century: New Perspectives', *Studi Musicali*, 10 (1981), pp. 197–216, especially pp. 205 and 207; H. M. Brown, 'Chansons for the Pleasure of a Florentine Patrician', *Aspects of Medieval and Renaissance Music: A Birthday Offering to Gustave Reese*, ed. J. LaRue (New York, 1966), pp. 56–66, especially p. 64 n. 22; and Sherr (see note 21), especially p. 637 n. 36.

the Sala di Manoscritti of the Biblioteca Nazionale Centrale in Florence suggested that the elaborate character of CorBC 95–6/ParisBNN 1817 may signify that a particular event prompted its copying, and it may be that its compiler consciously sought to assemble a repertory with so essentially Florentine a character, perhaps to celebrate Giulio's arrival in Florence and the beginning of his 'regency'; indeed, Giulio himself may have preferred a repertory that was different from that contained in others of his music books. On the other hand, it may be that one can exaggerate the extent to which works in the Roman repertory were available to Florentine scribes, even during the time of the Medici papacies; perhaps the simplest hypothesis of all is that the compiler exercised aesthetic preference, that he may have chosen not to include works by Roman composers even if they were available to him.

THE MUSIC-HISTORICAL IMPORTANCE OF CORBC 95–6/PARISBNN 1817: SOME OBSERVATIONS

If CorBC 95–6/ParisBNN 1817 was indeed Giulio's, it may be one of the more important documents we have for the evolution of the Italian madrigal. Pirrotta advanced a thesis concerning the *historical context* in which the new genre evolved:

Although only a little light can be cast on the initial stage and the course of development of the new genre, it may be taken as certain that most contributions to it originated in the cities of Florence and Rome, which were in close alliance under the Medici popes. . . . The transition to the madrigal-type . . . was probably effected in the entourage of Cardinal Giulio de' Medici during his stay in Florence (1519–23) and in the early years of his pontificate as Clement VII.[88]

Walter Rubsamen and James Haar advanced theses concerning the *stylistic antecedents* of the madrigal. Rubsamen[89] cited such genres as (1) the so-called 'new' chanson, exemplified by works like Ninot's

---

[88] 'Obgleich Anfangsstadium und Entwicklungswege der neuen Gattung noch wenig aufgehellt werden konnten, gilt es als sicher, dass die meisten Beitr. dazu aus den unter den Medicipäpsten eng verbündeten Städten Florenz und Rom stammten. . . . Der Übergang zum Madrigal-Typus . . . vollzog sich wahrscheinlich in der Umgebung des Kardinals Giulio dei Medici während seines Florentiner Aufenthaltes (1519–1523) und in den ersten Jahren seines Pontifikats als Clemens VII.' Pirrotta, 'Rom', *Die Musik in Geschichte und Gegenwart*, ed. F. Blume, 17 vols. (Kassel and Basle, 1949–86), XI, cols. 695–707, especially 706.

[89] 'From Frottola to Madrigal', *Chanson and Madrigal, 1480–1530*, ed. J. Haar (Cambridge, MA, 1964), pp. 51–72, especially pp. 62–4 and 67.

Et levez vous hau, Guillemette and Compère's *Alons fere nos barbes*, in which 'the music is textually bound and singable throughout the parts', 'sections of isometric (frottolistic?) homophony alternate with those in imitative polyphony, and portions in ternary meter enliven the basically duple rhythmic pattern', and '[t]hemes are light and folklike, often in repeated notes of equal value'; (2) polyphonically elaborated Italian popular melodies like Isaac's quodlibet *Donna di dentro* and Compère's *Che fa la ramancina* in which the popular melodies are used 'in an entirely vocal context, thus laying the groundwork both for the future villotta and the equivalence of textually conceived voice parts in the madrigal'; and (3) the works of Michele Pesenti, whom Rubsamen described as '[o]ne of the first Italian composers of the Cinquecento to write . . . works in textually conceived, imitative polyphony' and who 'participated . . . in the serious literary trend leading to the madrigal by setting to music two odes of Horace'. Haar suggested,

following an idea of . . . Rubsamen's, that [the madrigal's] roots are in the French chanson – not that of Claudin or Janequin but an earlier one, represented by the simpler pieces, sometimes dubbed 'modern' in style, in Petrucci's *Odhecaton, Canti B,* and *Canti C.* In other words this style of syllabically declaimed, completely vocal chordal polyphony with a gently imitative coloration is an Italian adaptation, as the so-called 'Parisian' chanson was a French adaptation, of an earlier prototype.[90]

CorBC 95–6/ParisBNN 1817 serves to connect the theses as to the context in which the madrigal evolved and its stylistic antecedents, since (in my view) it was prepared for Cardinal Giulio and a substantial proportion of the works it contains may be classified in the categories established by Rubsamen and Haar (its repertory

[90] J. Haar, 'The Early Madrigal', *Music in Medieval and Early Modern Europe*, ed. I. Fenlon (Cambridge, 1981), pp. 163–92, especially pp. 189–90. Iain Fenlon has argued similarly: he observed ('Context and Chronology of the Early Florentine Madrigal', *La letteratura, la rappresentazione, la musica al tempo e nei luoghi di Giorgione*, ed. M. Muraro [Rome, 1987], pp. 281–93, especially p. 284) that the French chanson was disseminated in Italy between 1460 and 1525 in four distinct manuscript traditions, the last of which was specifically Florentine and consists of sources written during the second and third decades of the sixteenth century: FlorBC 2442, FlorBN Magl. 107bis, FlorBN Magl. 117, FlorBN Magl. 121, FlorBN Magl. 164–7. This complex of sources forms CorBC 95–6/ParisBNN 1817's immediate context, and, as Fenlon remarked further, the French chanson was one of the elements in the Florentine musical culture in which the madrigal emerged.

In their recent book (see note 45), Fenlon and Haar have challenged Pirrotta's thesis about the importance of Medici patronage to the emergence of the madrigal. I myself am not prepared to abandon Pirrotta's thesis; indeed, for reasons that I hope to detail elsewhere, I believe it continues to be valid.

may thus be described as a kind of conspectus of madrigalian precursors). It contains the four works by Compère, Isaac and Ninot cited above and the anonymous quodlibet *Fortuna disperata/ Vidi la forosetta/ Vo m'avete svergogne*; the two quodlibets document an interest in polyphonic settings of Italian texts and belong, in Pirrotta's words, 'on a sensibly higher cultural level, since the task of combining simultaneously various already extant tunes required considerable skill in counterpoint'.[91] It also contains the two surviving motets by Pesenti, one of which Rubsamen rightly described as 'every bit as polyphonic and vocally conceived throughout the parts as are . . . [*Che farala che dirala* and *So ben che le non sa*, two of Pesenti's frottole]'. Indeed, Pesenti's role in the evolution of the madrigal has not yet been adequately assessed, but it must, in my view, have been an important one. He was, as Pirrotta remarked, an 'elegant . . . contrapuntist',[92] and he seems to have been the originator of the contrapuntal villotta in which all lines make use of popular melodic material, as Pirrotta also argued. The contrapuntal villotta bears a relationship to the contemporary French chanson, in that such works as the anonymous *Tambur tambur*, Josquin's *Entre je suis*, Févin's *Pardonnez moy* and Mouton's *Velecy velela*, all of which are contained in CorBC 95–6/ParisBNN 1817, are polyphonic arrangements of pre-existent popular melodies.[93]

Haar wrote that '[s]ome of the pieces cited by Rubsamen, . . . appear in the Florentine chanson manuscript Basevi 2442 and in the mixed source Magl. xix. 164–7; thus although the music was no longer new in the 1520s it was in currency in Florence at just the time Verdelot started his career there'. Such pieces may have been even more readily available to Verdelot than Haar suggested; as Giulio's associate in 1521, Verdelot would presumably have had access to such works as those in the repertory of Giulio's music

---

[91] *Music and Theatre from Poliziano to Monteverdi* (Cambridge, 1982), p. 86.
[92] See *Chanson and Madrigal* (note 89), p. 87.
[93] See N. Pirrotta, 'Novelty and Renewal in Italy: 1300–1600', *Studien zur Tradition in der Musik: Kurt von Fischer zum 60. Geburtstag* (Munich, 1973), pp. 49–65, especially pp. 59–60 and n. 19: 'Composers . . . used popular tunes . . . as material for contrapuntal elaboration in the special type [of frottola] called *villota* (somewhat parallel to some French chansons). . . . *Villote* and French chansons are often associated in prints and manuscripts of the period preceding the ascent of the madrigal; they probably met the demand for polyphonic pieces to be sung *a libro* by dilettanti, a habit which may have contributed to the all-vocal development of the madrigal.' On the chanson *Tambur tambur*, see B. J. Blackburn, 'Two Carnival Songs Unmasked: A Commentary on MS Florence Magl. xix. 121', *Musica Disciplina*, 35 (1981), pp. 121–78, especially pp. 135–6.

book, CorBC 95–6/Paris BNN 1817, a repertory that constitutes such crucial testimony to the Medici family's tastes in secular music during the years that witnessed the evolution of the Italian madrigal.

Andrew W. Mellon Foundation, Princeton

APPENDIX

Inventories of MSS CorBC 95–6/ParisBNN 1817 and VatP 1980–1
Note: Sigla for concordant manuscripts are those used in the *Census-Catalogue of Manuscript Sources of Polyphonic Music 1400–1550*, 5 vols., Renaissance Manuscript Studies 1 (Neuhausen-Stuttgart, 1979–88). Sigla for concordant prints are those used by the Répertoire International des Sources Musicales [RISM]; bibliographic information concerning anthologies is given in RISM B/IV/1, *Recueils imprimés, XVIe–XVIIe siècles*, ed. F. Lesure (Munich and Duisburg, 1960); bibliographic information concerning prints devoted to individual composers [Josquin: 1502 J 666, 1514 J 667, 1514 J 673, 1516 J 668, 1516 J 674, 1526 J 669, 1526 J 675, 1549 J 681, 1555 J 678, and (1559) J 676; Mouton: 1555 M 4017; and Willaert: 1539 W 1108 and 1545 reprint of 1539 W 1106] is given in the relevant volumes of RISM A/I, *Einzeldrucke vor 1800* (Kassel, 1971–86). The siglum 1560 *Bibliographie des éditions d'Adrian Le Roy . . .*, no. 68, refers to the print catalogued on pp. 91–4 of F. Lesure and G. Thibault, *Bibliographie des éditions d'Adrian Le Roy et Robert Ballard* (Paris, 1955); the print is not listed in RISM B/IV/1.

MS CorBC 95–6/ParisBNN 1817

The text incipit and foliation are given as they appear in the superius partbook. For each concordant source, inclusive foliation and composer ascription are provided, where known.

[1]   fols. 1ʳ–2ʳ, [anonymous], Ie nay dueil que de vous ne viegne
       BolC Q17, fols. 69ᵛ–71ʳ, A Agricola
       BrusBR 228, fols. 20ᵛ–22ʳ, anonymous
       FlorBN Magl. 178, fols. 0ᵛ–2ʳ, Alexander
       FlorBN BR 229, fols. 183ᵛ–185ʳ, Alexander agricola
       FlorR 2794, fols. 28ᵛ–30ʳ, Agricola
       LonBLR 20 A.xvi, fols. 24ᵛ–26ʳ, anonymous
       RegB C120, pp. 308–11, Agricola
       RomeC 2856, fols. 162ᵛ–164ʳ, Agricola
       SegC s. s., fols. cxiiiᵛ–cxivʳ, Alexander agricola
       VatG xiii.27, fols. 38ᵛ–40ʳ, Agricola

VerBC 757, fols. 34^v–36^r, anonymous
1501, fols. 42^v–44^r, Agricola

[2] fols. 2^r–2^v, [anonymous], Base moy
BrusBR ɪv.90/TourBV 94, fols. 22^v–23^v, anonymous
1502^2, fol. 38^r, Josquin
1520^3, fols. 17^v–18^r, anonymous
[c. 1535]^{14}, no. 33, anonymous

[3] fols. 2^v–3^v, [anonymous], Une playsant figlette
FlorBN Magl. 164–7, no. 69, anonymous
FlorC 2442, fols. 56^v–58^r, Loyset Compere
1504^3, fols. 9^v–10^r

[4] fols. 3^v–4^v, [anonymous], Youli mariner passe moy sena
FlorBN Magl. 164–7, no. 49, anonymous

[5] fols. 4^v–5^v, [anonymous], Veci la danse barbari

[6] fols. 5^v–6^r, [anonymous], Lordault lordault
BasU F.x.1–4, no 119, Josquin
BolC Q17, fols. 60^v–61^r, Nino petit
ParisBNF 1597, fols. 56^v–57^r, anonymous
RegB C120, pp. 266–7, Compere
1502^2, fols. 8^v–9^r, Compere

[7] fols. 6^r–7^r, [anonymous], Vostre bargeronette
BolC 17, fols. 65^v–66^r, Loyset Compere
FlorBN Magl. 178, fols. 73^v–74^r, Loyset Compere
VatG xɪɪɪ.27, fols. 41^v–42^r, anonymous
1501, fols. 46^v–47^r, Compere

[8] fols. 7^r–8^r, [anonymous], Et leve vo[us] o guigliermette
FlorC 2442, fols. 12^r–13^v, Ninot le petit
1504^3, fols. 81^v–83^r, anonymous

[9] fols. 8^r–9^r, [anonymous], Ie suis amie du forrier or alez
FlorBN Magl. 107bis, fols. 12^v–13^r, anonymous
FlorBN Magl. 164–7, no. 64, anonymous
VatG xɪɪɪ.27, fols. 104^v–105^r, Loyset Compere
1502^2, fols. 14^v–15^r, anonymous
[c. 1535]^{14}, no. 21, anonymous

[10] fols. 9^r–9^v, [anonymous], Gentil galans de france
FlorBN Magl. 164–7, no. 63, anonymous
1504^3, fols. 14^v–15^r, anonymous

[11] fols. 10^r–11^r, [anonymous], Alon fere no[us] barbes
CopKB 1848, pp. 2 and 15, anonymous
FlorBN Magl. 107bis, fols. 16^v–17^r, anonymous
FlorBN Magl. 164–7, no. 65, anonymous
SGallS 463, no. 178, Compere
1501, fols. 28^v–29^r, Compere

[12] fols. 11^r–11^v, [anonymous], Tambien mison pe[n]sada mari semi
bates
BolC Q17, fols. 73^v–74^r, anonymous
FlorBN Magl. 107bis, fols. 8^v–9^r, anonymous
FlorR 2356, fol. 14^v, anonymous
ParisBNF 1597, fols. LIV^v–LV^r, anonymous
RomeC 2856, fols. 145^v–146^r, anonymous

[13] fols. 11^v–12^v, [anonymous], Tambur ta[m]bur tambor

[14] fols. 12^v–13^v, [anonymous], Voles oir une chanson
FlorBN Magl. 164–7, no. 66, anonymous
VatG XIII.27, fols. 90^v–91^r, Loyset Compere [text is a contrafactum,
'De les mon getes']

[15] fols. 13^v–14^r, [anonymous], Si ie vo [sic: altus reads 'fet'] un chop
apres
BolC Q17, fol. 78^v, anonymous [text is a contrafactum, 'Tan bien']
1501, fols. 36^v–37^r, Japart [text is a contrafactum, 'Tan bien']

[16] fols. 14^r–15^r, [anonymous], Si ie vo[us] avoye pointe

[17] fols. 15^r–16^r, [anonymous], Ciascun me crie marietoy marie
1504^3, fols. 34^v–36^r, anonymous

[18] fols. 16^v–17^r, [anonymous], Fille vo[us] aves mal garde le pan
davant
BolC Q17, fols. 64^v–65^r, Ysac
BolC Q18, fols. 58^v–59^r, anonymous
CopKB 1848, pp. 400, 405, 424–5, anonymous
FlorBN Magl. 121, fols. 31^v–33^r, anonymous
FlorBN Magl. 178, fols. 70^v–72^r, Enriqus Ysac
FlorC 2442, fols. 78^r–79^v, yzac
SGallS 463, no. 137, anonymous [text is a contrafactum, 'Ave
sanctissima Maria']
VatG XIII.27, fols. 62^v–64^r, Ysach
VienNB Mus. 18810, no. 50, Henricus Ysaac

[19] fols. 17^v–18^r, [anonymous], Fortuna disperata/Vidi la forosetta
[altus]/Vo m'avete svergogne [tenor]

FlorBN BR 337, fols. 33^v–34^r, anonymous
FlorBN Magl. 164–7, no. 39, anonymous

[20]   fols. 18^v–19^r, [anonymous], Donna di dentro dalla tua chasa/Da[m]ene un poco [altus]/Fortuna d'un gran tempo [tenor]
FlorBN BR 229, fols. 154^v–156^r, Henricus Yzac

[21]   fols. 19^v–20^r, [anonymous], Entre ye suis en gra[n] penser
AugsS 142a, fols. 42^v–43^r, anonymous
BasU F.x.1–4, no. 51, Josquin
BrusBR 228, fols. 28^v–29^r, anonymous
FlorBN Magl. 164–7, no. 46, anonymous
FlorC 2439, fols. 24^v–25^r, Josquin
MunU 328–31, fols. 22^r, 58^r, 3^v, 13^v, anonymous
VienNB Mus. 18810, fols. 4^r, 4^r, 2^v, 3^v, Josquin de pres
1535^{11}, no. 37, Josquin [text is a contrafactum, 'In meinem sinn']
[c. 1535]^{13}, no. 87

[22]   fols. 20^r–21^r, [anonymous], Forsellement

[23]   fols. 21^r–21^v, [anonymous], Il estoit ung bon home
FlorBN Magl. 164–7, no. 68, anonymous
ParisBNF 1597, fols. 60^v–61^r, anonymous

[24]   fols. 22^r–22^v, [anonymous], Amor demoi

[25]   fols. 22^v–23^r, [anonymous], T[ ]
FlorBN Magl. 164–7, no. 47, anonymous
UlmS 237, fols. 22^r–22^v, anonymous

[26]   fols. 23^r–24^r, [anonymous], Maire de die

[27]   fols. 24^r–24^v, [anonymous], Laultre ior ie cievalcioie
FlorBN Magl. 164–7, no. 35, anonymous
1505^5, fol. 47^r

[28]   fol. 25^r, [anonymous], Che fa laramanzina
BolC Q17, fols. 62^v–63^r, Compere
FlorBN Magl. 164–7, no. 35, anonymous
1505^5, fol. 47^r

[29]   fols. 25^v–26^r, [anonymous], Substinuimus pacem
FlorBN Magl. 164–7, no. 35, anonymous
SGallS 461, pp. 46–7, h. ysacc
VatV 11953, fols. 5^r–6^r, H. Yzac
WittenL 1048

[30] fols. 26^v–27^v, [anonymous], O bone et dulcis d[omi]ne yh[es]u
      FlorBN ɪɪ.ɪ.232, fols. 117^v–118^r, Iosq[ui]n [index]
      FlorBN Magl. 164–7, no. 81, anonymous
      VerBC 758, fols. 44^v–46^r, anonymous
      1504^1, fol. 15^r [superius partbook], anonymous

[31] fols. 27^v–29^r, [anonymous], Alma rede[m]ptoris mater/Ave regina
      celorum [altus]
      FlorBN ɪɪ.ɪ.232, fols. 109^v–111^r, IOSQVIN
      FlorBN Magl. 164–7, no. 76, anonymous
      MilD 3, fols. 178^v–180^r, Jusq[ui]n depret
      UlmS 237, fols. 6^r–7^r [superius partbook], anonymous
      VatS 15, fols. 188^v–190^r, anonymous
      1505^2, fol. 2^r [superius partbook], Josquin [superius partbook]

[32] fols. 29^v–30^r, [anonymous], Elogeron no[us] seans
      BolC Q17, fols. 61^v–62^r, Yzac
      FlorBN BR 229, fols. 1^v–2^r, Henricus Yzac
      FlorBN Magl. 107bis, fols. 13^v–14^r, anonymous
      FlorBN Magl. 178, fols. 41^v–42^r, Yzac
      SGallS 463, no. 179, anonymous
      VatG xɪɪɪ.27, fols. 32^v–33^r, Ysach
      1501, fols. 45^v–46^r, anonymous

[33] fols. 30^r–30^v, [anonymous], Une [musque de Biscaye]
      BolC Q17, fols. 75^v–76^r, Josquin
      BolC Q18, fols. 74^v–75^r, anonymous
      FlorBN BR 229, fols. 149^v–150^r, Josquin
      FlorBN Magl. 178, fols. 16^v–17^r, Josquin
      RomeC 2856, fol. 85^r, Josquin de pres
      SevC 5-ɪ-43/ParisBNN 4379, fols. 113^v–114^r, anonymous
      VatG xɪɪɪ.27, fols. 27^v–28^r, Josquin
      1504^3, fol. 129^v, Josquin

[34] fols. 30^v–31^r, [anonymous], Vray dieu q[ue] pene messe
      BolC Q17, fols. 71^v–72^r, anonymous
      FlorBN Magl. 178, fols. 38^v–39^r, anonymous
      FlorC 2442, fols. 85^v–86^v, Gaspart
      VatG xɪɪɪ.27, fols. 87^v–88^r, anonymous [text is a contrafactum,
      'Quam diu che pen messe']
      1504^3, fol. 130^r, Compere

[35] fols. 31^v–34^v, [anonymous], Si oblitus fuero
      CambraiBM 125–8, fols. 37^v–38^r [superius partbook], anonymous
      DresSL 1/D/505, pp. 458–61, JA. Obrecht

FlorBN II.I.232, fols. 70^v–74^r, Ninot [index]
MunBS 3154, fols. 357^v–358^r, anonymous
SienBC K.I.2, fols. 192^v–196^r, anonymous
VatS 42, fols. 150^v–154^r, Jo. le petit
1504^1, fols. 11^v–12^r [superius partbook], anonymous

[36]   fols. 35^r–37^v, [anonymous], In illo tempore
FlorBN II.I.232, fols. 67^v–70^r, Ninot [index]
VatS 42, fols. 74^v–78^r, Jo. le petit

[37]   fols. 38^r–39^r, [anonymous], Palle, palle
BasU F.x.21 [text is a contrafactum, 'La bella']
FlorBN Magl. 107bis, fol. 43^r, anonymous
FlorBN Magl. 117, fols. 82^v–83^r, yzac
KönSU 1740 [text is a contrafactum, 'Alleluia, Hodie Christus
   natus est']
Kraków, Klasztor OO. Dominikanów [piece bears the designation
   'Capellae Leonis Papae']
LonBLE 3051/WashLC M6, fols. 1xxxi^v–1xxxiiii^r, anonymous
VatG XIII.27, fols. 0^v–2^r, H. Isach

[38]   fols. 39^r–42^v, [anonymous], Liber generationis
DresSL I/D/505, pp. 416–21, anonymous
FlorBN II.I.232, fols. 51^v–57^r, IOSQVIN
FlorBN Magl. 107bis, fols. 24^v–30^r, anonymous
LonRC 1070, pp. 192–203, anonymous
MunBS 10, fols. 127^v–145^r, Josquin de Press
ToleF 23, fols. iv^v–7^r, Josquin despres
UppsU 76c, fols. 64^v–67^r, Josquin des Pres
VatS 42, fols. 41^v–47^r, anonymous
1504^1, fols. 3^r–3^v [superius partbook], Josquin
1538^3, no. 37, Josquin [tenor partbook index]
1547^1, pp. 376–87, Iodoco
1555 J 678, fol. 3^r
1559^2, no. 8, IOSQVIN DE PRES

[39]   fols. 42^v–44^r, [anonymous], Tulerunt dominum
MunU 322–5, fols. 9^v–10^v, Josquinnus Auctor
SGallS 463, no. 111, Josquinus Pratensis
1503^1, fols. 30^v–33^r, anonymous
1519^2, no. 9, Pre Michael de Ver[ona]
1526^3 = reprint of 1519^2
1527 = reprint of 1519^2, 1526^3
1547^1, pp. 314–19, Isaac

[40] fols. 44v–46r, [anonymous], Quis dabit pacem
BolC Q20, no. 24, Isaac
FlorBN ii.i.232, fols. 128v–130r, YZACH
KasL 24, no. 46, H. Ysaac [text is a contrafactum, 'Jllumina oculos']

[41] fols. 46v–48r, [anonymous], Tota pulchra es
FlorBN ii.i.232, fols. 92v–94r, YZACH
SGallS 463, no. 110, Heinrichus Isaac
1547[1], pp. 268–71, Henricus Isaac Germanus Author

[42] fols. 48v–50r, [anonymous], Quis dabit capiti meo aquam
FlorBN ii.i.232, fols. 79v–81r, YZACH
VatG xiii.27, fols. 66v–68r, anonymous
1503[1], 69v–71r, anonymous

[43] fols. 50v–51r, [anonymous], Ie me levei laultre nuyt
FlorC 2442, fols. 17r–19v, Ninot le petit

[44] fols. 51v–52v, [anonymous] Pardo[n]nes moy se je foloye
FlorC 2442, fols. 69r–70v, Anton[ ] fevvin
[c. 1535][14], no. 12, anonymous

[45] fols. 52v–54r, [anonymous], Vele ci vele la
FlorC 2442, fols. 92r–94r, Mouton

[46] fols. 54r–55r, [anonymous], Se jay perdu mon amy

[47] fols. 55r–58v, [anonymous], Paratum cor meum
FlorBN Magl. 164–7, no. 72, anonymous
1539[9], no. 8, Iosquin
1555 J 678, fols. 8r–10r, Josquin

[48] fols. 58r–60r, [anonymous], Ecce tu pulchra es
BolC Q19, fols. 100v–101r, Josquin
BolC R142, fols. 17v–18r, Josquin
FlorBN ii.i.232, fols. 199v–200r, IOSQVIN
SevBC 1, fols. 84v–86r, Josquin
UlmS 237, fols. 12v–13r [superius partbook], anonymous
VerBC 758, fols. 40v–41r, anonymous
VerBC 760, fols. 18v–19r, Jusquin de pres
1502 J 666, final recto, Josquin. de. pres. [superius partbook]
1514 J 667 = reprint of 1502 J 666
1516 J 668 = reprint of 1502 J 666, 1514 J 667
1526 J 669 = reprint of 1502 J 666, 1514 J 667, 1516 J 668

[49] fols. 60r–62v, [anonymous], Prophetarum maxime

FlorBN II.I.232, fols. 31^v–35^r, YZACH
FlorBN Magl. 164–7, no. 71, anonymous
PadBC A17, fols. 98^v–101^r, anonymous
VatV 11953, fols. 1^v–4^r, hen yzack
1520^4, fols. 219^v–227^r, h. yzac [superius partbook]

[50]   fols. 63^r–65^v, [anonymous], Misericordias domini
FlorBN II.I.232, fols. 166^v–170^r, Iosquin [index]
1519^3, no. 8, Iosquin [superius partbook]
1526^4 = reprint of 1519^3
1537^1, no. 54, Iosquin [tenor partbook index]
1559^2, no. 6, IOSQVIN DE PRES

[51]   fols. 66^r–68^r, [anonymous], Quis dabit oculis
FlorBN II.I.232, fols. 185^v–187^r, Io m[out]on [index]
RegB C120, pp. 126–31, anonymous
VatC 234, fols. 136^v–139^r, anonymous
1519^2, no. 8, Jo. mouton [superius partbook]
1526^3 = reprint of 1519^2
1527 = reprint of 1519^2, 1526^3
1555 M 4017, fols. 4^r–5^v [superius partbook]
1559^2, no. 12

[52]   fols. 68^r–69^r, [anonymous], Factum est silentium
FlorBN II.I.232, fols. 48^v–51^r, IO. MOVTON
ModD 9, fols. 50^v–53^r, Jo. mouton
PadBC A17, fols. 129^v–131^r, anonymous
VatS 46, fols. 100^v–103^r, anonymous
VienNB Mus. 15941, fols. 59^v–61^v [altus partbook], mouton [tenor
    partbook index]
1519^1, no. 18, Io. mouton [superius partbook index]
1521^5, fols. 7^r–8^r [superius partbook], Io. Mouton [superius part-
    book index]
1526^2 = reprint of 1519^1

[53]   fols. 70^v–72^v, [anonymous], Gaude barbara beata
CambraiBM 125–8, fols. 1^v–2^r [superius partbook], anonymous
CivMA 59, fols. 60^v–62^r, anonymous
FlorBN II.I.232, fols. 163^v–166^r, Io: Mouto [index]
LonRC 1070, pp. 144–5, anonymous
MadM 6832, pp. 6–9, Joannes Monton
VatP 1980–1, fols. 65^v–66^v [tenor partbook], anonymous
1514^1 fols. 2^r–2^v [superius partbook], Io. mouton [superius part-
    book index]
1526^1 = reprint of 1514^1

[54]   fols. 73^r–^{v}, [anonymous], Missus est gabriel angelus
        AugsS 142a, fols. 36^v–38^r, Josquin[us]
        BolC R142, fols. 9^r–9^v, Josq[ui]n
        BrusBR 9126, fols. 177^v–178^r, Josquyn
        FlorBN ii.i.232, fols. 94^v–95^r, IOSQVIN
        FlorBN Magl. 164–7, no. 79, anonymous
        LonBLR 8.G. vii, fols. 23^v–25^r, anonymous
        ToleBC 10, fols. 31^v–34^r, Jusquin
        UlmS 237, fols. 12^r–12^v [superius partbook], anonymous
        UppsU 76c, fols. 67^v–68^r, Josquin des Pres
        VatS 63, fols. 47^v–48^r, anonymous
        1504^1, fol. 7^v [superius partbook], Josquini [superius partbook index]

[55]   fols. 73^v–74^v, [anonymous], [M]anus tue feceru[n]t me & plasmaveru[n]t
        CasAC D(F), fols. 41^v–42^r, anonymous
        VerBC 760, fols. 48^v–49^r, Al Danglon
        [1521]^6, fols. ix^r–x^r, Dom Michel

Concordant sources

AugS 142a: 21, 54
BasU F.x.1–4: 6, 21
BasU F.x.21: 37
BolC Q17: 1, 6, 7, 12, 15, 18, 28, 32, 33, 34
BolC Q18: 18, 33
BolC Q19: 48
BolC Q20: 40
BolC R142: 48, 54
BrusBR 228: 1, 21
BrusBR 9126: 54
BrusBR iv.90/TourBV 94: 2
CambraiBM 125–8: 35, 53
CasAC D(F): 55
CivMA 59: 53
CopKB 1848: 11, 18
DresSL i/D/505: 35, 38
FlorBN ii.i.232: 29, 30, 31, 35, 36, 38, 40, 41, 42, 48, 49, 50, 51, 52, 53, 54
FlorBN Magl. 107bis: 9, 11, 12, 32, 37, 38
FlorBN Magl. 117: 37
FlorBN Magl. 121: 18

FlorBN Magl. 164–7: 3, 4, 9, 10, 11, 14, 19, 21, 23, 25, 27, 28, 30, 31, 47, 49, 54
FlorBN Magl. 178: 1, 7, 18, 32, 33, 34
FlorBN BR 229: 1, 20, 32, 33
FlorBN BR 337: 19
FlorC 2439: 21
FlorC 2442: 3, 8, 18, 34, 43, 44, 45
FlorR 2356: 12
FlorR 2794: 1
KasL 24: 40
KönSU 1740: 37
Kraków, Klasztor OO. Dominikanów: 37
LonBLE 3051/WashLC M6: 37
LonBLR 8.G.vii: 54
LonBLR 20 A.xvi: 1
LonRC 1070: 38, 53
MadM 6832: 53
MilD 3: 31
ModD 9: 52
MunBS 10: 38
MunBS 3154: 35
MunU 322–5: 39
MunU 328–31: 21
PadBC A17: 49, 52
ParisBNF 1597: 6, 12, 23
RegB C120: 1, 6, 51
RomeC 2856: 1, 12, 33
SegC s. s.: 1
SevBC 1: 48
SevC 5-i-43/ParisBNN 4379: 33
SienBC k.i.2: 35
SGallS 461: 29
SGallS 463: 11, 18, 32, 39, 41
ToleBC 10: 54
ToleF 23: 38
UlmS 237: 25, 31, 48, 54
UppsU 76C: 38, 54
VatC 234: 51
VatG xiii.27: 1, 7, 9, 14, 18, 32, 33, 34, 37, 42
VatP 1980–1: 53
VatS 15: 31
VatS 42: 35, 36, 38

Concordant sources ordered by number of concordances

17: FlorBN Magl. 164–7
16: FlorBN II.I.232
10: BolC Q17, VatG XIII.27
7: FlorC 2442, 1504³
6: FlorBN Magl. 107bis, FlorBN 178
5: SGallS 463, 1501
4: FlorBN BR 229, UlmS 237, 1504¹

Index of compositions

Alma redemptoris mater/Ave regina celorum, Josquin, 31
Alon fere nous barbes, Compere, 11
Amor demoi, anonymous, 24
Base moy, Josquin, 2
Che fa laramanzina, Compere, 28
Ciascun me crie marietoy marie, anonymous, 17
Donna di dentro dalla tua chasa/Damene un poco/Fortuna d'un gran
  tempo, Isaac, 20
Ecce tu pulchra es, Josquin, 48
Elogeron nous seans, Isaac, 32
Entre ye suis en gran penser, Josquin, 21
Et leve vous o guigliermette, Ninot, 8
Factum est silentium, Mouton, 52
Fille vous aves mal garde le pan devant, Isaac, 18
Forsellement, anonymous, 22
Fortuna disperata/Vidi la forosetta/Vo m'avete svergogne, anonymous,
  19
Gaude barbara beata, Mouton, 53
Gentil galans de france, anonymous, 10
Ie me levei laultre nuyt, Ninot, 43
Ie nay dueil que de vous ne viegne, Agricola, 1
Ie suis amie du forrier or alez, Compere, 9
Il estoit ung bon home, anonymous, 23
In illo tempore, Ninot, 36
Laultre ior ie cievalcioie, anonymous, 27
Liber generationis, Josquin, 38
Lordault lordault, Compere, Josquin, Ninot, 6
Maire de die, anonymous, 26
Manus tue fecerunt me et plasmaverunt, Danglon, Pesenti, 55
Misericordias domini, Josquin, 50
Missus est gabriel angelus, Josquin, 54
O bone et dulcis domine yhesu, Josquin, 30

Palle, palle, Isaac, 37
Paratum cor meum, Josquin, 47
Pardonnes moy se je foloye, Fevin, 44
Prophetarum maxime, Isaac, 49
Quis dabit capiti meo aquam, Isaac, 42
Quis dabit oculis, Mouton, 51
Quis dabit pacem, Isaac, 40
Se jay perdu mon amy, anonymous, 46
Si ie fet un chop apres, Japart, 15
Si ie vous avoye pointe, anonymous, 16
Si oblitus fuero, Ninot, Obrecht, 35
Substinuimus pacem, Isaac, 29
T[ ], anonymous, 25
Tambien mison pensada mari semi bates, anonymous, 12
Tambur tambur tambor, anonymous, 13
Tota pulchra es, Isaac, 41
Tulerunt dominum, Isaac, Josquin, Pesenti, 39
Une musque de Biscaye, Josquin, 33
Une playsant figlette, Compere, 3
Veci la danse barbari, anonymous, 5
Vele ci vele la, Mouton, 45
Voles oir une chanson, Compere, 14
Vostre bargeronette, Compere, 7
Vray dieu que pene messe, Compere, Weerbeke, 34
Youli mariner passe moy sena, anonymous, 4

Index by composer

Agricola: Ie nay dueil que de vous ne viegne, 1
Compere: Alon fere nous barbes, 11; Che fa laramanzina, 28; Ie suis amie
    du forrier or alez, 9; Une playsant figlette, 3; Voles oir une chanson, 14;
    Vostre bargeronette, 7
Compere, Josquin, Ninot: Lordault lordault, 6
Compere, Weerbeke: Vray dieu que pene messe, 34
Danglon, Pesenti: Manus tue fecerunt me et plasmaverunt, 55
Fevin: Pardonnes moy se je foloye, 44
Isaac: Donna di dentro dalla tua chasa/Damene un poco/Fortuna d'un
    gran tempo, 20; Elogeron nous seans, 32; Fille vous aves mal garde le
    pan davant, 18; Palle palle, 37; Prophetarum maxime, 49; Quis dabit
    capiti meo aquam, 42; Quis dabit pacem, 40; Substinuimus pacem, 29;
    Tota pulchra es, 41
Isaac, Josquin, Pesenti: Tulerunt dominum, 39
Japart: Si ie fet un chop apres, 15

Josquin: Alma redemptoris mater/Ave regina celorum, 31; Base moy, 2;
Ecce tu pulchra es, 48; Entre ye suis en gran penser, 21; Liber generationis, 38; Misericordias domini, 50; Missus est gabriel angelus, 54; O
bone et dulcis domine yhesu, 30; Paratum cor meum, 47; Une musque
de Biscaye, 33

Mouton: Factum est silentium, 52; Gaude barbara beata, 53; Quis dabit
oculis, 51; Vele ci vele la, 45

Ninot: Et leve vous o guigliermette, 8; Ie me levei laultre nuyt, 43; In illo
tempore, 36

Ninot, Obrecht: Si oblitus fuero, 35

anonymous: Amor demoi, 24; Ciascun me crie marietoy marie, 17; Forsellement, 22; Fortuna disperata/Vidi la forosetta/Vo m'avete svergogne,
19; Gentil galans de france, 10; Il estoit ung bone home, 23; Laultre ior
ie cievalcioie, 27; Maire de die, 26; Se jay perdu mon amy, 46; Si ie vous
avoye pointe, 16; T[ ], 25; Tambien mison pensada mari semi bates,
12; Tambur tambur tambor, 13; Veci la danse barbari, 5; Youli
mariner passe moy sena, 4

MS VatP 1980–1

Composer ascriptions for the first and second pieces are given as they
appear in the index to MS VatP 1981 (no ascriptions are given in the
manuscript other than those reproduced here); text incipits are given as
they appear in the index to MS VatP 1980; genre designations as they
appear in the index to MS VatP 1980 are given in square brackets before
the text incipit; foliation is given as in the tenor partbook.

[1] fols. 1^r–6^v, fevi[n], Dite moy maues pense [mass]
     BolC Q19, fol. 141^v, fauim
     VatP 1982, fols. 57^v–64^r, anonymous
     VatS 16, fols. 102^v–117^r, Ant. de Fevin

[2] fols. 7^r–13^v, [La] rue, Missa incesament
     CambraiBM 4, fols. 58^v–69^r, anonymous
     JenaU 4, fols. 90^v–101^r, Petrus de la Rue
     JenaU 8, fols. 6^r–25^r, Petrus de la Rue
     MunBS C, fols. 71^r–99^r, Petrus de [la] rue
     NurGN 83795, fol. 41^v, anonymous
     's HerAB 72B, fols. 20^v–39^r, P. Rue
     VatG xii.2, fols. 225^v–242^r, anonymous
     VatS 154, fols. 30^v–49^r, anonymous
     WolfA A, fols. 28^v–54^r
     1549^{16}, nos. 59–62 [Pleni, Benedictus, and In nomine only]

[3] fols. 14^r–21^r, [anonymous], Missa descendi
BolC Q19, fols. 157^v–164^r, anonymous [Gloria and Credo only]
BudOS 20, fols. 78^v–83^r, H. J. [Agnus missing]
BudOS 24, fols. 30^v–32^r, 33^r–34^r, Henr: Jsac [Kyrie, Gloria and Credo only]
ModD 4, fols. 76^v–87^r, brumel
StuttL 45, fols. 69^v–92^r, Antonius Bruml [Agnus Dei iii incomplete]
VatP 1982, fols. 17^v–28^r, Brumel [Benedictus missing]

[4] fols. 21^v–27^r, [anonymous], Missa pange lingua
BrusBR iv.922, fols. 28^v–41^r, Josquin
BudOS 8
JenaU 21, fols. 1^v–18^r, anonymous
LeipU 49, fols. 4^r–12^r, Josquinus
MilA 46, fols. 61^v–72^r, Josquin
MunBS 260, nos 20, Josquin; 21, anonymous; 22, anonymous [Pleni, Benedictus and Agnus Dei ii only]
MunBS 510, fols. 42^v–63^r, anonymous
RegB C100, Josquini
RosU 49, no. 2, Josquin
ToleBC 16, fols. 20^v–38^r, Jusquin
VatG xii.2, fols. 186^v–200^r, anonymous
VatP 1982, fols. 140^r–151^r, Josquin
VatS 16, fols. 36^v–46^r, Josquin
VatSM 26, fols. 214^v–229^r, anonymous
VienNB 4809, fols. 1^v–22^r, Josquin
VienNB Mus. 18832, nos. 2, 3, 6 [Pleni, Agnus Dei ii and Benedictus only]
1539^2, no. vii, Josquin
1545^6, nos. li, Josquin; lii, anonymous [Pleni and Agnus Dei ii only]
1547^1, p. 321, Iusquini Pratensis [Pleni only]
[1559] J 676, no. ii, Josquin

[5] fols. 27^r–33^v, [anonymous], Missa [*sine nomine*]

[6] fols. 34^r–41^r, [anonymous], Missa Ave Maria
CambraiBM 18, fols. 168^v–183^r, anonymous
CasAC M(D), fols. 70^v–80^r, la Rue
CoimU 2, fols. 104^v–121^r
JenaU 12, fols. 18^v–32^r, anonymous
MechS s.s., fols. 49^v–62^r, anonymous
MontsM 773, fols. 30^r–43^r, anonymous
SubA 248, fols. 56^v–75^v
VatP 1982, fols. 46^v–57^r, P. dela rue

VatS 45, fols. 16^v–30^r, Pe. de la Rue
VienNB 15496, fols. 36^v–50^r
1516^1, fol. 19^v
1522, no. 2

[7] fols. 41^r–47^v, [anonymous], Missa anima mea

[8] fols. 48^r–52^r, [anonymous], Missa faisant regres
JenaU 3, fols. 1^v–14^r, Josquin de Pres
MunBS 510, fols. 24^v–41^r, anonymous
ToleBC 9
VatS 23, fols. 118^v–128^r, Josquin des Pres
VienNB 4809, fols. 90^v–108^r, anonymous
VienNB Mus. 15495, fols. 33^v–47^r, Josquin des Pres
1514 J 673, fol. 4^v, Josquin [title page]
1516^1, fols. 104^r–114^r, Josquin
1516 J 674 = reprint of 1514 J 673
1526 J 675 = reprint of 1514 J 673, 1516 J 674
undated reprint of 1514 J 673, 1516 J 674, 1526 J 675

fols. 52^v–62^v, blank

[9] fols. 63^r–64^r, [anonymous], [Motetti] Salvator Mundi
CasAC D(F), fols. 37^v–39^r, anonymous
SGallS 463, no. 124, Joannes Mouton
SGallS 464, fol. 12^v, anonymous
VallaC 5, fols. LVII^v–LIX^r, Jo. Mouton
VatG XII.4, fols. 20^v–24^r, Leriter
1520^2, fols. 5^r–6^r, anonymous
[c. 1521]^7, fols. 7^r–8^r, anonymous

[10] fols. 64^v–65^r, [anonymous], [Motetti] Miseremini
LeidGA 1441, fols. LXVI^v–LXIX^r, anonymous
MunBS 16, fols. 60^v–66^r, Johannes Mouton
SGallS 463, no. 136, Joannes Mouton
SGallS 464, fol. 12^r, anonymous
VatP 1976–9, fols. 62^v–64^r, anonymous
VienNB Mus. 15941, fols. 36^r–37^r, Richafort [index]
1519^1, no. 4, Richafort
1520^2, fols. 2^r–3^r, Josquin
1526^2 = reprint of 1519^1
1534^3, fols. 15^r–15^v, anonymous
1547^1, pp. 322–5, Joannes Mouton

[11] fols. 65^v–66^v, [anonymous], [Motetti] Gaude barbara
CambraiBM 125–8, fols. 1^v–2^r [superius partbook], anonymous

CivMA 59, fols. 60^v–62^r, anonymous
CorBC 95–6/ParisBNN 1817, fols. 70^v–72^r, anonymous
FlorBN ii.i.232, fols. 163^v–166^r, Io: Mouto [index]
LonRC 1070, pp. 144–5, anonymous
MadM 6832, pp. 6–9, Joannes Monton
1514^1, fols. 2^r–2^v [superius partbook], Io. mouton [superius partbook index]
1526^1 = reprint of 1514^1

[12] fols. 67^r–68^v, [anonymous], [Motetti] In Convertendo
BergBC 1209, fol. 36bis^v, anonymous
BolC Q19, fol. 84^v, Lupus
BolC Q20, no. 18, Lupus
StuttL 42, fol. 133^v, anonymous
TrevBC 7, fol. 84^v, Lupus
1532^{10}, p. 23, Lupus
1535^1, no. 5, Lupus
1539^9, no. 26, Lupus
1539^{12}, p. 43, Lupus
1545^4, p. 41, Lupus
1564^6, p. 42, Lupus

[13] fols. 68^v–70^r, [anonymous], [Motetti] Lauda Jerusalem
FlorL 666, fols. 10^v–14^r, Mr. Jam
GothaF A98, fol. 120^v, anonymous
KasL 24, no. 52, Josquin
1537^1, no. 49, Jo. Heugel

[14] fols. 70^v–71^v, [anonymous], [Motetti] Saluto te
FlorL 666, fols. 22^v–26^r, Adriano
LonRC 2037, fol. 31^v, Adrianus Willaert
1539 W 1108, no. 21, Adrianus Willaert
1545 reprint of 1539 W 1106, no. 23, Adrianus Willaert

[15] fol. 72^r, [anonymous], [Motetti] In illo Tempor[e]
BolC Q19, fol. 44^v, Andreas de silua
FlorL 666, fols. 84^v–85^r, Andreas
's HerAB 72C, fol. 67^v, anonymous
1520^1, no. 11, A. de silua
1521^6, no. 4, Andrea de silua

[16] fol. 72^v, [anonymous], [Motetti] In omni tribulatione
FlorL 666, fols. 79^v–80^r, Mouton
VerBC 760, fol. 6^v, anonymous
1521^5, no. 14, Moulu
1521^6, no. 3, Molu

[17] fol. 73^r, [anonymous], [Canzon[i]] Ne uos challie
SGallS 463, no. 191, Richafort
SGallS 464, fol. 8^r, Richafort
VienNB Mus. 18746, fols. 28^v–29^r, anonymous
1540^7, no. 47, Her. Math. Ver.
1544^{13}, fol. 7^r, Jo. Richafort

[18] fol. 73^v, [anonymous], [Canzon[i]] In Cessament
BerlPS 40013, fols. 169^v–170^r, anonymous [text is a contrafactum, 'Sic Deus']
GothaF A98, fols. 36^v–37^r, anonymous [text is a contrafactum 'Sic Deus']
MunBS 1508, no. 71, anonymous
NurGN 83795, fol. 166^r, anonymous [text is a contrafactum 'Sic Deus']
SGallS 463, no. 197, Petrus de la Rue
VienNB Mus. 18746, fol. 16^r, anonymous
WeimB B, fols. 96^v–97^r, anonymous [text is a contrafactum 'Sic Deus']
[c. 1521]^7, fol. 18^r, anonymous
1549 J 681, fol. xiii^v, Iosquin des prez [title page]
1552^{29}, anonymous
1560 *Bibliographie des éditions d'Adrian Le Roy. . . .*, no. 68, fol. 28^r, Delarue
1572^2, fol. 52^r, De La Rue

[19] fol. 74^r, [anonymous], [Canzon[i]] Petitte Camusete
BolC R142, fol. 32^v, Josquin
CopKB 1873
1545^{15}, fol. xi, Josquin des Pres [title page]
1549 J 681, fol. x^v, Iosquin des prez [title page]
1560 *Bibliographie des éditions d'Adrian Le Roy . . .*, no. 68, fol. 32^r, Josquin

[20] fol. 74^v, [anonymous], [Canzon[i]] Se conge prans
BolC A71
LeipU 49, fols. 188^v–189^r, Josquin [text is a contrafactum, 'Miserator et misericors Dominus']
SGallS 463, no. 211, Josquin
SGallS 464, fols. 8^v–9^r
1545^{15}, fol. viii, Josquin des Pres [title page]
1549 J 681, fol. vii^v, Iosquin des prez [title page]
1560 *Bibliographie des éditions d'Adrian Le Roy . . .*, no. 68, fol. 31^r, Josquin

[21]   fol. 75^r, [anonymous], [Motetti] Salua nos
       BolC Q19, fol. 22^v, Jo. moton
       BolC R142, fol. 57^r, Josquin
       FlorL 666, fols. 87^v–88^r, Mouton
       ModD 9, fol. 83^v, Mouton
       's HerAB 72C, fol. 46^v, Joannes Mouton
       StuttL 3, fol. 185^v, Joannes Mouton
       VatS 38, fol. 151^v, Jo. Mouton
       1521^6, no. 1, Jo. Mouton
       1540^7, no. 3, Joannes Mouton
       1542^{10}, no. 13, Willaert
       1558^4, no. 16, Mouton

fols. 75^v–86^v, blank

Concordant sources

BergBC 1209: 12
BerlPS 40013: 18
BolC A71: 20
BolC Q19: 1, 3, 12, 15, 21
BolC Q20: 12
BolC R142: 19, 21
BrusBR iv.922: 4
BudOS 8: 4
BudOS 20: 3
BudOS 24: 3
CambraiBM 4: 2
CambraiBM 18: 6
CambraiBM 125–8: 11
CasAC D(F): 9
CasAC (D): 6
CivMA 59: 11
CoimU 2: 6
CopKB 1873: 19
CorBC 95–6/ParisBNN 1817: 11
FlorBN ii.i.232: 11
FlorL 666: 13, 14, 15, 16, 21
GothaF A98: 13, 18
JenaU 3: 8
JenaU 4: 2
JenaU 8: 2
JenaU 12: 6

JenaU 21: 4
KasL 24: 13
LeidGA 1441: 10
LeipU 49: 4, 20
LonRC 1070: 11
LonRC 2037: 14
MadM 6832: 11
MechS s.s.: 6
MilA 46: 4
ModD 4: 3
ModD 9: 21
MontsM 773: 6
MunBS 16: 10
MunBS 510: 4, 8
MunBS 1508: 18
MunBS C: 2
NurGN 83795: 2, 18
RegB C100: 4
RosU 49: 4
's HerAB 72B: 2
's HerAB 72C: 15, 21
SGallS 463: 9, 10, 17, 18, 20
SGallS 464: 9, 10, 17, 20
StuttL 3: 21
StuttL 42: 12
StuttL 45: 3
SubA 248: 6
ToleBC 9: 8
ToleBC 16: 4
TrevBC: 12
VallaC 5: 9
VatG xii.2: 2, 4
VatG xii.4: 9
VatP 1976–9: 10
Vat P 1982: 1, 3, 4, 6
VatS 16: 1, 4
VatS 23: 8
VatS 38: 21
VatS 45: 6
VatS 154: 2
VatSM 26: 4
VerBC 760: 16

VienNB 4809: 4, 8
VienNB Mus. 15495: 8
VienNB Mus. 15496: 6
VienNB Mus. 15941: 10
VienNB Mus. 18746: 17, 18
VienNB Mus. 18832: 4
WeimB B: 18
WolfA A: 2
1514[1]: 11
1514 J 673: 8
1516[1]: 6, 8
1516 J 674: 8
1519[1]: 10
1520[1]: 15
1520[2]: 9, 10
1521[1]: 16
1521[6]: 15, 16, 21
[c. 1521][7]: 9, 18
1522: 6
1526[1]: 11
1526[2]: 10
1526 J 675: 8
1532[10]: 12
1534[3]: 10
1535[1]: 12
1537[1]: 13
1539[2]: 4
1539[9]: 12
1539[12]: 12
1539 W 1108: 14
1540[7]: 17, 21
1542[10]: 21
1544[13]: 17
1545[4]: 12
1545[6]: 4
1545 reprint of 1539 W 1106: 14
1545[15]: 19, 20
1547[1]: 4, 10
1549[16]: 2
1549 J 681: 18, 19, 20
1552[29]: 18
1558[4]: 21

(1559) J 676: 4
1560 *Bibliographie des éditions d'Adrian Le Roy* . . ., no. 68: 18, 19, 20
1564[6]: 12
1572[2]: 18
undated reprint of 1514 J 673, 1516 J 674, 1516 J 675: 8

Concordant sources ordered by number of concordances
5: BolC Q19, FlorL 666, SGallS 463
4: SGallS 464, VatP 1982
3: 1521[6], 1549 J 681, 1560 *Bibliographie des éditions d'Adrian Le Roy* . . ., no. 68
2: BolC R142, GothaF A98, LeipU 49, MunBS 510, NurGN 83795, 's HerAB 72C, VatG xii.2, VatS 16, Vien NB Mus. 18746, 1516[1], 1520[2], [c. 1521][7], 1540[7], 1545[15], 1547[1]

Index of compositions
Gaude barbara, Mouton, 11
In Cessament, Josquin, La Rue, 18
In Convertendo, Lupus, 12
In illo Tempor[e], de Silva, 15
In omni tribulatione, Moulu, Mouton, 16
Lauda Jerusalem, Heugel, Josquin, Mr. Jam, 13
Miseremini, Josquin, Mouton, Richafort, 10
Missa anima mea, anonymous, 7
Missa Ave Maria, La Rue, 6
Missa descendi, Brumel, Isaac, 3
Dite moy maues pense [mass], Fevin, 1
Missa faisant regres, Josquin, 8
Missa incesament, La Rue, 2
Missa pange lingua, Josquin, 4
Missa [*sine nomine*], anonymous, 5
Ne uos challie, Richafort, Werrecore, 17
Petitte Camusete, Josquin, 19
Saluto te, Willaert, 14
Salua nos, Josquin, Mouton, Willaert, 21
Salvator Mundi, Lhéritier, Mouton, 9
Se conge prans, Josquin, 19

Composer index
Brumel, Isaac: Missa descendi, 3
De Silva: In illo Tempor[e], 15
Fevin: Dite moy maues pense [mass], 1

Heugel, Josquin, Mr. Jam: Lauda Jerusalem, 13
Josquin: Missa faisant regres, 8; Missa pange lingua, 4; Petitte Camusete,
  19; Se conge prans, 20
Josquin, La Rue: In Cessament, 18
Josquin, Mouton, Richafort: Miseremini, 10
Josquin, Mouton, Willaert: Salua nos, 21
La Rue: Missa Ave Maria, 6; Missa incesament, 2
Lhéritier, Mouton: Salvator Mundi, 9
Lupus: In Convertendo, 12
Moulu, Mouton: In omni tribulatione, 16
Mouton: Gaude barbara, 11
Richafort, Werrecore: Ne uos challie, 17
Willaert: Saluto te, 14
anonymous: Missa anima mea, 7; Missa [*sine nomine*], 5

Early Music History (1991) Volume 10

MARTHA FARAHAT

ON THE STAGING OF MADRIGAL
COMEDIES

The brief life of the madrigal comedy spans the forty-year period
from 1590 to 1630. Coming at the end of the sixteenth century, the
genre marked the decline of the polyphonic madrigal style and
heralded the evolution of secular vocal music's emphasis on the
dramatic. As a genre, the madrigal comedy is not well known, and
its designation can lead to confusion, because the term refers to
collections of compositions that need not consist of madrigals or by
themselves form comedies. Nevertheless it is a term that retains
some usefulness in isolating a body of works from the late sixteenth
and early seventeenth centuries that share common elements. Not
until the most recent edition of *Grove's Dictionary* was there an entry
under the heading 'Madrigal Comedy'; earlier editions had described such works as madrigal operas, clearly an even more problematic term. The brief life of the genre – from Orazio Vecchi's
Selva di varia recreatione of 1590 to Banchieri's last publication, the
Trattenimenti da villa of 1630 – as well as the variety of types of
composition and of musical style to be found in these collections,
and the fact that there are so few of them, make it particularly
difficult to define more narrowly or more precisely. The composers
themselves seemed to have no special term for their works, either
failing to give them a generic subtitle, or calling them variously
comedia harmonica, *inventione*, *raggionamenti comici* and *genio madri-
galesco*, among other terms.[1]

Perhaps the best attempts to clarify the types of work which fall

---

[1]   These works are to be contrasted with publications of collections of textually unrelated
pieces and with madrigal cycles – books which set stanzas of a single poem. Where some
indication exists that a work was intended to be presented as a whole in performance by
virtue of either a particular subject matter or a set of characters, that implication is found
either in the title or in introductory remarks in the preface or dedication.

under the rubric 'madrigal comedy' was made by Cecil Adkins in the preface to his performance edition of *L'Amfiparnaso*.[2] Adkins devised a 'genealogical table of the madrigal comedy'[3] with four categories:

    i. Continuity provided by title only

    ii. Continuity provided by title and use of same characters throughout

    iii. Like ii, but all based on pastoral themes[4]

    iv. Continuity provided by plot and character development.

Only six works, written by just two composers, fall into category iv, yet it is this category for which the term 'madrigal comedy' is most appropriate, and from which it probably derives. All but one of these works, *L'Amfiparnaso* of Orazio Vecchi (the earliest to be composed), were written by Adriano Banchieri. Banchieri's five madrigal comedies with plot and character development are *La pazzia senile* (1598), *Il studio dilettevole* (1600), *Il metamorfosi musicale* (1601), *La prudenza giovenile* (1607) and *La saviezza giovenile* (1628).

The popularity of the madrigal comedy was short-lived; this may be explained in part by the concurrent fascination with the newly created medium of opera, a field from which Vecchi effectively distanced himself by declaring in the preface to *L'Amfiparnaso* that his work was 'not for the eyes but for the ears'. That statement is also the foundation for the conception, commonly held, that madrigal comedies were not intended to be dramatised and staged. A much simplified version of the argument goes like this:

---

[2] O. Vecchi, *L'Amfiparnaso*, transcr. and trans. C. Adkins, Early Musical Masterworks 1 (Chapel Hill, 1977), p. 15.

[3] Adkins's 'genealogical table' contains a number of factual errors which make it likely to mislead if used as a guideline. In category i, two of the works are incorrectly attributed: the 1592 *La nobiltà dell asino* . . . is not by Vecchi but by Banchieri, whereas the *Convito musicale* (1597) is by Vecchi, not Banchieri. Furthermore, *La nobiltà dell asino* contains very little music; its inclusion as a madrigal comedy, though not entirely without justification, requires explanation. The 1599 *Il Donatio* of Banchieri has a format different from most of the other works, but certainly uses the same characters throughout, and thus should be included under category ii rather than category i. Banchieri's 1630 publication, the *Trattenimenti da villa*, is based on pastoral themes and therefore belongs in category iii. Finally, the composer listed as 'P. Balsamino' must be Simone Balsamino; his only known musical composition is that listed in the table, the *Aminta musicale*. These errors notwithstanding, Adkins's table is useful as the first, perhaps the only, attempt to delineate and organise this short-lived genre which has so few compositions to define it.

[4] For our discussion, the distinction between ii and iii above is not essential. However, the distinction is not without merit, for the genre of the *favola pastorale* is closely related to this third category.

On the staging of madrigal comedies

Major premise: Vecchi's *L'Amfiparnaso* was definitely not to be staged.

Minor premise: Banchieri imitated Vecchi closely (some say almost exactly).

Conclusion: Banchieri's madrigal comedies were not to be staged.

The argument that the madrigal comedies were not to be staged has been accepted by nearly all musical scholars.[5] The same view, more elegantly rendered, was propounded by Einstein in *The Italian Madrigal*. As above, it is based primarily on the evidence given by Vecchi in the preface to *L'Amfiparnaso*. Vecchi, as quoted by Einstein, wrote: 'Moreover, the music is not interspersed with such pleasures for the sight as might relieve the one sense by the attentiveness of the other. However, those desirous of more action may refer every want to what is presupposed and inwardly expressed, and thus will they be able to form a complete idea of the play.'[6] Vecchi understood that his audience would want to see the play as well as hear it. Furthermore, he knew that the background of common understanding was great: his audience would have the correct presuppositions and inward expressions to fill in the gaps. Though much was left out in the presentation of the story line, the *commedia dell'arte* plots were so familiar to Vecchi's contemporaries that audiences would be able to understand and supply any missing links necessary for continuity.[7]

Since Banchieri's early works *La pazzia senile* and, especially, *Il studio dilettevole* are based on *L'Amfiparnaso*, the assumption has been that performance conditions would be approximately the same for all the others. Einstein's articulation of this view has been widely adopted. Referring to Vecchi, he states

With Vecchi the center of gravity is 'music as entertainment,' however great and serious a master he may have been otherwise. His so-called 'madrigal comedies', which are anything but comedies and which have no

---

[5] One scholar who espoused this view was Gustave Reese, who wrote: 'The late 16th century produced also a large body of "entertainment" music, with texts quasi-dramatic or otherwise suggested by action, though not intended for the stage.' *Music in the Renaissance* (New York, 1954), p. 433.

[6] Vecchi, *L'Amfiparnaso, op. cit.*, p. 15.

[7] Nino Pirrotta remarks on his understanding of Vecchi's intention: 'In other words, what he intended to do was not develop a comedy in an orderly fashion, but to evoke in the minds of his spectators the vision of a comedy being performed.' N. Pirrotta, *Music and Theatre from Poliziano to Monteverdi* (Cambridge, 1982), p. 115.

125

more to do with the theater, the stage, or the birth of the opera than Striggio's *Cicalamento*, follow after a long and fruitful preoccupation with the canzonetta.[8]

Einstein implies in his discussion of Banchieri that the same principles apply; Banchieri's works were modelled on Vecchi's and, although he made some modifications to the plots, the stories are nearly interchangeable.

Adriano Banchieri is Vecchi's real successor in so far as one can speak at all of a succession in this case, for Banchieri seems more like a small-scale Vecchi or a caricature of him. They were neighbors, so to speak, and it is hardly credible that they should not have known one another. ... The *Pazzia senile*, the first of Banchieri's madrigal comedies, first published in 1598 and reprinted at least five times ... makes the stuttering Pantalone the very center of the 'action' and accordingly uses the conventional three-voiced texture of the giustiniana; the whole might indeed be called a dramatized giustiniana in nineteen numbers.[9]

Banchieri's ... *Prudenza giovenile* of 1607, Opus xv, returns to the three-voiced texture of the giustiniana. ... The later and somewhat altered edition of 1628 is called the *Saviezza giovenile*. ... There is no need for us to discuss this work. It is simply a duplicate of the *Pazzia senile*.[10]

The similarity between all of these *commedia dell'arte*-related madrigal comedies is affirmed also by Nino Pirrotta, who describes Banchieri's works thus:

While Vecchi was careful to refrain from using the same pretext twice, as starting point for his inventions, one of his admirers and imitators, Banchieri, was less discreet. At least three times he attempted to reunite the two Parnassus – more than three times if one bears in mind that some of his so-called 'madrigal comedies' were each issued several times, on each occasion with alterations, additions and omissions. ... If you like, *La pazzia senile* (1598), *Il metamorfosi musicale* (1600) and *La saviezza giovenile* (1608) were three different performances of the same scenario, altered on each occasion to include a different dialogue, different retorts, and different musical *lazzi*.[11]

This insight by Pirrotta, however, may not go far enough; he is sufficiently cautious to avoid the claim that the pieces were staged. In the cases he cites, the *lazzi*, or slapstick acrobatic antics of the

---

[8]   A. Einstein, *The Italian Madrigal*, ii (Princeton, 1949), pp. 772–3.
[9]   *Ibid.*, pp. 802–3.
[10] *Ibid.*, pp. 812–13.
[11] Pirrotta, *op. cit.*, pp. 118–19.

commedia dell'arte clowns, are 'musical'. Pirrotta does not mean to imply that the music accompanies stage business. In a related context, discussing the intermedi of earlier staged theatrical productions, Pirrotta recognises that the similarity of situation was not necessarily a drawback to the effectiveness of a comic presentation:

In some ways what the *intermedi* were about was of only limited importance: subjects could be repeated, since what really mattered was the novelty of the way in which they were presented . . . although frequently a drummer and a fool are said to appear on stage, it is not always the same [there being] neither the same gestures nor the same music, but different inventions, costumes and music.[12]

Apparently, if Pirrotta accepted the idea that Banchieri meant his madrigal comedies to be staged, then his reservation regarding Banchieri's schematic plots, characters and situations would be nullified.

Laura Detenbeck, writing as recently as 1989, summarises the consensus, that these works were not acted out at all. She goes on to point out Banchieri's greater sensitivity to action, noting both his economy of characters and his more coherent plots, and she describes in detail his attention to the theatrical structures of the *commedia dell'arte*, following the traditions as outlined by Giacomo Oreglia.[13] Banchieri on all points is shown to have been more theatrically orientated than Vecchi. In Detenbeck's opinion, viewed in a purely theatrical perspective, these works invite staging. She does not attempt to provide *evidence* that they were intended for the stage, other than substantiating the claim that they conform to dramatic *commedia* traditions,[14] and noting several points in the plot where stage directions are implicit. She observes:

'Bizarre Humour' enters to deliver the prologue, in which he presents the first concrete evidence that the piece was intended for performance before an audience: 'Illustrious spectators, I have come out here into your presence to make reverence to you . . .' He tells who he is and then bids silence 'because I see Pantalone who humbly approaches, to begin the Senile Madness' (p. 5). Banchieri has included implicit stage directions in

[12] *Ibid.*, p. 51.
[13] 'Before the curtain rose, an actor spoke the prologue, which usually had no direct relation to the subject of the performance; in the intervals between the acts it was the custom to present brief intermezzos, often delightfully burlesque character sketches.' G. Oreglia, *The Commedia dell'Arte*, trans. L. F. Edwards (London, 1968), p. 12.
[14] L. Detenbeck, 'Dramatized Madrigals', *The Science of Buffoonery: Theory and History of the Commedia dell'Arte*, ed. D. Pietropaolo (Toronto, 1989), pp. 59–68.

the text in the manner typically used by Renaissance playwrights. . . . Act 2 rediscovers Pantalone and Burattino. . . . This scene indicates another implicit stage direction: Doralice must appear at a window or in a doorway, unseen by the two characters on stage, in order to overhear their conversation.[15]

While arguing against the notion that some of the madrigal comedies may have been meant for the stage, Pirrotta recognises Banchieri's competence in the field of drama:

An eager polygraph, as well as a musical composer, performer and theoretician, Banchieri also wrote, under the pseudonym of Camillo Scaligeri della Fratta, a whole series of comedies, in a mixture of languages and dialects, with associated *intermedi*, at times 'visible', at times 'invisible'. He therefore knew all that he needed to about comedy, but in his musical comedies he worked even more schematically than Orazio Vecchi, and actually his plots, characters and situations are merely slight variations on those of *L'Amfiparnaso*. At most the roles of the two old men are at times reversed: instead of allowing his daughter to marry Doctor Graziano, Pantalone himself becomes the luckless hopeful suitor. However, most important of all, especially for the *intermedi*, of which there were none in *L'Amfiparnaso*, but which here played an important part, is the fact that the comedy is each time set somewhere new; this allows the author to vary the local colour and to have the masquerades refer to different characteristic trades.[16]

Both Banchieri's five comedies and Vecchi's *L'Amfiparnaso* have similar structures. All consist of approximately twenty compositions. Most begin with a prologue and end with a *licenza* – conventions borrowed from Italian theatre. All are organised into acts and scenes. There are, nonetheless, some obvious differences between the two composers' works. Vecchi's tend to be longer and more elaborate than Banchieri's. Banchieri wrote for three vocal parts, instead of the five used by Vecchi, but he preferred to have six singers; this disposition of voices permits of greater identification of a vocal part with a specific dramatic role. (It is interesting to note that it is only in these *commedia dell'arte*-related works that Banchieri scored for three voices. He used five for all of the other madrigal comedies – those that fall in the first three of Adkins's categories.) Banchieri's acts are separated by intermedi of the sort described by Pirrotta above, while Vecchi's acts have no such dividing numbers.[17]

---

[15] *Ibid.*, pp. 63–4.
[16] Pirrotta, *op. cit.*, pp. 118–19.
[17] The one exception to this in *L'Amfiparnaso* occurs in the middle of Act 3, with the scene

The question of staging, or lack of it, was one that Vecchi felt compelled to address. It remains a problem for performances of *L'Amfiparnaso* even today. Contemporary staging often incorporates some form of mime, using either puppets or live performers, in wilful disregard of Vecchi's stated intentions. The Italian musicologist Carlo Perinello made an attempt to reconcile the apparent contradiction between what he would intuit – that these works demanded to be staged – and the words of Vecchi.[18] His solution was to retain the five-part vocal texture, but to distinguish between characters, associating particular voices with specific dramatic roles, and making that voice dominant when that character was supposed to be singing. The other voices were then used in an orchestral, accompanying fashion. Ernest Newman summarised Perinello's vision thus:

Leaving the music virtually entirely intact he individualizes in his own practicable score now this vocal line, now that, in such a way that each of them could be delivered with perfect verisimilitude by a living actor [as against the marionette solution sometimes used] or in a stage setting with the madrigal complex enveloping these solo parts in the way that the orchestral complex envelops a solo part in an opera of today.[19]

Though in sympathy with this treatment, neither Newman nor Perinello would maintain that this was Vecchi's intention.

Although there exists a variety of possibilities when performances of these works are attempted today, none of these solutions is entirely convincing, and little historical justification is offered for anything other than a series of sung miniatures. Most of the pieces are quite brief, the shortest a mere twenty breves. Yet, being aware of Banchieri's competence in writing comedies, it defies our credulity to suppose, with all the humour, satire and melodrama contained in these works, that they were not, at least at times, staged with the trappings of acts, costuming and at least minimal scenery. Indeed, evidence from Banchieri himself supports this intuition. Though several scholars have noted his writing on the

---

between the female servant Francatrippa and the Hebrews inside their house. Although this does not mark the end of an act, it functions in a similar manner, having no obvious relationship to the 'action' of the main plot, and serving only to delay the resolution of the drama.

18 See C. Perinello, ed., *Orazio Vecchio: L'Amfiparnaso* (Milan, 1938), pp. iii–xiii, and *idem*, 'L'Amfiparnaso: comedia harmonica d'Horatio Vecchi', *Rivista Musicale Italiana*, 41 (1937), pp. 1–23, especially 21–3.

19 E. Newman, 'L'Amfiparnaso', *Sunday Times* [London] (22 Dec 1946).

subject, he has not been taken seriously, for a variety of reasons.[20] Banchieri's most elaborate instructions for staging are found in the preface of La prudenza giovenile, published in 1607. He indicates two different ways of performing the comedy. The first, 'the way of singing the comedy in a simple manner', iterates some rules similar to those he included at the beginning of several of his earlier madrigal comedies. Briefly, 'One of the three singers of the terzetti, before the music, should read aloud the title of the scene, names of the participants and arguments: one [should] sing with deliberation [pausatamente], and gracefully, anticipating the non-Tuscan words, and some few harmonic novelties, and that is all.'[21] The alternative means of presentation is outlined in a much more lengthy description of recommendations for performance. Because it is crucial to an understanding of Banchieri's plan, it is included here in its entirety.

If you wish to perform the said comedy musically, you must choose a room which is not too large and as closed as possible (so that the voices and instruments can be enjoyed more fully), and in a corner of that room put a pair of large carpets on the floor, together with a stage set (back-drop) with two buildings; these will make an attractive scene. [This is a typical construct for plays of the time – two buildings, one on either side, each with windows from which characters can talk to each other.] On the sides of that setting place two chairs, one at the right, the other at the left.

---

[20] Probably the most significant reasons are, first, the fact that the preface to L'Amfiparnaso is so well known and so very clear on the subject of staging. Since the plots of Banchieri's madrigal comedies are similar to that of L'Amfiparnaso, the tendency has been to assume that they are also similar in the manner in which they should be staged. Perhaps, however, the import of that preface is quite contrary to this supposition: Vecchi may have felt that he had to write at length to justify his attempt to go against the natural presumption of the times; perhaps without that preface one and all would, without a second thought, have proceeded to stage L'Amfiparnaso. The second reason for the prevailing view against staging comes, I believe, from a confusion over the publication of La prudenza giovenile. The second edition of this work, La saviezza giovenile, is found in Bologna. Since the second edition is complete, whereas the first lacks the two lower partbooks, scholars have chosen to work from the later publication. The date of that publication has also been mistaken through Gaetano Gaspari's handwritten preface, copied from the 1607 edition, being affixed to the later one. Banchieri's observations on how the comedy might be performed were much more important in 1607 than they would have been if written in 1628 when he had already finished nearly all of his madrigal comedies, and after opera had been in vogue for more than twenty years.

[21] 'Modo da tenersi incantare semplicemente la Comedia di PRUDENZA GIOVENILE. / Uno de gli tre cantori de terzetto in terzetto, avanti la Musica, leggerà forte il titolo della Scena, nomi de gli Intercantori, e Argomenti: Si canta pausatamente, e con gratia, antivedendo le parole non Toscane, alcune novità di Armonie; e ciò basti.' A. Banchieri, La prudenza giovenile (Venice, 1607), p. 3.

Behind the set place benches for the singers, in such a way that they will be about a hand's distance from each other, with their faces turned towards the audience. Behind the singers have a pleasing ensemble of lutes, clavicembali, or other instruments, tuned in 'tuono corista'. Over the stage set sew a large curtain, which will cover [conceal] the singers and instrumentalists, and with the following instructions [the work] will commence.

Be sure that the singers and actors [*Recitatori*] look over the music, prose and verse, beforehand, for unfamiliar elements and dialects.

The singers will perform from their partbooks [*sopra gli libri*] (since they are not to be seen), and if singing falsetto is desired, three will suffice; however if it is more convenient, it would be better to have six [singers], two soprano, two tenor, alto and bass, singing and keeping silent as the music dictates, giving spirit to the happy words, affect to the mournful ones, and articulating intelligibly everything with the good judgement of a prudent singer.

Drawing on a copy of the following original, the Recitanti should learn their parts from memory (as they will be seen) and accompany the music with every readiness as to place and time [tempo?].

It will also be necessary to have one who is not [directly] involved to help the singers, instrumentalists and actors in case of need.[22]

With this introduction *La prudenza giovenile* presents a most convincing case for assuming some sort of staging, one so strong that it must be asked what the motivation can be for questioning it.

The evidence is minutely detailed. At the beginning of the book, Banchieri sets out a list of 'Intercantori, et dicitori' (Figure 1).

---

22 'Volendo recitare la sudetta Comedia musicalmente, sia necessario ritriarsi entro una stanza non molto grande, & può chiusa che si poule (acciò le Voci, & Stromenti meglio si posino godere,) Et in un'angolo di detta stanza porre un paio di Tappeti grandi sopra il pavimento, insieme una prospettiva con doi cantonate, che rendino vaghezza à i circonstanti. In detta Scena si porranno due Sedie, l'una à man destra, l'altra alla sinistra. Dietro la prospettiva si porranno banzuole per gli Cantori, in modo che sijno distanti un palmo l'un dall'altro, con gli visi voltati verso gli Audienti. Dietro à gli Cantori vi sarà un vagho Concerto di Lauto, Clavecemboli, à altri Stromenti, accordati in Tuono Corista. Di sopra la prospettiva si cucirà una tela in modo grande, che faccia cuperto sopra gli Cantori, & Suonatori, & con l'ordine seguente si darà principio.

Avertendo, che gli Cantori, & Recitatori antivedino prima la Musica, Prosa, & Rima, il tutto per le novità, & parole non Toscane.

Gli Cantori canteranno sopra gli libri, (per essere inapparenti,) & volendo cantare alla bastarda saranno tre: tuttavia essendovi commodità meglio sariano in sei, Dui Soprani, Dui Tenori, Alto, & Basso, cantando & tacendo secondo le occasioni, dando spirito alle parole allegre, affetione alle meste, & pronuntiar con voci intelligibili, tutto à giuditio del prudente Cantore.

Gli Recitanti devono imparare quello gli tocca alla mente, (per essere apparente) cavandone le copie dal seguente originale, & con ogni prontezza à luoco & tempo accompagnare la Musica.

Et sarà anco necessario uno non interessato, che aiuti gli Cantori, & Suonatori, & Recitanti, (occorrendo.)' *Ibid.*, pp. 3–4.

131

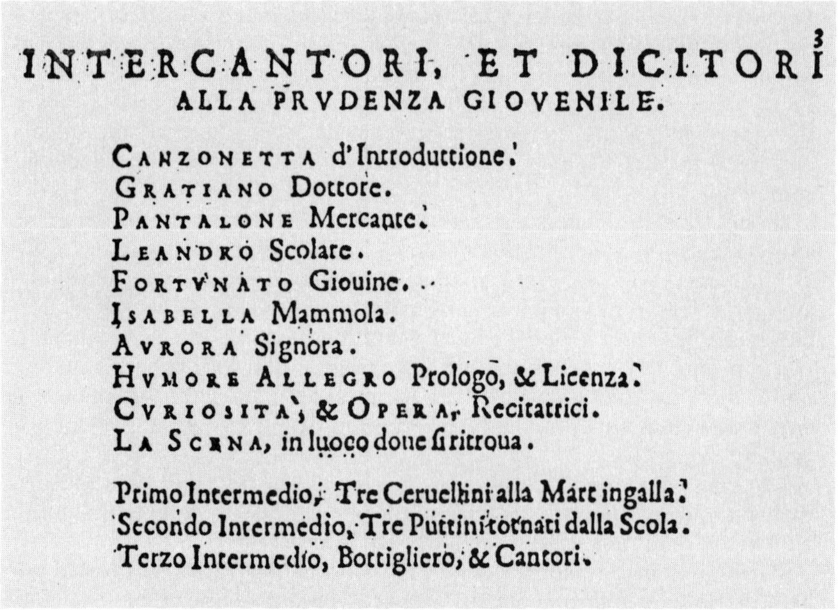

Martha Farahat

INTERCANTORI, ET DICITORI³
ALLA PRVDENZA GIOVENILE.

CANZONETTA d'Introduttione.
GRATIANO Dottore.
PANTALONE Mercante.
LEANDRO Scolare.
FORTVNATO Giouine. .·
ISABELLA Mammola.
AVRORA Signora.
HVMORE ALLEGRO Prologo, & Licenza.
CVRIOSITA', & OPERA, Recitatrici.
LA SCENA, in luoco doue fi ritroua.

Primo Intermedio, Tre Ceruelkini alla Mart ingalla.
Secondo Intermedio, Tre Puttini tornati dalla Scola.
Terzo Intermedio, Bottigliero, & Cantori.

Figure 1   List of participants in Adriano Banchieri, *La prudenza giovenile* (Bologna, 1607), p. 3.

Included are: (a) the *dramatis personae*: Pantalone, Gratiano, their servants, and so on, (b) 'Humore Allegro' (familiar from Banchieri's earlier madrigal comedies), who declaims the prologue and *licenza* as in the practice of the *commedia erudita*, and (c) two additional figures (*recitatrici*), Curiosità and Opera. All these performers are presented in one continuous list. I submit that this is a list of cast members who are 'apparenti', or visible.[23] The *intercantori* are to be differentiated from the *cantori*. Their name implies that they are 'between' – in this case, between the audience and the source of the music, the *cantori* and *suonatori*.[24] Near the end of Act 1, Banchieri even specifies the position of two of the characters. He indicates 'Gratiano in strada, Aurora alla finestra'.[25] With one important exception, the *cantori*, as Banchieri explained in his

23 'Intercantori' is not found in either current or historical Italian dictionaries. It is probably Banchieri's creation, a portmanteau word combining 'interlocutori' and 'cantori'.
24 The designation 'intercantori' may also imply that these are the characters who interact with each other in song, cf. *interlocutori*.
25 *Prudenza*, p. 26.

132

instructions, were not meant to be seen. The last of the comedy's three intermedi involves a Bottigliero (wine merchant) and the *cantori*. (See the more detailed discussion of the third intermedio below.) Again, by making it clear that in this one case the singers are to appear on stage, Banchieri implies stage action.

Banchieri provides additional instructions for the singers and instrumentalists, and for the movements of Opera (indicated here as Endeavour) and Curiosità (here translated as Novelty), during the performance. He begins with an 'Ordine in dar principio', or 'beginning instructions'. The instrumentalists may play a concerto of their own choosing which should have a final chord of G Dorian ('G sol, re ut, per b. molle') in order to give the singers their pitches for the coming 'canzonetta d'introduttione'.[26] Banchieri then digresses to explain his views on the relationship of poetry to music, and of the characteristics of perfection in each. He concludes his introduction with a statement about what will be seen in the theatre: 'but now, in this Theatre you will hear not separated, but united Poetry and Music, that exist together to create for you an artful Comedy, that being an invention not before heard of, they can be sure of offering you more than a little enjoyment, following the Maxim that all new things are pleasing'.[27]

Endeavour introduces Novelty, and some spoken dialogue ensues. When the dialogue is finished, Endeavour makes a bow and withdraws to the chair at the right of the stage, leaving Novelty to continue. Addressing the audience, Novelty says that she has investigated with all diligence around the stage in order to discover what is to occur and has found that 'with new inventions is to be represented musically a graceful and virtuous Comedy entitled *La prudenza giovenile*, divided into three acts, with four scenes in each, and ornamented not only with intermedi, but also with sweet *con*-

---

[26] 'Gli leggiadri Suonatori con un vagho Concerto à gusto loro, il quale habbia la sua corda finale in G sol, re ut, per b. molle, daranno principio, obligando à detto finale, acciò gli Cantori possino principiar assolutamente.' The introduction is followed by the appearance of Prudenza Giovenile, ornately dressed, who recites a speech during two promenades: 'Finita la Canzonetta d'Introduttione uscirà in Scena PRUDENZA GIO-VENILE (chiamata in soggietto OPERA) vagamente ornata, e date dui passaggiate recitarà questa Prosa.'

[27] 'mà hora in questo Teatro, udirete non separate, mà conteste insieme Poesia, e Musica, che in un' istesso tempo sono per recitarvi, un'artificiosa Comedia, che per essere inventione non più sentita, si puole assicurare sia per porgere non poca dilettatione, stando quella gran Massima, che tutte le cose nuove piaciono'.

certi of voices and instruments, together with a Prologue and Licenza, recited by the Humore Allegro'.[28]

Novelty goes on to give the setting and synopsis of the plot,[29] after which she observes that the singers wish to present the first intermedio. She retires to the chair at stage left to listen while the singers perform an introductory intermedio, preceded by a 'toccatina'[30] played by the instrumentalists. When the intermedio is finished, Endeavour rises, goes to centre stage and says:

> Here is Humore Allegro, who confidently promises
> you who surround him that your boredom will be banished.
> He then observes Gratiano, with a curious poem.[31]

Note that Novelty says (1) that there are new inventions to be found, (2) that a comedy will be presented and (3) that the comedy will be *ornamented* (my italics) not only with intermedi, but also with the music of voices and instruments. Should we assume that the comedy consisted entirely of these ornamentations, or is there something more that is being ornamented? I would argue that in the use of the word 'ornament' is the implication that something else must exist to which ornamentation is added. Unlike in the previous madrigal comedies (*La pazzia senile* and *Il studio dilettevole*), here Humore Allegro does not introduce himself until midway

---

[28] 'Cortesi Auditori, in, che la CURIOSITÀ sono, per sodisfattione vostra, et interesse mio, hò investigato con ogni diligenza possibile, dentro e fuori di questa Scena, quello siasi per fare, e hò ritrovato, si deve con nuova inventione rapresentare musicalmente una vagha, e virtuoso Comedia, intitolata, PRUDENZA GIOVENILE, divisa in tre Atti, quattro Scene per ciascuno, ornata non solo di spassevoli Intermedii, mà parimente di soavissimi Concerti di voci e istromenti, insieme Prologo e Licenza recitato dall' Humor Allegro.'

[29] 'Il soggietto della Favola sarà diviso in duoi Capi. Hora imaginatevi questa sia la nostra nobiliss. Città di N. entro la quale habita un Vecchio per nome, cognome, patria, e professione chiamato Gratiano Forbesoni da Francolino, Dottor insolentissimus in utroque, trioque, quatroquie, e cinque oche, il qual bell'Humore ritrovandosi per fogliola una vagha Giovinetta per nome Isabella, tratta con Messer Pantalone de Bisognosi mercante de fighi sechi, e sara che salate, volergliela dare per moglie; mà ciò inteso dal Sig. Leadro Scolare innamorato di detta Isabella, si sposano insieme senza saputa de i vecchi. Hora mò Gratiano non per altro fine cerca levarsi Isabella di casa, se non per esser egli innamorato della Signora Aurora, sperando con tale occasione ridursela in casa: mà che? ciò inteso da l Sig. Fortunato amante di Aurora, si sposano insieme, essendo scacciato il povero Gratiano con inguirie e villanie. Di nodi, che gli poveri vecchi insensati restano burlati nella loro Pazzia Senile, e le dui Copie di felici amanti godonsi per la loro Prudenza Giovenile. In tanto volendo gli Cantori recitare il primo Intermedio, mi ritiro à sentire.'

[30] This may be simply a chord which gives the singers their pitches.

[31] 'Ecco l'Allegro Humor, che baldanzoso / Promette à i circonstanti un Fuggi l'otio / Poi vedendo Gratian l'ode curioso.'

through his piece. In the earlier works, his role might be seen as similar to a personage in a mascherata, that is, 'io sono . . .'. Here, however, the identity of the speaker is clearer or, perhaps, less important than the information he is conveying.

We are confronted with the central performance question of this work. Is it conceivable that Banchieri would go to such lengths to describe the stage and its accoutrements, detailing the dress of two characters, Endeavour and Novelty, and then have the dramatic action played out in song without any visible characters or singers? The question arises repeatedly as the work progresses.

Endeavour returns to her chair, and the singers sing 'Circonstanti state à udir'. At this point the partbook shows a woodcut of the figure of a man dressed in close-fitting garments, knee breeches and a ruff, wearing a sword, and gesturing as though speaking (Figure 2). When the Prologue is over, Novelty resumes centre stage and says:

> Poor lovesick Gratiano
> With little hope from the beautiful Aurora
> Threatens Love with his many words?[32]

Novelty returns to sit down, and the singers sing 'Pavarazz Duttor'.[33] Here again we have a woodcut, this time of the Doctor standing in front of a similar set, and gesturing (Figure 3). In a similar manner the comedy continues. Before each song the argument is spoken by either Endeavour or Novelty. Not every song is preceded by a woodcut, but woodcuts are interspersed liberally throughout the print (Figures 4 and 5).

In a discussion of the staging of *Aminta*, Adriano Cavicchi, quoting Ercole Bottrigari's manuscript *Dialogo delle scene e dei teatri*, has shown that woodcuts in sixteenth-century printed editions were sometimes representations of the actual stage for a given drama.[34] These were included either prescriptively (that is, to show how the stage should appear) or perhaps after the fact, showing what one staging of the drama actually looked like.

---

[32] 'Il povero Gratiano innamorato / Con poca speme della bell' Aurora / Minnaccia Amor con lui molto adirato?'

[33] As found preceding each song, here is the direction 'Ritorna CURIOSITÀ a sedere, e cantano gli Cantori.'

[34] A. Cavicchi, 'La scenografia dell'*Aminta* nella tradizione scenografica pastorale ferrarese del sec. xvi', *Studi sul teatro veneto fra rinascimento ed età barocca*, ed. M. T. Muraro (Florence, 1971), p. 58.

PROLOGO DELL' HVMORE ALLEGRO.

CANTORI.

Circonstanti state à vdir
Quanto qui vi son per dir,
Sentirete hor hor cantar
Strauaganze à tutt'andar.
Io mi chiamo ALLEGR' HVMOR
Alla barba di color,
Ch'ogni tratto col ceruell'
Fanno in aria vn gran castell'.
Fa la la la la la la
Tutt'in tuono passo in quà,
Per vdir' anch' io il Dotror,
Che si lagna per Amor.

Figure 2   'Prologo dell'Humore Allegro', from Adriano Banchieri, *La prudenza giovenile* (Bologna, 1607), p. 8.

P Auarazz Duttor ·
   Cancar viegn' all' Amor, e i ſuò bulzun,
Vinticiqu ſganaſſun
Mi ghe dò ſel accatt:
E ſe dag pò in tel matt
Ag' ſpezz le frizz' e l'arch con gran fracaſs,
E immediate ag' piſs' in tel carcaſs.

Figure 3   Gratiano: 'Pavarazz Duttor', from Adriano Banchieri, *La prudenza giovenile* (Bologna, 1607), p. 10.

V Agha, e gentil' Aurora,
Qnando farà quell' hora ?
Che il mifero mio cor efca di dogl:e,
Con effermi fedel', e cafta moglie ?

Figure 4   Fortunato: 'Vagha, e gentil'Aurora', from Adriano Banchieri, *La prudenza giovenile* (Bologna, 1607), p. 30.

D Olorofi tormenti, afpri martiri,
  Stretti lacci, e catene,
Fiere pafsioni, e pené,
Pianti, fofpiri, e doglie,
E quanto mal s'accoglie,
Tutto venghi vèr mè còn tirannia,
Pur ch'id fia in gratia d'Ifabella mia.

Figure 5   Leandro: 'Dolorosi tormenti', from Adriano Banchieri, *La prudenza giovenile* (Bologna, 1607), p. 20.

The third intermedio of the *Prudenza* differs from the others in that it involves action on the part of the singers. The characters involved are the singers and a wine seller ('Bottigliero, & Cantori'). The Bottigliero induces the singers to drink a glass of wine in order to sing the final act more happily ('più allegramente'). Banchieri gives the direction 'Here the virtuous singers, with much encouragement among themselves, finally drink a glass of wine at one gulp, the better to sing well.' But these instructions are *not* included in the material to be announced or sung by Endeavour or Novelty.[35] This constitutes a marked deviation from the previous flow of the comedy.

Finally, following the *licenza*, both Novelty and Endeavour stand up, and the instrumentalists gracefully play a balletto, which is to be danced by the two. Upon finishing the dance, Endeavour says to the audience, 'If you ask me, most gentle observers [*spettatori*], you have been virtuously and charmingly entertained, with pleasure of a special kind: For your part, please condescend to show us your gratitude, by applause and with these words: "Long live the pleasing style / Of the Prudenza Giovenile."'

For this madrigal comedy, then, in addition to providing music, Banchieri specified the set, the participants, including the *commedia dell'arte* principal characters, and those elements which were not part of the common conceptual framework of his audience – the garb and movements of Endeavour and Novelty, and the single instance in which the singers appeared for a drink and, presumably, a bow. (This is perhaps a precursor of, a cultural antecedent to, the bow given today by the opera orchestra, usually before the last act.)

But *La prudenza giovenile* is not our only source of evidence that Banchieri envisioned the staging of at least some of his works. In correspondence regarding the *Vivezze di Flora e Primavera* (1622)[36] we find further evidence of staging. Banchieri had already prepared the way for this in the dedication of *La prudenza*, in which he said, 'These lively arguments of mine, embellished boldly with new inventions and beauty, were determined to appear, hoping to find

---

[35] 'Qui gli virtuosi Cantori, con molti inviti trà loro, alla fine si bevono un bichier di vino, tutti à un tratto, per puoter piu cantare più allegramente. . . . Et finito il Canto in mezo la Scena CURIOSITÀ dice.' *Prudenza*, end of Act 2.

[36] A madrigal comedy falling into Adkins's category III.

favour when they were seen, and I and they together promise to provide good welcome to their virtuous brother entitled *Fior gradito*, who hopes to show his great worth soon.'[37]

It is not certain that this is a reference to the *Vivezze di Flora e Primavera*, but it is a possibility: that work is based on Roberto Poggiolini's book of poetry entitled *Flora idillio*, the frontispiece to which indicates that the poems contained therein were to be recited with music at the monastery of San Michele in Bosco, in the Accademia dei Floridi. The copy of Poggiolini's *Flora* which survives in the library of the University of Bologna is in all likelihood a printed programme of a particular evening at the academy. This copy is actually signed by Banchieri, but within the text, after a group of songs and recitations, we find the annotation: 'Idillio Poesia del Caval. Roberto Poggiolini. Posta in Musica da Gieronimo Giacobi, e Adriano Banchieri.' As recorded in his published correspondence, the *Lettere armoniche*, Banchieri invited both Poggiolini and Padre D. Domenico Luchi, abbot of San Michele in Bosco, to the festivities. The letter to Poggiolini is of particular interest. Banchieri wrote:

You are invited to enjoy the fruits of your engaging work, on the second of next May, in our Accademia dei Floridi of San Michele in Bosco. Your most beautiful Flora, beautiful in herself, but appearing in the guise of a bride, wedded to the ingenious harmonies of Girolamo Giacobbi, Domenico Benedetti and myself, will be performed in a Theatre of Springtime ... this will also be accompanied by two shepherds representing Fiorito Aprile and Dilettoso Maggio. The staging will be sumptuous, the music appropriate, and the actors [*Recitanti*] will perform admirably.[38]

In the text published by Banchieri in Bologna in the name of the academy, we find a description of the stage set and the participants.

---

[37] Dedication to *La prudenza giovenile*: 'A queste mie vive ragioni, ... e tutta ardita, e baldanzosa, con nuove inventioni, e vaghezze s' è resoluta uscire, sperando esser favorita de quando ciò gl' avverrà, io e lei insieme promettiamo darne buona relatione à un suo virtuoso fratello intittolato FIOR GRADITO, il qual desidera con studio maggiore mostrare il valor suo frà poco tempo.'

[38] Banchieri, *Lettere armoniche* (Bologna, 1628), p. 35: 'Invito V. Sig. per li due del seguente Mese di Maggio à godere i frutti del suo vivace ingegno nella nostra FLORIDA ACADEMIA di S. Michele in Bosco. Comparirà in Teatro di Primavera la sua bellissima FLORA, bellissima per se stessa; mà in guisa di vaga sposa ornata di gioie armoniche, intrecciate dal Sig. D. Girolamo Giacobbi, dal Sig. Domenico Benedetti, e da me ancora, che la renderanno maggiormente maestevole; sarà anche accompagnata da duo Pastori rappresentanti Fiorito Aprile, e Dilettoso Maggio. L'apparato sarà sontuoso, la Musica proportionata, e i Recitanti di compita sodisfattione . . .'.

The frontispiece indicates 'recitanti, concertanti', 'Choro di stromenti musicali', 'Choro di voci musicali', 'Primavera recita', 'Aprile recita, e canta', 'Maggio recita e canta' and 'Apparato del theatro'. In other words, there will be an instrumental ensemble, a choral ensemble, recitations by Primavera, Aprile and Maggio, and solo singing by (at least) Aprile and Maggio. When the curtain opens, Banchieri says,

> you will hear a sweet chorus of instruments which cannot be seen, and you will see a grove with beautiful flowers, surrounded by woods, all reminiscent of the site of the Accademia dei Floridi of San Michele in Bosco. At the front of the stage appears the coat of arms of Cardinal Borghese, protector of the academy, at the right that of Testa Sanese, and at the left, that of Lucchi Bolognese. Each of these shall have a star inserted, and on the stage above will be played the idyll *Flora*. The idyll begins with a chorus. While the scene opens, lamps are lit. As the music finishes, Primavera comes into view, ornately dressed with embroidered flowers, herbs and gold, and on her right and left are two shepherds who represent April and May.[39]

Again, there can be no question but that this work was to be staged. Furthermore, though we do not have a retrospective account of the performance, we know that plans for it advanced to the point of the libretto being printed and the honoured guests invited.

If we accept the idea that madrigal comedies were intended to be staged, the books of music which are our record of these works may be viewed either as the scenario of the comedy to be performed or perhaps as something akin to a libretto for the musical part of the drama. At the time under consideration, a scenario for a *commedia dell'arte* performance contained the information needed by the professional actors in a troupe. That information was the skeleton of the performance to be done, and the players would then add specific stage business and dialogue in order to flesh out the drama.

---

[39] A. Banchieri, *Flora idillio* (Bologna, 1622), dedication: 'udì soavissimo Choro di stromenti musicali inapparenti, e videssi un ridente pratodi variati FIORI, attorniato da verzure boschereccie, tutto alludendo al sito della Florida Academia di S. Michele in Bosco; in frontespiqio l'arme dell'Ill.mo Sig. Card. Borghese Protettore dell'Accademia, à man destra l'arme del Testa Sanese, e à man sinistra l'arme de i Lucchi Bolognesi, nelle cui due armi Testi, e Lucchi, vien inserto una STELLA, sopra la quale leggiadramente scherza il vago idillio intitolato FLORA. CHORO DI VOCI IN MUSICA / . . . Mentre gli aprono il sen accesi lampi.

Finita la musica comparve i vista la vaga PRIMAVERA riccamente ornata di FIORI, erbe, & oro, i candida veste, e con lei, a man destra & a sinistra dui Pastori significanti APRILE, e MAGGIO.

That part which was not written down changed from performance to performance, while that which was written or memorised was played similarly in each performance. Banchieri's partbooks, understood as musical scenarios, contain the part of the drama which remained constant from one performance to another. The many printings of the *Pazzia* are an indication of the work's popularity.[40] Viewed as librettos, the books provide (in addition to the music itself) enough material, in the *argomenti* which precede each piece of music, to supply the reader with the gist of the action.

The evidence is conclusive: whether or not we find in Banchieri's writing satisfactory solutions to and detailed clarification of specific problems of staging, we may state with confidence that Banchieri must have envisioned the dramatised staging of at least two of his madrigal comedies. How extensive that staging should be was presumably, then as now, a matter of individual taste, flair and budgetary concerns, as well as the availability of actors, singers and instrumentalists, to say nothing of the stage area itself. Musicologists have taken Vecchi at his word, believing that he did not conceive of *L'Amfiparnaso* as a work to be staged with action. If we also take Banchieri to mean what he says, then we must believe that he did intend several of his works to be staged. That he did not write specifically contradicting Vecchi may mean, not that he agreed with Vecchi, but that he felt no need to elaborate on the obvious, the prevailing assumption, that these works should be staged.

[40] Mischiati lists eight printings, O. Mischiati, *Adriano Banchieri (1568–1634): Profilo biografico e bibliografia della opera* (Bologna, 1971). Brian Mann has found reference to an additional print (1617) in Kraków; he has not yet seen this edition himself.

Early Music History (1991) Volume 10

PAULA HIGGINS

PARISIAN NOBLES, A SCOTTISH PRINCESS, AND THE WOMAN'S VOICE IN LATE MEDIEVAL SONG*

For Lewis Lockwood on his sixtieth birthday

Perhaps the best-known songs of Antoine Busnoys are those whose texts conceal in acrostics or puns some form of the name 'Jacqueline d'Aqueville' (for the song texts and translations see Appendix 1). The first letters in each line of *A vous sans autre* (no. 2) and *Je ne puis vivre ainsi toujours* (no. 3) yield the acrostics 'A Iaqveljne' and 'Jaqueljne d'Aqvevjle' respectively; the first line of *A que ville est abhominable* (no. 4) makes a pun on the surname 'Aqueville'; and the incipit of *Ja que lui ne si actende* (no. 1) forms an

* This article is based on Chapter 4 of my dissertation 'Antoine Busnois and Musical Culture in Late Fifteenth-Century France and Burgundy' (Ph.D. dissertation, Princeton University, 1987), pp. 161–212. It has been extensively rewritten and supplemented with new research undertaken with the generous financial support of a Women's Studies Faculty Research Grant from Duke University in summer 1989 and an ACLS Fellowship for Recent Recipients of the Ph.D. for 1989–90. Earlier or condensed versions of this study were presented at the Fourteenth Annual Conference on Medieval and Renaissance Music, King's College, London, 15 August 1986, with the title 'Busnois's Hacqueville Songs: Musical Autobiography or Historical Fiction?'; at the Annual Meeting of the American Musicological Society, Austin, Texas, 28 October 1989, with the title 'Parisian Nobles, a Scottish Princess, and the Woman's Voice in Fifteenth-Century Song'; and with the present title at the conference 'Power of the Weak? The Authority and Influence of Medieval Women', Centre for Medieval Studies, University of Toronto, 23 February 1990. I wish to thank Margaret Bent, David Fallows, Michael Long and Reinhard Strohm for valuable comments on earlier drafts of this essay.

Abbreviations of manuscripts and archival sources cited in the text are as follows: F-Pn=Paris, Bibliothèque Nationale, with abbreviations for the following *fonds*: fr.=fonds français; n.a.f.=nouvelles acquisitions françaises; DB=Dossiers bleus; F-Pan=Paris, Archives Nationales, with abbreviation for the following *fonds*: MC=Minutier Central de la Ville de Paris; B-Br=Brussels, Bibliothèque Royale; Roh=Berlin, Staatsbibliothek der Stiftung Preussischer Kulturbesitz, Kupferstichkabinett MS 78.B.17 ('Rohan Chansonnier'); Niv=Paris, Bibliothèque Nationale, Département de la Musique, Rés. Vmc. Ms. 57 ('Chansonnier Nivelle de La Chaussée'); Dij=Dijon, Bibliothèque Municipale, MS 517; Lab=Washington, DC, Library of Congress, M2.1 L25 Case ('Laborde Chansonnier'); Wolf=Wolfenbüttel, Herzog-August-Bibliothek, MS Guelf. extrav. 287; Mel=New Haven, Yale University, Beinecke Library, MS 91 ('Mellon Chansonnier'); Jard=*Le jardin de plaisance et fleur de rethoricque* (1509).

ambiguous series of monosyllables that can also be read as the name 'Jaqueline'.

In 1927 Eugénie Droz and Geneviève Thibault revealed that a 'Jacqueline de Hacqueville' was a fifteenth-century Parisian noblewoman married to a counsellor in the Parlement of Paris, a fact which signalled to them Busnoys's contact with the cultural milieu of that city.[1] Since then, all others commenting on the songs have accepted their autobiographical significance and have assumed that they attest to Busnoys's otherwise unknown activity in Paris where he had a romantic liaison with the woman in question.[2] Attempting to pinpoint a more specific time-frame for the creation of the songs, Leeman Perkins ordered them chronologically to reflect the course of a short but heated affair between Busnoys and Hacqueville during the summer of 1461 or 1465.[3]

[1]　E. Droz, G. Thibault and Y. Rokseth, eds., *Trois chansonniers français du XVe siècle*, Documents Artistiques du XVe Siècle 4 (Paris, 1927; repr. New York, 1978), pp. xi and 118.

[2]　G. Reese, *Music in the Renaissance* (New York, 1959), p. 101; H. M. Brown, *Music in the Renaissance* (Englewood Cliffs, 1976), p. 84; L. L. Perkins, 'Antoine Busnois and the d'Hacqueville Connection', *Musique naturelle et musique artificielle: In memoriam Gustav* [sic] *Reese*, ed. M. B. Winn, Le Moyen Français 5 (Montreal, 1979), pp. 49–64; M. Picker, 'Busnois [de Busne], Antoine', *The New Grove Dictionary of Music and Musicians*, ed. S. Sadie, 20 vols. (London, 1980), III, p. 504. On *Je ne puis vivre*, see also W. Arlt, 'Vom Überlieferungsbefund zum Kompositionsprozess: Beobachtungen an den zwei Fassungen von Busnois' "Je ne puis vivre ainsy"', *Festschrift Arno Forchert zum 60. Geburtstag am 29. Dezember 1985*, ed. G. Allroggen and D. Altenburg (Kassel, 1986), pp. 27–40.

[3]　Perkins's article (see note 2) was the first serious attempt to determine the precise nature of Busnoys's 'Hacqueville Connection'. Perkins added a fifth song, *A une dame jay fait veu*, to the original group because the colours blue and yellow mentioned in the text are those featured in the Hacqueville family arms. But the Hacqueville arms include not only blue and yellow, but silver and sable as well: 'un escu d'argent au chevron de sable chargé de cinq aiglettes d'or et accompagné de trois testes de paon arrachées d'azur'. See Tours, Bibliothèque Municipale, MS 1182, fol. 274^v and F. A. A. de La Chesnaye-Desbois, *Dictionnaire de la noblesse*, 3rd edn, 19 vols. (Paris, 1863–76; repr. Nendeln, 1969), III, p. 192. Moreover, the extant sources for the poem do not agree on the colours. The text of *A une dame* in Dij, which contains all of the Hacqueville songs, translated reads 'blue and white' instead of 'blue and yellow', and in the poetry anthology F-Pn fr. 1719, fol. 113, the word 'jaune' is crossed out and replaced by 'noir'. Blue and white are in fact the colours mentioned in the text of *Ja que lui ne si actende*, where the poet declares that the colours her lover will wear are those of her name, one 'perse' (blue-green) and the other 'blanche'. Blue and white are also the colours of the flowers decorating *A que ville est abhominable* in Dij, fols. 18^v–19 (see below, p. 150), significant not only because Dij alone transmits all of the Hacqueville songs, but especially because of its primacy as a source of Busnoys's music. If colour symbolism is the rationale for adding a piece to the group, it would seem reasonable to expect the songs to refer consistently to the same colours. Therefore, the song may belong to the group, but not quite for the reasons Perkins proposed. In this study I shall focus only on the four songs whose references to Jacqueline are explicit. My subsequent work on the Hacqueville songs has led me to conclusions differing considerably from those of Perkins, but I am indebted to the structural framework and stimulating point of departure his article provided.

Traditional thinking about the Hacqueville songs presumes that Busnoys himself wrote their texts as well as the music, and that they record his genuine sentiments stemming from an emotional involvement with Hacqueville; in other words, that the empirical author, Busnoys, and not his poetic persona, is the protagonist of the poems. While nineteenth-century philologists fully embraced the notion of 'personal' or 'autobiographical' poetry, especially with regard to late medieval poets like François Villon, most literary critics today categorically reject the idea, insisting upon the absolute distinction between the poet and the persona of the text.[4] Thus, Villon's poetry, which is also rife with acrostics and name games, has been described by some as 'as personal as any poetry has ever been', while others maintain that to equate the empirical author with the persona of the text imbues poetic discourse with the authority or reliability of a historical document, thereby allowing extrinsic fact or supposition to bear upon literary judgement.[5]

Similarly, Guillaume de Machaut's *Livre du voir-dit*, which purports to be a chronicle of the poet's literary exchange and love affair with 'Toute Belle', has provoked highly-charged debates about the extent to which it is based on real episodes in the poet's life.[6] Since 1875, when Paulin Paris proclaimed the identity of Machaut's Toute Belle as that of a verifiable French noblewoman of the 1360s,[7] some have accepted the story as literal autobiography, while others have claimed that Machaut's 'True Story' is but a colossal hoax,[8] undoubtedly inspired in part by a long line of 'erotic pseudo-autobiographies' in which a male poet ventriloquises the voice of an allegedly fictive female interlocutor.[9] Somewhere

---

[4] For a useful summary of the conflicting views on personal poetry see N. J. Lacy, 'Villon in his Work: the *Testament* and the Problem of Personal Poetry', *L'Esprit Créateur*, 18 (1978), pp. 60–9.

[5] Lacy, 'Villon', pp. 62–3.

[6] W. Calin, 'Le livre du voir-dit', *A Poet at the Fountain: Essays on the Narrative Verse of Guillaume de Machaut*, Studies in Romance Languages 9 (Lexington, KY, 1974), p. 167.

[7] P. Paris, ed., *Guillaume de Machaut: Le livre du voir-dit* (Paris, 1875; repr. Geneva, 1969), pp. xxii–xxiv. The name is concealed in an anagram formed by rearranging the first eight letters of verse 9030 together with all of the letters of verse 9029. See below, p. 174.

[8] See Calin, 'Le livre du voir-dit', pp. 169–72, for a summary of various positions on the 'truth or fiction' of Toute Belle. Calin staunchly upholds the arguments of G. Hanf who was the first to attempt to prove that the *Voir-dit* was entirely a work of fiction. See 'Ueber Guillaume de Machauts Voir dit', *Zeitschrift für romanische Philologie*, 22 (1898), pp. 145–96.

[9] See G. B. Gybbon-Monypenny, 'Guillaume de Machaut's Erotic 'Autobiography': Precedents for the Form of the *Voir-dit*', *Studies in Medieval Literature and Languages in Memory of*

between the two extremes, most critics consider the 'truth or fiction' of the female character a tangential issue at best and at worst an insoluble problem that is ultimately irrelevant to an interpretation of the text.[10]

Clearly, then, given the current climate of opinion among literary critics, the 'sincerity' of Busnoys's Hacqueville poems cannot be taken for granted. Busnoys, as we know, was as much esteemed as a poet as he was as a composer; but even if he wrote the Hacqueville poems, how can we know the nature and extent of their autobiographical significance, if any? We probably cannot, but that does not mean the problem has to end there. The critical stance taken by the late Edward Lowinsky, who attempted in one of his last articles to reconcile the divergent viewpoints on autobiographical readings of late medieval poetry, might be useful to consider here. Challenging the prevalent notion that autobiographical elements in a poem are immediately suspect once the topos is discovered to be traditional, Lowinsky argued that when documentary evidence of a concordance between life and poetry exists (as in the cases of Deschamps, Villon, Charles d'Orléans, and Christine de Pizan), a poem can be read both as a poem and as a personal, or autobiographical, expression; but the absence of such documentary evidence does not necessarily rule out an autobiographical interpretation. For Lowinsky, the specificity, originality and intensity of a given poem should be entitled to weigh as heavily as does documentary evidence.[11]

Adopting these criteria for the sake of the argument, then, can it be established that Busnoys's Hacqueville poems are sufficiently 'specific, original and intense' to warrant their acceptance as 'sincere' expressions of Busnoys's emotions, rather than those of his poetic persona? The cryptograms contained in the four poems are indeed highly specific, and the author has displayed great ingenuity and originality in devising poetic schemes that exploit this particular woman's name. Perkins noted that while *Ja que lui ne* (no. 1) and *A vous sans autre* (no. 2) are almost emblematic of the conventional

---

Frederick Whitehead, ed. W. Rothwell, W. R. J. Barron, D. Blamires and L. Thorpe (Manchester, 1973), pp. 133–52.

10 K. Brownlee, *Poetic Identity in Guillaume de Machaut* (Madison, 1984), p. 239, n. 25.

11 E. E. Lowinsky, 'Jan van Eyck's *Tymotheos*: Sculptor or Musician? With an Investigation of the Autobiographic Strain in French Poetry from Rutebeuf to Villon', *Studi Musicali*, 13 (1984), pp. 33–105, especially p. 68.

courtly love lyric, *Je ne puis vivre* (no. 3) betrays an intensity of expression absent from the first two poems.[12] Indeed, the language is more extreme and rife with hyperbole: he cannot stand it any longer, he needs some comfort for his pain, and in a scarcely veiled erotic allusion asks very specifically for 'just one hour, or less, or more . . .'; he walks around in 'a hundred circles', 'stays up all night' and then, 'drowning in tears', cries out to God in vain 'Vengeance!' for his plight because he realises that 'pity', which he has invoked in line 5 of *A vous sans autre*, is 'sleeping'.

The last song, *A que ville* (no. 4), is almost unsurpassed in the fifteenth-century song repertory for the caustically sarcastic language used to repudiate the same woman who until then consumed the poet's thoughts.[13] Adjectives like 'abominable', 'detestable' and 'vituperable' are rarely encountered in courtly discourse; the extreme language and intensity of expression seem to blur the boundaries between poet and persona.

Besides specificity, originality and intensity, a number of other factors hint at the author's personal involvement. First, textual acrostics and topical references do often provide gratuitous clues about otherwise unknown connections between poets and the individuals named. For example, at least two of the names appearing in Dufay's acrostics correspond to people he knew in Cambrai.[14] Similarly, the only other individuals alluded to in Busnoys's works, the Count of Charolais and Johannes Ockeghem, also involve real-life contacts.[15] Secondly, the contrapuntal manipulation of musical motifs in retrograde and inversion is a hallmark of Busnoys's style, and the cryptic verbal canons he devised to conceal their resolutions betray his delight in riddles of all kinds. Word

---

[12] Perkins, 'Antoine Busnois', p. 53.

[13] Noting that the 'harshness of tone and bitterness of sentiment' are virtually unmatched in the vernacular verse of the period, Perkins earmarked this song as signalling the demise of the 'affair' between Busnoys and Jacqueline. Perkins, 'Antoine Busnois', p. 54.

[14] Robert Auclou and Petrus de Castello. See D. Fallows, *Dufay* (London, 1982), pp. 29–31, 60–1. Fallows noted that most of Dufay's songs containing acrostics must have been completed before 1440, 'possibly giving clues to hitherto unsuspected travels and associations in his early years' (p. 54).

[15] Both are mentioned in the text of *In hydraulis*. Busnoys worked for Charles, Count of Charolais, who later became Duke of Burgundy, from *c.* 1467 to 1477, and he was in all likelihood a personal acquaintance of Ockeghem, since they both worked contemporaneously at the church of St-Martin of Tours in the early 1460s. See P. Higgins, '*In hydraulis* Revisited: New Light on the Career of Antoine Busnois', *Journal of the American Musicological Society*, 39 (1986), pp. 41–61 and p. 76.

games in general, then, might be viewed as the literary manifestation of his most outstanding musical trait. Thirdly, one must be somewhat sceptical of an author/persona distinction in the case of a poet like Busnoys who, in a passage of ostensibly self-deprecatory homage to Ockeghem, did not hesitate to announce his own name as the composer of the ostentatiously virtuosic motet *In hydraulis*.[16] Similarly, in *Anthoni usque limina*, he constructed a clever Latin text dedicated to his patron saint as a pretext for flaunting his own name,[17] wrote a playful verbal canon to ensure that the reader would not miss it,[18] and conceived the whole piece in two symmetrical halves in which the number of tactus (108) in each section corresponds to the cipher of his last name.[19]

Then there is the question of audience. One might well ask what is the point of embedding cryptograms in the texts of four musical works unless the author expects someone to find them. The only manuscript that contains all four of the Hacqueville songs is Dij, the source of nearly half of Busnoys's secular output. The first 'Hacqueville' song transcribed therein, *A que ville est abhominable*, seems to have had the special attention of the artist.[20] A striking woman in red appears in the superius initial in the upper left-hand corner of the verso (see Figure 1), similar to one inhabiting an initial 'J' of *Je ne puis vivre* on fol. 38ʳ of the same manuscript. This opening is the only one of the some seventy decorated folios in the manuscript that contains coloured flowers of any kind,[21] and moreover, the flowers are blue and white, the two colours mentioned in the text of *Ja que lui ne*. Dij's version of the incipit is especially noteworthy because it gives away the pun. The variant 'est' for 'et' results not in the reading 'oh, how vile and abomin-

---

[16] 'saluteris tuis meritis per me Busnois illustris comitis de Chaulois [sic] indignum musicum'.

[17] Busnoys's full name is concealed in the opening and concluding phrases of the text '*Anthoni usque* limina . . . Fiat in omni*bus noys*'.

[18] 'Alpha et o cephasque deutheri / cum pos decet penulti[mum] queri / actoris qui nomen vult habere'. See C. L. W. Boer, *Het Anthonius-Motet van Anthonius Busnois* (Amsterdam, 1940), p. 16.

[19] That is, by assigning numerical values to the letters of Busnoys's last name (spelled with a 'y', as in the manuscript Brussels, Bibliothèque Royale, MS 5557) in accordance with the rules of gematria (a=1, b=2, etc.), the sum total of the letters equals 108.

[20] E. Barret pointed this out some years ago in 'A Critical Edition of the Dijon Chansonnier: Dijon, Bibliothèque de la Ville, MS 517 (Ancien 295)', 2 vols. (Ph.D. dissertation, George Peabody College for Teachers of Vanderbilt University, 1981), I, p. 36.

[21] *Ibid.*

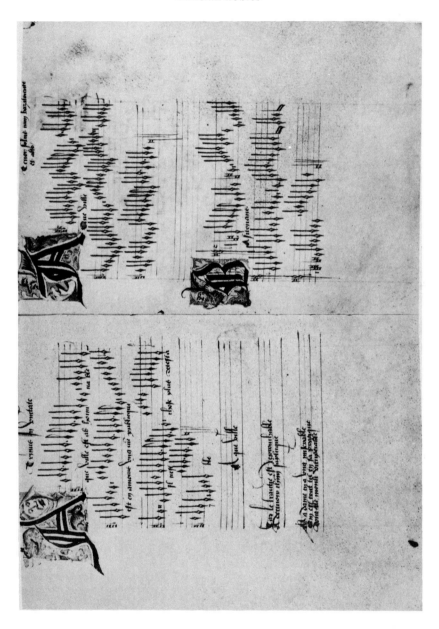

Figure 1 *A que ville est abhominable*, Dij, fols. 18^v–19

able', as in Roh, the only other textual source, but literally 'Aqueville is abominable.' Also curious is the label 'Basitonans' given to the contratenor part in the lower right half of the recto, the only piece of some 160 in the manuscript bearing this designation. Since the piece carries no composer attribution, the scribe may well have cryptically encoded one using the initial 'B' of the word 'Basitonans' and the tenor's initial 'A' directly above it; that is, 'A[ntoine] B[usnoys]'.

Furthermore, while quantitative arguments are not the most compelling, the frequent recurrence of Jacqueline de Hacqueville's name does seem to signify more than a passing interest on the composer's part;[22] and apart from their clever poems, fascinating text-critical issues and rich biographical implications, the Hacqueville songs, as many have noted, represent some of Busnoys's finest secular music.[23]

If, then, there is at least the possibility that the songs stemmed from episodes in Busnoys's life, how can the truth or fiction of Jacqueline de Hacqueville be irrelevant, as some literary critics would claim? If some kind of genuine interaction between Busnoys and the woman in question prompted their creation, surely the songs would have biographical, if not autobiographical, implications for her as well. Proceeding from the assumption that further knowledge of this woman or her family could conceivably shed new light on the circumstances surrounding the genesis of the musical complex, I searched Parisian archives and libraries for more information. In the course of that investigation, new details emerged not only about the Parisian noblewoman herself, but about still another woman with the same name. In the following discussion I shall highlight the social, cultural and historical contexts surrounding these two late medieval women, thereby bringing to the foreground

---

[22] Perkins, 'Antoine Busnois', pp. 50–1.

[23] Several writers have described *Je ne puis vivre ainsi* as one of the most extraordinary songs in the fifteenth-century literature. C. Vanden Borren concluded his *Études sur le quinzième siècle musical* (Antwerp, 1941) with an extract from this piece beginning with the modulating sequence on 'Quelque confort' and ending with the close of the *A* section. He remarked: 'Il y a là en un bref espace, un tel flot de mélodie, une telle suavité dans la rencontre des voix, que le plus pur génie ne peut être dénié à l'inventeur des pareilles délices.' (p. 281). George Perle considered 'the wonderful subtlety and ingenuity of [Busnoys's] rhythmic ideas' exhibited in this song 'probably unsurpassed in the entire history of music'; 'The Chansons of Antoine Busnois', *Music Review*, 11 (1950), p. 94. For another discussion of the piece, see Higgins, 'Antoine Busnois', pp. 35–43.

issues that have traditionally been regarded as tangential, insoluble and irrelevant, and consigning to the margins the original subject of inquiry – Busnoys and his music.[24] In the final analysis this shift in paradigm offers neither a tidy resolution of the enigma surrounding Busnoys's songs, nor the definitive identification of one true woman associated with them, but rather a theoretical prism reflecting a broader spectrum than has existed heretofore of the ways in which Jacqueline de Hacqueville or women like her might have participated in the literary and musical culture of the late Middle Ages.

II

Exactly who was the Parisian noblewoman Jacqueline de Hacqueville, long immortalised in textbooks and liner notes as Busnoys's 'loved one', 'lady love' and 'mistress'? As with most medieval women, the extant documents mention her only as a footnote in the lives of her father, brothers, husband and male children. This information is nevertheless invaluable in permitting a partial reconstruction of her social, political and cultural environment. The original act of the *succession* of her father's estate, dated 16 June 1482, which survives in the Minutier Central de la Ville de Paris,[25] is especially useful in definitively identifying her parents, her grandparents, her siblings and their spouses, thereby correcting the confused and inaccurate lineages of her family recorded by seventeenth- and eighteenth-century amateur genealogists. Her father, Jacques de Hacqueville,[26] one of the wealthiest cloth mer-

---

[24] An extensive discussion of the music of the Hacqueville songs will be published in my book *Antoine Busnoys and Musical Culture in the Late Middle Ages* (Oxford, forthcoming).

[25] F-Pan MC, Étude viii/4. 16 June 1482 is the date recorded on the act of *succession* of the estate; but an eighteenth-century copy of a now lost original document states that he was already deceased by 4 April 1474 (F-Pn DB 343 (Hacqueville), fol. 22ᵛ). A time-lag involved in the settlement of his estate undoubtedly accounts for the discrepancy between the two dates.

[26] He was evidently the son of Jean de Hacqueville, a *marchand drapier* of Paris, and Jacqueline Dourdine. This contradicts information given in de La Chesnaye-Desbois, *Dictionnaire de la noblesse*, iii, pp. 189–90, where it is stated that his father was Jean de Hacqueville, one of the deputies in 1463 from Paris to the court of Louis xi at Tours. This Jean de Hacqueville must have been Jacques's brother mentioned in the *succession* along with a deceased sister, Jehanne de Hacqueville. Another brother, Nicolas de Hacqueville, for whom Jacques had served as a *testataire*, died before 29 April 1439 (F-Pn DB 343 (Hacqueville), fol. 36). After the death of Jacques's father, his mother remarried,

chants of Paris,[27] counted the French royal court among his clients.[28] Her mother, Gillette Hennequin, was an educated noble-woman whose family included a long line of lawyers and counsellors in the Parlement of Paris, the supreme judicial body of France's *ancien régime*.[29] Jacques de Hacqueville and Gillette Hennequin were married in 1444[30] and had at least nine children, whose names and occupations, together with those of their spouses, are given in Appendix 2. Of these, five were still minors – that is, under the age of eighteen – in 1474,[31] and since Jacqueline was not among them, she was in all likelihood born some time between 1445 and 1457.[32] By 1474[33] she had married Jean Bochart or Bouchart, a distinguished member of the Parlement of Paris who served under kings Louis xi, Charles viii and Louis xii.[34] She and

to one Pierre de Tremblay. Except where noted in parentheses, all of the foregoing information is taken from the original act of *succession* of the estate of Jacques de Hacqueville, F-Pan MC, Étude viii/4, 16 June 1482.

27 His name is frequently encountered in Parisian municipal documents and in the registers of *compagnies françaises*, the guild associations of France. See J. Favier, *Le commerce fluvial dans la région parisienne au XVe siècle*, i: *Le registre des compagnies françaises (1449–1467)* (Paris, 1975), p. 67 (refs. 584, 610, 705, 768, 956, 1035).

28 A payment to him dated 19 May 1464 is entered in the household accounts of Louis xi for five ells of violet satin used to fashion a short robe for the king for the forthcoming Feast of Pentecost (F-Pan KK 59, fol. 37). See Higgins, 'Antoine Busnois', p. 176, n. 331, for a transcription of the document.

29 Dame d'Attichy, she later acquired the seigneurie of Onz-en-Bray from Gaspard de Montchevalier (de La Chesnaye-Desbois, *Dictionnaire de la noblesse*, iii, p. 190). An undated autograph letter of hers to Jean Bourré, seigneur du Plessis, asked him to intercede with the king on behalf of her son-in-law Gauchier Vivien, who was married to her daughter Jehanne (F-Pn fr. 20429, pièce no. 15). At some point after her husband's death she acquired a dwelling known as the 'Séjour du roi', near the Pont de Charenton in Paris. According to J. Lebeuf (*Histoire de la ville et de tout le diocèse de Paris*, 15 vols. (Paris 1754–8), ii, p. 366) this was a gift from Louis xi.

30 F-Pn DB 343 (Hacqueville), fol. 36. I have reconsidered my perhaps unduly cautious position (Higgins, 'Antoine Busnois', p. 177, n. 333) on this source which consists of eighteenth-century copies of registers of the Auditeur du Châtelet. The reference states that Jacques de Hacqueville 'a épousé' Gillette Hennequin on 30 April 1444.

31 F-Pn DB 343 (Hacqueville), fol. 22^v, 4 April 1474. The minor children listed there are Nicolas, Raoul, Ragonde, Henry and Jean.

32 In other words, none of the five minor children could have been born before 1457. It is likely, then, that the remaining siblings, including Jacqueline, had been born between 1445 (the year following her parents' marriage) and 1457.

33 The exact date of Hacqueville's union with Bochart is unknown. According to eighteenth-century copies of original fifteenth-century documents she was already married to him in 1474. See F-Pn DB 343 (Hacqueville), fol. 36^v.

34 Membership in the Parlement of Paris carried considerable prestige. Considered as an extension or embodiment of the king's honour, the Parlement had to be respected as such at all costs. Severe penalties were imposed upon anyone – whether an ordinary citizen or a high-ranking official of the realm – who dared to utter a word against one of its members, even the lowliest *huissier*, living or deceased. (F. Aubert, *Histoire du Parlement de*

her husband were still living in 1503[35] and died some time between then and March 1508.[36] They had undoubtedly resided in the parish of St-Benoît-le-Bétourné in Paris since they were both entombed in that church.[37]

In keeping with the tendency of Parisian social and political orders of the *ancien régime* to perpetuate themselves, Jacqueline de Hacqueville's sisters were also married to members of Parlement or to elite officers of the crown, and her brothers were high-ranking ecclesiastics, advocates in the Parlement or functionaries of the French court. Nicolas de Hacqueville, a counsellor and president in the Paris Parlement, canon of Notre-Dame of Paris, provost of St-Martin of Tours, and abbot of the Augustinian abbey of Livry, was a prime mover in the ecclesiastical reform movement in the Paris of Erasmus and Standonck before his death in 1501.[38] Con-

---

Paris de l'origine à François Ier (1250–1515), 2 vols. (Paris, 1884), I, p. 124). Among the numerous examples of individuals punished for insulting a member of the Parlement were two gentlemen who were imprisoned in the Conciergerie when numerous insulting and injurious statements against a deceased counsellor were found in their dossiers. The target of their insults, according to the document, was 'the late Maistre Jehan Bochart', Jacqueline's husband. (*Ibid.*, p. 124, n. 1, citing F-Pan X[1a] 1511, fol. 208). The document in question states that the guilty parties were imprisoned on 28 July 1508, thus leaving no doubt that the 'late Maistre Jehan Bochart' refers to the elder Jean and not to his son Jean, who died in 1532. For further references to Jean Bochart see E. Maugis, *Histoire du Parlement de Paris de l'avènement des rois Valois à la mort d'Henri IV*, 3 vols. (Paris, 1913–16; repr. New York, 1967), *infra*.

[35] M. Fournier, *La faculté de décret de l'Université de Paris au XVe siècle*, III (Paris, 1913), p. 444, n. 2, citing F-Pn Clairambault 765, p. 403.

[36] Maugis, *Histoire du Parlement*, III, p. 135, gives Bochart's date of death as 24 June 1507. The *inventaire après décès* of his son, dated 19 September 1532, provides the *terminus ante quem* for the death of Jacqueline de Hacqueville. The first item on the inventory of papers attesting to his territorial holdings and inheritance of capital is a *brevet*, dated 22–3 March 1508 (n.s.), containing the *succession* of his parents, both of whom are referred to as 'deffunctz'. See Higgins, 'Antoine Busnois', p. 185, n. 363.

[37] F-Pn DB 104 (Bochart), fol. 1[v], and Maugis, *Histoire du Parlement*, III, p. 135. F-Pn DB 343 (Hacqueville), fol. 36[v], also says that Jacqueline de Hacqueville was interred with her husband at St-Benoît, 'vis à vis l'image de la Magdaleine près le jubé'. Their sarcophagus must have been impressive, judging from a contemporary allusion to it. A contract made in February 1525 between a Parisian tombsmith and the deacon of Paris, Jacques Barthomier, for the creation of a tomb specified that it must be 9 feet long by 4 feet wide 'en laquelle aura deulx personnaiges engravez d'homme et de femme, avecques pareille ou meilleur ouvraige estant à la tombe de feu monsieur Bochart, qui est à Sainct-Benoist'; see E. Coyecque, *Recueil d'actes notariés relatifs à l'histoire de Paris et de ses environs au XVIe siècle*, I (1498–1545) (Paris, 1905), no. 568. Significantly, Ockeghem held a chaplaincy in this little-studied church which was also the parish of François Villon's youth. See Higgins, 'Antoine Busnois', pp. 187–8.

[38] See P. Piolin, ed., *Gallia christiana in provincias ecclesiasticas . . .*, 16 vols. (Paris, 1870–99), VII, cols. 154 and 836; Maugis, *Histoire du Parlement*, III, pp. 114 and 131; A. Renaudet, *Préréforme et humanisme à Paris pendant les premières guerres d'Italie (1494–1517)*, Bibliothèque de l'Institut Français de Florence (Université de Grenoble), 1st series, 6 (Paris, 1916),

Paula Higgins

temporaries compared him to King David, who, having dedicated his days to affairs of state, spent his nights with his instruments contemplating the mysteries of heaven.[39] Nicolas de Hacqueville's musical interests are further corroborated by the French theologian, mathematician and musical theorist Jacques Lefèvre d'Estaples (Jacobus Faber Stapulensis) who dedicated his treatise *Elementa musicalia* of 1496 to him.[40]

Of Jacqueline's eight children,[41] Nicolas Bochart, undoubtedly her brother's namesake, must also have had serious musical training since he held the office of *chantre* in the cathedral of Beauvais in the 1530s, a post which conferred responsibility for all musical aspects of the church's activities.[42] Evidence of musical interests in

pp. 182–3 and *infra*. His affiliations with Notre-Dame of Paris and St-Martin of Tours raise the question of his acquaintance with Busnoys and especially with Johannes Ockeghem, who, as we know, held important positions at both institutions. Given his age, though, any contact with either composer probably came about after the Hacqueville songs had been written.

39 'De eo vulgo ferebatur, quod more regis David negotia peragebat in die, nocte vero in psalterio et cythara coelestia secreta ruminabat'; *Gallia christiana*, VII, col. 836, and Renaudet, *Préréforme et humanisme*, p. 182.
40 'Elementa musicalia ad clarissimum virum Nicholaum de Haqueville presidentem Parisiensem'. See 'Febvre (Jacques Faber ou Le) surnommé Stapulensis', *Biographie universelle*, ed. F.-J. Fétis, 8 vols., 2nd edn (Paris, 1860–70), III, pp. 196–7, and G. Thibault, 'Busnois', *Die Musik in Geschichte und Gegenwart*, ed. F. Blume, 14 vols. (Kassel and Basle, 1948–61), II, col. 517. Perkins's statement of the reverse ('Antoine Busnois', p. 59), that is, that Hacqueville was the author of the treatise and dedicated it to d'Estaples, is incorrect. For more on Lefèvre d'Estaples see M. Ruhnke, 'Faber Stapulensis, Jacobus [Le Febre, Jacques]', *The New Grove Dictionary*, VI, p. 345, and Renaudet, *Préréforme et humanisme*, *infra*.
41 The names and occupations of her eight children are as follows: (1) Antoine Bochart, seigneur de Farinvilliers, counsellor in the Parlement of Paris, then *maître des requêtes de l'hôtel*, married to Françoise Gayand (daughter of Louis Gayand, lieutenant general of Clermont in Beauvaisis, and of Jeanne de Feuquiere), with whom he had one daughter; (2) Jean Bochart (II), seigneur de Noroy and Champigny, *avocat* in the Parlement of Paris under François I, married to Jeanne Simon, daughter of Philippe Simon, counsellor in the Parlement, and niece [*recte* sister] of Jean Simon, Bishop of Paris, who gave him the territory of Champigny in honour of his marriage; (3) Pierre Bochart, seigneur de Onzen-Bray, official of Beauvais; (4) Henry Bochart, abbot of Sully, near Fontevrault, where he is buried; (5) Nicolas Bochart, canon and *chantre* of the cathedral of Beauvais; (6) Magdeleine Bochart, wife of Nicolas le Coq, counsellor to the king and president of the Cour des Aides in Paris; (7) Louise Bochart, wife of Louis Rouillart, sieur de Gandin, counsellor in the court of Parlement; (8) Guillemette Bochart, wife of Antoine de Badouvillers, seigneur de La Varenne, near Montereau-saut-Yonne. (F-Pn DB 104 (Bochart), fols. 1–4ᵛ). For further bibliographical information on the Bochart children see Higgins, 'Antoine Busnois', pp. 181–9.
42 Although not explicitly stated, his designation as 'chanoine et chantre' would seem to refer to the office of *chantre* at the cathedral and not to his being a 'singer' there. The *chantre* was responsible for all singers, choirboys and masters of the choirboys, an administrative position that would have required considerable expertise in music.

156

Hacqueville's family are relevant to establishing the likelihood of her own musicality, since women performers and composers from later periods frequently came from dynasties of musicians.[43] The Hacqueville-Bochart family also commands attention from historians as the matrilineal ancestors of Louis XIII's most illustrious statesman. Suzanne de La Porte, mother of Armand-François du Plessis, the Duke and Cardinal of Richelieu, was the daughter of Claude Bochart, the only child of Hacqueville's eldest son, Antoine.[44] Privy as they were to the powerful world of king's counsellors, magistrates, ecclesiastics and humanist intellectuals surrounding the French court and the Sorbonne, the Hacqueville-Bochart clan was clearly among the most elite of the realm. But however conducive the cultural milieu might have been to facilitating Hacqueville's access to music and literature, this still brings us no closer to explaining satisfactorily her role, if any, in the creation of some of Busnoys's best songs. To complicate matters further, there was at least one other Jacqueline de Hacqueville, temporally removed from the Parisian noblewoman by roughly twenty years, whose historical context suggests an even more likely connection with Busnoys than the Parisian noblewoman. This Jacqueline de Hacqueville was a *damoiselle d'honneur* (maid of honour) to the

---

[43] Francesca Caccini (1587–*c.* 1640) and Elisabeth-Claude Jacquet de la Guerre (*c.* 1666–1729) are perhaps the best-known examples. For examples of sixteenth-century Italian women from musical families see A. Newcomb, 'Courtesans, Muses, or Musicians? Professional Women Musicians in Sixteenth-Century Italy', *Women Making Music: The Western Art Tradition, 1150–1950*, ed. J. Bowers and J. Tick (London, Urbana and Chicago, 1986), pp. 99–101.

[44] Apparently the eldest son, Antoine Bochart is the most mysterious of the Bochart children. His title of Seigneur de Farinvilliers, evidently inherited from his father, removes virtually any doubt that he was one of Jacqueline's sons. Although contemporary documents indicate that he was a member of the Parisian Parlement, his name does not turn up in any of the published histories of the institution (F-Pn DB 104 (Bochart), fol. 2). His daughter Claude married François de La Porte, an *avocat* in the Parisian Parlement. For financial details concerning their marriage contract see Higgins, 'Antoine Busnois', p. 182, n. 352. Claude Bochart later gave birth to Suzanne de La Porte, mother of Armand-François du Plessis, Cardinal Richelieu. See de La Chesnaye Desbois, *Dictionnaire de la noblesse*, xv, col. 948, and E. W. Marvick, *The Young Richelieu: A Psychoanalytic Approach to Leadership* (Chicago and London, 1980), pp. 45–62. Antoine Bochart's Christian name seems to have had no antecedent within the Hacqueville or Bochart families as was customary. It would be frivolous at this point to imagine that this could signal some further connection with Antoine Busnoys, but the coincidence is intriguing.

Paula Higgins

dauphine Marguerite d'Écosse, first wife of the future King Louis XI.[45]

III

Certain events in the short life of the Scottish princess Margaret Stuart (1424–45) may well have spawned many a fairy tale. The eldest daughter of King James I of Scotland and Queen Joan Beaufort, she went to France at the age of twelve to wed the reluctant young dauphin Louis in extravagant nuptial festivities held at Tours in 1436.[46] Many anecdotes blending myth and reality sur-

[45] G. L. E. du Fresne de Beaucourt, *Histoire de Charles VII*, 6 vols. (Paris, 1881–91), IV, p. 89, n. 3, lists one 'Jacqueline de Hacqueville', aged twenty-four years, together with a 'Marguerite de Hacqueville' among the *damoiselles d'honneur* of the dauphine. Unfortunately, he failed to cite his source or its date, indicating only that the list had been compiled 'after contemporary documents', of which he had amassed a formidable number for his still unsurpassed six-volume study of Charles VII. From subsequent references it is clear that Beaucourt had used C. P. Duclos's *Histoire de Louis XI*, 3 vols. (The Hague, 1745–6), for much of the section relating to Marguerite d'Écosse. Duclos does mention a 'Marguerite de Hacqueville', but Jacqueline is here given the surname 'de Bacqueville' and is listed as twenty-five years of age. See Duclos, *Histoire de Louis XI*, III (The Hague, 1746), p. 37. If Duclos was Beaucourt's source it is difficult to explain the discrepancies of both orthography and age. Moreover, several of the women Beaucourt cites are not mentioned by Duclos.

For these reasons it seems probable that Beaucourt and Duclos used different original documents. Inasmuch as the minuscules 'b' and 'h' are commonly confused in fifteenth-century palaeography, Beaucourt probably read the name as Hacqueville, and Duclos as Bacqueville. M. Thibault, *La jeunesse de Louis XI, 1423–1445* (Paris, 1907), p. 510, n. 4, observed the discrepancy between Beaucourt's orthography and that of Duclos and says that Beaucourt undoubtedly thought Marguerite de Hacqueville and Jacqueline were sisters. In H. Menu, 'Charles VII et la dauphine Marguerite d'Écosse à Châlons-sur-Marne (4 mai–18 août 1445)', *Annuaire administratif, statistique, historique et commercial de la Marne* (1895), p. 555, they become 'les deux sœurs Marguerite et Jacqueline de Hacqueville'. Sisters do seem to have been frequently placed at court together, judging from the pairs of women with identical family names who turn up among the attendants of princesses. For example, other ladies-in-waiting of the dauphine and the queen included Annette and Jeanne de Cuise, Marguerite, Jeannette and Antoinette de Villequier, Jeanne and Marguerite Bradefer; the ladies-in-waiting to the wife of Philippe, King of Navarre, in 1339 and 1340 included Jehanne and Margot de Helnet (F-Pn n.a.f. 9175, fols. 640 and 642ᵛ); ladies-in-waiting to Jehanne de Laval, second wife of René d'Anjou, in 1464–8 included Marguerite and Lyonne Cossu (*ibid.*, fol. 675).

On the basis of these examples, to which dozens more could be added, the likelihood seems strong that Jacqueline and Marguerite de Hacqueville were sisters, and that Duclos's reference to Jacqueline de Bacqueville is probably a misreading or a typographical error. In any case, since the Parisian noblewoman's parents were married in 1444, and since the dauphine's lady-in-waiting was about twenty-four years old in that year, she cannot possibly be the Parisian woman at an earlier stage in her life.

[46] King James I of Scotland (1394–1437), poet and author of *The Kingis Quair* (ed. J. Norton-Smith, Oxford, 1971), evidently enjoyed a considerable posthumous reputation as a performer and composer of music, according to the testimony of John Fordun, John

158

round this mysterious princess, dubbed 'the melancholy dauphine' by her biographer, and whose dying words were 'Fy de la vie! Ne m'en parlez plus!'[47] A cause for much concern at court was her apparent inability to produce an heir, which doctors attributed to a lack of sleep, to drinking too much vinegar, eating sour apples and wearing her belts too tight.[48] But others less kindly drew their own

Major and Alessandro Tassoni, discussed at length by the anonymous author of a curious late eighteenth-century monograph (also containing an edition of *The Kingis Quair*) entitled *Poetical Remains of James the First, King of Scotland* (Edinburgh, 1783), pp. 5–7 and 195ff.

Much has been written about Louis's reluctance to marry Marguerite d'Écosse, who had been chosen for him by his father Charles VII as part of a politically strategic alliance with James I of Scotland. Scholars disagree as to the reasons for his evidently intense dislike of her, but there seems to be no basis whatever for the often repeated and profoundly misogynous testimony of the sixteenth-century English chronicler Richard Grafton that her poor hygiene and bad breath drove him away: 'the lady Margaret, maryed to the Dolphin, was of such nasty complexion and evill savored breath, that he abhorred her company as a cleane creature doth a caryon'. See Beaucourt, *Histoire de Charles VII*, IV, p. 90, n. 1.

[47] The most celebrated, if apocryphal, tale about her involves the poet Alain Chartier. As the story goes, the dauphine came upon Chartier sleeping on a bench, and bent over and kissed him on the mouth. When her stupefied companion exclaimed, 'My Lady, I am astonished that you have kissed such an ugly man!' she replied, 'I have not kissed the man, but rather the precious mouth which has been the source of so many good and virtuous words.' P. Champion, *Histoire poétique du quinzième siècle*, Bibliothèque du xvᵉ Siècle 27, 2 vols. (Paris, 1923), I, pp. 131–2, citing J. Bouchet, *Annales d'Aquitaine*. The story is summarily dismissed by all modern scholars as being totally without foundation, since Alain Chartier was dead by the time Marguerite came to France in 1436. And since she was only four years old when Chartier visited the Scottish court in 1428, it is further presumed that she would have been too young to appreciate his talents. It should be pointed out, however, that we know very little about the education of medieval children and therefore have no basis upon which to form assumptions of any kind about the literary capacity of a privileged noble child reared in the sophisticated literary, artistic, and musical climate that the court of James I evidently provided. Moreover, whether apocryphal or not, the story, which seems to have originated in the mid-sixteenth century, illustrates the extent to which folklore about the dauphine's literary interests must have survived in the popular memory at least a century beyond her own lifetime. For more information on Marguerite d'Écosse see Champion, *La dauphine*; L. A. Barbé, *Margaret of Scotland and the Dauphin Louis* (London, 1917), pp. 114–49; R. S. Rait, *Five Stuart Princesses* (Westminster, 1902), pp. 3–46; Beaucourt, *Histoire de Charles VII*, IV, pp. 89–111; Duclos, *Histoire de Louis XI* (1745–6); A. Vallet de Viriville, *Histoire de Charles VII*, 3 vols. (1863–5), III, pp. 81–90; Le Roux de Lincy, *Les femmes célèbres de l'ancienne France* (Paris, 1848); Thibault, *La jeunesse de Louis XI*, pp. 503–51.

[48] 'M. de Charny dit qu'il avoit entendu qu'elle n'étoit point habile à porter enfans, et si ainsi étoit qu'elle allât de vie à trespassement, il faudra marier monseigneur le Dauphin à une autre qui fût encline à porter enfans; et lors il qui parle [Jamet de Tillay] dit qu'il avoit ouy dire à madame Dubois Menart qu'elle mangeoit trop de pommes aigres et de vinaigre et se ceignoit aucunefois trop serrée aucunefois trop lâche, qui étoit chose qui empêchoit bien à avoir enfans'. Duclos, *Histoire*, III, p. 47. Especially valuable for its nugget of medieval popular wisdom concerning female infertility, this commentary bears a striking similarity to the nineteenth-century 'cult of female invalidism', whereby 'tight-lacing, fasting, vinegar-drinking, and similar cosmetic or dietary excesses were all parts of a physical regimen that helped women either to feign morbid weakness or actually to

conclusions when the courtier Jamet de Tillay claimed to have discovered Jean d'Estouteville, seigneur de Blainville and Torcy, and another unidentified gentleman in the dauphine's darkened chambers late one night, together with her ladies-in-waiting,[49] and proceeded to decry the 'great lewdness' of the situation.[50] Eight months later, when the twenty-one-year-old princess fell ill and eventually died on 16 August 1445 at Châlons-sur-Marne, the official cause was given as pneumonia. Rumours at court, however, suggested that her already debilitated state of health had been exacerbated by the insinuations of infidelity perpetrated by the courtier Jamet de Tillay. The troubled Charles vii ordered two legal inquests into the cause of her death at which many ladies and gentlemen of the court

"decline" into real illness'. See S. Gilbert and S. Gubar, *The Madwoman in the Attic: The Woman Writer and the Nineteenth-Century Literary Imagination* (New Haven, 1979), p. 25. For a compelling discussion of infirmity and sickness as 'physical evidence of mental and physical purity' as well as a provocative analysis of the 'cultural apotheosis of the sublime consumptive' in *fin-de-siècle* art see B. Dijkstra, *Idols of Perversity: Fantasies of Feminine Evil in Fin-de-Siècle Culture* (Oxford, 1988), pp. 25–36. The striking and even more bizarre medieval analogue for this behaviour is the subject of a brilliant and compelling study by C. W. Bynum, *Holy Feast and Holy Fast: The Religious Significance of Food to Medieval Women* (Berkeley, 1987). Taking as her point of departure the centrality of food and food imagery to women's lives, Bynum argues that the various food practices of medieval women 'frequently enabled them to determine the shape of their lives – to reject unwanted marriages, to substitute religious activities for more menial duties within the family, to redirect the use of fathers' or husbands' resources, to change or convert family members, to criticize powerful secular or religious authorities, and to claim for themselves teaching, counseling, and reforming roles for which the religious tradition provided, at best, ambivalent support' (p. 220). Bynum's conclusions would seem to take on a certain relevance to Marguerite d'Écosse in the light of Louis's alleged animosity towards her.

49 (First deposition of Jamet de Tillay, 1 June 1446) 'dit qu'environ Noel, l'an 1444, un soir environ neuf heures de nuit, autrement du jour ne du temps ne se recorde, le roi étant à Nancy en Lorraine, lui qui parle [Jamet de Tillay] et Messire Regnault de Dresnay, chevalier, allèrent en la chambre de ladite dame, laquelle étoit lors couchée sur sa couche, et plusieurs de ses femmes étoient autour d'elle; aussi y étoit Messire Jean d'Estouteville, seigneur de Blainville, appuyé sur la couche de ladite dame, et un autre qu'il ne connoît; et pour ce que ladite dame étoit en sadite chambre sans ce que les torches fussent allumées, il qui parle dit audit messire Regnault, maître d'hôtel de ladite Dame, que c'étoit grande paillardie à lui et autres officiers de ladite dame, de ce que lesdites torches étoient éteintes à allumer, et dit qu'il dit lesdites paroles pour le bien et honneur de ladite dame et de sa maison'; Duclos, *Histoire*, iii, p. 42.

50 Tillay's suspicions were perhaps excessively heightened by the highly charged sexual climate of the French royal court, where Charles vii was alleged to have routinely availed himself of the ladies-in-waiting of both the dauphine and the queen, who included his most celebrated mistress Agnes Sorel. See F. F. Steenackers, *Agnès Sorel et Charles vii: Essai sur l'état politique et moral de la France au xvᵉ siècle* (Paris, 1868), pp. 250–9.

were required to testify.[51] The sworn deposition of Jamet de Tillay unwittingly provides an exceptionally rare glimpse into the private circle of this late medieval princess who seems to have had a passion for writing poetry shared and encouraged by her ladies-in-waiting. Tillay blamed the dauphine's illness on her female attendants, who he claimed kept her up all night writing rondeaux and ballades:

the said Nicole asked him [Jamet de Tillay] what was wrong with her, and what caused her illness and [Jamet] answered that the doctors said she had much rancour in her heart, which was harmful to her and exacerbated by lack of sleep; and then the said Nicole replied that the doctors had told him the same thing, and also added: 'If only she had not had that woman [in her service]!' 'Who?' said [Tillay]. Nicole answered, 'Marguerite de Salignac'. And Tillay retorted: 'Nor Prégente, nor Jeanne Filloque!' Asked why he said such things, he answered that he had heard that they were the ones who kept her up too late writing rondeaux and ballades.[52]

When interrogated further as to what he had told King Charles VII about his daughter-in-law's death, Tillay gave the following testimony:

---

[51] Including Duclos's 'Jacqueline de Bacqueville', who testified about comments the dauphine made on her deathbed: 'Jacqueline de Bacqueville, âgée de vingt-cinq ans ou environ, jurée, ouïe et examinée sur ce que dessus est dit par nous commissaires dessusdits, le vingt-cinquième jour d'octobre audit an [1445]: Dit et dépose par son serment qu'environ la mi-août, dernièrement passée, elle qui parle étant à Chaalons [sic] en la chambre de madame la Dauphine, le jour que madite Dame tréspassa, elle ouït que maistre Robert Poitevin disoit à madite dame qu'elle avoit pardonné à tout le monde, et madite dame répondit audit maître Robert: Non ai vraiment; et par trois fois lui dit lesdites paroles. Et adonc madame de Saint Michel, et autres Demoiselles étant illec, dirent à madite dame qu'il falloit qu'elle pardonnât à tout le monde, si elle vouloit que Dieu lui pardonnât; et adonc madite dame dit tout haut qu'elle pardonnoit à tout le monde de bon coeur et requéroit à Dieu qu'il lui voulsist pardonner. Interrogée si à cette heure que madite dame répondit audit maître Robert les paroles: Non ai vraiment, si elle nomma personne: Dit que non. Interrogée si paravant la maladie de madite dame, ne durant icelle, elle n'ouït point madite dame parler d'aucunes personnes à qui elle eût malveillance: Dit que non, et plus n'en sçait, sur tout diligemment enquise et examinée. Ainsi *signé* G. le Boursier et Bigot.' Duclos, *Histoire*, III, pp. 36–7.

[52] (Second deposition of Jamet de Tillay, 23 August 1446) 'ledit Nicole lui demanda ce qu'elle avoit, et d'où procédoit cette maladie, et il qui parle [Jamet de Tillay] lui répondit que les médecins disoient qu'elle avoit un courroux sur le coeur, qui lui faisoit grand dommage, et aussi que faute de repos lui nuisoit beaucoup; et lors ledit Nicole dit que lesdits médecins lui en avoient autant dit, et aussi dit: Plût à Dieu qu'elle n'eût jamais eu telle femme à elle! Et quelle, dit il qui parle? Et lors ledit Nicole lui répondit: Marguerite de Salignac. Et il qui parle lui dit: Plût à Dieu, ne aussi Prégente, ne Jeanne Filloque [*recte* Filleul]! Requis pourquoi il dit lesdites paroles, dit pour ce qu'il avoit ouï dire que c'étoient celles qui la faisoient trop veiller à faire rondeaux et balades.' Duclos, *Histoire*, III, pp. 47–8.

and the king asked him if she were pregnant, and [Tillay] answered no, as the doctors had said. And the king asked him what caused her illness; and [Tillay] said that it came from a lack of sleep, as the doctors had said, and that she frequently stayed up so much that it was often dawn before she went to bed; and sometimes my lord the dauphin had been asleep for some time before she joined him, and often she was so busy writing rondeaux that she sometimes wrote a dozen in a day, which was not good for her. And when the king asked if that could give her headaches, my lord the treasurer, Maistre Jehan Bureau who was present said, 'Yes, if she does it too much; but these [i.e. writing poetry] are pleasurable things.'[53]

Any allusion to the creative process in the late Middle Ages is unusual enough, but this one is unmatched as a sworn eyewitness account of the literary creativity of late medieval women. And it is transparently clear from Tillay's lengthy version of events that he strongly disapproves of her activities. Writing poetry was not only distracting the dauphine from her marital duties, it was contributing to her moral depravity, and worst of all, it 'was not good for her' – it was making her sick. A compendium of the negative attitudes towards creativity directed at women writers, artists and composers from the beginning of recorded history,[54] Tillay's

---

[53] 'Et lors le roi lui demanda si elle étoit impédumée; et il qui parle répondit que non, comme disoient les médecins. Et le roi lui demanda, d'où procède cette maladie, et il qui parle lui dit qu'il venoit de faute de repos, comme disoient les médecins, et qu'elle veilloit tant, aucunefois plus, aucunefois moins, que aucunefois il étoit presque soleil levant avant qu'elle s'allât coucher, et que aucunefois monseigneur le Dauphin avoit dormi un somme ou deux avant qu'elle s'allât coucher, et aucunefois s'occupoit à faire rondeaux, tellement qu'elle en faisoit aucunefois douze pour un jour, qui lui étoit chose bien contraire. Et lors le roi demanda si cela faisoit mal à la tête, et monsieur le trésorier maître Jean Bureau, là présent, dit: Oui, qui s'y abuse trop; mais ce sont choses de plaisance.' Duclos, *Histoire*, III, p. 54.

[54] The morals of creative women in music, literature and art have historically tended to be viewed with suspicion. For examples of the notion that music-making, and especially music composition, was dangerous to a woman's chastity see J. Bowers, 'The Emergence of Women Composers in Italy, 1566–1700', *Women Making Music*, pp. 139–41. In later centuries, women composers like Corona Schröter feared that publication of their music would be perceived almost as an act of promiscuity. See M. Citron, 'Women and the Lied, 1775–1850', *Women Making Music*, p. 230. Many creative women were the targets of innuendo. The sixteenth-century poet Louise Labé, for example, was accused of granting sexual favours to the men of Lyons (A. R. Jones, 'City Women and their Audiences: Louise Labé and Veronica Franco', *Rewriting the Renaissance: The Discourses of Sexual Difference in Early Modern Europe*, ed. M. W. Ferguson, M. Quilligan and N. J. Vickers (Chicago, 1986), pp. 302–3). The seventeenth-century English writer and playwright Aphra Behn was considered a 'shady lady' (Gilbert and Gubar, *The Madwoman*, p. 63), and the composer and singer Barbara Strozzi (1619–1664?) is reputed to have been a Venetian courtesan (E. Rosand, 'The Voice of Barbara Strozzi', *Women Making Music*, p. 172). Since many creative women clearly did have libertine attitudes towards sexuality, such suspicions were not always without foundation. Indeed, given the stigma of impropriety associated with any public acknowledgement by a woman of her creative

testimony echoed in part that of the doctor who had performed the autopsy. Stopping short of linking the dauphine's illness directly to her creative endeavours, the doctor nevertheless diagnosed her lung disease as having originated in her brain, which had been weakened by her habit of staying up so late and thereby rendered more vulnerable to a probable infection that eventually travelled to her lung.[55]

Tillay accused three women of aiding and abetting the dauphine in her literary pursuits: Marguerite de Salignac, Prégente de Melun and Jehanne Filleul, all three of whom were ladies-in-waiting to the dauphine and Queen Marie d'Anjou along with Jacqueline de Hacqueville.[56] And lest the credibility of Tillay's testimony be challenged as a self-serving pretext for getting himself off the hook, it is fortunate that external evidence corroborates the literary activities of all three women. Concerning Marguerite de Salignac, the first of the ladies mentioned, the *Jardin de plaisance* transmits a poem con-

activities, it is probably no coincidence that women who did publish their work were those who seem to have been least concerned about notions of respectability, or whose respectability was presumably beyond question (e.g. nuns). As Newcomb ('Courtesans, Muses', p. 102), Rosand ('The Voice', p. 172) and others have pointed out, a long tradition of serious music-making by courtesans existed in Venice. Curiously, though, the subject has never been pursued in a scholarly study. The degree of literary cultivation among certain Venetian courtesans must have been high, to judge from Pietro Aretino, who said of one: 'She knows by heart all Petrarch and Boccaccio and many beautiful verses of Virgil, Horace, Ovid, and a thousand other authors.' Quoted in J. Burckhardt, *The Civilization of the Renaissance in Italy* (New York, 1958), p. 394, n. 2. With regard to women writers in the nineteenth century, morality and respectability became so closely linked to economic success that they could no longer risk the kind of sexual innuendo surrounding a woman like Aphra Behn. See Gilbert and Gubar, *The Madwoman*, pp. 63–4.

[55] 'Il luy semble que ladicte maladie principalement luy est venue pour ce que ladicte dame vieilloit trop, parquoy se corrompoit son sang et les humeurs de son corps; son cervel s'en affoiblissoit et nature envoye toujours au plus foible du corps et iceluy qu'elle trouve plus brecié les superfluitez ou humeurs corrompues. Dont en son cervel s'est engendré un rume, lequel a esté cause de engendrer un appostume en son dit cervel. Et peult estre que de son dit cervel peult estre tombé par manière de une gouture partye de ces humeurs corrompues sur les parties de son poulmon, qui a esté cause de ulcerer son dit poulmon, comme a esté trouvé par effet.' Deposition of Guillaume Léotier, in F-Pn Dupuy 762, fol. 51ᵛ, quoted in Beaucourt, *Histoire de Charles VII*, IV, pp. 106–7, n. 3. My interpretation of Léotier's report as implicitly associating the dauphine's literary endeavours with the cerebral origin of her lung disease receives striking corroboration in Erasmus's colloquy 'The Abbot and the Learned Woman', where the ignorant Abbot Antronius, parroting popular wisdom, warns his erudite interlocutor Magdalia that 'Books destroy women's brains'; see *The Colloquies of Erasmus*, trans. N. Bailey, I (London, 1878), p. 380. For similar examples of women whose creative activities were thought to have had pathological consequences see Gilbert and Gubar, *The Madwoman*, pp. 55–6.

[56] Jehanne Filleul and Marguerite de Salignac were *damoiselles d'honneur* to Marguerite d'Écosse, and Prégente de Melun, *damoiselle d'honneur* to Marie d'Anjou, Charles VII's queen. See Beaucourt, *Histoire de Charles VII*, IV, p. 90, n. 4.

cealing an acrostic of her name,[57] significant in light of the two Hacqueville acrostics that survive in the same source. Prégente de Melun, another of the ladies mentioned by Tillay, had borrowed a copy of the courtly narrative *Clériadus*[58] from Marie of Cleves, Duchess of Orléans, who had to send one of her servants to the French court to retrieve it.[59] This not only provides further concrete evidence of literary exchanges between the French royal court and that of Orléans, but also seems to hint at the existence of a kind of literary subculture among the women of the two courts.[60] Finally, a bergerette ascribed to Jehanne Filleul, the third lady-in-waiting, survives in the poetry collection F-Pn fr. 9223.[61] This manuscript preserves dozens of poems by other of the dauphine's courtiers

[57] E. Droz and A. Piaget, eds., *Le jardin de plaisance et fleur de rhétorique*, II (Paris, 1925), p. 205. Steenackers (*Agnès Sorel*, p. 257, n. 2) records a gift from the king of 192 livres 10 sous in the year 1454 to Marguerite de Salignac 'to have a room for her lying-in'. Steenackers, who never mentions the literary interests of Marguerite d'Écosse's ladies and assumes, often with little justification, that they were all mistresses of Charles VII, attributes this rather generous gift to Marguerite de Salignac to a probable 'accouchement clandestin'. Among the most frequently recorded payments to women in the accounts of both male and female magnates, gifts for a *gésine* (lying-in) are usually accorded to attendants of his consort at her behest, or to the wives of loyal male servants.

[58] *Clériadus* undoubtedly refers to the courtly narrative *Clériadus et Méliadice* discussed by Christopher Page as a rich source of information concerning late medieval performance practices. See 'The Performance of Songs in Late Medieval France: A New Source', *Early Music*, 10 (1982), pp. 441–50. Evidence that Marie of Cleves owned a copy of the narrative which she in turn lent to the female attendants at the French royal court is interesting in light of Page's observations' concerning its 'evidence of a French aristocratic and possibly royal provenance' (p. 442) since 'the author speaks of the chivalry, the court and the king of France in the most flattering terms' (p. 450). An edition of *Clériadus et Méliadice* has appeared since the publication of Page's article: G. Zink, ed. *Clériadus et Méliadice: Roman en prose du XVe siècle* (Paris and Geneva, 1984).

[59] According to A. Vallet de Viriville (*Histoire de Charles VII*, 3 vols. (Paris, 1863), III, pp. 85–6, n. 1): 'Le 18 août 1450, Marie de Clèves, duchesse d'Orléans, envoie un messager d'Yèvre-le-Châtel à Corbeil, où était la reine, pour recouvrer des mains de Prégente de Melun, dame de la reine, un roman de chevalerie intitulé *Clériadus*, que la duchesse avait prêté à Prégente.' The now lost document in question, one of ten items included under no. 852 in the *Catalogue des archives de M. Le Baron de Joursanvault, contenant une précieuse collection de manuscrits, chartes et documents originaux* (Paris, 1838), p. 145, was subsequently acquired by the Bibliothèque du Louvre, which was destroyed by fire in 1871. Included under the same catalogue number was a document of 1470 referring to Regnault le Queux and Robert du Herlin who had given the duchess 'certains livres par eulx fais de ballades et rondeaulx'. The latter document was published by [Léon-Emmanuel] le comte de Laborde, *Les ducs de Bourgogne*, 3 vols., III (Paris, 1852), p. 403, no. 7060, who listed as its call number Bibliothèque du Louvre, F145³.

[60] The concept of a separate tradition of women's literary culture is central to the pioneering work of Gilbert and Gubar (see note 48) as well as to that of the literary critic Elaine Showalter, *A Literature of their Own: British Women Novelists from Brontë to Lessing* (Princeton, 1977).

[61] *Hélas mon amy sur mon ame*, fol. 46, ed. Raynaud, *Rondeaux*, p. 76. See below, p. 182, for the complete text.

(including her nocturnal companion the Seigneur de Torcy),[62] several poems set to music by Busnoys and his contemporaries,[63] and an otherwise unknown rondeau attributed to Busnoys.[64] Still another of the dauphine's ladies, the fifteen-year-old Annette de Cuise, though not among the guilty parties cited by Tillay, seems to have been the custodian of several of the dauphine's books and papers, including 'un livre qui parle d'amours' and another of 'chansons et ballades'.[65] Annette de Cuise and her sister Jeanne, a lady-in-waiting to Queen Marie d'Anjou, were siblings of the poet Anthoine de Cuise whose name is attached to some dozen rondeaux in F-Pn fr. 9223, including *Les douleurs dont me sens tel somme* set to music by Dufay.[66]

Since the dauphine's circle of female attendants included a woman named Jacqueline de Hacqueville, the fact that one of the Hacqueville songs – *Ja que lui ne si actende* – happens to be in a woman's voice takes on a new significance. By 'woman's voice' I mean that the gender endings of adjectives and other textual allusions make it clear that the speaker or persona is a woman. Of course the use of a woman's voice does not necessarily mean that a poem was actually written by a woman, as literary critics are quick to point out. The editor of the Mellon Chansonnier's version of the

---

[62] F-Pn fr. 9223 transmits thirty-four poems by three male courtiers in the dauphine's circle: Blosseville (29), Tanneguy du Chastel (3), and Jean d'Estouteville, seigneur de Torcy et Blainville (2). Torcy's rondeau *N'ai ge pas esté bien party* follows that of Jehanne Filleul in the same manuscript. For the most recent biographical information on these poets see B. L. S. Inglis, ed., *Le manuscrit B. N. nouv. acq. fr. 15771* (Paris, 1985), pp. 19–24 (Blosseville), pp. 35–6 (Tanneguy du Chastel) and pp. 58–60 (Seigneur de Torcy).

[63] *Les douleurs dont me sens tel somme*, fol. 8ᵛ, text by Anthoine de Cuise, set to music by Dufay; *Nul ne me doibt de ce blasmer*, fol. 14ᵛ, text by Monsieur d'Orvilier, anonymous musical setting in Dij, fols. 142ᵛ–143ʳ; *C'est par vous que tant fort soupire*, fol. 18, text by Meschinot, anonymous musical setting in Dij, fols. 50ᵛ–51ʳ; *J'en ay le dueil et vous la joye*, fol. 59, text by Blosseville, anonymous musical setting in Dij, fols. 144ᵛ–145; *Malleureux cueur que veulx tu faire?*, fol. 62ᵛ, text by Le Roussellet, musical setting by Dufay in Lab, fols. 26ᵛ–28, and Wolf, fols. 25ᵛ–27; *Qu'elle n'y a je le maintien*, fol. 104, text by Anthoine de Cuise, anonymous musical setting in Dij, fols. 109ᵛ–110; *En tous les lieux ou j'ay esté*, fol. 101, text by Monsieur Jacques, musical setting by Busnois in Dij, fols. 83ᵛ–85, and Niv, fols. 44ᵛ–46; *A ceste foiz je me voy*, fol. 56, text by C. Blosset, anonymous musical setting in Dij, fols. 64ᵛ–65; *Quant jamais aultre*, fol. 60ᵛ, text by Le Roussellet, anonymous musical setting in I-Pu 362, fols. 56ᵛ–58.

[64] *Lequel vous plairoit mieulx trouver*, fol. 98, ed. Raynaud, *Rondeaux*, p. 153.

[65] Deposition of Annette de Cuise, F-Pn Dupuy 762, fol. 53: 'Interrogée sy elle a aucune chose en garde de madicte dame, dict que non, fors un livre qui parle d'amours, et de chansons et ballades, et aucunes lettres d'estat qui sont en son coffre lequel elle auroye avec le bagaige de la Roine'.

[66] For the most recent biographical information on Anthoine, Jeanne and Annette de Cuise, see Inglis, *Le manuscrit B.N. nouv. acq. fr. 15771*, pp. 29–33.

text equivocated about the gender of its voice[67] and claimed that in any case the authors of this and of six other woman's songs in Mellon were probably all men, since Christine de Pizan 'was the only woman poet of the day to make a name for herself'.[68] Significantly, the same critical tactic reverberates in the work of Machaut scholars arguing against Toute Belle's authorship of the poems attributed to her in the *Voir-dit*. If such a woman poet existed, they claim, 'she would have been noticed by her contemporaries. But they say nothing of Agnes de Navarre, Péronne d'Armentières, or any other lady poet until Christine de Pisan'.[69] Besides overlooking

---

[67] Garey noted that the incipit *Ja que lui ne si actende* could be read either as 'Let Jacqueline wait' or 'Although he doesn't expect it'. See his discussion of the text of this poem in Perkins and Garey, *Mellon Chansonnier*, II, pp. 242–3.

[68] Perkins and Garey, *Mellon Chansonnier*, II, p. 74.

[69] Since 'her poems are of the same high quality as his', and the style of her lyrics 'indistinguishable' from Machaut's, employing 'identical rhyme, meter, imagery, and diction', they cannot possibly have been written by her. '. . . the brilliant young poetess existed only in Guillaume de Machaut's imagination. A fictional character, she is not to be identified with Péronne d'Armentières or anyone else who actually lived in the fourteenth century.' (Calin, p. 170, upholding the arguments of G. Hanf). Especially noteworthy is the assumption that Péronne's poems would necessarily have been inferior in quality to those of Machaut. The alleged indistinguishability of Toute Belle's lyrics from Machaut's notwithstanding, when the late Machaut scholar Sarah Jane Williams examined the poems she found striking divergences from Machaut's standard procedure at every turn: 'Whereas ballades far outnumber rondeaux elsewhere in Machaut's literary and musical repertory, the proportion is reversed in the *Voir Dit*, where rondeaux outnumber ballades thirty to nineteen.' As Williams points out, this may well be due to the fact that Toute Belle initiated the lyric exchange with a rondeau, and that the form was an easy one for her to grasp. Moreover, the first few rondeaux attributed to Toute Belle 'are written in forms of the rondeau rarely if ever found in Machaut's work elsewhere'. The third rondeau sent by Toute Belle is unique among all Machaut's others in alternating long with short lines; two of the virelais have only a single stanza, instead of three; and her ballade *Regrete la compaignie* and the virelai *Cent mille fois esbahie* both have only two instead of three stanzas, an irregularity commented upon by Machaut in the text. See 'The Lady, the Lyrics and the Letters', *Early Music*, 5 (1977), pp. 462–8. Another study, using a computer-aided linguistic analysis of the poems, demonstrated that there are in fact striking qualitative differences in the vocabularies of the poems attributed to Machaut and Péronne respectively. See N. Musso, 'Comparaison statistique des lettres de Guillaume de Machaut et de Péronne d'Armentière dans le Voir-dit', *Guillaume de Machaut: Colloque, Table Ronde, Reims, 19–22 avril 1978* (Paris, 1982), pp. 175–93. Musso's evidence was challenged by literary critics on the grounds that the apparent linguistic differences might have been deliberately created by Machaut. This, however, seems to me the strongest evidence in favour of the existence of Péronne or a woman like her. Even if Machaut wrote the poems himself, attempting to emulate the written prose of a young woman, this presupposes (a) that he probably knew of women writers and (b) that he perceived qualitative 'differences' in their writing to the point of having concrete notions about how they would manifest themselves in a literary text. Whether or not gender difference can be discerned in literary texts is a controversial topic being heatedly debated in late twentieth-century literary critical circles. Machaut was indeed remarkably ahead of his time if he perceived such subtle distinctions some six centuries ago. My thanks to Professor Lawrence Earp for drawing my attention to Musso's article.

the long history of women writers and poets spanning the millennium before Christine de Pizan,[70] these statements are contradicted by the closely related poetry anthologies F-Pn fr. 9223, mentioned earlier, and F-Pn n.a.f. 15771, which together bear attributions to five women: the dauphine's lady-in-waiting Jehanne Filleul,[71] Marie of Cleves (Madame d'Orléans),[72] Mademoiselle de Beau Chastel,[73] Jammette de Nesson,[74] and Queen Marie d'Anjou.[75]

---

[70] For the most recent study of medieval women writers see P. Dronke, *Women Writers of the Middle Ages: A Critical Study of Texts from Perpetua (d. 203) to Marguerite Porete (d. 1310)* (Cambridge, 1984). In the book's preface, Dronke comments on the extent to which these works have been unjustly undervalued in the past and gives a few notable examples of the paradoxical attempts even until recent times either to accept their authenticity and trivialise them, or to reject their authenticity on the basis of their high quality and therefore attribute them to men.

[71] *Hélas mon amy sur mon ame*, F-Pn fr. 9223, fol. 46, 'Jehanne Filleul', ed. Raynaud, *Rondeaux*, pp. 76–7; F-Pn n.a.f. 15771, fol. 38ʳ, 'Jehanne Fillieul', ed. Inglis, *Le manuscrit*, p. 146. The poem also survives anonymously in Roh, fol. 178ʳ (ed. M. Löpelmann, *Die Liederhandschrift des Cardinals de Rohan (XV. Jahrh.)*, Gesellschaft für romanische Literatur 44 (Göttingen, 1923), p. 343), F-Pn fr. 1719, fol. 121ʳ, and Jard, fol. 81 (ed. Droz and Piaget, *Le jardin*, no. 212).

[72] *En la forest de Longue Actente*, 'Madame d'Orléans', F-Pn fr. 9223, fol. 26ᵛ, ed. Raynaud, *Rondeaux*, p. 43; F-Pn n.a.f. 15771, fol. 2ʳ, 'Madame d'Orléans', ed. Inglis, *Le manuscrit*, p. 73; F-Pn fr. 1104, fol. 87ᵛ, 'Madame d'Orléans'; F-Pn fr. 25458, fol. 415ʳ, 'Madame d'Orléans'. The poem survives anonymously in F-Pn fr. 1719, fols. 4ᵛ, 64ᵛ, 129ʳ; Roh, fol. 64ᵛ; Carpentras, Bibliothèque Municipale, MS fr. 375, fol. 50ᵛ; London, British Library, MS Harley 6916, fol. 171ᵛ; F-Pn fr. 1722, fol. 76ᵛ.

[73] *En ce monde n'a saint ne saincte*, 'Madamoiselle de Beau Chastel', F-Pn fr. 9223, fol. 69, ed. Raynaud, *Rondeaux*, p. 113. The poem survives anonymously in Roh, fol. 204ʳ, ed. Löpelmann, *Die Liederhandschrift*, pp. 408–9.

[74] *C'est pour me receller les biens*, F-Pn fr. 9223, fol. 36ᵛ, 'Jammette de Nesson', ed. Raynaud, *Rondeaux*, p. 59; F-Pn n.a.f. 15771, fol. 39ʳ, 'Denesson a ja', ed. Inglis, *Le manuscrit*, p. 148. The poem survives anonymously in F-Pn fr. 1719, fol. 44ʳ.

[75] *Pour tous les maulx d'amours guerir*, F-Pn n.a.f. 15771, fol. 34, 'Recepte de la Raine', ed. Inglis, *Le manuscrit*, p. 137. The poem survives anonymously in F-Pn fr. 1719, fol. 75ʳ; Roh, fol. 202ᵛ; Carpentras, Bibl. mun. MS 375, fols. 55ʳ, 65ʳ; F-Pn fr. 25458, fol. 441ʳ; F-Pn fr. 1104, fol. 92ᵛ; London, British Library, MS Harley 6916, fol. 181ᵛ; and F-Pn n.a.f. 7559, fol. 68ʳ. The attribution 'Recepte de la Raine' in all likelihood refers to Queen Marie d'Anjou. See A. Angremy, 'Un nouveau recueil de poésies françaises: Le MS B. N. nouv. acq. fr. 15771', *Romania*, 95 (1974), p. 4. The dauphine's household was incorporated with that of Queen Marie d'Anjou, with whom she travelled constantly. Marie d'Anjou was the sister of Duke René d'Anjou, another of the noble literary amateurs of his day. Champion published the poem as a work of Charles d'Orléans because it appears in his autograph manuscript without an attribution. The existence of several other poetic 'recipes' 'for curing the ills of love' by other poets suggests that it was among those themes developed at the Orléans court such as 'je meurs de soif auprès de la fontaine'. B. Inglis (*Le manuscrit*, p. 206) has suggested the possibility that 'la Raine' could also refer to Jeanne de Laval, 'reine de Sicile', second wife of René d'Anjou. Inglis cited the existence of another 'recepte' similar to this one attributed to Jean de Lorraine (son of René, and stepson of Jeanne de Laval) in support of this hypothesis. In light of the evidence presented here concerning the close interaction among the women of the French court and the Orléans court, as well as the numerous pieces by French court poets surviving in the manuscript, it would seem more likely that a non-specific reference to 'the queen' would be to the Queen of France, Marie d'Anjou.

Paula Higgins

With the exception of Marie of Cleves, only a single poem by each of them has survived, but at least Jammette de Nesson, niece of the poet Pierre de Nesson, must have written a good deal more. In his *Champion des dames*, Martin le Franc juxtaposed her literary production with that of Christine de Pizan and called her 'the other Minerva', so it seems unlikely that he formulated his opinion of her on the basis of one poem.[76] And what do we make of the sole bergerette attributed in the same manuscripts to Jehanne Filleul? Should we assume that she exhausted her imagination in writing it? And what of Marguerite de Salignac and Prégente de Melun, the other women cited by Tillay, not to mention Marguerite d'Écosse herself who, if we take him at his word, sometimes wrote a dozen poems in a day?[77] How do we weigh the independent evidence of sworn depositions and contemporary documents attesting to the otherwise unknown literary creativity of a circle of medieval women

[76] See A. Thomas, 'Jammette de Nesson et Merlin de Cordebeuf', *Romania*, 35 (1909), pp. 82–94; Raynaud, *Rondeaux*, p. xxviii; and Inglis, *Le manuscrit*, pp. 48–50. The very context in which Le Franc chose to mention her is telling: L'Adversaire, one of the interlocutors in the poem, admonishes Franc-Vouloir, Christine de Pizan's enthusiastic panegyrist, for neglecting to mention Jammette de Nesson (Thomas, p. 82). This seems to betray the author's awareness of how the work of noteworthy women can be overlooked. In any case one might well ask what motivated Le Franc to write a 24,000-verse poem drawing attention to the unsung accomplishments of women, the full text of which has never been edited.

[77] To put this remark in perspective, a dozen poems a day would have exceeded the '100 verses' Machaut claimed to be capable of writing when he was having a good day. Even accounting for the possibility of Tillay's exaggeration, this is still a considerable output. Marguerite d'Écosse might well have been a female analogue of Charles d'Orléans. Yet, surprisingly, of the dozens of scholars who have mentioned her activities as a poet none seems to have considered this possibility; all have contented themselves with presuming the mediocrity of her poetic gifts, even though her poetry seems not to have survived. See for example P. M. Kendall, *Louis XI: The Universal Spider* (New York, 1971), p. 63: 'Like her father, James I of Scotland, Margaret was enamoured of poetry, though it is doubtful – none of her compositions has survived – that she possessed her father's genius'; and J. Cleugh, *Chant royal: The Life of King Louis XI of France* (New York, 1970), p. 60: 'No examples of Margaret Stuart's verses survive . . . she fervently admired Alain Chartier and Charles of Orléans . . . it is improbable, however, that she attained the heights of lyrical imagination and delicacy of statement which they achieved.' Such statements, of which there are many more examples, are emblematic of the ways in which the literary and musical creations of women, even when they have survived, have historically tended to be dismissed without a reading or hearing. The subject with regard to women writers has been treated in a witty, polemical and powerfully sobering work by D. Spender, *The Writing or the Sex? Or, why you don't have to read women's writing to know it's no good* (New York, 1989). I raised similar questions with regard to musical creativity and women composers from the late eighteenth century to the twentieth in my paper 'In her Brother's Shadow: The Musical Legacy of Fanny Mendelssohn Hensel', *Proceedings of 'The Changing Patterns of Our Lives: Women's Education and Women's Studies', A Sesquicentennial Symposium at Duke University, 3–5 March 1989* (Durham, NC, 1989), pp. 37–49.

168

against the powerful silence of contemporary authors and paucity of attributions that seem to deny their very existence? In a period when the boundaries between poet and composer were still somewhat fluid, this question takes on more dramatic proportions if we juxtapose it with the apparent invisibility of female composers of polyphony in the fourteenth and fifteenth centuries.[78]

The critical argument *ex vacuo* that unquestioningly accepts the non-existence of other creative women underscores how 'exceptional women' in literature, art and music continue to function in critical discourse not as signifiers of a more widespread general tendency, but rather as the exceptions who prove the rule of woman's creative sterility. Without wishing to exaggerate unduly the role of women in the literary and musical culture of the late Middle Ages, I would nevertheless suggest that the evidence which reveals that at least half a dozen women in a single court of the 1440s were writing poetry that survives in the same manuscripts from which many texts set to music were drawn would seem to dispel the notion that Christine de Pizan was the only woman of the Middle Ages writing poetry. This is not to accord these women the presumably 'professional' status Christine de Pizan enjoyed (although one should wonder about 'the other Minerva', Jammette de Nesson). But even if their literary activities were those of courtly amateurs, this is no reason to dismiss them. That Anthoine de Cuise, Jacques de Savoye and Le Roussellet were courtly amateurs has not prevented scholars from investigating their potential connections with the composer Guillaume Dufay and other composers who set poems by each of them. Nor has Charles d'Orléans seemed

---

[78] Both M. V. Coldwell (*'Jougleresses* and *Trobairitz*: Secular Musicians in Medieval France', *Women Making Music*, pp. 55–6) and H. M. Brown ('Women Singers and Women's Songs in Fifteenth-Century Italy', *Women Making Music*, pp. 64–5) try to explain the absence of polyphonic compositions attributed to women from the fourteenth to sixteenth centuries. Coldwell attributes this to political considerations and Brown to the exclusion of women from cathedral schools. Curiously though, precisely the same obstacles existed for women composers from the mid-sixteenth century on, and they somehow managed to circumvent them. Brown is much closer to the mark, in my view, when he suggests that perhaps women were composing music but could not admit to doing so (p. 64). Given the vast number of pieces surviving anonymously in musical manuscripts from the fourteenth to sixteenth centuries, it would not be at all surprising if works by women were among them. The more fundamental question that needs to be raised is this: since there is abundant evidence that women in convents and monasteries, as well as aristocratic women, did compose monophonic music up to *c.* 1300 and polyphonic music from 1566 on, often against considerable odds, what would have stopped them from doing so during the intervening 250 years?

to suffer excessively from scholarly neglect, despite his status as the noble 'amateur par excellence' of the late Middle Ages. Apart from the difficulty of defining 'professional' and 'amateur' in a period when such distinctions in the literary and musical culture may have been more apparent than real, Howard Brown has recently provided further evidence that courtly amateurs – men and women alike – regularly performed secular music at court, reinforcing a point made by Heinrich Besseler some years ago.[79]

And lest Marguerite d'Écosse's circle risk dismissal as an aberration, one might also wonder about that of Marie of Cleves, the Duchess of Orléans, for whom two attributed poems survive and whose literary interaction with the women of the French court has already been noted. The autograph signatures of several of her ladies-in-waiting appearing in her personal copy of poems by Alain Chartier attest to the likelihood of their participation at least as an audience for, if not as creators of, courtly poetry.[80] Marguerite d'Autriche's literary coterie also merits closer scrutiny since the names of no fewer than four of her female attendants appear in the margins of some dozen poems in one of her personal poetry albums.[81]

Ignorance of the active participation of women in the writing of courtly poetry, as well as misconceptions about women's literacy, could conceivably fuel the notion that late medieval song texts in a woman's voice were written by men.[82] But even the information

[79] Brown, 'Women Singers and Women's Songs', pp. 67 and 83–4, n. 28.

[80] P. Champion, 'Un "Liber amicorum" du xvᵉ siècle: Notice d'un manuscrit d'Alain Chartier ayant appartenu à Marie de Clèves, femme de Charles d'Orléans', *Revue des Bibliothèques*, 20 (1910), pp. 320–36.

[81] On the poetry albums of Marguerite d'Autriche see E. Gachet, *Albums poétiques de Marguerite d'Autriche* (Brussels, 1849), and M. Françon, *Albums poétiques de Marguerite d'Autriche* (Cambridge, MA, and Paris, 1934). The parallel of Marguerite d'Autriche's court with that of the dauphine Marguerite d'Écosse is striking in light of the fact that Marguerite d'Autriche was raised at the French court and imbued with its literary traditions. Hers may represent yet another circle of courtly women who emulated and participated in the literary interests of their lady. In any case, the names appearing in B-Br 10572, whether or not they are those of the authors, include those of at least four of her ladies: Madamoiselle de Planci, Madamoiselle de Huclam, Madamoiselle de Vère, and Madamoiselle de Baude. The music-historical importance of Marguerite d'Autriche's court was brought to scholars' attention by M. Picker, ed., *The Chanson Albums of Marguerite of Austria: MSS 228 and 11239 of the Bibliothèque Royale de Belgique, Brussels* (Berkeley, 1965).

[82] For eye-opening accounts of women's education and erudition in the Middle Ages and Renaissance see J. M. Ferrante, 'The Education of Women in the Middle Ages in Theory, Fact, and Fantasy', *Beyond their Sex: Learned Women of the European Past*, ed. P. H. Labalme (New York and London, 1980), pp. 9–42; P. O. Kristeller, 'Learned Women of

presented here is not entirely new: at least a dozen historians and philologists alike from the mid-eighteenth century to the early twentieth have discussed Marguerite d'Écosse and her ladies-in-waiting in some detail.[83] But one would never know this from the four sentences accorded her in the most recent study of Charles VII published in 1974, by far the most accessible and the only one existing in English. There any residual evidence of her literary interests all but vanishes in a passage of cryptic ambiguity: 'she died at 21 allegedly worn out by her over-fertile poetic imagination'.[84]

Evidence that women did participate in the writing of courtly poetry, and probably in greater numbers than has hitherto been supposed, challenges the widespread assumption that the authors of all texts in a woman's voice were men. Regrettably, the undoubtedly substantial poetic legacy of Marguerite d'Écosse disappeared among her papers, of which Louis XI ordered the destruction shortly after her death in 1445.[85] But there is little question but that some of her works, those of her ladies, and others by the handful of women poets acknowledged in F-Pn fr. 9223 and n.a.f. 15771 survive among the not insubstantial number of anonymous texts in a woman's voice transmitted in other poetry collections of the fifteenth century. In fact, all of the texts attributed to women in F-Pn fr. 9223 and n.a.f. 15771 are transmitted anonymously in several other poetry anthologies of the period.[86] In light of the repeated claims by literary critics that poems in a woman's voice were all written by men, it is curious that the few anthologies that do give authors' names fail to corroborate this assertion. None of the 188 poems ascribed to male authors in F-Pn fr. 9223, and none of the eighty-six poems attributed to men in F-Pn n.a.f. 15771, is written in a woman's voice. Of the five poems attributed to women in the same sources, three are in a woman's voice and two in a neutral

---

Early Modern Italy: Humanists and University Scholars', *Beyond their Sex*, pp. 91–116; and the classic article by C. Jourdain, 'Mémoire sur l'éducation des femmes au moyen âge', *Mémoires de l'Institut National de France: Académie des Inscriptions et Belles Lettres*, 28 (1874), pp. 79–133.

[83] See note 47 for the bibliography concerning Marguerite d'Écosse.

[84] M. G. A. Vale, *Charles VII* (Berkeley, 1974), p. 96. Vale's account provides a useful example of how a historian's ideological perspective inevitably shapes the resulting historical construct.

[85] Beaucourt, *Histoire de Charles VII*, IV, p. 189.

[86] See notes 71–5 above for the sources in which these poems survive anonymously.

voice. Another woman's poem in F-Pn fr. 9223 bears no author's name. On the basis of this admittedly limited but at least consistent statistical evidence, it seems plausible that when writing individual lyric poems in the *formes fixes* men and women tended to use the gendered voice of their own sex, unless of course they adopted the gender-masking alternative of the neutral voice, an option that would for obvious reasons have been particularly attractive to women poets. Many women, such as the sixteenth-century Lyonnaise poet Pernette du Guillet, wrote in a neutral voice so that their poems, taken out of context, might be assumed to have been written and experienced by a male persona.[87] In fact, if we add to the poems by the five women mentioned here a second poem attributed to Marie of Cleves,[88] an interesting statistic emerges: of six poems attributed to women, three are in a woman's voice and three in a neutral voice. With due acknowledgement of the limits of this sample, it would appear nevertheless that women were just as likely to employ the shroud of the neutral voice as the woman's voice. It is not outside the realm of possibility, therefore, that poems by women survive among the many courtly texts in a neutral voice. In other words, while songs in a woman's voice do constitute only a small percentage of fifteenth-century poetry anthologies,[89] there is no reason to make the essentialist assumption that women who did write poetry would have necessarily confined themselves to the woman's voice. For that matter, if male poets could ventriloquise a woman's voice, what would theoretically prevent any woman poet from ventriloquising a male voice as did some of the trobairitz (women troubadours) and Christine de Pizan herself in several of her *débats* between male and female interlocutors? The complex theoretical issue of gendered voice vs. the gender of the poet becomes a critical one for music historians because at least one authority on medieval performance practice made the demonstrably specious claim that 'medieval music making was an all male affair' since songs are 'almost invariably written from the man's point of view'.[90]

[87] F. Rigolot, 'Gender vs. Sex Difference in Louise Labé's Grammar of Love', *Rewriting the Renaissance*, p. 298.

[88] *Habit le moine ne fait pas*, 'Madame d'Orléans', F-Pn fr. 1104, fol. 94.

[89] Poems in a woman's voice make up only 2% of F-Pn fr. 9223, but about 10% of Roh.

[90] D. Munrow, 'On the Performance of Late Medieval Music', *Early Music*, 1 (1973), pp. 197–8. This notion, which seems to be based on an unfounded assumption about the

IV

In light of the foregoing, then, I should like to consider the possibility that Jacqueline de Hacqueville wrote the text of *Ja que lui ne*, leaving aside for the moment the question of 'which' Jacqueline. Besides cultural setting and grammatical viewpoint, several unusual pieces of circumstantial evidence enhance this possibility. While studying the song texts of the Chansonnier Nivelle de La Chaussée, I was struck by several curiously emblematic, almost ungrammatical,[91] incipits, which seemed contrived as if to conceal some latent meaning. Upon further examination, half a dozen of them yielded anagrams, that is, entirely new words and phrases made by scrambling the letters of the incipit.[92] One of them, the anonymous *Pour les biens qu'en vous je parçoy*, which happens to be in a woman's voice, contains an anagram which reads 'Ces vers pour Bunoys, Jaqueline' or 'these verses for Bunoys, Jaqueline', as shown in Example 1. For the benefit of the sceptic I hasten to mention that there is a venerable medieval literary tradition of

Example 1. Anonymous, *Pour les biens qu'en vous je parçoy*, Chansonnier Nivelle de La Chaussée, fol. 12.

POUR LES BIENS QU'EN VOUS JE PARÇOY

=

CES VERS POUR BUNOYS, JAQUELINE

non-existence of women in medieval musical culture, is contradicted by the significant numbers of women musicians known to have performed publicly, at least in the secular sphere, before medieval and renaissance princes and princesses. See especially the documents and literary references cited in C. Wright, *Music at the Court of Burgundy, 1364–1419: A Documentary History*, Musicological Studies 28 (Henryville, Ottawa and Binningen, 1979), pp. 183–6; Y. Rokseth, 'Les femmes musiciennes du xiie au xive siècle', *Romania*, 61 (1935), pp. 464–80; Coldwell, '*Jougleresses* and *Trobairitz*', pp. 39–61; Brown, 'Women Singers and Women's Songs', pp. 62–89; and C. Page, *Voices and Instruments of the Middle Ages: Instrumental Practice and Songs in France, 1100–1300* (Berkeley and Los Angeles, 1986), pp. 156–9. Evidence of active participation by women in the vocal performance of secular music of the Middle Ages has important implications for the late twentieth-century medieval performance practice industry, which, with notable exceptions, still tends to be dominated by all-male vocal groups.

[91] 'Ungrammaticality', as defined by M. Riffaterre, 'ranges from utter nonsense to obscurity to what are perceived as metaphors, but metaphors in which the semantic transfer seems somehow deviant' ('Intertextual Scrambling', *Romanic Review*, 68 (1977), p. 197). For a good example of the 'ungrammaticality' of a fifteenth-century incipit see the last item in Example 7.

[92] An anagram, which involves scrambling and rearranging letters in words or phrases, is read horizontally and should not be confused with an acrostic, which is a name or phrase formed vertically from the first letters of each line of a poem.

concealing proper names and phrases in anagrams.[93] It is precisely by means of an anagram that Machaut reveals his own and Toute Belle's identities in the final verses of the *Voir-dit*. He tells the reader that the names of the author and his lady can be found by taking 'the ninth verse from the end and then the first eight letters of the eighth. There you will see our names clearly.' The verses in question and the resultant anagram which are given in Example 2a read 'Guillaume de Machaut, Peronelle d'Armentiere'.[94] Alternative solutions of this anagram, such as the one given in Example 2b, have been proposed by various scholars,[95] but nobody denies the

Example 2. Machaut, *Le livre du voir-dit*, verses 9029 and 9030 ('the ninth verse from the end and the first eight letters of the eighth from the end').

(a) Paulin Paris's resolution, correcting the 'mistaken' FAME to DAME.

POUR LI CHANGIER NULLE AUTRE DAME

MADAME LE

=

GUILLAUME DE MACHAUT, PERONELLE D'ARMENTIERE

(b) Jacqueline Cerquiglini's reworking of the same anagram, using the actual rhyme FAME at the end of verse 9029.

POUR LI CHANGIER NULLE AUTRE FAME

MADAME LE

=

GUILLAUME DE MACHAUT, PERRONNE FILLE A A[I]MER

[93] On the history of anagrams see especially E. Kuhs, *Buchstabendichtung: Zur gattungskonstituierenden Funktion von Buchstabenformationen in der französischen Literatur vom Mittelalter bis zum Ende des 19. Jahrhunderts* (Heidelberg, 1982) which, despite its rather limited coverage of the Middle Ages, gives some idea of the vast number of publications on the subject, particularly in the sixteenth and seventeenth centuries; A. Canel, 'Histoire de l'anagramme, principalement en France', *Revue de Rouen*, 9 (1841), pp. 162–71 and 193–204; and R. Lebègue, 'Les anagrammes de Villon à Malherbe', *Académie des inscriptions et belles lettres*, *Institut de France: Comptes rendus des séances de l'année* (1969), pp. 243–50. The anagram in Example 1 leaves the letters 'P' and 'o' unused.

[94] Despite his assertion to the contrary (p. xxiii), Paris adds two Es and one T, and leaves one A unused, to arrive at this solution of the anagram, at odds with the one he gives on p. 370 n. 1: 'Perone d'Armantiere [et] Guillaume de Machau'. Moreover he prints 'nule' in verse 9029 instead of 'nulle'. This was noted by J. Cerquiglini, *'Un engin si soutil': Guillaume de Machaut et l'écriture au XIVe siècle*, Bibliothèque du xvᵉ Siècle 48 (Paris, 1985), pp. 233–4. See her lengthy critique of Paris's methodology on pp. 223–43.

[95] Cerquiglini, pp. 233–43. Cerquiglini's resolution 'Guillaume de Machaut, Perronne fille a amer' is based on her disagreement with Paulin Paris's alteration of the rhyme 'fame', which appears in all the manuscripts, to 'dame' and a variant spelling of the word 'nule' and 'nulle'. Another solution of the anagram, 'Guillaume de Machaut amera fille Perronne', was proposed by H. Suchier, 'Das Anagramm in Machauts *Voir dit*', *Zeitschrift für romanische Philologie*, 21 (1897), pp. 541–5. Other 'signature' anagrams appearing in

existence of anagrams in Machaut's poetry. Similarly, the anonymous author of the fourteenth-century *La clef d'amors*, who concealed his identity and that of his lady in an elaborately constructed, still undeciphered anagram,[96] gives a compendium of formulas for devising anagrams that conceal proper names.[97]

Anagrams have long been the subject of much controversy among Villon scholars. Convinced that Villon's poetry was saturated with anagrams, Tristan Tzara, the high priest of the Dada movement, became obsessed with deriving a foolproof system for deciphering them.[98] Anagrams enjoyed an enormous vogue in French court circles from the mid-sixteenth century on and attained such widespread popularity by the end of the century that, according to one contemporary, 'everyone is doing them and some are even making a business of it'.[99] Their history goes back at least to the Hebrew Kabbala, and the Greek poet Lycophron is said to have composed several of them for Ptolemy in the third century BC.[100] Their rapid proliferation in the sixteenth century is generally attributed to the rise of humanism. A few of the more famous anagrams of the period are given in Example 3.

[96] Machaut's works include the one at the end of *Le confort d'ami*: 'Guillaume de Machaut, Charles roi de Navarre' (vv. 3968–70); and at the end of *La prise d'Alexandrie*: 'Guillaume de Machaut, Pierre roi de Chipre e de Iherusalem' (vv. 244–5). See Cerquiglini, pp. 235–6. Cerquiglini's resolution is not without its own problems however, as P.-Y. Badel noted in his review of her book (*Romania*, 106 (1985), pp. 550–61). While her argument that the *Voir-dit* anagram should correspond structurally to those in other of Machaut's works is basically sound, that anagram would be more truly parallel to Machaut's others if it were to say 'Péronne, *x de y*' with *x* being a title and *y* being a territory, as Badel suggests. Although Badel does not mention this, Paris's resolution is actually closer to Machaut's others in that there is at least a *y*, and if one assumes the *x* to be understood: Guillaume de Machaut, Peronelle [dame] d'Armentière'. Moreover, as Badel noted, it is doubtful whether the phrase 'fille a amer' would have had any medieval significance.

[97] *La clef d'amors*, ed. A. Doutrepont, Bibliotheca Normannica 5 (Halle, 1890; repr. Geneva, 1975), pp. 125–6, vv. 3377–425. This text is for the most part a virtual French translation of Ovid's *Ars amatoria*, but the sections on anagrams are unique to it.

[97] *La clef d'amors*, Appendix, pp. 127–35.

[98] See J. Dufournet, 'Tzara et les anagrammes de Villon', *Nouvelles recherches sur Villon*, Bibliothèque du xvᵉ Siècle 45 (Paris, 1980), pp. 249–73. For an explanation and critique of Tzara's system, which involved the arrangement of letters in symmetrical positions around a movable axis, see L. D. Stults, 'A Study of Tristan Tzara's Theory concerning the Poetry of Villon', *Romania*, 96 (1975), pp. 433–58.

[99] 'Aujourd'huy ceste invention est si commune, que chacun s'en mesle, voire, y en a qui en font marchandise.' Canel, 'Histoire de l'anagramme', pp. 167–8, quoting Estienne Tabourot, a sixteenth-century authority on anagrams and author of *Les bigarrures et touches du Seigneur des Accords* (Paris, 1585). Tabourot may have been related to Jehan Tabourot (1520–95), who published the well-known dance treatise *Orchésographie* (1588) under the pseudonym 'Thoinot Arbeau', an anagram of his real name.

[100] Lebègue, 'Les anagrammes', p. 243.

Example 3.

FRANCOIS RABELAIS[a]

SERAFINO CALBARSI

ALCOFRYBAS NASIER

HENRI DE VALOIS[a]

DIEU LE HARNOIS

PIERRE DE RONSARD[a]

SE REDORE PINDARE

LOUYSE DE LORRAINE[b]

L'OR DE HENRY VALOIS

MARIE TOUCHET[c]

JE CHARME TOUT

[a] These are perfect anagrams.
[b] Canel, 'Histoire de l'anagramme', p. 193. This anagram adds an H and leaves out an E.
[c] Marie Touchet was the mistress of Charles IX. Canel, 'Histoire', p. 193. This is a perfect anagram using all the letters of the woman's name.

Although clearly at the zenith of literary fashion during the late sixteenth century and beyond, anagrams were routinely used in the fifteenth century and earlier. Besides the well-known examples by Machaut and the author of *La clef d'amors* previously mentioned, Christine de Pizan signed her name in anagram in the refrain of the last of her *Cent ballades* (Example 4);[101] the fifteenth-century artist Jean Colombe signed several of his illuminations with the name 'Molbeco' (Example 5);[102] the poetry manuscripts of Marguerite d'Autriche give the names of authors in pseudo-anagrams that can be easily resolved by dropping the first and last letters of each word and reading the remaining letters in retrograde (Example 6);[103] and the fifteenth-century poetry collection Roh contains at least half a dozen poems with incipits containing anagrams of women's names

[101] S. Huot, *Lyric Poetics and the Art of Compilatio in the Fourteenth Century* (Ph.D. dissertation, Princeton University, 1982), p. 233.
[102] See P. Chenu, 'Le livre des offices pontificaux de Jean Coeur, archevêque de Bourges', *Mémoires de la Société des Antiquaires du Centre*, 48 (1938–41), p. 27, and C. Schaefer, 'Nouvelles observations au sujet des heures de Laval', *Arts de l'Ouest* (Rennes, 1980), p. 45.
[103] Françon, *Albums poétiques de Marguerite d'Autriche*, p. 53. Françon believes that the attributions in B-Br 10572, the only album containing poems without music, are 'dedications' or 'allusions' to the people who 'inspired' the poems, rather than to authors' names.

that are signalled with inscriptions in the manuscript itself (Example 7).[104] The title of another poem in Roh, *Pour bien vous veoir le nom tourner/D'une dame bien atournée*,[105] might even be a direct allusion to the practice of devising anagrams on a woman's name. The existence of acrostics and word games in Busnoys's texts has long been acknowledged by scholars, but the same texts have never been scrutinised for anagrams, which are another common, if less apparent, manifestation of the same fascination with cryptograms.

Example 4. Christine de Pizan: refrain of Ballade 100.

En escrit ai mis mon nom
En escrit=Crestine

Example 5. Signature appearing in illuminations of the fifteenth-century artist Jean Colombe.

M O L B E C O

=

C O L O M B E

Example 6. Names attached to poems in B-Br 10572, poetry album of Marguerite d'Autriche.

X A M I   B E L L E S I O M E D O   B E D Z   C E D U A B O[a]

M A   D E M O I S E L L E   D E   B A U D E

Z E L I   A D R A T S A B O   S E D Z   I N O B R U O B A[b]

L E   B A S T A R D   D E   B O U R B O N

[a]   Françon, *Les albums poétiques*, p. 170, no. 63.
[b]   Françon, *op. cit.*, p. 163, no. 56.

[104]   The inscriptions explicitly identify the given phrase as being the 'nom tourné' ('turned' or 'twisted' name) of a particular woman. Several of the poems contain acrostics on the same names, leaving no doubt as to the intentionality of the anagrams. Roh also includes the names of other women in acrostics (names formed by reading down the first letter of each line): Jehanne de Cambray, wife of the Parisian Parlement member Henry de Marle; Perrette de Raye; and Jehanne Cenami, wife of the Lucchese banker Giovanni Arnolfini. Roh transmits some 60% of Niv's song texts, including those for 50% of its unique pieces, and for nine of Busnoys's eleven songs. These circumstances enhance the possibility that the text of *Pour les biens* transmitted therein (no. 78), with a musical setting unique to Niv and possibly by Busnoys, does contain an intentional anagram alluding to Busnoys and Jacqueline.
[105]   Löpelmann, *Die Liederhandschrift*, p. 290.

Example 7.

Celle qui est *du ranc de charité*[a]
du ranc de charité=Catherine du Drac
Ce que tant ayme *du ranc de charité*[b]
du ranc de charité=Catherine du Drac
Checun y tarddera souvent[c]
Checun y tarddera=Catheryne du Drac
Gracieuse entre mile et belle[d]
gracieuse entre mile=Marguerite Lencisée
Feru suis du vent de *la bise*[e]
la bise=Isabel
Ma foy seure *vrite germa*[f]
vrite germa=Marguerite

[a] Löpelmann, *Die Liederhandschrift*, no. 52, pp. 73–4. This poem also contains an acrostic on the same name. Catherine du Drac was a verifiable Parisian noblewoman of the fifteenth century, the daughter of an illustrious member of the Parisian Parlement. The du Drac and Hacqueville-Bochart families seem to have been closely related. The Parisian Jacqueline de Hacqueville served as godmother to Madeleine du Drac born on 'St Thomas's day, 1503' and her daughter-in-law Jeanne Simon, married to her son Jean Bochart, stood up for Annette du Drac in 1515. See J. de Launay, 'Une sainte-veuve parisienne au xvi[e] siècle', *Annuaire du Conseil Héraldique de France*, 21 (1908), pp. 170 and 172.

[b] Löpelmann, *op. cit.*, no. 53, p. 74. This poem also contains an acrostic on the same name.

[c] Löpelmann, *op. cit.*, no. 480, pp. 306–7. Annotation in Roh: '*Checun y tarddera* est le nom tourné de *Catharine* [sic] *du Drac*'.

[d] Löpelmann, *op. cit.*, no. 406, p. 267. Annotation in Roh: '*gracieuse entre mile* est le nom tourné de *Marguerite Lencisée*'. I have thus far been unable to identify this woman.

[e] Löpelmann, *op. cit.*, no. 481, p. 307. Annotation in Roh: '*la bise* est le nom tourné de *Ysabel*'.

[f] Löpelmann, *op. cit.*, no. 397, p. 262. Annotation in Roh: '*vrite germa* est le nom de *Marguerite* tourné'.

One obvious candidate for a potential anagram is the text of the song *Bel Acueil le sergant d'amours*, the first piece in the Mellon Chansonnier, a manuscript made for Beatrice of Aragon and which bears formal dedications to her elsewhere in the manuscript. Not surprisingly, the song's incipit conceals her name (Example 8). The name itself uses only fifteen of the twenty-five letters in the incipit, but it is possible that the remaining letters form some kind of descriptive phrase.[106] According to contemporary practice, a

[106] I have so far been unsuccessful in establishing a phrase that would satisfactorily use all of the remaining letters, although perhaps significantly the word 'MUSE' is among them.

Example 8. Busnoys, *Bel Acueil le sergant d'amours*, incipit from the Mellon Chansonnier, fol. 1ᵛ.

BEL ACUEIL LE SERGANT D'AMOURS

=

BEATRICE D'ARAGON

certain amount of liberty was accorded in the creation and resolution of anagrams.[107] An anagram was 'imperfect' if many of the letters remained unused, or if letters had to be used more than once. It was considered 'perfect' if all of the letters of the phrase could be used without repetition.[108] There were also several degrees of sophistication in anagrams. Imperfect anagrams, like those attributed to Villon, conceal only the name of one person or several people, while others concealed an entire verse or phrase.[109] However perfect or imperfect the anagram in *Bel Acueil*, it seems unlikely that the embedding of Beatrice of Aragon's name therein is coincidental, because besides the open dedications to her in two other places in the manuscript, further symbolic and numerological references have been uncovered by Leeman Perkins and Jaap van Benthem.[110] Significantly, Mellon transmits a unique spelling of the word *sergent* as *sergant*, that is, with an 'a', without which the anagram does not work.

Returning to the putative anagram in *Pour les biens* that would conceal a 'dedication' to 'Bunoys', one must admit that it would certainly be in the same ludic spirit as the puns and acrostics on Jacqueline's name. Even if we dismiss the possibility of an anagram

---

[107] Canel, 'Histoire de l'anagramme', p. 169.

[108] Lebègue, 'Les anagrammes', pp. 243–4.

[109] See the examples given in Canel, 'Histoire de l'anagramme', pp. 168–71.

[110] Perkins noted the symbolic location of *Bel Acueil* as the first piece in the chansonnier, interpreting it as a song of welcome or greeting for the young princess (*Mellon Chansonnier*, I, pp. 1, 19–20, 32). Jaap van Benthem ('Concerning Johannes Tinctoris and the Preparation of the Princess's Chansonnier', *Tijdschrift van de Vereniging voor Nederlandse Muziekgeschiedenis*, 32 (1982), pp. 24–9) took Perkins's conclusions several steps further in pointing out the correspondence of the first two initials, B and A, with those of her name and the coincidence that the manuscript consists of three sections, each of nineteen pieces and each ending with a reference to Beatrice. The reason for division by nineteen, according to Benthem, is that it represents the numerical equivalent of 'T', the first letter of 'Tinctoris', the compiler and arranger of the manuscript. He also showed that the number of notes in the tenors of several pieces corresponds to the cipher of her name. Worth mentioning, too, is the coincidence that Beatrice of Aragon's initials are those of Busnoys's name in retrograde, something Busnoys was unlikely to have missed.

in *Pour les biens* a number of other factors suggest its connection with Busnoys. First, the iconographic emblem of a boar or swine appears in the contratenor initial of *Pour les biens* and in three other places in Niv, twice in pieces attributed to Busnoys in the manuscript and once in Binchois's *Tout a par moy*.[111] Curiously, the same figure is also found in the Dijon and Copenhagen chansonniers in pieces ascribed to Busnoys. Several examples of these creatures are shown in Figure 2. An attribute of St Anthony Abbot, the swine accompanies him in fifteenth-century illuminations as a symbol of the demons of sensuality and gluttony he vanquished in the desert.[112] Since Anthony Abbot was Busnoys's patron saint, the swine may well represent a kind of iconographic signifier of Busnoys.

Secondly, the fifth and sixth lines of *Pour les biens* correspond to the two opening verses of Busnoys's *Cent mille fois le jour*, cited by Pierre Fabri as an example of the bergerette.[113] As shown in Example 9, the only difference between the two verses is the voice of the persona. Even allowing for the standard clichés of late medieval texts, the likelihood of an intertext here seems strong.[114]

Example 9. Anonymous, *Pour les biens*, lines 5 and 6:

Mille fois le jour a par moy
Je me souhaite vostre dame.

Busnoys, *Cent mille fois*, lines 1 and 2:

Cent mille fois le jour du moins
Je me souhaite o vous, ma dame.

[111] David Fallows has informed me that in his opinion *Tout a par moy* is in the style of neither Binchois nor Frye, and is probably by Busnoys, an attribution that would seem to be corroborated by the iconographical evidence discussed here. There is also the possibility that the artist simply misread or confused the attribution to 'Binchois' as 'Busnois', which still happens frequently today.

[112] G. Ferguson, *Signs and Symbols in Christian Art with Illustrations from Paintings of the Renaissance* (New York, 1954), p. 18.

[113] P. [Le Fèvre, *dit*] Fabri, *Le grand et vrai art de pleine rhétorique*, ed. A. Héron, 3 vols. (Rouen, 1890; repr. Geneva, 1969), II, p. 73.

[114] Significantly, Roh transmits Busnoys's text with a slightly altered incipit: instead of 'Cent mille fois le jour' the incipit reads 'Mille fois le jour', corresponding even more closely with the lines in *Pour les biens*. See Löpelmann, *Die Liederhandschrift*, pp. 152–3. For some thoughts on the intertextuality of fifteenth-century music see Higgins, 'Antoine Busnois', pp. 144–60.

Figure 2 Decorated initials featuring boar or swine in the Dijon Chansonnier (Dij), the Chansonnier Nivelle de La Chaussée (Niv) and the Copenhagen Chansonnier (Cop)

Anon., *Pour les biens*, Niv, fol. xi

Binchois, *Tout a par moy*, Niv, fol. xxvii

Busnoys, *C'est vous en qui*, Niv,
fol. xxxiii^v

Busnoys, *Vous marchez*, Niv, fol. lix

Busnoys, *C'est bien maleur*, Dij, fol. 25   (Busnoys) *Quant vous me ferez*, Cop, fol. 30

Paula Higgins

Perhaps the most striking evidence that *Pour les biens* was written by Jacqueline de Hacqueville lies in its textual similarities to the poem in F-Pn fr. 9223 attributed to another of the dauphine's ladies-in-waiting, Jehanne Filleul (Example 10). Besides being

Example 10. Jehanne Filleul, *Hélas mon amy sur mon ame*, F-Pn fr. 9223, fol. 46.

*Hélas! mon amy, sur mon *ame*
Plus qu'aultre *famme*
J'ay de douleur si largement,
Que nullement
Avoir confort je ne puis *d'ame*

J'ay tant de dueil en ma pencée
Que trespassée
Est ma leesse depiecza:

A l'eure que m'eustes laissée
Seulle esgarée
Tout mon plaisir se trespassa.

Dont maleureuse je me *clame*
Par Nostre *Dame*
D'estre voustre si longuement,
Car clerement
**Je cognoys que trop fort vous *ame*,
Hélas! mon amy [sur mon ame]

(Alas, my friend, I swear
that, more than any other woman,
I have such great pain
that I'll never have any peace of mind.

My mind is full of so much grief
that only [if I were] dead would my sorrow disappear.

The moment you left me alone, cast aside,
All my pleasure ceased

182

Parisian nobles

Of which I proclaim myself unhappy,
by Our Lady,
to be yours for so long,
because clearly,
I see that I love you too much.)

Anonymous, *Pour les biens qu'en vous je parçoy*, Niv, fol. x^v.

Pour les biens qu'en vous je parçoy
*Mon amy je prens sur mon *ame*
**Que tant et si fort je vous *ame*
Que point a demy ne vous voy.

Mille foys le jour a par moy
Je me souhaite vostre *dame*
    Pour les biens

Car s'ainsi estoit sur ma foy
Que jamais il se trouvast *ame*
Qui vist de plus eureuse *femme*
Que je seroye sur ma foy.
      Pour les biens . . .

(For the good things I perceive in you,
my friend, I swear
that I love you so much and so strongly
that you don't see even half of it.

A thousand times a day,
I wish to be your lady.
    For the good things I perceive in you . . .

Because if that were the case, I swear,
one would never find
another woman living
happier than I would be.
    For the good things I perceive in you . . .)

poems in a 'woman's voice', there are obvious resemblances between lines 1 and 16 of *Hélas* and lines 2 and 3 of *Pour les biens* (indicated with asterisks). They also share five rhymes on 'ame': ame (3 times), famme, and dame. In *Hélas* it is the A rhyme; in *Pour les biens*, the B rhyme. Each time the word 'ame' itself recurs as a rhyme in each poem it is used in the same three grammatical senses: as the noun 'soul'; as the verb 'love'; and in the vocative expression 'mon amy . . . sur mon ame'. The rhymes 'ame', 'dame', and 'famme' are of course among the most common in late medieval poetry. But the rhyme 'ame' itself had special significance at Marguerite d'Écosse's court as a pun on her initial 'M', as two poems by her courtier Blosseville make explicit.[115]

The themes of the two poems are clearly dissimilar: in *Hélas* a woman laments the end of a relationship and in *Pour les biens* a woman transparently declares her love. Yet they share a striking directness of expression in addressing the recipient in the second person and of affection in the use of the expression 'je vous ame'. There is no other Busnoys text in the masculine voice in which the lady is addressed so openly as with the words 'I love you' – he cries hot tears, writhes and complains, agonises over her absence, and pleads for her mercy in the most urgent tone, but never does he address a woman saying 'je vous ame'. And it is hardly to be expected that he would, since the persona of *A vous sans autre* admits that he could 'never . . . be so bold' as to tell the woman how he feels. In fact, the closest any of Busnoys's song texts comes to an equivalent expression of intimacy is line 3 of *Ja que lui ne*, 'je l'aime plus qu'assez' (I love him more than enough), for which I shall shortly propose an attribution to Jacqueline de Hacqueville. This is not the place to explore the complex, contradictory, controversial and yet tremendously compelling theory of *écriture féminine*,[116] which

---

[115] *Celle pour qui je porte l'M*, ed. Raynaud, *Rondeaux*, p. 72, and *Vous qui parlés de la beauté d'Elaine*, a complainte on the death of Marguerite d'Écosse, line 6: 'd'une pour qui bien devons priser l'M' (ed. Raynaud, *Rondeaux*, p. 108). Significantly, both of these poems employ the same rhymes on 'ame' as *Hélas mon amy* and *Pour les biens*: ame, dame, fame, blasme, and reclame. These puns were very much in keeping with other rebuses in vogue at the court of Charles VII, such as 'Rien sur L n'a regard', a pun on 'surelle' or 'sorel', the surname of Agnes Sorel, mistress of Charles VII. See Steenackers, *Agnès Sorel et Charles VII*, pp. 340–1.

[116] For the most lucid account of *écriture féminine*, a concept heavily indebted to the work of the French feminist critic Hélène Cixous, see T. Moi, *Sexual/Textual Politics: Feminist Literary Theory* (London, 1985), pp. 102–26. For a cogent critique of *écriture féminine* as a powerful yet problematic literary concept see A. R. Jones, 'Writing the Body: Toward an

suggests that textuality is inextricably linked with sexuality. Suffice it to say for the moment that a more careful scrutiny of the subtle linguistic or contextual differences in medieval texts known to have been written by women could provide important clues to the female authorship of anonymous texts. Some of these possibly gender-specific textual strategies might include: the exaggeration of the traditional humility topos evident in the works of Hildegard of Bingen, Hrotsvitha, and other women writers;[117] the departure from accepted grammatical conventions involving gender, found in the work of Louise Labé (1524?–1566);[118] the feminist revision of myths, such as the alternative version of the creation story that turns up in the poetry of Christine de Pizan and Marie de Romieu (1545?–1590?);[119] and new twists to traditional plots that serve to empower or highlight the actions of women characters, as in the works of Marie de France.[120] Along the same lines, the

Understanding of *l'Ecriture féminine*', *The New Feminist Criticism: Essays on Women, Literature, and Theory*, ed. E. Showalter (New York, 1985), pp. 361–77.

[117] A recent study by J. Ferrante ('Public Postures and Private Maneuvers: Roles Medieval Women Play', *Women and Power in the Middle Ages*, ed. M. Erler and M. Kowaleski (Athens, GA, 1988), pp. 213–29) discusses the subtle rhetorical strategies by which medieval women writers exploited the subordinate roles men expected of them as devices for facilitating self-empowerment. Hildegard and Hrotsvitha, for example, exaggerate the conventional humility topos by excessive use of diminutives and self-deprecatory allusions to themselves as 'poor little women', 'ignorant little things', while at the same time levelling devastating critiques at some of the most powerful men of their day.

[118] Rigolot, pp. 287–98. Rigolot focused on 'the possible misuse of gender forms as a sexually-coded index of self-expression . . . Since Renaissance love discourse has been shared by male and female writers, it seems that one possible approach is to look for bizarre or incongruous elements in female-authored texts and find out if they can be interpreted as revealing sex differentiation.' (p. 288)

[119] By a 'feminist revision' I mean a critical reinterpretation of a woman's role which has traditionally been viewed as negative or subordinate (such as that of Eve) that casts her in a more favourable light or superior position. Perhaps the best example is that which appears in Christine de Pizan's *L'epistre au dieu d'amour* (1399), vv. 245–53, where she claims that woman, and not man, was the superior creation because she was made from better-quality material – a human rib made by God ('le plus noble des choses terrien-nes') – and not from the slime of the earth ('du lymon de la terre'), as Adam was. Significantly, the same twist to the creation story is echoed in Marie de Romieu's *Brief discours: que l'excellence de la femme surpasse celle de l'homme* (1591), vv. 31–6: 'la matière de chair est-elle pas plus belle . . . que n'est celle qui fut formée du limon?' For editions of both poems see *The Defiant Muse: French Feminist Poems from the Middle Ages to the Present: A Bilingual Anthology*, ed. D. C. Stanton (New York, 1986), pp. 14–28 and 46–63. Given the overwhelming tendency in medieval and renaissance culture to view Mary and Eve as bipolar opposites of supreme goodness and evil incarnate, the sympathetic portrayals of Eve by Christine de Pizan in vv. 258–70 of the poem mentioned above are also striking. I plan to discuss these and other examples in a study currently in progress entitled '"From Adam's Rib": Feminist Exegeses of Genesis I–III'.

[120] M. Freeman ('The Power of Sisterhood: Marie de France's "Le Fresne"', *Women and Power in the Middle Ages*, pp. 250–64) demonstrates how Marie de France creates a

predominance of women's names in the acrostics, anagrams and other linguistic cryptograms mentioned here may well offer further evidence of the tendency to fantasise about letters, hieroglyphs and calligraphies apparent in a large number of literary and pictorial works by women from the eleventh to twentieth centuries. Such appropriations of the alphabet, according to Gilbert and Gubar, represent subversive attempts by women to 'authorise' the female signature within a patriarchal system of language that by definition consigned them to the margins or excluded them altogether.[121]

I should like to return now to the poem *Ja que lui ne si actende* (Appendix 1, no. 1), which I mentioned in passing at the outset of this article, concurring with Perkins's assessment of it as 'emblematic' of the courtly love lyric. But is it really? In poems nos. 2–4 the male persona begs the distant lady to 'have pity on me' (no. 2, ll. 5–6), claims that 'never could he be so bold' as to tell her outright what he feels (no. 2, ll. 7–8), tells her to study his poem so that she will 'have mercy on him' (no. 3, ll. 9–11), curses the heavens while drowning in tears because she will not grant him any (no. 3, ll. 14–16) and finally, accusing her of being heartless, renounces her as detestable, vituperable and abominable (no. 4). Given Busnoys's harsh portrayal of the *belle dame sans merci* in these three poems, how do we then account for the poem *Ja que lui ne*? In light of the three references to masculine pronouns in lines 1, 5 and 11 ('Although *he* doesn't expect it . . ., thus *he* has the privilege . . ., *he* will see . . .') the voice is clearly that of a woman.[122] But listen to what she says: 'I love him more than enough for everyone to perceive it . . . More than ever I shall cling so close to his side that he will clearly see that I do ever improve his lot.' What happened to the merciless lady? Is this the aloof, unfeeling Jacqueline portrayed in the other three texts? If Busnoys had indeed written this text ventriloquising the

---

'uniquely feminine' version of a well-known legend by 'revers[ing] the procedures associated with the Griselda model' with the result that 'the domain of women, formerly private, hidden, and inconsequential, has been publicly commemorated'.

[121] See S. Gilbert and S. Gubar, 'Ceremonies of the Alphabet: Female Grandmatologies and the Female Authorgraph', *The Female Autograph*, ed. D. C. Stanton (Chicago, 1987), pp. 21–48. The fact that many of these textual cryptograms are employed by men addressing a female audience seems to corroborate further the idea that women were particularly fascinated with the alphabet and its various permutations.

[122] The argument for the woman's voice in the poem can only be made unequivocally given the context of the other three poems alluding to Jacqueline de Hacqueville and of course presumes a heterosexual relationship. Otherwise the possibility of homosexual interactions would need to be considered seriously.

voice of the woman, as some critics would claim, why would he give her voice only to contradict everything he has said and thereby impugn his own testimony about her? Inasmuch as the courtly love dynamic thrived on the principle of the lady's unattainability, remoteness and, above all, her silence, is there not something peculiarly dissonant about the numerous fifteenth-century song texts in a woman's voice, such as *Ja que lui ne, Pour les biens* and *Hélas mon amy*, that seem to give the lie to the male poet's portrayal of the cruel and indifferent woman by retorting 'but I do love you!' or, lamenting, 'I loved you too much and now you've gone' – all of which seem eerily reminiscent of the directness of expression that characterises several *cansos* by the trobairitz?[123] This is not to suggest a return to the biological essentialism that has traditionally marred the critical reception of women writers by labelling it as 'more emotional', 'confessional' or 'closer to nature' and hence less intellectually challenging than that of male poets. Nor is it to suggest, as did Alfred Jeanroy, that women poets as 'slaves to tradition, incapable of analytic effort' mindlessly 'exploited existing themes' by inverting the gender roles.[124] Rather, it serves to

---

[123] See especially the Countess of Dia's *A chantar m'er de so qu'ieu non volria* and *Estat ai en greu cossirier*, as well as Clara d'Anduza's *En freu esmai et en greu pessamen* in M. Bogin, *The Women Troubadours* (New York and London, 1980), pp. 84–9 and 130–1. As this article was going to press, I came across the recent study by J. Ferrante, 'Notes Toward the Study of a Female Rhetoric in the Trobairitz', *The Voice of the Trobairitz*, ed. W. D. Paden (Philadelphia, 1989), pp. 63–72. Her observations about rhetorical strategies in a small group of troubadours and trobairitz whose periods of literary activity seem to have been roughly contemporaneous reveal that women poets 'rarely use the second person for anyone but the lover', while male poets 'are as likely to address their fellow men as their ladies' (pp. 64–5).

[124] Bogin, *The Women Troubadours*, p. 68. The view that the women troubadours took over male themes and changed the gendered voice is surprisingly prevalent despite its patent invalidity. In an otherwise pioneering and insightful article, Howard Brown ('Women Singers and Women's Songs', p. 77) makes a similar claim about fifteenth-century songs in a woman's voice, which he acknowledges were probably written by women. Moreover, such arguments fail to note the ideas expressed by women that are never expressed by men, or that would be virtually inconceivable coming from men. A study by A. Tavera claims that extremely close readings of texts by the trobairitz, phrase by phrase, word by word, reveal more than a dozen ways in which these poems are completely distinct from those found in pieces by male troubadours. See 'A la recherche des troubadours maudits', *Exclus et systèmes d'exclusion dans la littérature et la civilisation médiévales*, Sénéfiance 5 (Aix-en-Provence, 1978), pp. 137–62. Although the author's perspective is marred by his attribution of these differences to a biologically determined 'feminine' nature, some of his remarks about the specific textual differences are perceptive and worthy of closer examination. The observations of Ferrante (see note 123) further corroborate the idea that there are discernible rhetorical differences in the language employed by the troubadours and trobairitz.

reinforce the observation made by recent scholars that women who dared to write love poetry could not simply 'invert the roles' because the courtly-love tradition by definition demanded their silence. As Ann Rosalind Jones has argued with regard to the renaissance poets Pernette du Guillet and Louise Labé, women poets working within a literary tradition created by and over-whelmingly predominated by men, need 'to be interpreted with an awareness of their authors' specificity as women, a historical speci-ficity shaped by sexual ideologies and the exclusion of women from the world of letters'. Once the gender of the poet changes, the rules of the game are rewritten:

if a woman poet expresses her love for a man in the Neoplatonic mode, she ceases to be the transcendent ideal called upon . . . Likewise, a woman who analyzes her suffering in the absence of her lover, in the Petrarchan mode, reverses the relationship on which Petrarchan poetry depends: the distance and silence of the lady versus the pain and longing, hence the speech, of the lover. To speak as a woman in either of these discourses is to contradict the role they assign to women: the opaque target of the mascu-line gaze, of male desire, of male praise and persuasion. By virtue of their sex, early women poets challenged the rhetorical and symbolic order on which love poetry was based.[125]

What I am proposing, then, is that Jacqueline de Hacqueville probably did have some special meaning for Antoine Busnoys, not necessarily as his mistress or loved one, but rather as a participant in a creative musical-literary exchange with him, of which the texts of the pieces discussed here, *Ja que lui ne* and *Pour les biens*, might be two surviving examples. And if the erotic pseudo-autobiography recurs as a topos in the history of Western literature, it is equally true that a venerable tradition of authentic poetic and epistolary exchanges between men and women dates back to antiquity.[126] Significantly, three of the four poems by women poets in F-Pn fr. 9223 discussed earlier, those by Marie of Cleves, Jammette de

---

[125] A. R. Jones, 'Assimilation with a Difference: Renaissance Women Poets and Literary Influence', *Yale French Studies*, 62 (1981), pp. 135–53.

[126] Some examples include Venantius Fortunatus and Queen Radegunde, St Jerome and Paula, Heloise and Abelard, the troubadours and trobairitz, Christine de Pizan and Eustache Deschamps, Pernette du Guillet and Maurice Scève, Louise Labé and Olivier de Magny, among others. See Dronke, *Medieval Women Writers*, pp. 84–106, for further examples, especially the extraordinary testimony by the biographer of St Jón, first Bishop of northern Iceland (d. 1121), concerning the existence of a traditional game between women and men that involved the exchange of amorous verses in late eleventh-century Iceland (p. 105).

Nesson, and Jehanne Filleul, are lyric exchanges with men (Charles d'Orléans, Tanneguy du Chastel and an anonymous male poet) and contain identical rhyme schemes and intertextual allusions.[127] Another of the woman's songs in the Chansonnier Nivelle de La Chaussée shares similar rhymes and other textual similarities with a poem by C. Blosset preserved in F-Pn fr. 9223.[128]

Whether the Scottish princess's lady-in-waiting, the Parisian noblewoman married to Jean Bochart several decades later, or still another woman was Busnoys's interlocutor are issues that cannot yet be resolved conclusively. The strength of the circumstantial evidence would seem to argue in favour of the lady-in-waiting, but it seems clear that Busnoys could not have written the Hacqueville songs in the 1440s.[129] If we were to admit the possibility that the lady-in-waiting entered the service of Queen Marie d'Anjou after the dauphine's death and remained there well into the 1450s, as did Jehanne Filleul,[130] Prégente de Melun,[131] Marguerite de

---

[127] Although not specifically designated 'réponse', the poem of Madame d'Orléans, 'En la forest de Longue Actente' immediately follows that of Charles d'Orléans on the same theme, and shares many of the same A-rhyme words. The exchange between Jammette de Nesson and Tanneguy du Chastel is explicit. In the margin of the folio where Nesson's poem appears is the inscription: 'la response est de l'autre costé par faulte du relieur.' The relationship between these two poems is even more striking: not only do they share both A and B rhymes, they reproduce every one of the same rhyme words in identical sequence, but in different grammatical context. Especially noteworthy are the incipits of the two poems. Nesson's reads: 'C'est pour me receller les *biens*' and Tanneguy's 'Puis qu'en moy cuidez tant de *biens*', both of which seem to echo the incipit of the anonymous poem 'Pour les *biens* qu'en vous je parçoy' (italics mine). A poem to which Jehanne Filleul's *Hélas mon amy sur mon ame* seems to be a response immediately precedes it in *Le jardin de plaisance*, I, fol. 81[v]. It too contains an allusion to *biens*, in line 3. At least one of these exchanges was initiated by the woman, that of Jammette de Nesson. Similarly, in Machaut's *Voir-dit* it was Toute Belle who launched the exchange of poems by sending Guillaume a rondeau, and significantly, over half the *Voir-dit*'s lyrics are pairs of pieces with related subjects, rhymes and verse forms (see Williams, 'The Lady', p. 465).

[128] *Plus voy mon mignon plus le prise*, Niv, fols. 75[v]–76, shares many rhymes and textual similarities with the poem by C. Blosset, *Plus vous regarde trop plus fort je vous prise* in F-Pn fr. 9223, fol. 53. Compare *Chansonnier Nivelle de La Chaussée* (*Bibliothèque nationale, Paris, Rés. Vmc, ms. 57, ca1460*), ed. P. Higgins (Geneva, 1984), fols. 75[v]–76, with Raynaud, *Rondeaux*, pp. 88–9.

[129] This statement is based solely on received opinion about the datings of manuscripts transmitting his secular works which in turn tend to assume a date of composition relatively close to the date of compilation. We have almost no information about the chronology of Busnoys's works with the exception of *In hydraulis*, which was almost certainly written between 1465 and 1467, and we still have no idea of exactly when he was born.

[130] '[April 1449] A Jehanne Filleul, damoiselle de la Royne, que le roy lui a donné pour lui aidier à avoir robée et soy mectre en point pour aler acompaigner ma dame Helienor d'Escoce en l'Austeriche.' F-Pn fr. 23259, pièce 18. Éléonore d'Écosse était la sœur de the dauphine.

[131] '[February 1447] A Prégente de Meleun, l'une des damoiselles de la Royne, la somme de

Salignac[132] and other of the dauphine's ladies, we come much more comfortably close to a temporal and geographical situation in which the songs could conceivably have been written. Marie d'Anjou, of course, lived almost exclusively in the Loire valley, particularly in the city of Tours, where Busnoys is now known to have been active by 1461 at the latest. Even so, this would still alter somewhat dramatically the existing notions of the chronology of Busnoys's musical output.[133] On the other hand, the Parisian noblewoman herself might very well have been sent to court to serve as a lady-in-waiting to some princess. Daughters of the lesser nobility routinely filled the ranks of ladies-in-waiting to princesses and monarchs and, like their male counterparts, were sent to court to be educated until their marriage. The number of Hacqueville family members who were habitués of French court circles would undoubtedly have facilitated her placement at court.[134] It is also possible that Busnoys himself spent an as yet undocumented period of residence in Paris, as scholars have often surmised, possibly as a student at the university. If such was the case, Busnoys might have been retained as a private tutor to the Hacqueville children, a practice that was especially common among members of the wealthy merchant classes and lesser nobility.

Whether Jacqueline de Hacqueville might also have been a musician and whether her own creativity could conceivably have

---

LXXV L. XVII S. VI D. tournois laquelle somme ledit seigneur lui a donnée ou mois de decembre pour avoir une robe pour elle'. F-Pn fr. 23259, pièce 6. Melun was still in the queen's service in 1461 (F-Pn n.a.f. 9175, fol. 347ᵛ).

[132] Steenackers, *Agnès Sorel*, p. 257, n. 2.

[133] I shall address the broader music-historical implications of a redating of Busnoys's musical activities to the 1450s in my forthcoming *Antoine Busnoys and Musical Culture*. On Busnoys's activity in Tours in 1465 see Higgins, '*In hydraulis*', pp. 70–6. Evidence of his activity in the cathedral of that city by 1461 at the latest comes from an unpublished document discovered by Pamela Starr and discussed in her paper 'Rome as the Center of the Universe', given at the National Meeting of the American Musicological Society, Baltimore, November 1988. Although the document itself is dated February 1461, the incident to which it alludes might well have occurred a year or two earlier.

[134] Jacqueline's father had business connections with the French court (see above, pp. 153–4), her mother's family (the Hennequins) included members of Parlement and royal advisers, and her uncle Jean de Hacqueville was a deputy to Louis XI in Tours in 1463, while Busnoys would have been living there. Given the extraordinary number of lawyers and counsellors in the male line of the Hacqueville-Bochart family, the fact that Jacqueline's great-granddaughter, Suzanne de La Porte (Richelieu's mother), was a lady-in-waiting to Queen Louise of Lorraine in 1580 (de La Chesnaye-Desbois, *Diction-naire de la noblesse*, xv, col. 948) may suggest that a tradition of ladies-in-waiting existed in the female line of the family. Indeed, the Jacqueline and Marguerite de Hacqueville at Marguerite d'Écosse's court in the 1440s may have been related to the Parisian family.

extended into the realm of musical composition are questions that must be sidestepped until we can gain more information about the ultimately more important question that has been generated in this discussion: what role did female poets and musicians play in the literary and musical culture of the late Middle Ages?[135] It is precisely with regard to this question that the 'truth or fiction' of literary characters like Machaut's Toute Belle assume an importance for the music historian that is perhaps lost on the literary critic whose concern is limited to the text itself. According to Machaut, Toute Belle was a gifted young woman from a noble family and 'the best singer born in a hundred years' who allegedly sought him out for his music.[136] And she is sufficiently literate musically to read and perform Machaut's compositions, many of which he claims to have written at her behest. While Machaut does underscore Toute Belle's exceptionality as a singer ('la mieulz chantans qui fust née depuis cent ans'), he fails to note anything at all unusual about a matter of much greater import: she is sufficiently fluent in the reading of polyphonic music to the point that she instantly recognises his attempt to pass off a reworking of an old piece of music under the guise of a new work.[137] If this woman was a product of Machaut's imagination, we need at the very least to ask why it is that he portrays her as being so gifted at music and poetry and, moreover, why he so readily and unabashedly acknowledges that she has the stuff to beat him at his own game. Because the identity of the woman has recently been viewed as a tangential and indeed irrelevant issue, literary critics and music historians alike

---

[135] Other of Busnoys's song texts written from a woman's point of view include: *Joye me fuit et douleur me court seure*, *Seule a par moy en chambre bien parée*, *Ung plus que tous est en mon souvenir* and *Je suis venue vers mon amy* (the last carries a conflicting attribution to Hayne van Ghizeghem). See Brown, 'Women Singers and Women's Songs', p. 76, for a list of songs from the woman's point of view in I-Fn 229.

[136] Williams, 'The Lady, the Lyrics', p. 462; citing Paris, *Le livre du voir-dit*, p. 4.

[137] Unable to keep up with Toute Belle's demands for new music, Machaut sent her an old piece for which he had composed a new tenor and contratenor, but she complained that she had already seen it before and demanded something new. Williams, 'The Lady', p. 464, citing Paris, pp. 242 and 250. The text of the relevant exchange is as follows: (Machaut): 'Je vous envoie un rondel noté, dont je fis pieça le chant et le dit. Sy y ay fait nouvellement teneure et contreteneure. Si, le vueilliez savoir, car il me semble bon.' (Paris, p. 242) (Toute Belle): 'J'ay éu. I. rondel noté que vous m'avez envoié, mais je l'avoie autrefois éu et le scay bien. Si vous prie que vous me vueillez envoier des autres, et se vous avez nuls des virelaiz que vous féistes avant que vous m'éussiez veue, qui soient notez, si m'en vueilliez envoier, car je les ay en grant desir de savoir, et par especial *L'ueil qui est le droit archier.*' (Paris, p. 250)

191

seem to have overlooked the fact that, in its portrayal of Toute Belle as a strong, independent, assertive, exceptionally literate and musically gifted woman, the *Voir-dit* is something of a feminist text.[138] Therefore, unless we must now count Machaut among the prototypical authors of utopian feminist fiction, I think we have to assume that, whether she was Peronne d'Armentières or someone else, Toute Belle must have had some basis in the poet's reality. The literary evidence would concord nicely with the numerous courtly documents from the period alluding to performances by female vocalists and serve in turn to reinforce the notion that these women were indeed capable of performing polyphonic art music, a point about which some music historians remain peculiarly sceptical. Perhaps the fictive Toute Belle was based on a lady-in-waiting at one of the many courts at which Machaut served during his lifetime. This would explain not only her seemingly itinerant existence, but especially her interests in literature and music; for it is undoubtedly in an aristocratic setting that she would have heard the music and poetry of Machaut which prompted her to seek him out in the first place.

Significantly, it is precisely the cultural ambience of the secular princely courts that yielded the literary and musical works of the women troubadours (trobairitz) and trouvères;[139] and it is precisely from the same courtly circles that the professional female virtuoso singer emerged in Italy during the second half of the sixteenth century.[140] The renowned singing ladies at the court of Ferrara appeared officially on the books not as musicians but as 'ladies-in-waiting', a function that scarcely hints at the significance of their vital musical role at court.[141] Similarly, the late renaissance painter Sofonisba Anguissola was employed as a lady-in-waiting to the Queen of Spain.[142] Just as many male composers and artists of the

---

[138] By 'feminist' I mean a text in which women are portrayed in a positive light as intelligent, strong-willed, gifted and accomplished, as opposed to negative portrayals of them as deceitful, destructive, stupid, weak and incompetent. Positive views of women are especially striking within the context of the 'viral antifeminism' and its 'discourse of misogyny' which according to one leading critic 'runs like a rich vein throughout the breadth of medieval literature'. See R. H. Bloch, 'Medieval Misogyny', *Representations*, 20 (1987), p. 1.

[139] See especially Coldwell, '*Jougleresses* and *Trobairitz*', pp. 39–61.

[140] See Newcomb, 'Courtesans, Muses or Musicians?', pp. 90–115.

[141] Newcomb, pp. 93–4.

[142] G. Pollock, *Vision and Difference: Femininity, Feminism and the Histories of Art* (London, 1988), p. 42.

late Middle Ages served secular princes under the rubric *varlet de chambre*,[143] ladies-in-waiting in all likelihood performed analogous roles in the households of princesses. Some of the best-known patrons of fifteenth-century music were women who also wrote poetry, played musical instruments, and had serious interests in polyphonic music, including Beatrice of Aragon,[144] Marie of Burgundy,[145] Marguerite d'Autriche,[146] Isabella d'Este,[147] and Anne of Brittany.[148] It is well known that all of these women employed some of the best-known male composers of their day, and it seems unlikely that they would have chosen to surround themselves with women with whom they shared little in common.[149]

---

[143] Baude Cordier, Hayne van Ghizeghem, Adrien Basin and Antoine de Longueval, among many others.

[144] Beatrice of Aragon was the destinee of the Mellon Chansonnier, as well as the dedicatee of no fewer than three theoretical treatises by Tinctoris. Surely this signals a far greater interest in and understanding of polyphonic music than the passive status she is generally accorded, as patron of music and musicians, would suggest.

[145] Daughter of Charles the Bold, Marie of Burgundy took over the Burgundian court chapel, which included Busnoys, on her father's death in 1477. The court organist Pietre Beurse gave her daily lessons on the clavichord. See Higgins, '*In hydraulis*', p. 68.

[146] On Marguerite d'Autriche's musical education and interests see Picker, *The Chanson Albums of Marguerite of Austria*, pp. 14–15. I too wonder, as does Picker, if Marguerite might have tried her hand at musical composition 'as a natural extension of poetic composition and as a result of her evident interest in music'.

[147] Isabella d'Este sang and played the lute, viol, lira da braccio and keyboard instruments. She employed several of the foremost frottolists of the day, including Bartolomeo Tromboncino and Marchetto Cara, and maintained a continuous correspondence with native Italian poets whose imitations of Petrarch she encouraged and solicited. See W. F. Prizer, 'Isabella d'Este and Lucrezia Borgia as Patrons of Music: The Frottola at Mantua and Ferrara', *Journal of the American Musicological Society*, 38 (1985), pp. 1–33, especially pp. 5, 13, 17, 18, and 30. Prizer's study underscores the major impact Isabella's evidently passionate interests in poetry and music had on the development of the frottola as a genre and on native Italian music in general. Her courtly circle offers a paradigm of how a woman or women operating by necessity in cultural spheres separate from the mainstream (i.e. those cultivated and nurtured by their male consorts) – in this case, secular music, vernacular poetry and *bas instruments*, as opposed to sacred music, Latin texts and *hauts instruments* – could give rise to entirely new styles and genres.

[148] On Anne of Brittany's patronage and musical establishment see S. Bonime, 'Anne de Bretagne (1477–1514) and Music: An Archival Study' (Ph.D. dissertation, Bryn Mawr College, 1975). Unfortunately this study gives no information on Anne's own musical education and interests. Some details of her education, as well as her literary, artistic and musical interests, however, are given in Le Roux de Lincy, 'Détails sur la vie privée d'Anne de Bretagne, femme de Charles VIII et de Louis XII', *Bibliothèque de l'École des Chartes*, 11 (1849), pp. 148–71.

[149] For example, the woman named 'Pacquette' who sang with the two famous blind vielle players at the Burgundian Feast of the Pheasant in 1454 was a lady from the household of the duchess (Isabel of Portugal): 'une damoiselle de l'ostel de ladicte duchesse'. See D. Fallows, 'Specific Information on the Ensembles for Composed Polyphony, 1400–1474', *Studies in the Performance of Late Mediaeval Music*, ed. S. Boorman (Cambridge, 1983),

We need to gain deeper insights into these and many other
questions about the role of women as active agents in the creation
and propagation of musical culture in the late Middle Ages. Surely
one of the most perplexing is the absence of a single musical composition attributed to a woman between *c.* 1300 and 1566,[150] followed by a proliferation of publications of polyphonic music by
women from 1566 on.[151] Can these really be the fruits of a musical
creativity sprung forth fully formed from a musical void? There is
little question but that further investigation into the daily musical
activities in female convents, monasteries and béguinages,[152]
studies of the musical manuscripts produced therein,[153] inventories
of women's libraries,[154] and a closer scrutiny of court payment
records of various princesses will shed important light on issues

p. 139. Similarly, among the chansons sung at the wedding festivities for Charles the
Bold and Margaret of York in 1468 was *Bien venue la belle bergère* sung for Margaret by
Madame de Beaugrant, the governess of Charles's daughter Mary, riding a lion who
sang the tenor. See R. Strohm, *Music in Late Medieval Bruges* (Oxford, 1985), p. 99.

[150] The explanation proposed by Coldwell ('*Jougleresses* and *Trobairitz*', p. 55) that 'when
Salic law prohibited the passage of the French crown through women, women were no
longer able to compete as composers with men' clearly begs many questions.

[151] On publications by women composers in Italy see Bowers, 'The Emergence of Women
Composers', pp. 116–67.

[152] Fundamental studies include M. Brenet's pioneering 'La musique dans les couvents de
femmes depuis le moyen âge à nos jours', *La Tribune de Saint-Gervais*, 4 (1898), pp. 25–31,
58–61, 73–81; Rokseth, 'Les femmes musiciennes'; and A. B. Yardley, '"Ful weel she
soong the service dyvyne": The Cloistered Musician in the Middle Ages', *Women Making
Music*, pp. 15–38, which despite the author's unduly modest claim to the contrary (p. 30)
shows more than ample cause for a major revision in the common understanding of
sacred music in the Middle Ages. Strohm (*Music in Late Medieval Bruges*, pp. 62, 70, 107
and 160, nn. 8 and 9) drew attention to the musical activities of the Rich Clares and the
béguines of Bruges as music teachers, music scribes, performers, and possibly conduits of
polyphonic music.

[153] Studies of musical manuscripts produced in female monasteries and convents will shed
some sorely needed light on the thoroughly unexplored subject of women's musical
literacy and creativity in the late Middle Ages. See Yardley, '"Ful weel"', pp. 26–7, for a
working list of polyphony surviving in manuscripts from medieval nunneries.

[154] A recent study attempting to assess the extent of women's ownership of manuscripts is
that of S. G. Bell, 'Medieval Women Book Owners: Arbiters of Lay Piety and Ambas-
sadors of Culture', *Women and Power in the Middle Ages*, ed. Erler and Kowaleski, pp. 149–
87. The number of women destinees of music manuscripts of the fifteenth century speaks
strongly in favour of a high level of musical literacy among elite and noble women. The
most notable examples include: the Mellon Chansonnier (Beatrice of Aragon); the
chansonniers B-Br 228 and 11239 (Marguerite d'Autriche); and F-Pn fr. 1596
(Marguerite d'Orléans). The devotional song-motet, *Ave regina* by Walter Frye, which
opens both the Wolfenbüttel and Laborde chansonniers could signal the destination of
both manuscripts for female aristocratic patrons. Significantly, the Pixérécourt chansonnier (F-Pn fr. 15123), the shape of whose Italian shield identifies its owner as a woman,
also opens with a song-motet: *O pulcherrima mulierum*. The textual allusions to the virgin
Mary, queen of heaven, in these dedicatory pieces could well signal their destination for
terrestrial female magnates.

relating to the creation and diffusion of music by late medieval women.

I should like to conclude with two images that illustrate the central points raised here. On the cover of a recent collection of essays entitled *Rewriting the Renaissance*, there is a famous drawing of Sir Thomas More's family by Hans Holbein. The central position in the drawing is occupied by Margaret Giggs, More's adopted daughter and a Greek scholar, who is bending over More's father and pointing out something in a book. In a later oil-painting of the same drawing the woman who had figured so prominently in the original was relegated to the margins.[155] I am reminded of a well-known photograph of the aging Liszt in which he is seated at a piano in Weimar, hands poised to begin a musical work. On seeing a print of virtually the same picture I was stunned to discover that Liszt is not alone in the room: scarcely three feet away is a striking woman violinist who, on further investigation, proved to be one Arma Senkrah, née Harness. Long consigned to music-historical oblivion, Senkrah was a Canadian virtuoso who toured extensively in Europe during the 1880s, and who in 1885 was an habituée of the circle of Liszt, with whom she performed publicly.[156] These random examples of how women have been literally 'cut out of the picture' are powerful metaphors of how they have tended in the past to be seen as marginal and dispensable to the historical enterprise. Music historians have always recognised the necessity of placing the study of music within its appropriate cultural and historical contexts. Perhaps it is now time to acknowledge that the historical variable of gender, once shifted to the centre of a critical discourse, cannot fail to have an unexpected and often powerfully transformative impact on our understanding of music not only in the late Middle Ages, but throughout the history of Western culture.

University of Notre Dame

---

[155] Ferguson, Quilligan and Vickers, eds., *Rewriting the Renaissance*, p. x.

[156] See *Franz Liszt: Briefe aus ungarischen Sammlungen, 1835–1886*, ed. M. Prahacs (Kassel etc., 1966), Brief 589, pp. 283 and 446. The most recent study of Liszt, E. Burger's *Franz Liszt: A Chronicle of his Life in Pictures and Documents* (Princeton, 1989), includes a full-page reproduction of the photograph in question (picture no. 607), together with a quotation from August Stradal's memoirs. Stradal suggested that Senkrah had 'dragged [Liszt] off to the photographer's studio' where the photograph was taken and subsequently distributed copies of it autographed by Liszt for publicity purposes, thus accounting for the fact that she always played to full houses throughout Europe. Curiously, Burger fails to mention whether Albert Morris Bagby and Brod Korb, who flank Liszt at the piano in a photograph taken in the same studio (picture no. 606), had also coerced Liszt there. Perhaps Senkrah had dragged them there on the same occasion as well.

APPENDIX I

The Hacqueville songs: texts and translations

1.
Ja que lui ne si actende[1]
Car tous autres sont cassez
Et je l'aime plus qu'assez
Affin que chascun l'entende.

Aussi il a tel renom
de porter a sa plaisance

Deux des lectres de mon nom
L'une perse et l'autre blanche.

Plus que jamais de sa bende
Me tendray et de si pres
Qu'il voirra bien par expres
Que son fait tousiours amende.
 Ja que lui ne . . .

(Although he doesn't expect it,
For all others have been driven to despair,
I love him more than enough
For everyone to perceive it.

Moreover he has the privilege
Of wearing at his pleasure

Two of the letters of my name:
One blue and the other white

More than ever I shall cling
so close to his side
that he will clearly see
That I do ever improve his lot.
 Although he doesn't expect it . . .)

---

[1] Dij, fols. 61ᵛ–62ʳ.

2.

A vous sans autre me viens rendre[2]
Il m'est force qu'ainsi le face
A ce me contraint votre grace
Qui tant est belle doulce et ten[d]re

Vueillez vo pitié condescendre
Envers moi qui de prime face
    A vous sans autre . . .

Le vous dire n'ose entreprendre
Jamais en moi n'eust tant d'audace
Ne au moins pretendant estre en grace
En tant que honneur se peut estendre
    A vous sans autre . . .

(To you and no other I come in surrender;
So must I do perforce.
To this your grace constrains me,
[your grace] which is so gentle, sweet and tender.

Please deign to have pity
Upon me, who, at first sight
    To you and no other I come in surrender . . .

I dare not tell you how I feel
Never could I be so bold
Aspiring nevertheless to be in your favour –
To the extent that honour will allow.
    To you and no other I come in surrender . . .)

---

[2]   Dij, fols. 21^v–22^r.

3.

Je ne puis vivre ainsi tousiours[3]
Au mains que j'aye en mes doulours
Quelque confort
Une seule heure au mains au fort
Et tous les jours
Leaument serviray amours
Jusqu'à la mort.

Noble femme de non et d'armes
Estripvez à ce dicté cy

Des jeulx pleurant à chaudes larmes
Affin qu'aiez de moi mercy.

Quant a moy je me meurs bon cours
Veillant les nuitz faisant cent tours
En criant fort
Vengence à dieu, car à grant tort
Je noye en plours
Lors qu'au besoing me fault secours
Et pitié dort.
            Je ne puis vivre . . .

(I cannot live like this forever
Unless I have some comfort for my pain
Just one hour, or less – or more
And every day
I'll serve the god of love faithfully
Unto death.

Woman, noble in name and arms,
pay close attention to this poem

so that, eyes streaming with hot tears
you may have mercy on me

As to me, I am wasting away,
Awake at night, walking in a hundred circles
Crying aloud to God
Vengeance! for most unjustly
I'm drowning in tears.
Just when I need it
I get no help,
And Pity sleeps.
            I cannot live like this forever . . .)

[3]   Dij, fols. 37ᵛ–39ʳ.

4.

A que ville est abhominable[4]
Est en amours ung cueur publique
Il n'est chose plus detestable
   A que ville . . .

Car le traictié est reprouchable
A decevoir chacun s'aplicque
   A que ville . . .

Madame en a ung miserable
Qui est tout tel en sa pratique
Dont elle [est] moult vituperable.
   A que ville . . .

(Ah, how vile and abominable
in love is a public heart,
Nothing, I think, is more detestable.

Because the declaration is reprehensible,
seeking [as it does] to deceive everyone
   Ah, how vile and abominable . . .

My lady has a pretty miserable [heart],
which is entirely in keeping with her behaviour,
for which she is most deserving of vituperation.
   Ah, how vile and abominable . . .)

APPENDIX 2

Children of Jacques de Hacqueville and Gillette Hennequin
(from *Succession* of Jacques de Hacqueville, 6 June 1482; Paris, Archives
   Nationales, Minutier Central de la Ville de Paris, Étude viii/4)
(1) 'Maistre Henry de Hacqueville maistre ès arts, religieux en l'eglise de
   Fontaines les Meaulx'
(2) 'Jehan de Hacqueville mineur d'ans'
(3) Katherine, wife of 'Jehan Laisé, seigneur de Précy'
(4) 'Raoul de Hacqueville trésorier du camp du roy nostre dit seigneur'[5]
(5) Jehanne, wife of 'Gauchier Vivien marchand bourgeois de Paris'[6]
(6) Jacqueline, wife of 'Maistre Jehan Bouchart, conseiller du Roy nostre
   dit seigneur en sa court de parlement'

---

[4] Dij, fols. 18ᵛ–19ʳ.
[5] He was already in this position by 3 August 1481. See F-Pan KK 63, fol. 128ᵛ. He was a
   lay *marguiller* in the church of St-Severin in 1493.
[6] She later became abbess of the Abbey of Longchamps. See *Gallia christiana* (note 38
   above), vii, col. 947. In 1504 she renounced her right to inheritance in favour of the
   abbey (F-Pan MC Étude viii/8).

(7) Charlotte, wife of 'Maistre Jaques de Wignacourt, notaire et secretaire du Roy nostre dit seigneur et controlleur de sa chancelerie ou palais à Paris'[7]

(8) 'Maistre Nicole de Hacqueville aussi conseiller du Roy nostre dit seigneur en sa dicte court de parlement et chanoine en l'eglise de Paris'[8]

(9) Ragonde, wife of 'Maistre Pierre Poingnant semblablement conseiller dicellui seigneur en ladicte court'[9]

---

[7] For a lengthy biographical entry on Wignacourt see A. Lapeyre and R. Scheurer, *Les notaires et secrétaires du roi sous Louis XI, Charles VIII, et Louis XII, 1461–1515: Notices personnels et généalogiques*, 2 vols. (Paris, 1978), II, p. 318, no. 668.

[8] For additional information see *Gallia christiana*, VII, cols. 154 and 836.

[9] For further information on Pierre Poignant, see Maugis, *Histoire du Parlement de Paris*, III, p. 112. He is not to be confused with his son Pierre le jeune, who was married to Guillemine La Grasse. Poignant the elder died before 1497 and after his death Ragonde de Hacqueville married Jean de Miraulmont.

Early Music History (1991) Volume 10

SUSAN RANKIN

THE EARLIEST SOURCES OF NOTKER'S SEQUENCES: ST GALLEN, VADIANA 317, AND PARIS, BIBLIOTHÈQUE NATIONALE LAT. 10587*

Iste libellus habet versus modulaminis apti
Ut ventum teneat qui velit esse tenax

'This little book has verses of composed *modulamen*, so that he who wishes to be retentive may hold on to his breath.' With this elegiac distich Notker Balbulus concluded the preface dedicating his *Liber ymnorum* to Liutward, Bishop of Vercelli, abbot of Bobbio, archchaplain and chancellor to the then emperor, Charles the Fat.[1] The collection of sequences must have been sent to Liutward during 884, since by December of that year Notker had broken off work on his *Metrum de vita sancti Galli*, mentioned in the preface to the *Liber ymnorum* as in the process of preparation.[2] The genesis of the book of sequences can be traced farther back: Notker tells in his preface how, on showing verses to his teacher Iso, corrections were pro-

---

* I would like to dedicate this study to Helmut Hucke, for whose sixtieth birthday its first version was prepared.
[1] The classic edition and study of the *Liber ymnorum* is by W. von den Steinen, *Notker der Dichter und seine geistige Welt*, 2 vols. (Berne, 1948). See also R. L. Crocker, *The Early Medieval Sequence* (Berkeley, 1977), with an English translation of Notker's preface (pp. 1–2). In the distichon reproduced above, *modulamen* (meaning 'melody' or the like) is used in the genitive singular; the translation is thus more literal than that of Von den Steinen: 'Dies Büchlein bringt Verse mit zugehörigem melodischem Vortrag' (*Notker der Dichter*, II, p. 11), where *mit* corresponds less directly to a music–text relationship in which the quintessential factor is that texts are composed to fit pre-existent melodies. I thank David Howlett and Michael Lapidge for their advice on the translation of this distich.
[2] Von den Steinen, *Notker der Dichter*, I, pp. 507, 526. On Notker's literary works see P. Stotz and H. Haefele, 'Notker I. von St Gallen', *Die deutsche Literatur des Mittelalters Verfasserlexikon*, VI (2nd edn, Berlin and New York, 1987), cols. 1186–210.

201

posed. Later he presented some 'little verses' to his teacher Marcellus (the Irish monk Moengal) who 'with joy' collected them on parchment scrolls (*rotulae*) and gave them to his students to sing. Marcellus died at St Gallen in 871, Iso in the same year at the monastery of Moutier-Grandval, where he had been sent to teach some time previously.[3] Many of the 'versus modulaminis apti' must have been composed already by 871.

In its explanation of the development of the artistic personality, the preface to the *Liber ymnorum* remains one of the most fascinating historical sources of the ninth century. The very fact of its existence, as well as the detail of Notker's preface, stimulates inquiry in many directions. For the history of musical transmission in the early Middle Ages, those questions range from the most concrete to conceptual aspects. Did the *Liber ymnorum*, in its original form of 884, contain musical notation?[4] What was, by that time, the state and manner of use of musical notation at St Gallen – by then the home of a large scriptorium, rich in books and favoured by the younger members of the Carolingian dynasty?[5] And in what way did Notker understand the relation of melodies to verses, and, in consequence, the potential relation between written music and written text? If the practice in East Frankish prosers of notating sequence melismas in unbroken neume groups beside the texts sung to them rather than above the text (as in early chant books and, from that point on, most Western notations up to the present day) goes back to Notker's time, then it may be explained as the outcome of a conceptual division inherent in Notker's explanation of his compositional procedure (or that proposed by Iso): 'Singulae

[3] The date of Iso's departure from St Gallen is not known. During that period when both Iso and Moengal taught at St Gallen, the Irish monk had the responsibility for the inner (monastic) school, the native Alemann that of the outer (canonic) school. On Iso see especially J. Duft, 'Iso monachus – doctor nominatissimus', *Churrätisches und st. gallisches Mittelalter: Festschrift für Otto P. Clavadetscher*, ed. H. Maurer (Sigmaringen, 1984), pp. 129–71.

[4] For the most recent discussions see H. Hucke, 'Die Anfänge der Bearbeitung', *Schweizer Jahrbuch für Musikwissenschaft*, 3 (1982), pp. 15–20, and 'Zur melodischen Überlieferung der Tropen', *Liturgische Tropen*, ed. G. Silagi, Münchener Beiträge zur Mediävistik und Renaissance-Forschung 36 (Munich, 1985), pp. 107–24; A. Haug, *Gesungene und schriftlich dargestellte Sequenz: Beobachtungen zum Schriftbild der ältesten ostfränkischen Sequenzenhandschriften* (Neuhausen-Stuttgart, 1987), especially 'Notker und die Neumenschrift', pp. 20–1.

[5] On Latin literary culture at St Gallen see W. Berschin, *Eremus und Insula: St Gallen und die Reichenau im Mittelalter – Modell einer lateinischen Literaturlandschaft* (Wiesbaden, 1987), with detailed bibliography. On script and literacy at St Gallen see R. McKitterick, *The Carolingians and the Written Word* (Cambridge, 1989), *passim*, especially ch. 3.

motus cantilenae singulas syllabas debent habere'.[6] As described and as transmitted, these 'versus modulaminis apti' involve the bringing together of two distinct arts, poetry and music.

Moving from St Gallen to a more European dimension, Notker's story of the monk of Jumièges who, fleeing from the Viking onslaught, brought to St Gallen an antiphoner 'in quo aliqui versus ad sequentias erant modulati' has led to discussion of whether the French antiphoner contained musical notation or not.[7] After repeated attacks along the Seine during the decade after 841, the Normans established their domination in the whole area surrounding Jumièges (which lies relatively close to the mouth of the Seine). The years 856–62 brought the worst and most far-reaching invasions into Frankish territory. We do not know at what date the monks of Jumièges finally abandoned their home, but those of the neighbouring abbey of St Wandrille fled when their buildings were burned in January 857. The *latest* date of copying of the 'Jumièges Antiphoner' must be estimated in the 850s, thus very close to the earliest 'dated' neume notations and fifty years earlier than the first *extant* notated chant books. And yet, what could Notker's words 'in which verses to the sequences were artfully formulated' mean but that the 'sequences' to which he refers were notated?

While our knowledge of the Jumièges Antiphoner is unlikely ever to reach beyond speculation, study of the early transmission of the *Liber ymnorum* may help to answer crucial questions about East Frankish musical culture in the late ninth century. Until now, however, no sources of either Notker's verses or the dedicatory preface have been recognised as copied before the mid-tenth century;[8] a troper and proser from the Benedictine monastery of St

---

6   On the contrast between East and West Frankish patterns of transmission, and their relation to compositional procedures, see K. Schlager, 'Beobachtungen zur frühen Sequenz in ost- und westfränkischer Überlieferung', *Gordon Athol Anderson (1929–1981): In memoriam*, 2 vols. ed. L. Dittmer, Musicological Studies 39 (Henryville, Ottawa and Binningen, 1984), pp. 531–43.

7   See especially Hucke, 'Überlieferung', pp. 107–8. On the authenticity of Notker's report see Johannes Duft, 'Le "Presbyter de Gimedia" apporte son antiphonaire à Saint-Gall', *Jumièges: Congrès scientifique du XIIIe centenaire*, 2 vols. (Rouen, 1955), II, pp. 925–36, and 'Wie Notker zu den Sequenzen kam', *Zeitschrift für schweizerische Kirchengeschichte*, 56 (1962), pp. 201–14.

8   W. von den Steinen, 'Die Anfänge der Sequenzendichtung', *Zeitschrift für schweizerische Kirchengeschichte*, 40 (1946), pp. 190–212 and 241–68, especially 253; 41 (1947), pp. 19–48 and 122–62; see also Von den Steinen, *Notker der Dichter*, II, pp. 192ff, 'Zur Überlieferungsgeschichte des Liber ymnorum', and Crocker, *Early Medieval Sequence*, pp. 5 and 425–6.

Susan Rankin

Alban at Mainz (London, British Library, Add. MS 19768) dating from this period includes fourteen of Notker's sequences, while the prosers in St Gallen, Stiftsbibliothek, MS 381, and Einsiedeln, Stiftsbibliothek, MS 121, both copied in the last quarter of the tenth century, have been considered the earliest extant witnesses of Notker's dedication and preface.

But there exist two earlier sources which have hardly been taken into account, the first unnoticed in the Vadiana collection in St Gallen until Bernhard Bischoff recognised the texts as Notker's (in his catalogue of 1864, Scherrer had given the text incipits under the title 'Sechs Hymnen mit alten Musikzeichen'),[9] the second neglected – presumably because of its fragmentary state – and wrongly dated in the standard publications.[10] Both St Gallen, Vadiana 317, and Paris, Bibliothèque Nationale, MS fonds lat. 10587, date from the late ninth–early tenth century, this second without any doubt copied during Notker's lifetime (d. 912). Thus, the long gap between Notker's attested but lost collection of the 880s and the mid- to late tenth-century sources vanishes. Indeed, the possibility that the original dedicatory copy of the *Liber ymnorum* still exists, albeit in fragmentary form, is proposed by Hartmut Hoffmann in connection with his revised dating of the Paris manuscript.[11] Whether the actual dedicatory copy or not, this Paris fragment constitutes the first part of a proser arranged in typical St Gallen fashion: dedication, preface, incipit notice, followed by sequences in liturgical order. The Vadiana manuscript, on the other hand, shows a different form of transmission: a small collection of sequences copied into blank pages in a non-liturgical context.

These two sources bring important new aspects to the discussion of the early transmission of Notker's sequences, especially since

[9] G. Scherrer, *Verzeichniss der Manuscripte und Incunabeln der Vadianischen Bibliothek in St Gallen* (St Gallen, 1864), pp. 84–6; B. Bischoff, 'Bücher am Hofe Ludwigs des Deutschen und die Privatbibliothek des Kanzlers Grimalt', *Mittelalterliche Studien*, 3 (Stuttgart, 1981), pp. 187–212, especially 199. The Vadiana collection is housed in the Kantonsbibliothek (earlier the Stadtbibliothek). I thank Frau Helen Thurnheer of the Kantonsbibliothek for her kind assistance during my visits to the library. I also thank Bernhard Bischoff for his generous help concerning the dating of hands in the Vadiana manuscript.

[10] Although used by Von den Steinen for his *Liber ymnorum* edition, the fragment was not mentioned in H. Husmann, *Tropen- und Sequenzenhandschriften*, RISM B/v/1 (Munich, 1964). On the dating, see under the manuscript description below.

[11] H. Hoffmann, *Buchkunst und Königtum im ottonischen und frühsalischen Reich*, 2 vols. (Stuttgart, 1986), I, p. 390. I am most grateful to Professor Hoffmann for sending me copies of his photographs from the Paris manuscript.

both contain musical notation. In view of their significance as the two earliest witnesses of Notker's soon famous compositions, I shall present here descriptions of the codicological situation of the two sources and discussion of their origins. The consequences of the redating of Paris 10587 for our knowledge of the original *Liber ymnorum*, in particular its dedication notice and layers within its repertory, are studied; and, finally, I return to the discussion of musical notation at St Gallen and transmission of the sequence repertory.

ST GALLEN, VADIANA 317 (V)

The present codex is a miscellany and contains the following items:[12]

(1) fols. 1ʳ–13ʳ: *Ammonitiones sancti Basilii*
(2) fols. 13ᵛ–15ᵛ: sequences (without rubrics or melody titles):

Festa Christi (str. A–8 only)	[Epiphany]
Summi triumphum	[Ascension]

This has neumes over the first line (syllabic notation), and in the margin line by line down to str. 10 (melismatic notation), all in the same ink as the text. The first melismatic group is written above the capitals A E U A.

Laurenti David magni martyr	[St Laurence, 10 August]
Dilecte Deo Galle perenni	[St Gallen, 16 October]
Laude dignum	[St Otmar, 16 November]
Quid tu virgo mater	[for a martyr]

Immediately following this, lines 9–18 of fol. 15ᵛ show signs of erasure. Fols. 13ᵛ and 14ʳ are reproduced in Figure 1.

(3) fol. 15ᵛ, lines 19–22: Boethius, *Consolatio*, book 3, carmen 7, ll. 1–6
INCIPIT VERSUS BOETII/HABIT HOC VOLUPTAS OMNIS . . .
6 lines only; in the same hand as the sequences.
(4) fols. 16ʳ–23ᵛ: *Vita sancti Findani*
(5) 12 blank paper pages
(6) fols. 24ʳ–55ᵛ: *Acta apostolorum*
Begins and ends incomplete (ch. 6.5–28.20).
(7) 6 blank paper pages
(8) fols. 56ʳ–68ᵛ: *Ammonitio sancti Pauli qualiter demonstraverat ei dominus videri bonum et malum*
(9) fol. 68ᵛ: hymn *Ut queant laxis*
In a tiny script of s. xi.

---

[12] See the entries in Scherrer, *Vadianische Bibliothek*, pp. 84–6, and A. Bruckner, *Schreibschulen der Diözese Konstanz: St Gallen*, Scriptoria Medii Aevi Helvetica: Denkmäler Schweizerischer Schreibkunst des Mittelalters 2–3 (Geneva, 1936 and 1938), II, p. 54.

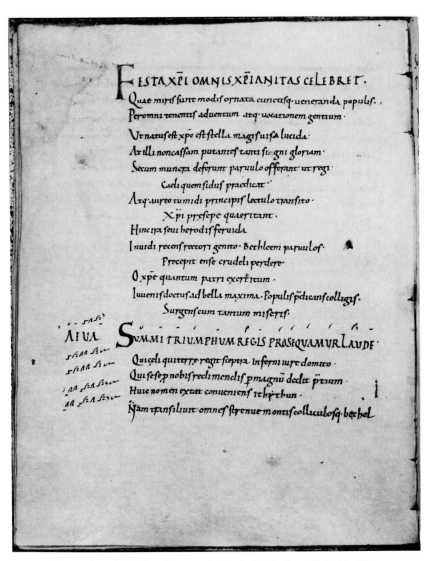

Figure 1a   St Gallen, Kantonsbibliothek, Vadiana 317, fol. 13ᵛ

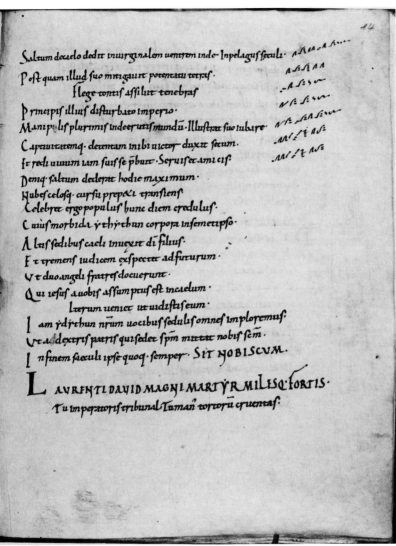

Figure 1b   Vadiana 317, fol. 14^r

(10) fols. 69^r–^{v}: pen trials
   The recto is very much discoloured, suggesting that it might once have served as an outside cover.
(11) fols. 70^r–77^v: *Liber magni Aurelii Casseodori Senatoris de Anima*
(12) fols. 78^r–86^v: *Andreae Presbyteri Chronicon*
   Incomplete: missing the first and last folio.

Some of these fascicles may not have been brought together before the mid-fifteenth century. The binding incorporates part of a fourteenth-century charter across the spine, while paper leaves bound inside the volume (see items 5 and 7 above) have a crown watermark found on papers from southern German and Swiss regions during the period 1454–70.[13] All parts of the codex were copied between the mid-ninth century and the end of the tenth; some are written in St Gallen book hands, while at least one (item 12) was copied by a hand trained further south, in Chur or northern Italy.

The sequences and fragment of one of Boethius' songs were copied into pages left blank after the *Ammonitiones Sancti Basilii*. The *Ammonitiones*, sequences and song fragment are contained within the first two gatherings, of eight and then seven folios; of a sixteenth folio – which presumably contained the continuation of the *Versus Boetii* – only a stub remains. One other part of Codex 317 appears closely linked with these first two gatherings; the quaternion constituted by fols. 70–7 (item 11) has the same dimensions, ruling and number of lines per page (22). The hand is also very similar to that which copied the *Ammonitiones Sancti Basilii*.[14] Items 1 and 11 are thus likely to have been copied in the same place during the same period.

That this copy of the *Ammonitiones Sancti Basilii* was in St Gallen by the late ninth century is confirmed by Bischoff's identification of it as part of a volume once owned by Grimald, abbot of St Gallen from 841 until his death in 872.[15] One of the most influential men ever to be associated with the abbey, Grimald held key posts under two successive Carolingian kings, as chaplain to Louis the Pious, then as chancellor (833) and later archchaplain (848) to Louis the

---

[13] The watermark is Crown-I, 325a, in G. Piccard, *Die Kronenwasserzeichen, Findbuch I* (Stuttgart, 1961).
[14] Scherrer, *Vadiana*, p. 86, and Bruckner, *Schreibschulen*, II, p. 54.
[15] Bischoff, 'Bücher', p. 199.

German.[16] Grimald bequeathed his personal collection of books to the abbey; according to a list copied between 883 and 896 (Stiftsbibliothek 267, pp. 30–2), this ran to thirty-four volumes.[17] The list includes the item *Librum Valerii Cimiliensis episcopi et de vita Karoli imperatoris et Admonitiones sancti Basilii in una sceda*, identified by Bischoff as Vatican City, Biblioteca Apostolica Vaticana, MS Reg. lat. 339, fols. 7–38, and Vadiana 317, pp. 1–25. According to the description, Grimald's volume had no solid binding, but was preserved 'in una sceda' – literally a sheet (presumably of parchment). Later, like many of his books, this was taken apart and recombined with other material, only one part remaining in St Gallen.[18]

It is not known precisely where the named texts were copied; a chrismon drawn twice on fol. 13ʳ of Vadiana 317 is close to that used by Dominicus, a notary working in Regensburg, the home of Louis's court.[19] However, the group of sequences and Boethius verses were added after Grimald's death; the thin and untidy hand bears the characteristics of early tenth-century work.[20] By this time the two gatherings containing the *Ammonitiones sancti Basilii* were most likely in the monastic library at St Gallen.

Among the six sequences are included two in honour of St Gallen's most highly venerated saints: Gallus, Irish monk and founder of the abbey,[21] and Otmar, the first abbot (719–59, elected abbot 744). The Otmar sequence, *Laude dignum*, was probably composed not by Notker but by a younger person within his immediate circle, one extremely familiar with Notker's poetic technique (Von den Steinen's *Andreasdichter*). The other five sequences, for the feasts of

16 In addition to Bischoff, 'Bücher', see the entry for Grimald in J. Duft, A. Gossi and W. Vogler, *Die Abtei St Gallen* (St Gallen, 1986), pp. 105–7, and D. Geuenich, 'Beobachtungen zu Grimald von St Gallen, Erzkappelan und Oberkanzler Ludwigs des Deutschen', *Litterae medii aevi: Festschrift für Johanne Autenrieth*, ed. M. Borgolte and H. Spilling (Sigmaringen, 1988), pp. 55–68.

17 The list is edited by P. Lehmann, *Mittelalterliche Bibliothekskataloge Deutschlands und der Schweiz*, I: *Die Bistümer Konstanz und Chur* (Munich, 1918), pp. 87–9.

18 Bischoff, 'Bücher', pp. 193ff.

19 Bischoff, 'Bücher', p. 212.

20 In a letter of 14 February 1987 Bischoff revises his earlier opinion of the date of this hand; in *Mittelalterliche Studien* (p. 199), he had estimated that the sequences were added towards the end of the ninth century.

21 Recent discussion has confirmed the older, much disputed tradition that Gallus had come from Ireland with Columbanus; see W. Berschin, 'Gallus abbas vindicatus', *Historisches Jahrbuch*, 95 (1975), pp. 257–77.

Epiphany, Ascension, Laurence, Gallus and a martyr, are all Notker's own.

The first sequence to be copied, *Festa Christi*, is incomplete, lacking the five concluding strophes. The texts of this and the following four sequences (i.e. all except *Quid tu virgo*) contain a number of serious errors, as well as variants from other St Gallen sources; the texts are collated with Von den Steinen's edition in the Appendix. These text errors frequently involve the inclusion of one or more extra letters (*surgens* for *sugens*: *Festa Christi*; *coniunctorum* for *coniunctum*: *Laude dignum*). Traces remaining after erasure show how in several places someone corrected some of these mistakes (*singni* corrected to *signi*: *Festa Christi*; *manipulis* corrected to *maniplis*: *Summi triumphum*). A further level of error involved the wrong division of words, creating nonsense (*sidu seximium* for *sidus eximium*: *Laude dignum*; *placere pleas* for *pace repleas*: *Dilecte Deo Galle*). Lastly, ae is sometimes written out, sometimes replaced by e with *cauda*, but very often written as plain e; this is all the more surprising, given that, throughout the ninth and tenth centuries, St Gallen copyists took great care to use ae or e *caudata* where necessary.

Was this the work of a young or incompetent scribe, someone who barely understood the Latin words he copied (or heard)? Or was the scribe working from an already corrupt exemplar and himself trying to correct the text as he went along? The first five texts are all laid out in verse lines, with the first and often the last line in rustic capitals, as was the practice at St Gallen. That part of the sixth text (*Quid tu virgo*) which appears on fol. 15^v is not arranged in this way, but copied continuously with as many words as possible on each ruled line. This more economic use of space might have been forced on the scribe by the presence of something else (now erased) on lines 9–18 of the page. It might, at the same time, relate to the use of two different exemplars for the first five and the sixth sequences; for *Quid tu virgo* has *no* errors, variants from St Gallen readings, or e's lacking *caudae* in the relevant places.

The neumes written alongside *Summi triumphum* transmit the same melodic version as later St Gallen sources (see Figure 2), except for strophe 3, 'Huic nomen', where V has the long melisma corresponding to strophe 4 rather than the relevant shorter version; this can surely be considered a simple copying error. In typical St Gallen fashion, the word *Alleluia* is shortened to AEUA (rather

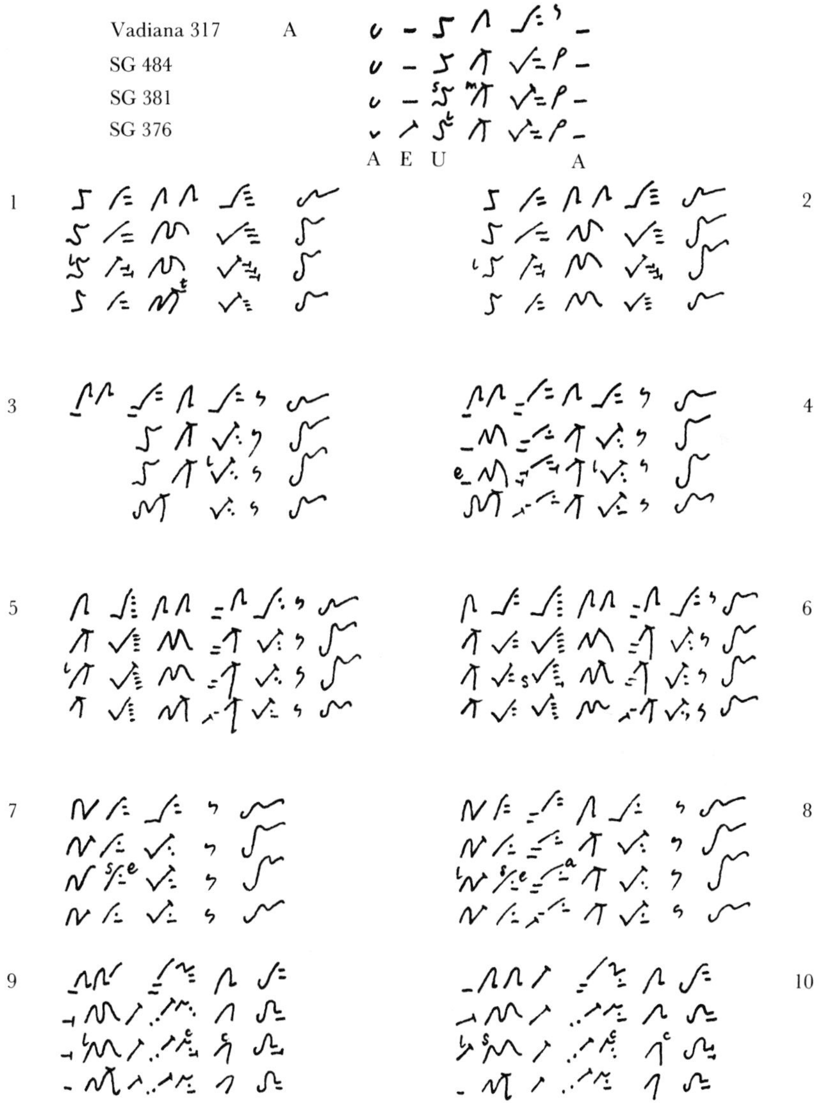

Figure 2   Melismatic notations for *Summi triumphum*, strophes A-10

211

than AEUIA) and written in the margin beside the first text line.[22] Compared with the notation of the famous cantatorium (Stifts-bibliothek 359), as well as the later St Gallen prosers, the neumes of V make little use of the potential for variation in the writing of any one sign. In addition, there are no episemas or significative letters. The *punctum* and *tractulus*, differentiated as · and - in the other St Gallen sources, are not distinguished. The *clivis* is consistently writ-ten ∧, without any change in the length of the descending stroke; in strophe 5, for example, where Stiftsbibliothek 484, 381 and 376 all indicate a large interval by ∧ (in diastematic sources a falling fifth), V uses the same sign as for a fall of a second. Nor does the scribe use the *porrectus flexus* /∧⸜, but instead writes a double *clivis* ∧∧ . On the other hand, the *oriscus* takes two forms: �961 and ∿, this second corresponding to the first element of a *pressus minor* (↗) in the notations of MSS 484, 381 and 376. Since the neumes of V appear to have been written at the same time as the text, and possibly even using the same pen, the text scribe was probably responsible. Clearly, he understood the relation of the musical notation to the text, writing each portion of the melisma beside the relevant text phrase. And the consistency with which he wrote individual signs suggests that he had been trained and knew well how to write neumes, even if his script has none of the elegance of the cantatorium's notation. Lastly, while almost all aspects of his neume script agree with recognised models of St Gallen practice, the wide angle of the *pes* ⟋ (rather than ✓) and the use of a second *oriscus* sign both suggest contact with more northern East Frankish notations.[23]

Like the contrast of corrupt and correct text versions, the inclu-sion of notation for ten strophes of one sequence only cannot be explained in any obvious and simple way. It may or may not have a bearing on the situation that, among the six sequences, *Summi triumphum* alone is not related to a pre-existing *Alleluia* iubilus.[24]

---

[22] On the abbreviated version of *Alleluia*, see Haug, *Gesungene und schriftlich dargestellte Sequenz*, p. 37.
[23] For example, the Mainz Troper (British Library Add. 19768) has exactly the same wide-angled *pes*.
[24] Concerning the relation of Notker's sequences to alleluia melodies see B. Stäblein, 'Notkeriana', *Archiv für Musikwissenschaft*, 19–20 (1962–3), pp. 84–99, and Crocker, *Early Medieval Sequence*, *passim*, especially pp. 12–13.

Figure 3   Writing frames in Paris, Bibliothèque Nationale, MS fonds latin 10587

PARIS, BIBLIOTHÈQUE NATIONALE LAT. 10587
(P)

Since no detailed physical description of the manuscript has yet been published, I give one here:

Fols. i+8+i (modern foliation in ink, top right recto: 1–6 in one hand, 7+8 in another). Parchment, 155×120 mm, all leaves with rounded outer corners. Written space (fols. 1ʳ–3ᵛ) 84×82 mm; (fols. 4ʳ–8ᵛ) 84×103 mm. 13 written lines per page. Dry-point ruling, with no sign of pricking visible; writing frames as shown in Figure 3.

Script: Fine St Gallen book hand, the same throughout, using dark-brown ink. Red capitals, with blue filling on fols. 2ʳ and 5ʳ.

Musical notation: fols. 5ʳ–8ᵛ, St Gallen neumes in vertical margins, in a lighter ink than the text; the marginal alleluia inscriptions are written by the text hand; fols. 5ʳ–6ᵛ, interlinear neumes (Swiss–German), which could have been added shortly after the book was 'finished'.

Collation: ɪ₆ (FHHFFH.HFFHHF)+ɪɪ₂ (HF.FH). Nothing is missing from the centre of ɪ, but an outer bifolium has probably been lost; the single bifolium of ɪɪ neither continues directly from ɪ nor forms the centre of ɪɪ (see Figure 4 below).

Binding: Modern boards (after 1867); on spine 'Notkeri Balbuli fragmenta'.

Inscriptions: 'les f. 7 et 8 ont été acquis en 1867 dans un lot de fragments de mss.' and 'Volume de 8 feuillets 13 Mars 1900' (front flyleaf recto); four lines written in very light brown ink (?s. xv), and subsequently largely erased (fol. 1ʳ, upper margin); stamp of the Bibliothèque Royale and 'Supplᵗ. 1.1000' (fol. 1ʳ, lower margin); 'A ? tu es che ami jjh(esu)m' (fol. 2ᵛ, upper margin, cursive late medieval script); 'Notkerus Balbulus coenobita S. Galli confessor xpi' (fol. 7ʳ, upper margin, modern hand); 'Notkerus Balbulus coenobita S. Galli confessor xpi' (fol. 8ᵛ, lower margin, modern hand).

Susan Rankin

Provenance: From the number 'Supplément latin 1000' on fol. 1ʳ, it can be surmised that fols. 1–6 entered the Bibliothèque Royale in the 1820s or 30s.[25]

The fragment's eight folios include:
1ʳ–4ᵛ the dedication to Liutward 'Summi sanctitatis' (in rustic capitals), the preface 'Cum adhuc iuvenulus', the incipit notice, followed by
5ʳ–6ᵛ the sequences *Natus ante saecula* and *Hanc concordi* (A–6.2 only), then
7ʳ⁻ᵛ *Laus tibi Christe qui humilis* (A–8 only), and
8ʳ⁻ᵛ *Festa Christi* (5.3–12.2 only).[26]

Guided by the arrangement of sequences in other copies of the *Liber ymnorum*, the typical St Gallen hair/flesh arrangement of leaves (from the first outer folio HFFH etc.), the absence of pricking holes for the ruling (always visible on the outer folios of the gathering in St Gallen manuscripts), and the ruling pattern (fols. 1–3 without, fols. 4–8 with a second column), the position of these eight leaves within two gatherings can be reconstructed as in Figure 4. Fols. 4ᵛ–5ʳ are reproduced in Figure 5.

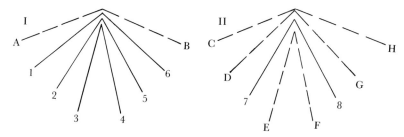

Figure 4   Reconstruction of the first two gatherings of the fragment Paris, Bibliothèque Nationale, MS fonds latin 10587

Dating. Delisle's *Inventaire des manuscrits latins* . . . (1863) gives the date of this fragment as 'xi s', and Von den Steinen's *Notker der Dichter* has 'etwa Anfang 11. Jahrh.', while Hoffmann's recent

---

[25]   The numbering of the 'supplément latin', the last shelfmark system to precede the present one, appears to follow a rough chronological pattern. The numbers 1005–16 were given to a collection of manuscripts bought from the sale of the Bibliothèque de Rosny in 1837 (see L. Delisle, *Le cabinet des manuscrits de la Bibliothèque impériale*, ɪɪ (Paris, 187?), p. 294; the numbers 1017 and 1018 went to the Gradual of St Evroul (now fonds lat. 10508) and to the seventeenth-century copy of the Office of the Circumcision of Sens, both manuscripts recorded as entering the library in 1837.

[26]   The numbering of strophes is based on the edition by Von den Steinen, *Notker der Dichter*, ɪɪ; for details of what is preserved, see also his description of the manuscript (ɪɪ, p. 204).

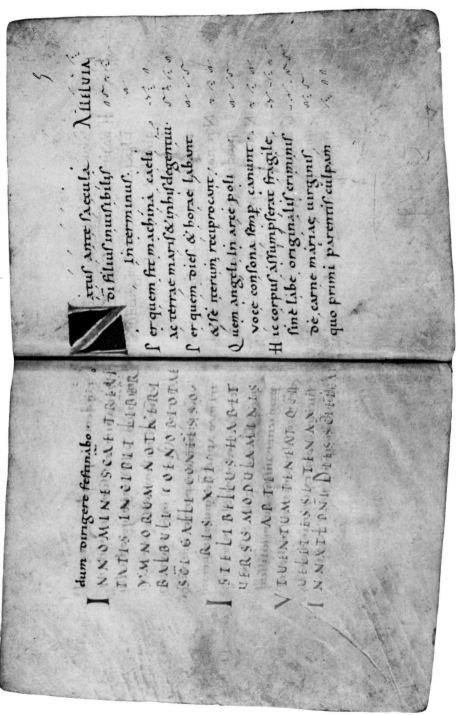

Figure 5   Paris, Bibliothèque Nationale, MS fonds latin 10587, fols. 4ᵛ–5ʳ

215

study of Ottonian scriptoria proposes 'der Zeit um 900'.[27] This discrepancy of dates can be relatively easily explained by the continuity of calligraphic style in St Gallen manuscripts of the late ninth, tenth and eleventh centuries. A type of Caroline minuscule script developed at St Gallen in the second half of the ninth century retained its essential characteristics, undergoing only minor changes, throughout this period.[28] But the archives of the monastery are uniquely well preserved, and, with the charters as reference material, a group of test criteria can be used to date St Gallen scripts in specific periods.[29] In its use of particular letter and ligature forms (and in the absence of others), as well as in its roundness, the degree of differentiation between different letter forms, and an overall impression of lightness and grace, the script of P points unequivocally to the late ninth or very early tenth century.[30] It is the same type of script at roughly the same point in its evolution as that of the cantatorium (Stiftsbibliothek 359), although P's scribe never uses the open a *α* of which the cantatorium's scribe was so fond.[31] More significantly, the hand of P is closely akin to that of the famous *Evangelium longum* (Stiftsbibliothek 53 – so called because of its shape, determined by the ivory plaques carved by the monk Tuotilo for its binding), and the decoration of the capitals in P, with blocks of contrasting colour within the rectangular space of the letter, matches a technique used throughout the gospel book exactly. Much of the history of this book is known

[27] L. Delisle, *Inventaire des manuscrits latins conservés à la Bibliothèque impériale sous les nos 8823–18613 du fonds latin* (Paris, 1863); Von den Steinen, *Notker der Dichter*, II, p. 204, and Hoffmann, *Buchkunst*, I, p. 390.

[28] Hoffmann, 'St Gallen', *Buchkunst*, I, pp. 366ff; see also Bruckner, *Schreibschulen*, II, pp. 24–45, and N. Daniel, 'Die Sankt Galler karolingische Minuskel in der zweiten Hälfte des neunten Jahrhunderts', *Handschriften des zehnten Jahrhunderts aus der Freisinger Dombibliothek* (Munich, 1973), pp. 11–43.

[29] On the St Gallen charters of this period see H. Wartmann, ed., *Urkundenbuch der Abtei Sanct Gallen*, I: *700–840* (Zürich, 1863), II: *840–920* (Zürich, 1866); O. P. Clavadetscher and P. Staerkle, eds., *Die Dorsualnotizen der älteren St. Galler Urkunden* (St Gallen, 1970); and M. Borgolte, D. Geuenich and K. Schmid, *Subsidia Sangallensia*, I: *Materialen und Untersuchungen zu den Verbrüderungsbüchern und zu den älteren Urkunden des Stiftsarchivs St. Gallen* (St Gallen, 1986).

[30] See Hoffmann, *Buchkunst*, I, p. 390, for a precise description of the letter forms of this script.

[31] *Cantatorium no 359 de la Bibliothèque de Saint-Gall (IXᵉ siècle)*, Paléographie Musicale, 2nd series, 2 (Tournai, 1924); a more recent facsimile edition (with less clarity, but including the extra material at the beginning and end of the manuscript) is *Die Handschrift St. Gallen Stiftsbibliothek 359 Cantatorium*, Monumenta Palaeographica Gregoriana 3 (Münsterschwarzach, n.d.).

from Ekkehart IV's report:[32] it was copied by Sintram, a scribe famed for the elegance and fluency of his script, and clearly regarded as 'the best scribe' working in the monastery in the last decade of the ninth century.

The marginal neumes are also entirely consistent with the cantatorium's notation; in all senses, they can be described as classic St Gallen neumes. Using the same basic neume shapes and axis as those of the cantatorium, they also show a good degree of differentiation in the use of individual signs, a clear distinction between *punctum* and *tractulus*, use of a slanted *tractulus* ♪ (rather than ♪), the lengthening of a descending stroke *♪* , *pes* ✓ and *pes quassus* ✓, *porrectus flexus* ♪ (implying lengthening of the third or fourth element), *pressus minor* ∴ and *maior* ⌒. Other signs include the *porrectus* ∿ , *pes stratus* ⨍, *bistropha* ∾ , *epiphonus* ℰ and *quilisma* ⌣ (and, of course, the various combinations of *virga* and *punctum* with other signs). Episemas are much in evidence, but there are no significative letters.

Content and origin. The earlier date helps to explain certain differences between P and other St Gallen prosers. Von den Steinen had been puzzled by the contradiction in P between features which clearly pointed to an origin in St Gallen (presentation and incipit notice) and the fact that the Christmas prose *Eia recolamus* was not included. Other St Gallen collections (Stiftsbibliothek 381, 376, 380, 378, 382, 375), as well as one copied by a St Gallen hand for Minden (1024–7; earlier Berlin, Staatsbibliothek der Stiftung Preussischer Kulturbesitz, cod. theol. lat. 4° 11, now in Kraków), all place the Nativity sequence *Eia recolamus* between Notker's *Natus ante saecula* (always first in the *Liber ymnorum*-based collections) and Notker's Stephen sequence *Hanc concordi*. According to Von den Steinen's philological study, *Eia recolamus* did not form part of Notker's *Liber ymnorum*; rather it was composed – probably at St Gallen – in the early tenth century.[33] Its omission from the series in P is thus entirely consistent with the date of *c.* 900 proposed by Hoffmann.

Besides the extremely characteristic script, the form of words adopted for the incipit notice points unequivocally to an origin at St

[32] See J. Duft and R. Schnyder, *Die Elfenbein-Einbände der Stiftsbibliothek St. Gallen* (Beuron, 1984).
[33] Von den Steinen, *Notker der Dichter*, I, pp. 560–2.

Susan Rankin

Gallen: IN NOMINE SANCTAE TRINITATIS INCIPIT LIBER YMNORUM
NOTKERI BALBULI COENOBIOTAE SANCTI GALLI CONFESSORIS CHRISTI.
The epithet 'Balbulus' appears consistently in the incipit notices of
other St Gallen prosers (Stiftsbibliothek 381, 378 and 380)[34] but
never outside the abbey. Of course, within the monastic com-
munity at St Gallen, the use of 'Balbulus' had the clear purpose of
differentiating between Notker 'the composer of sequences' (as he
was remembered in the St Gallen *Necrologium*: MS 915) and any
other monks named Notker, in particular Notker 'Piperisgranum'
(the doctor, d. 975) and, later, Notker Labeo, also named Teutoni-
cus (the famous translator from Latin to German, *c.* 950–1022).
More importantly, the original form of incipit notice must have
been composed by Notker himself, and it is clear from his other
writings (*Formelbuch, Gesta Karoli* and one of the Stephen hymns)
that he was accustomed to describe himself as 'balbus et edentulus'
('stammering and toothless').[35]

However, the incipit notice in P differs significantly from those in
other St Gallen and closely linked sources (see Table 1). Of special
interest is P's unique opening formula 'In nomine sanctae
trinitatis', contrasting with the later expressions 'In christi nomine'
and 'In nomine domini'. All three correspond to invocations used
at the beginning of charters belonging to the abbey, the first
exclusive to royal charters,[36] the other two typical of charters written for private individuals. In an age marked by theological dis-
agreements over the nature of the Trinity, the use of a Trinitarian
formula had both theological significance and political overtones;[37]
Notker's incipit notice must be read against the history of imperial
practice since the beginning of the century.

Among other signs of Byzantine influence in the imperial
charters of Charlemagne (i.e. those composed after his coronation
as Holy Roman Emperor on 25 December 800) is the new invoca-

---

[34] For a variety of reasons, the incipit notice is missing from the St Gallen prosers in
Stiftsbibliothek 376, 382 and 375.
[35] Von den Steinen, *Notker der Dichter*, I, pp. 366 and 520.
[36] Wartmann, *Urkundenbuch*, nos. 344 (19 Oct 833), 433, 434, 435, 449, 453, 454, 477, 479,
503, 519, 527, 569, 570, 573, 586, 587, 588, 590, 591 etc.; see also the catalogue of
invocations by L. Santifaller, 'Über die Verbal-Invokation in den älteren Papst-
urkunden', *Römische historische Mitteilungen*, 3 (1958/9 and 1959/60), pp. 18–113; on
Trinitarian invocations see especially pp. 42, 93–101.
[37] See the highly informative study by H. Fichtenau, 'Zur Geschichte der Invokationen und
"Devotionsformeln"', in H. Fichtenau, *Beiträge zur Mediävistik*, II: *Urkundenforschung*
(Stuttgart, 1977), pp. 37–61.

218

Table 1 *Incipit notices in sources of the 'Liber ymnorum'*

P:	In nomine sanctae trinitatis	incipit Liber ymnorum
SG 381/380:	In christi nomine	incipit Liber ymnorum
SG 378:	[no invocation]	incipit Liber ymnorum
Einsiedeln:	In nomine domini	incipit Liber ymnorum
Minden:	In nomine domini Iesu Christi	incipit Liber ymnorum
P:		Notkeri Balbuli
SG 381/380:		Notkeri Balbuli
SG 378:		Notkeri Balbuli
Einsiedeln:		Notkeri magistri
Minden:	ad sequentias modulatorum Notkeri	
P (only):	coenobiotae sancti Galli confessoris Christi	

tion: 'In nomine patris et filii et spiritus sancti'.[38] Although the Trinitarian emphasis was not maintained by Charlemagne's son and successor as Emperor, Louis the Pious,[39] it re-emerged in the royal charters of Charlemagne's grandson, Louis the German, now as: 'In nomine sanctae et individuae trinitatis'. This form of invocation was retained by successive East Frankish rulers – Charles the Fat, Arnulf, Louis the Child, followed by the Ottonian dynasty. Notker's own collection of charter models (in the so-called *Formelbuch*),[40] indicates his clear awareness of these variations, the first three of his five models for royal charters beginning: 'In nomine sanctae et individuae trinitatis', 'In nomine dei et domini nostri Iesu Christi' and 'In nomine patris et filii et spiritus sancti',[41] thus with precisely the formulas associated with three successive East Frankish rulers.

Notker owed his knowledge of Carolingian chancery practice to more than the royal charters making grants to St Gallen: it was Grimald, later abbot of St Gallen and probably Notker's mentor, who, as chancellor to Louis the German in 833, had composed the

---

[38] Fichtenau, 'Invokationen', p. 41 and n. 12.
[39] Louis the Pious's charters begin 'In nomine domini dei et salvatoris nostri Iesu Christi'. Besides distinguishing his charters from those of his father, Louis's formula alludes directly to his programme of European unification under a Christian regime.
[40] On the *Formelbuch* see the *Verfasserlexikon*, cols. 1194–8, and especially W. von den Steinen, 'Notker des Dichters Formelbuch', *Zeitschrift für schweizerische Geschichte*, 25 (1945), pp. 449–90.
[41] Ed. K. Zeumer, *Formulae Merowingici et Karolini aevi*, Monumenta Germaniae Historica, Legum sectio v (Hanover, 1886), 395–7.

first charters to use the formula 'In nomine sanctae et individuae trinitatis'.[42] Whether it was Grimald himself or theologians and liturgists at Louis's court who were responsible for the new invocation, it seems likely that the exact form of words chosen was influenced by recent theological discussion, not least the three books entitled 'Sermo de fide sanctae et individuae trinitatis',[43] written by Charlemagne's learned adviser, Alcuin. Grimald's own copy of Alcuin's most admired dogmatic work became the property of the library of St Gallen after his death.[44] The preface to Alcuin's work begins 'In nomine sanctae trinitatis' . . .

There can be no doubt that Notker's use of the Trinity invocation deliberately imitates the royal charter formula, and in this sense represents 'correct etiquette', since the addressee of Notker's little book at the time of composition of the preface held the offices of archchaplain and chancellor to the emperor (Charles the Fat). But Grimald's ownership of a copy of Alcuin's study, and direct knowledge of theological discussions of Trinitarian matters at the Carolingian court, must be considered equally important in influencing St Gallen's most learned scholar. Notker's formula not only underlines the close association between the abbey of St Gallen and the royal house, but also pays homage to the greatest intellectual of the age. That this element in the incipit notice was altered by later scribes indicates that reference to the Trinity had lost its immediate political and theological relevance. The later formulas are blander, of a kind used over hundreds of years by individuals of any standing.

The ending of P's incipit notice again differs from the St Gallen versions in MSS 381, 378 and 380, copied in the late tenth and mid-eleventh centuries; the description of Notker as 'a monk of St Gallus, confessor of Christ' is absent from these later sources. Presumably 100 years or more after Notker's death in 912, such a personal identification had become unnecessary, whereas in the first period of dissemination of Notker's *Liber ymnorum* in the late ninth century – and especially when it was first assembled and copied into the volume dedicated to Liutward – the authorial identification with St

---

[42] Santifaller, 'Verbal-Invokation', p. 96, and Fichtenau, 'Invokationen', pp. 42ff.
[43] Alcuin, *Opera omnia*, ed. J.-P. Migne, *Patrologia latina*, ci (Paris, 1851), cols. 9–58.
[44] The list of books in Grimald's private collection includes the entry 'Albini ad Karolum de fide libri III et eiusdem ad Fridogisum de sancta trinitate'; Lehmann, *Mittelalterliche Bibliothekskataloge*, p. 89.

Gallus held considerable significance, connecting the end of the preface with the beginning (where the dedicatee, Liutward, is addressed as 'Abbatique coenobii sanctissimi columbani ac defensori cellulae discipuli eius mitissimi galli'). And again, as with the epithet Balbulus, the form of words 'coenobiota sancti Galli' can be associated directly with an 'authentic' Notker source. For an entry made in MS 14 of the Stiftsbibliothek in Notker's own hand begins 'Ego notkerus. indignus coenobiota sancti galli. cum adhuc adolescentulus', these last words corresponding directly to the beginning of the *Liber ymnorum* preface 'Cum adhuc iuvenulus'.[45]

That Notker himself is the most likely person to have formulated the incipit notice in the form in which it appears in P leads on to the further question whether P itself represents a fragment of the original dedicatory copy of the *Liber ymnorum*, as proposed by Hoffmann.[46] Apart from the early date and the form of the incipit notice, both format and quality of the little book suggest that this might well be the case. The fact that the hand which copied P is not Notker's own is not a serious argument against. While he would undoubtedly have overseen the preparation of Liutward's copy, he might well have assigned the task of copying it to another scribe. The script is regular, fluent (with very few signs of original erasure) and well formed, and thus of high quality; also, of course, Notker was well placed to choose a scribe from among pupils to whom he had probably taught the art of writing.[47]

The copy sent to Liutward must have been small, most likely without substantial binding, as implied by the incipit notice description 'libellus'.[48] But the unpretentious format denoted by *libellus* by no means implies a lack of care in preparation, and Notker's dedication amply demonstrates his awareness of the high position held by the abbey's friend and patron, Liutward. The Paris frag-

---

[45] Stiftsbibliothek 14 consists, up to the middle of p. 331, of a collection of Old Testament books copied in a hand of s. ix[1]. The lower half of p. 331 is reproduced in Von den Steinen, *Notker der Dichter*, II, Tafel 3. On Notker's hand see *idem*, I, p. 520, and S. Rankin, '*Ego itaque Notker scripsi*', *Revue Bénédictine*, 101 (1991, forthcoming).

[46] Hoffmann, *Buchkunst*, I, p. 390.

[47] The pattern of Notker's organisation of the work of other scribes can be traced in several books remaining in the Stiftsbibliothek; see Rankin, '*Ego itaque Notker scripsi*'.

[48] On the relation of *libelli* to liturgico-musical transmission, see M. Huglo, 'Codicologie et musicologie', *Miscellanea codicologica F. Masai dicata*, ed. P. Cockshaw, M.-C. Garand and P. Jodogne (Ghent, 1979), pp. 71–82; and M. Huglo, *Les livres de chant liturgique* (Turnhout, 1988), pp. 64ff.

ment fits the description *libellus* well: small, no sign of any original binding (rather the opposite, since the lost first folio did not include any part of the dedication, and may thus have served as protection) and lacking elaborate decoration (even the first capital 'N' of *Natus ante saecula* is a simple painted capital). On the other hand, the script is of a high quality and uses few abbreviations, the words are well spaced, aiding comprehension of new texts, the margins allowed around the writing space are wide and contain no (original) markings, and the layout shows careful consideration of appearance (as for example in the presentation of the incipit notice, with short lines centred). These scribal procedures can be recognised in other manuscripts produced in the St Gallen scriptorium during this period, while the lack of special decoration seems to be an aspect of liturgical book production. Only the highest grade of liturgical books (gospel books, psalters and so on) were treated more lavishly. In the cantatorium (a book considered fine enough to be bound between carved ivory plates) only the first letters of the opening rubric and chant (p. 24 *Dominica prima* and p. 25 *Ad te levavi*) were enlarged and painted in outline, using flourishes and scrolling leaves.

Nevertheless, while the presentation of the Paris book – described by Hoffmann as 'einfach aber schön' – allows of its consideration as part of the dedication copy, there are other possibilities. Notker's preface explains how his proses were written out on single unbound pieces of parchment (*rotulae*). In addition to these, the abbey must have owned its own *Liber ymnorum* exemplar, prepared as a model for that to be sent to Liutward, or as a copy of it.[49] The Paris fragment could equally well represent such a 'house copy', although its cleanness and lack of marginal markings argue against its use by the cantors of the abbey in liturgical situations. A substantial problem is posed by the sequence *Laus tibi Christe qui humilis*, part of which appears on fol. 7. Although this text is transmitted by the earliest sources of the *Liber ymnorum* known to him, Von den Steinen argued that it had been composed by a Notker pupil, its technique and content being inferior to that of the other early Innocents sequence, *Laus tibi Christe qui sapit*.[50] The

---

[49] Von den Steinen, *Notker der Dichter*, II, pp. 192ff.
[50] *Idem*, I, pp. 347ff. He describes *Laus tibi Christe qui humilis* in these terms: 'Die Sequenz, in Sankt Gallen früh neben die notkerische gestellt, aber auswärts wenig verbreitet, hat viel

reconstruction of P's first two gatherings allows for the inclusion of:

5ʳ–6ʳ	*Natus ante saecula*	Nativity	25 December
6ʳ–[Bᵛ]	*Hanc concordi*	Stephen	26 December
[Bᵛ–Cᵛ]	[*Johannes Jesu Christo* and	John, apostle	27 December
[Cᵛ–Dᵛ]	another sequence (or vice versa)]		
7ʳ–[Eʳ]	*Laus tibi Christe qui humilis*	Innocents	28 December
[Eʳ–Fᵛ]	[*Gaude Maria*]	Nativity octave	1 January
[Fᵛ]–8–[Gʳ]	*Festa Christi*	Epiphany	6 January

The space between *Johannes Jesu Christo* and *Laus tibi Christe qui humilis* could well have been filled by *Laus tibi Christe qui sapit*;[51] it was not unusual to find two sequences for one feast in the St Gallen collections, and Von den Steinen's reconstruction of Notker's original includes two sequences for each of the Ascension and Dedication feasts. If Von den Steinen's assessment of the authorship of the two Innocents sequences is correct, then we must accept either that Notker included another poet's work in his own collection, or that P represents not the original *Liber ymnorum*, but another more broadly based and slightly later St Gallen collection. P may indeed be a model of the kind of exemplar sent out from St Gallen to other monasteries; sequences composed at St Gallen by Notker and his contemporaries were clearly in circulation in East Frankish regions early in the tenth century.

The Vadiana manuscript shows the copying of Notker's sequences in a manner not previously associated with St Gallen, where patterns of transmission from the late tenth century on are dominated by the large proser collections. This small collection corresponds more closely to those in two other manuscripts, one French and one Italian, both dating from the same late ninth–early tenth-century period. On fols. 57ʳ–60ᵛ of Verona, Biblioteca Capitolare, MS 90, a group of five sequence texts is copied as part of a large collection of Carolingian rhythmical poetry.[52] Munich clm 14843, a miscellany

---

und gut von dem Meister des Hymnenbuches gelernt ... So wären lebendige Verbindungen mit Notker viele zu zeigen.' 'This sequence – at St Gallen set alongside Notker's [Laus tibi Christe qui sapit] at an early date, but not widely transmitted outside the monastery – has absorbed much of the art of the "*Liber ymnorum* Master" ... in many respects, deep connections with Notker's work can be demonstrated.'

51   I have calculated this precisely, comparing numbers of words per page in the extant parts of P with the lengths of missing texts.

52   For more details of the Verona sequences see Von den Steinen, 'Anfänge', *Zeitschrift für*

probably from St Aper, Toul, includes ten sequence texts, copied with tropes and alleluia verses (fols. 93^r–103^v).[53] These two collections share four concordances; all of their sequence texts are of West Frankish origin, excepting Notker's *Benedicta semper sancta*, added by a later hand on fol. 77 of the Verona manuscript. Besides their miscellaneous contexts, the three sequence collections have one further significant characteristic in common, for the texts of the Verona and Toul manuscripts are also fairly corrupt. The Verona scribe appears not to have understood properly what he was copying, while the Toul scribe had a great deal of trouble with endings. In all three cases, the sophisticated language and formulations of the new sequence verses proved too difficult even for trained scribes.

In contrast to this kind of source, Notker's *Liber ymnorum* represented a new departure, its systematic approach of collecting one poet's work in a special book itself unique in ninth-century liturgical practice. Of course, Notker explains in his preface how he had shied away from the idea proposed to him by Marcellus: to collect his verses in a book and present them to a great man; only later, encouraged by his brother Othar, did he dare to compile the *Liber ymnorum* and, by sending it to Liutward, effectively 'publish' it. Aware of the exceptional quality of his poetry, Notker in his preface conveys both pride and humility in presenting his verses to an extremely well-placed patron. It is in this context that we can now set the little Paris fragment; whether it belonged within the copy sent to Liutward or not, there can be no doubt that it lies close to Notker's original. And, in an unequivocal manner, it confirms rather than contradicts all our impressions of the progressive nature of musical culture at St Gallen in the late ninth century, for the *Liber ymnorum* evidently included musical notation from the very beginning, written in the margins alongside the text, in the layout which later characterised the whole East Frankish transmission. A system of ruling in double columns, a wide one for the text, a thinner one for the melismatic notation, is already present (see

schweizerische Kirchengeschichte, 40 (1946), pp. 253–6; for a study of the whole manuscript see G. G. Meersseman, 'Il codice XC della Capitolare di Verona', *Archivio Veneto*, 104 (1975), pp. 11–44.

[53] The sequences and their relation to the rest of clm 14843 are discussed in Von den Steinen, 'Anfänge', *Zeitschrift für schweizerische Kirchengeschichte*, 40 (1946), pp. 256–63; see also Husmann, *Tropen- und Sequenzhandschriften*, pp. 78–9.

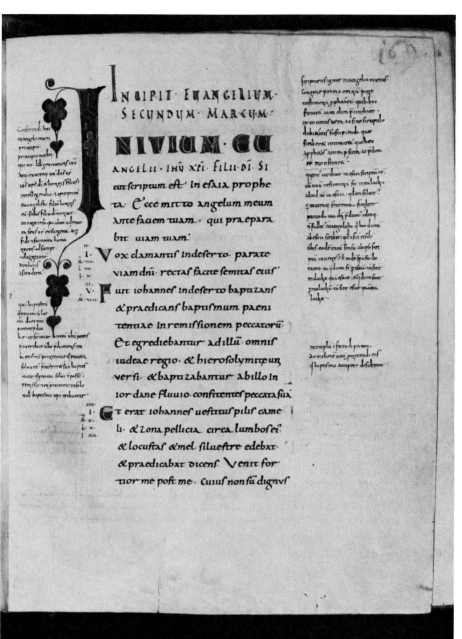

Figure 6   St Gallen, Stiftsbibliothek, MS 50, p. 169

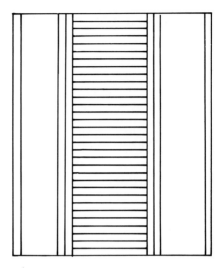

Figure 7   Writing frame in St Gallen, Stiftsbibliothek, MS 50

Figure 3 above). The practice of ruling in columns of unequal width was hardly novel: the preparation of parchment for any substantially glossed text would have required it. Only here, in order not to conflict with the status of the main text, and to allow for the greater number of words in the gloss, a smaller text hand would be used, calling for closer ruling of horizontal lines within the thinner column (or their omission altogether). A glossed gospel book copied at St Gallen in the late ninth or early tenth century (Stiftsbibliothek 50) is ruled with a wide central column and two thinner ones on either side, the side columns having no ruled horizontal lines. Figure 6 shows page 169 of MS 50, Figure 7 its ruling.[54]

The Paris notations tell more than this: direct comparison of them with the late tenth- and eleventh-century St Gallen notations for the same material indicates an extreme continuity in the transmission.[55] Figure 8 shows the notations in six St Gallen sources for

[54]   Page 255 of Stiftsbibliothek MS 50 is reproduced in Bruckner, *Schreibschulen*, II, Tafel 18.

[55]   For the texts, not only of St Gallen sequences, but of those of the whole 'German' (East Frankish) tradition in general, Von den Steinen has noted the same tendency towards conservatism in transmission ('sie sind fast immer fehlerlos überliefert'), contrasting with West Frankish transmission, in which variants were commonly introduced (*Notker der Dichter*, I, p. 84).

1 Natus ante saecula
  dei filius
  invisibilis, interminus,

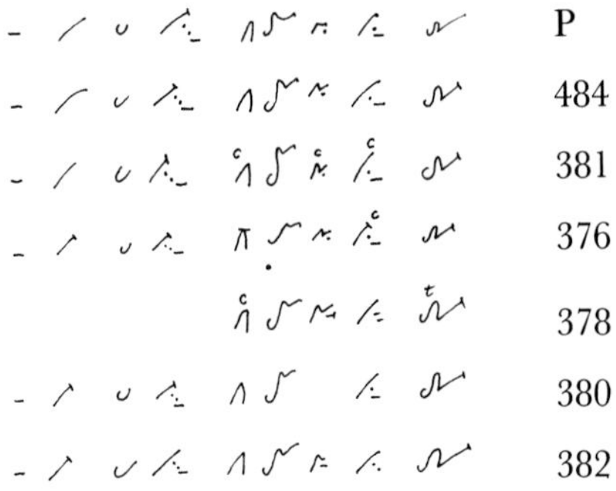

	P
	484
	381
	376
	378
	380
	382

2 Per quem fit machina
  caeli ac terrae,
  maris et in his degentium,

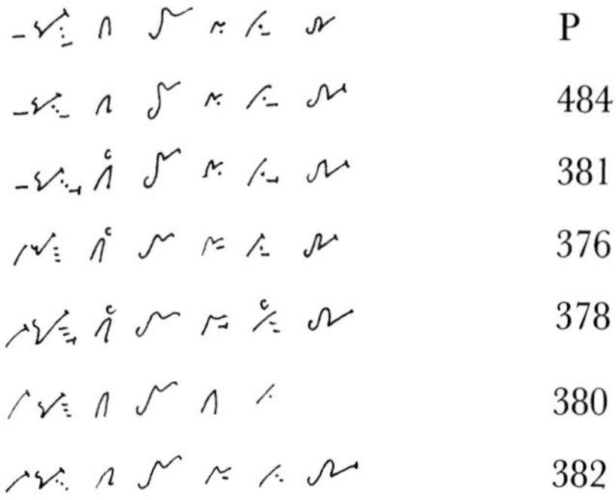

	P
	484
	381
	376
	378
	380
	382

3 Per quem dies et horae
    labant
  et se iterum reciprocant,

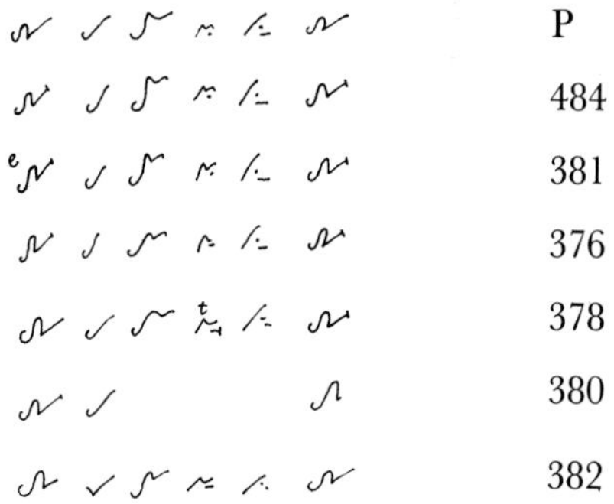

	P
	484
	381
	376
	378
	380
	382

Figure 8 Melismatic notations for the sequence *Natus ante saecula* in seven St Gallen sources

227

4 Quem angeli in arce poli
   voce consona semper
     canunt:

P
484
381
376
378
380
382

5 Hic corpus assumpserat
    fragile
  Sine labe
  originalis criminis
  de carne Mariae virginis,
  quo primi parentis culpam
  Aevaeque lasciviam
    tergeret.

P
484
381
376
378
380
382

6 Hoc praesens diecula
    loquitur
  Praelucida,
  adaucta longitudine,
  quod sol verus radio sui
  luminis vetustas mundi
  depulerit genitus tenebras.

P
484
381
376
378
380
382

Figure 8 *continued*

228

7 Nec nox vacat novi
   sideris luce,
   quod magorum oculos
   terruit scios:

Neumes	Source
	P
	484
	381
	376
	378
	380
	382

8 Nec gregum magistris
   defuit lumen
   quos praestrinxit claritas
   militum dei.

Neumes	Source
	P
	484
	381
	376
	378
	380
	382

9 Gaude, dei genitrix,
   quam circumstant
       obstetricum vice
   concinentes angeli
   gloriam deo.

Neumes	Source
	P
	484
	381
	376
	378
	380
	382

Figure 8 *continued*

10 Christe patris unice,
    qui humanum nostri
      causa formam
    assumpsisti, refove
    supplices tuos,

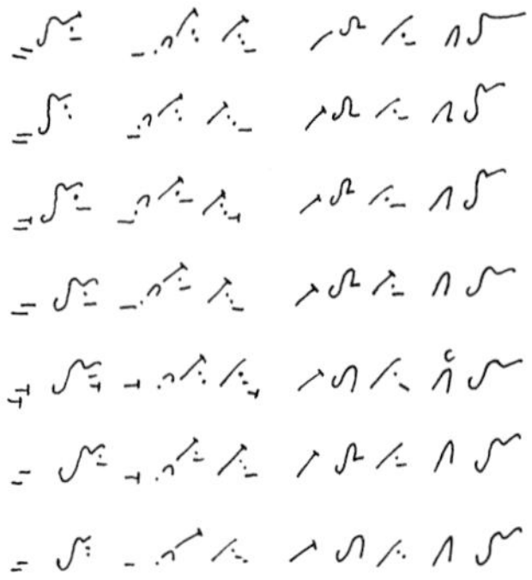

P
484
381
376
378
380
382

11 Et quorum participem te
      fore
    dignatus es, Jesu,
    dignanter eorum
    suscipe preces,

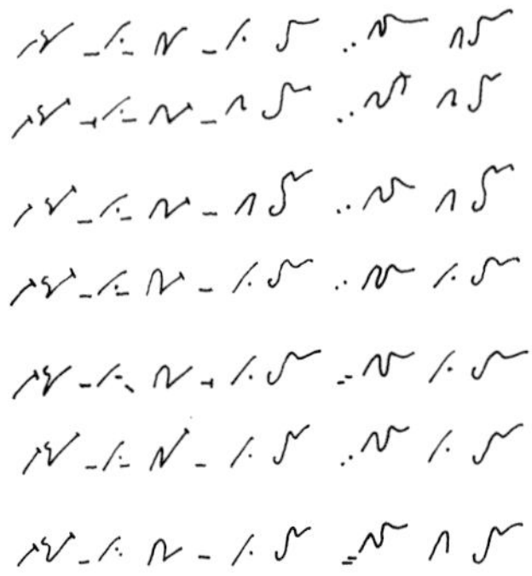

P
484
381
376
378
380
382

12 Ut ipsos divinitatis tuae
    participes, deus,
    facere digneris,
    unice dei!

P
484
381
376
378
380
382

Figure 8 *continued*

230

the sequence *Natus ante saecula* (melody *Dies sanctificatus*) beside those of P. The detail of neume division (which does not always correspond to word divisions, since one neume group may stretch across more than one word), the nature of the individual signs used to convey a melodic movement and, by implication, the melodic readings, remain overwhelmingly the same. It is not so much the non-variance of melodic readings which is striking; an oral tradition could equally well maintain such continuity. But the conservation of notational detail and lack of 'variant' notations could have been upheld only in a situation where written transmission was the norm *from the outset*.

An interesting dimension of the comparison of the Paris notations with those of later sources is the information it provides about the place of episemas and significative letters in the written tradition. Apparently, the letters represent a potential for clarification which may be desired by (or required of) individual scribes, but they are not a fixed part of what is copied. Episemas seem to come somewhere between this individual pragmatic approach and what is considered fixed in ink and parchment. In some parts of the melodies episemas are applied unvaryingly; in others they appear in some sources, but not in all.

While there was nothing in Notker's prefatory hexameter 'Iste libellus habet versus modulaminis apti' to prove the actual notation of the melodies as well as his verses, it no longer appears necessary to argue that his texting of the *melodiae longissimae* was conceived as 'a substitute musical notation'.[56] From the cantatorium, variously dated between 900 and 925 (and on the basis of the script, I believe towards the earlier part of that period), it could be established that the highly characteristic, detailed and inflected St Gallen notation was well in place by the year 900. What we now know of the early transmission of the *Liber ymnorum* points to the fact that all essential aspects of this neume script were already developed by the 880s (with the single exception of the significative letters).[57]

---

[56] This is the sense in which I understand the arguments presented by Haug: 'Wenn er auswendig gewusst wird, leistet der dem Melisma angepasste Text eine schriftanaloge Hilfe beim Festhalten der Melodie, auch ohne selber aufgeschrieben zu sein' (*Gesungene und schriftlich dargestellte Sequenz*, p. 20).

[57] Their absence in P in no way implies that they had not yet been thought of at this time; in any case, the historical tradition which linked them with Notker has every chance of being authentic. See J. Froger, 'L'épître de Notker sur les "lettres significatives" ', *Études grégoriennes*, 5 (1962), pp. 23–71.

231

While the role of the Vadiana sequence collection in transmission of the *Liber ymnorum* appears marginal, the Parisian fragment leads into a central St Gallen situation, offering precise
information and many valuable points of orientation in the context
of current scholarly debate on the early transmission of chant, the
origin and function of notation, the nature of the sources and the
relation of music and text.

Emmanuel College, Cambridge

APPENDIX

Readings in Vadiana 317

These are here collated with the edition by Von den Steinen, to which all
strophe numbers refer.

Festa Christi
    4 *signi*: originally *singni*, *n* erased.
    7 *saevi*: *sevi*; *praecipit*: *precepit*.
    8 *exercitum*: *exertitum*, with c written above t; *sugens*: *surgens*.

Summi triumphum regis
    3 *Idithun*: *ithythun*.
    4 *montes*: *montis*.
    8 *maniplis*: originally *manipulis*, *u* erased.
    11 *polosque*: *celosque*; *praepeti*: *prepeti*; *transvolans*: *transiens*.
    12 *Idithun*: *ythythun*.
    13 *expectet*: *exspectet*; *affuturum*: *adfuturum*.
    15 *Idithun*: *ydythun*.
    16 *a dextris*: originally *ad dextris*, *d* erased.

Laurenti David
    3 large erasure following *Sprevisti*.
    6 *vitae*: *vite*.
    7 *Caesaris*: *Cesaris*; *contemnis*: *contempnis*.
    8 *vane*: *igne*.
    9 *praefectus*: *prefectus*.
    10 *Gaudet*: originally *gaudent*, *n* erased; *favo*: originally *favor*, *r* erased.
    11 following *David*, large erasure.

Dilecte deo
 2 *oboediens*: *obediens*; *arduae*: *ardue*.
 3 *praedia*: *predia*.
 4 *ludicra nati*: *ludi cranati*.
 6 *praetulisti*: *pretulisti*.
 7 *pretio*: *precio*.
13 *pace repleas*: *placere pleas*.

Laude dignum
 3 *Hic*: *Hinc*; *sidus eximium*: *sidu seximium*.
 5 *praeceptis*: *preceptis*; *promptus*: *proptus*.
 8 *curando*: *c* first written as *a*, corrected by dots (not erasure).
 9 *coniunctum*: *coniunctorum*.
 Z *regnat*: *regat*.

Early Music History (1991) Volume 10

Rob C. Wegman

PETRUS DE DOMARTO'S *MISSA SPIRITUS ALMUS* AND THE EARLY HISTORY OF THE FOUR-VOICE MASS IN THE FIFTEENTH CENTURY*

In 1449, the records of the church of Our Lady at Antwerp mention a new singer, Petrus de Domaro (see Figure 1).[1] He does not reappear in the accounts of 1450, and those of the subsequent years are all lost. Musical sources and treatises from the 1460s to 80s call him, with remarkable consistency, P[etrus] de Domarto, and reveal

*   I should like to thank Margaret Bent, Jaap van Benthem, Julie Bray, Barbara Haggh, David Fallows, David Kidger, Andrew Kirkman, Chris Maas, Adelyn Peck and Ronald Woodley for reading the first draft of this article and offering valuable suggestions. I owe a special debt to Reinhard Strohm (the first to recognise the historical significance of Domarto's *Missa Spiritus almus*) for generously sharing with me his many perceptive observations.

   The manuscript sigla used here are as follows. AostaS D19: Aosta, Biblioteca del Seminario Maggiore, MS A¹D19; BrusBR 5557: Brussels, Koninklijke Bibliotheek, MS 5557; LucAS 238: Lucca, Archivio di Stato, MS 238; ModE M.1.13: Modena, Biblioteca Estense, MS α.M.1.13 (*olim* lat. 456); MunBS 3154: Munich, Bayerische Staatsbibliothek, Mus. ms. 3154; MunBS Germ. 810: Munich, Bayerische Staatsbibliothek, MS Germ. 810 ('Schedelsches Liederbuch'); NapBN 40: Naples, Biblioteca Nazionale, MS vi E 40; ParisBNN 4379: Paris, Bibliothèque Nationale, nouvelles acquisitions françaises, MS 4379; PozU 7022: Poznań, University Library, MS 7022; TrentC 87–92: Trent, Castello del Buon Consiglio, MSS 87–92; TrentM 93: Trent, Museo Diocesano, MS BL ('Trent 93'); VatS 14, 15, 51: Vatican City, Biblioteca Apostolica Vaticana, Cappella Sistina, MSS 14, 15 and 51; VatSP B80: Vatican City, Biblioteca Apostolica Vaticana, MS San Pietro B80; VerBC 755: Verona, Biblioteca Capitolare, MS DCCLV.

1 First published in J. van den Nieuwenhuizen, 'De koralen, de zangers en de zangmeesters van de Antwerpse O. L.-Vrouwekerk tijdens de 15e eeuw', *Gouden jubileum gedenkboek van de viering van 50 jaar heropgericht knapenkoor van de Onze-Lieve-Vrouwekatedraal te Antwerpen* (Antwerp, 1978), p. 38. Domarto served as a vicar-singer in the left choir of the church; he received a *signum* or *loot* for every service in which he participated. The *loten* were marked 'J', 'Sp' and 'M', and differed in value according to the type of service: 2¼ Brabant groats for 'M' (Matins), 1 groat for 'J' (unknown) and 5 miten [=$\frac{5}{24}$ groat] for 'Sp' (Lesser Hours). Altogether 49 *loten* are recorded for Domarto between 24 June and 24 December 1449, equivalent to a total sum of nearly 33 Brabant groats. The payments survive in Antwerp, Cathedral Archive, Rekeningen van de kapelanen 1430–1450 (register 142):
'petrus de domaro xxj signa [J] valent xxj groten' (fol. 205ᵛ);
'petrus de domaro xxv signa [Sp] valent v groten v miten' (fol. 208ᵛ);
'petrus de domaro iij signa [M] valent vj groten xviij miten' (fol. 210ʳ; see Figure 1).

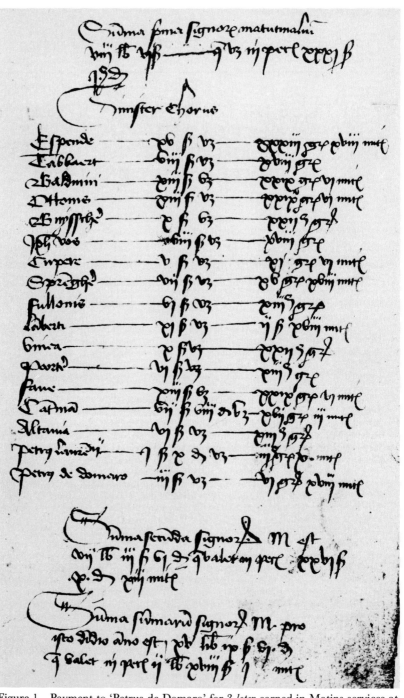

Figure 1 Payment to 'Petrus de Domaro' for 3 *loten* earned in Matins services at the church of Our Lady, Antwerp, between 24 June and 24 December 1449 (Antwerp, Cathedral Archive, Rekeningen van de kapelanen 1430–50 (register 142), fol. 210ʳ). For transcription of payment and explanation see note 1.

that he was an internationally famous composer in the third quarter of the fifteenth century.[2]

Domarto's surviving output consists of two masses and two songs. The three-voice *Missa quinti toni irregularis* existed by 1458, and is attributed to him both in its main source, VatSP B80, and in Tinctoris's *Liber imperfectionum notarum* of 1474–5.[3] The earliest surviving copy of the four-voice *Missa Spiritus almus*, in TrentC 88, must date from around 1462. The latter mass is also transmitted in four later sources: LucAS 238, PozU 7022, VatS 14, and ModE M.1.13.[4] Again there is no shortage of attributions. All sources

The maximum number of *loten* that could be accumulated between 24 June and 24 December was approximately 190. A total of 33 *loten* suggests a stay of at least three or four weeks. Reinhard Strohm has suggested that Domarto worked at Antwerp as a 'visiterer', i.e., a visiting priest who sang in the choirstalls – a common arrangement in musical centres in the Low Countries (private communication, 20 February 1990).

[2]   Reinhard Strohm has tentatively identified Domarto with Pierre Maillart *dict* Petrus, who had been a choirboy at Notre Dame in Paris in 1405, was a chaplain of Philip the Good in 1436–51, and died in 1477. See: R. Strohm, *Music in Late Medieval Bruges* (Oxford, 1985), pp. 25 and 124; more on Maillart in B. H. Haggh, 'Music, Liturgy, and Ceremony in Brussels, 1350–1500' (Ph.D. dissertation, University of Illinois at Urbana-Champaign, 1988), p. 626.

The surname '[de] Domarto' is exceedingly rare. I have come across only three other occurrences of the name in the fifteenth century. The earliest is in a document of the Court of Hainaut, dating 1417, which mentions a Josse de Dommart, merchant in Paris; see L. Devillers, ed., *Cartulaire des comtes de Hainaut*, VI/1 (Brussels, 1896), p. 36. A Reginaldus de Dom(m)arto worked as master of the choirboys in Lille, 1457–8 (see below). And a Michiel Domart was clerk of the Audit Chamber at Mechlin in 1476; see J. T. de Smidt and E. I. Strubbe, *Chronologische lijsten van de geëxtendeerde sententiën en procesbundels berustende in het archief van de Grote Raad van Mechelen* (n.p., 1966), p. 113. Gérard de la Garde (d. 1345), cardinal and professor of theology at Paris, was variously styled G. de Gerria/Guardia and G. Domarus/de Daumaro/Damarus; see A. Franklin, *Dictionnaire des noms, surnoms et pseudonymes latins de l'histoire littéraire du moyen âge [1100 à 1500]* (Hildesheim, 1966), pp. 281–2.

Reinhard Strohm suggests that Petrus de Domarto may have come from the little town Domart-en-Ponthieu, near Doullens, in the diocese of Amiens (*Music in Late Medieval Bruges*, p. 124). This assumption is strengthened by the presence, in 1457–8, of a Reginaldus de Dom(m)arto as master of the choirboys at the church of St Pierre at Lille, 90 km north-east of Domart-en-Ponthieu (R. Strohm, 'Insular Music on a Continental Island', paper read at the February Meeting of the Royal Musical Association, London, 4 February 1989).

[3]   Christopher Reynolds has argued that the scribe of VatSP B80, Nicholas Ausquier, copied Domarto's *Missa quinti toni irregularis* from a lost source dating from 1458 (C. Reynolds, 'The Origins of San Pietro B80 and the Development of a Roman Sacred Repertory', *Early Music History*, 1 (1981), pp. 257–304). The title of the mass (which is in Bb Lydian) comes from Tinctoris's *Liber imperfectionum notarum*; see A. Seay, ed., *Johannis Tinctoris opera theoretica*, Corpus Scriptorum de Musica 22/I (n.p., 1975), p. 154. Ausquier's copy of the mass lacked the Kyrie; a later scribe added a Kyrie ascribed to Egidius Cervelli. The Sanctus also appears in TrentC 89, fols. 57^v–58^r.

[4]   TrentC 88, fols. 401^v–410^r; LucAS 238, fols. 11^v–17^r; VatS 14, fols. 38^v–47^r; ModE M.1.13, fols. 117^v–129^r; and PozU 7022, fols. II/8^r–9^v and II/11^r–12^v. For the date of TrentC 88, see S. E. Saunders, 'The Dating of the Trent Codices from their Watermarks,

except PozU 7022 (where most of the mass, including the first page, is missing) ascribe the cycle to '[P.] de Domarto'. Moreover, Tinctoris mentions both mass and composer four times in his *Proportionale musices* of 1472–3 (three times with musical examples) and once in his *Liber de arte contrapuncti* of 1477 (again with a musical example). Domarto's two songs, *Je vis tous jours* and *Cheluy qui est tant plain de deul*, survive in three chansonniers from the 1460s to 80s.

Domarto's reputation in the fifteenth century is puzzling. A recent writer called him 'Tinctoris's perennial whipping boy'.[5] It is indeed remarkable that in his *Proportionale* Tinctoris blamed Domarto for incorrectly using the mensuration signs O2, C3 and ₵ in *Spiritus almus*, even though several other composers committed the same errors.[6] And when the theorist could find no fault in Domarto's vertical juxtaposition of the signs C and ₵ (in the same

---

with a Study of the Local Liturgy of Trent in the Fifteenth Century' (Ph.D. dissertation, King's College, University of London, 1983), pp. 87–91. The layer of LucAS 238 containing the *Spiritus almus* cycle was copied in Bruges presumably in 1467–9 (Strohm, *Music in Late Medieval Bruges*, pp. 120–3 and 193). PozU 7022 is discussed in M. Perz, 'The Lvov Fragments: A Source for Works by Dufay, Josquin, Petrus de Domarto, and Petrus de Grudencz in 15th-Century Poland', *Tijdschrift van de Vereniging voor Nederlandse Muziekgeschiedenis*, 36 (1986), pp. 26–51. Domarto's mass is found in the second gathering, which dates from the third quarter of the fifteenth century. Adalbert Roth has proposed a date of *c.* 1474 for VatS 14; see A. Roth, 'Studien zum frühen Repertoire der Päpstlichen Kapelle unter dem Pontifikat Sixtus' IV. (1471–1484): Die Chorbücher 14 und 51 des Fondo Cappella Sistina der Biblioteca Apostolica Vaticana' (Ph.D. dissertation, University of Frankfurt am Main, 1982), pp. 237–40. ModE M.1.13 was copied in Ferrara in 1481; see L. Lockwood, *Music in Renaissance Ferrara 1400–1505* (Oxford, 1984), pp. 222–4. Three of the five sources (TrentC 88, VatS 14 and ModE M.1.13) transmit the full cycle. PozU 7022 contains two trimmed leaves with portions of the Credo and Sanctus, and a few snippets with music for the Kyrie and Gloria. LucAS 238 contains portions of the Kyrie, Gloria, Sanctus and Agnus.

[5] R. Taruskin, 'Antoine Busnoys and the *L'homme armé* Tradition', *Journal of the American Musicological Society*, 39 (1986), p. 284.

[6] Seay, ed., *Johannis Tinctoris opera theoretica*, II (n.p., 1978), pp. 48–9, 55 and 56. Some of Tinctoris's comments were echoed by Franchinus Gaffurius in his *Tractatus practicabilium proportionum* of *c.* 1481–3 (unpublished; the treatise survives in Bologna, Civico Museo Bibliografico Musicale, MS A 69; see C. A. Miller, 'Early Gaffuriana: New Answers to Old Questions', *The Musical Quarterly*, 56 (1970), pp. 373–83). The relevant passages are: 'don Marto [*sic*] in Missa spiritus almus proportionam duplam unica binarij scilicet numeri ziphra pluries inconuenienter signauit' (fol. 5ʳ), and the list of composers committing the 'inexcusable error' of *prolatio maior* augmentation: 'Busnoÿs in Missa Lome arme et Bernardus ycart in Missa de Amor tu dormi et don Marto in missa spiritus almus atque Gaspar in Missa Venusbant' (fol. 12ᵛ). Gaffurius's comments have little independent value; his treatise is strongly influenced by the views of Tinctoris, with whom the young man had discussed matters of music theory during his stay at Naples in 1478–80 (cf. A. Atlas, *Music at the Aragonese Court of Naples* (Cambridge, 1985), pp. 80–2, and Miller, *op. cit.*, pp. 377–8).

mass), he stated, almost reluctantly, that the practice was 'tolerable'.[7] In his *Liber de arte contrapuncti*, Tinctoris criticised *Spiritus almus* again (along with Busnoys's song *Maintes femmes*), now for incorrectly handling a passing dissonance.[8] Finally, he reprimanded Domarto in the *Liber imperfectionum notarum* for erroneously imperfecting a dotted long in the *Missa quinti toni irregularis*.[9]

Evidently Tinctoris did not think very highly of Domarto's skills. At the same time it is puzzling that the theorist gave so much attention to his masses, for they could well have been over twenty years old by the time his treatises were written, and their relevance to a man whose opinions reflected the tastes and ideals of the 1470s rather than the 1450s must have been limited.[10] Yet the wordings of Tinctoris's criticisms seem to suggest that he blamed the composer not so much for committing the errors as for introducing them. For instance, while Domarto had 'sinned intolerably' by using C as a sign of augmentation, other composers – such as Ockeghem, Busnoys, Regis, Caron and Faugues – had merely 'imitated him in this error'. Similarly, it was Domarto who had 'failed many times' in using O2 as equivalent to ₵ in perfect minor modus (rather than to Φ⏐), and although Busnoys, Regis and others had done the same, Tinctoris considered this no excuse for *his* having done it in the first place. Busnoys in particular seems to have been a follower of Domarto. Although a generation younger, he is criticised in one breath with Domarto in the *Liber de arte contrapuncti*. And in the *Liber imperfectionum notarum* it is 'Busnoys and many others' who imitate Domarto and Barbingant in their erroneous practice of imperfecting dotted longs.

It would appear that by singling out Domarto as the culprit for errors that were widely committed in the 1470s, Tinctoris was obliquely attesting to his influence, for good or bad, on composers of the Ockeghem generation.[11] That impression is confirmed when

---

[7] *Opera theoretica*, IIa, pp. 45–6.

[8] Seay, ed., *Johannis Tinctoris opera theoretica*, II (n.p., 1975), p. 139.

[9] Tinctoris objected to this also in Barbingant's song *L'homme bany*; cf. *Opera theoretica*, I, pp. 153–4.

[10] I have argued elsewhere that the years 1455–75 saw profound changes in the style, scope and production of polyphonic masses (R. C. Wegman, 'The Anonymous Mass *D'ung aultre amer*: A Late Fifteenth-Century Experiment', *The Musical Quarterly*, 74 (1990), pp. 566–94). By the mid-1470s, Domarto's *Missa Spiritus almus* must have sounded noticeably antiquated (see below).

[11] This was noted earlier by Strohm, *Music in Late Medieval Bruges*, p. 124.

the theorist describes both him and Jean Cousin as composers 'non parvae auctoritatis'.[12] And it accords well with the fact that the *Spiritus almus* Mass survives in no fewer than five musical sources, copied as far apart as Italy, Flanders and Poland and together spanning the period *c.* 1462–81 (see note 4 above). Of all the Continental four-voice masses that were composed before about 1460, none seems to have enjoyed more widespread and enduring fame than Domarto's.[13]

But what distinguishes the *Spiritus almus* Mass from other four-voice cycles of the period? Why was the mass so famous? If it was an influential work, where can its influence be traced? These questions take us into one of the most shadowy phases of Renaissance music history, the early development of the four-voice mass. If studied in that context, Domarto's *Missa Spiritus almus* does indeed appear to have been a seminal work. It casts new light on the early development of Johannes Ockeghem, and can be shown to have been a major influence on Antoine Busnoys. Domarto's mass appears in the late fifteenth-century repertory as an isolated piece, and its context can be reconstructed only by carefully evaluating other pieces that seem to fit it in some way. But the light that these pieces shed on the *Missa Spiritus almus* is reflected by that mass, and illuminates them in turn. What emerges is the contours of a new pattern in the fascinating but dark history of fifteenth-century music.

Domarto's *Missa Spiritus almus* belongs to the small group of fifteenth-century cycles that are based not on entire chants, but only on internal sections of chants. Its cantus firmus is the final phrase 'spiritus almus' from the responsory *Stirps Jesse* for Marian feasts, transposed up a fifth. The text of the responsory runs: '℟. The tree of Jesse brought forth a twig, and the twig a flower:* and upon this

---

[12] *Opera theoretica*, IIa, p. 56.

[13] In the eighteenth century, Domarto was among the first fifteenth-century composers to regain his former fame. In his letter to Eugenio de Ligniville of 3 March 1767, Padre Martini mentioned 'Firmino Caron, Gio[vanni] Regis, Antonio Busnois, Pietro de Domart, Enrico Isaac, Giacomo Obrect, Giovanni Okenheim, Jusquin del Prato, etc.' as especially proficient in the art of canonic writing (see A. Schnoebelen, ed., *Padre Martini's Collection of Letters in the Civico Museo Bibliografico Musicale in Bologna* (New York, 1979), pp. 331–2). The source of Padre Martini's information is unclear; it cannot be Tinctoris, since the latter never made a statement to this effect. Martini did have access to his treatises, though; see *Tinctoris opera theoretica*, I, p. 10.

flower rests *the nourishing spirit*. ℣. The twig is the Virgin, the Mother of God, the flower her son' (words of cantus firmus in italics).[14] Other masses based on internal sections of chants include the anonymous English *Caput* Mass, the anonymous *Missa Thomas cesus*, Ockeghem's *Missa Ecce ancilla Domini* and Obrecht's *Missa Sicut spina rosam*.[15]

Domarto's reasons for singling out the phrase 'spiritus almus' were probably of a liturgical or theological nature. The tree of Jesse symbolises the genealogy of the Virgin Mary, and the reference to the Holy Spirit is to be seen as an allusion to the virgin birth.[16] Other evidence tends to confirm the special significance of the 'spiritus almus' melody: Antoine Busnoys used the entire responsory *Stirps Jesse* as a cantus firmus in his motet *Anima mea liquefacta est*,[17] and he, too, placed special emphasis on the final section of the chant. It is worth taking a closer look at Busnoys's setting.

Anima mea is a three-part motet in so-called treble-dominated scoring, for top voice and two equal parts approximately a fifth

---

[14] '℞. Stirps Jesse virgam produxit, virgaque florem:* et super hunc florem requiescit *spiritus almus*. ℣ Virga dei genitrix virgo est, flos filius eius' (after Isaiah 11:1). The cantus firmus was identified by Strohm, *Music in Late Medieval Bruges*, p. 124. The responsory *Stirps Jesse* is printed in the *Processionale monasticum* (Solesmes, 1893), p. 186. A responsory which is musically identical with *Stirps Jesse* is *Comedetis carnes*, for Corpus Christi; see *Liber usualis* (Tournai, 1962), p. 927.

The head-motif of the mass seems to quote the trope *Spiritus alme adest* for the Introit of the Mass of the Holy Ghost, *Spiritus domini* (Strohm, *Music in Late Medieval Bruges*, p. 124). In this context it is worth pointing out that Domarto's head-motif is itself quoted at the beginning of the anonymous motet *Salve mundi gloria*, a setting of a *Salve regina* trope (MunBS 3154, fols. 67ᵛ–69ʳ; edition in T. Noblitt, ed., *Der Kodex des Magister Nicolaus Leopold*, Das Erbe deutscher Musik 80 (Kassel, 1987), pp. 230–7). This motet was copied in a layer whose paper has been dated 1476 (T. Noblitt, 'Die Datierung der Handschrift Mus. ms. 3154 der Staatsbibliothek München', *Die Musikforschung*, 27 (1974), p. 41). In several ways this interesting piece seems to be a musical reflection of Domarto's mass (cf. the descriptive analysis of the cycle below): it is in D Dorian, with generally low ranges, unusual ficta, slow harmonic movement, and little imitation in the full passages. Beyond the head-motif, however, the motet shares little with the *Missa Spiritus almus* in terms of melodic content. So long as the cantus firmus (in the lowest voice) has not been identified, and the *Salve regina* trope located, it is difficult to assess the significance of the apparent relationship.

[15] The cantus firmi of these masses were identified by Manfred Bukofzer (*Studies in Medieval and Renaissance Music* (New York, 1950), pp. 229–30 and 308–9) and Reinhard Strohm (see Reynolds, *op. cit.*, p. 285).

[16] See Strohm, *Music in Late Medieval Bruges*, p. 124, with implicit cross-reference to p. 71. Barbara Haggh informed me that high solemn Masses of the Holy Spirit and the Virgin Mary were common at important funerals (private communication, 16 January 1990; cf. Haggh, *op. cit.*, p. 351). This combination could perhaps explain Domarto's choice of cantus firmus and suggest that the *Missa Spiritus almus* was written for a funerary context.

[17] Edition in A. Smijers, ed., *Van Ockeghem tot Sweelinck*, I (2nd, revised edn, Amsterdam, 1952), pp. 22–6.

lower. The responsory *Stirps Jesse* is stated in one of the latter voices, the tenor, but two extended statements of chant appear in the top voice when the tenor is silent. The first occurs at the beginning (bars 1–15), the other about two-thirds of the way through (bars 87–107). Both statements relate to the proper tenor statements as quasi-fore-imitations. In the most reliable source, BrusBR 5557,[18] the chant statements in the top voice are supplied with two simultaneous texts: the appropriate words of *Anima mea* and, written through the staves, those of *Stirps Jesse* (not printed in Smijers). The texting of the top voice in the two passages is as follows: 'Anima mea liquefacta est'/'Stirps Jesse' (bars 1–15), and 'tulerunt pallium meum custodes murorum'/'spiritus almus' (bars 87–107). The beginning of the chant, and its final phrase 'spiritus almus', are thus given special emphasis. The parallelism between the two top-voice statements was probably intentional. Although *Anima mea* is through-composed, the music is interrupted in bar 86 by a drawn-out chord on A major (in D Dorian), just before the 'spiritus almus' quotation in the top voice starts. The contratenor has here a *signum congruentiae*, which suggests that a midpoint division analogous to that in a courtly song is intended. The suspicion that Busnoys implied a structural division is strengthened by the fact that the following duo opens in almost exactly the same way as does the introductory duo at the beginning of the motet.

So the 'spiritus almus' phrase is highlighted by Busnoys in three interrelated ways: first, by reserving to that phrase the 'second section' of the motet; secondly, by the extended top-voice statement of the phrase, foreshadowing the statement in the tenor; and thirdly, by the structural position of that statement in the motet as a whole. There is thus reason to believe that Busnoys's *Anima mea* and Domarto's *Missa Spiritus almus* were written for similar Marian contexts, in which the final section of *Stirps Jesse* apparently carried independent significance. A direct geographical or historical connection between the two works seems unlikely, however, for

---

[18] Busnoys's *Anima mea liquefacta est* appears as an anonymous composition in VatS 15, fols. 239ᵛ–242ʳ. In BrusBR 5557 the motet was copied presumably under the composer's supervision, on paper datable to 1476–80. See F. Warmington, '"A Very Fine Troop of Bastards?": Provenance, Date, and Busnois's Role in Brussels 5557', paper read at the annual meeting of the American Musicological Society, Philadelphia, 1984; for the date see R. C. Wegman, 'New Data Concerning the Origins and Chronology of Brussels, Koninklijke Bibliotheek, Manuscript 5557', *Tijdschrift van de Vereniging voor Nederlandse Muziekgeschiedenis*, 36 (1986), p. 14.

Domarto and Busnoys seem to have used different versions of the responsory. Example 1 gives a vertical alignment of their cantus firmi, together with two plainchant versions, one from 's-Hertogenbosch and the other from the Use of Sarum. Domarto and Busnoys appear on the whole to be in agreement; most of the discrepancies between their versions can be attributed to differences in embellishment (for instance, notes 28–31 in Example 1). However, in the final part of the melody Domarto is closer to 's-Hertogenbosch, Busnoys to Sarum (notes 39, 43, and 47). Although it must therefore be concluded that the two composers used different versions of *Stirps Jesse*, Busnoys's motet helps to pro-

Example 1. Comparison of cantus firmus statements of the melisma 'spiritus almus' from the responsory *Stirps Jesse*, in (a) Antoine Busnoys, *Anima mea liquefacta est/Stirps Jesse* (tenor, top voice) and (b) Petrus de Domarto, *Missa Spiritus almus*. The original chant is given in (c) according to the Sarum Antiphonal* and in (d) from a 's-Hertogenbosch Antiphonal.**

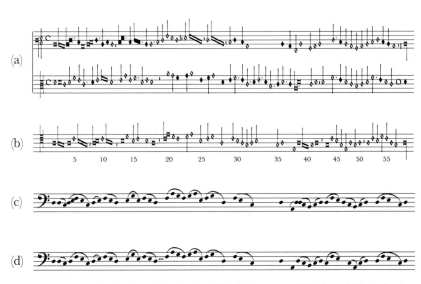

*   W. H. Frere, ed., *Antiphonale Sarisburiense*, The Plainsong and Mediaeval Music Society (repr. Farnborough, 1966), p. 519.
** 'Codex Smijers', now in the possession of the Confraternity of Our Lady at 's-Hertogenbosch; see A. Smijers, ed., *Van Ockeghem tot Sweelinck*, ɪ (2nd, revised edn, Amsterdam, 1952), p. 22.

vide the context in which Domarto's choice of the 'spiritus almus' melody is to be understood.

The *Missa Spiritus almus* employs schematic cantus firmus manipulation.[19] When this technique is applied, the cantus firmus remains unchanged in its notated form throughout the cycle. As a sounding voice, however, it appears in various transformations derived from the notated form with the help of different external clues to its interpretation (usually mensuration signs or verbal canons). The schematic procedures by which the different tenors are derived are essentially non-musical: intervals, notes and note values are treated as isolated particles with manipulable properties rather than as elements of a musical structure.

The type of schematic manipulation employed by Domarto is mensural transformation.[20] Throughout the mass the *Spiritus almus* tenor is invariably notated as in Example 2a, except that the number of breve rests varies from section to section.[21] Variety is provided by presentation in different mensurations (see Table 1), leading to differences in the rhythmic interpretation of the tenor. Example 2b shows the various rhythmic shapes which the tenor assumes. The example gives the relative durations of the tenor notes, not in terms of fixed tempo units but in multiples of minims. This allows direct comparison between tenor statements in different mensurations, irrespective of whether diminution or augmentation has been applied.[22] As can be seen at a glance, the tenor assumes four different rhythmic shapes in the course of the mass, all derived from the same notational archetype.

It could be argued that the changes of mensuration need not have been introduced with the express purpose of generating rhythmic permutations – indeed, that the latter may well have been fortuitous by-products of some other purpose, for instance, the creation of rough length relationships. That objection can safely be dismissed. Length relationships were almost certainly not Domarto's primary concern. If we add up, for each mensuration, the relative durations given in Example 2b, we arrive at the total

[19] The following description is based on R. C. Wegman, 'Another Mass by Busnoys?', *Music & Letters*, 71 (1990), p. 5.
[20] This term was coined by Reinhard Strohm in his paper 'The Music of the 1450s', Fifteenth Annual Conference on Medieval and Renaissance Music, Southampton, 1987.
[21] The breve rests are not indicated in the example; they always precede sections A and B.
[22] See Wegman, 'Another Mass by Busnoys?', p. 6, n. 18.

Example 2. Petrus de Domarto, *Missa Spiritus almus*: (a) notation of mass tenor; (b) relative durations of cantus firmus notes in the mensurations O, C, ☉, ₵, and C3 (counted in multiples of minims)

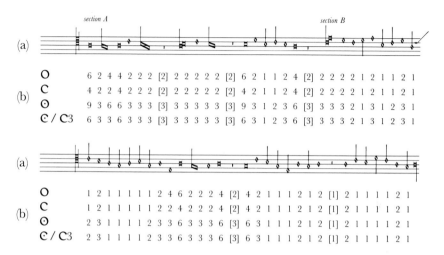

(a)

(b)

O	6 2 4 4 2 2 2 [2] 2 2 2 2 2 [2] 6 2 1 1 2 4 [2] 2 2 2 2 1 2 1 1 2 1
C	4 2 2 4 2 2 2 [2] 2 2 2 2 2 [2] 4 2 1 1 2 4 [2] 2 2 2 2 1 2 1 1 2 1
☉	9 3 6 6 3 3 3 [3] 3 3 3 3 3 [3] 9 3 1 2 3 6 [3] 3 3 3 2 1 3 1 2 3 1
₵ / C3	6 3 3 6 3 3 3 [3] 3 3 3 3 3 [3] 6 3 1 2 3 6 [3] 3 3 3 2 1 3 1 2 3 1

(a)

(b)

O	1 2 1 1 1 1 1 2 4 6 2 2 2 4 [2] 4 2 1 1 1 2 1 2 [1] 2 1 1 1 1 2 1
C	1 2 1 1 1 1 1 2 2 4 2 2 2 4 [2] 4 2 1 1 1 2 1 2 [1] 2 1 1 1 1 2 1
☉	2 3 1 1 1 1 2 3 3 6 3 3 3 6 [3] 6 3 1 1 1 2 1 2 [1] 2 1 1 1 1 2 1
₵ / C3	2 3 1 1 1 1 2 3 3 6 3 3 3 6 [3] 6 3 1 1 1 2 1 2 [1] 2 1 1 1 1 2 1

Table 1 *Structure of Domarto, 'Missa Spiritus almus'*

Section	Signature	Tenor signature	Cantus firmus phrase	Relative length[a]	
Kyrie I	O	O	AB	72	
Christe	[₵]	C	AB	64	208
Kyrie II	O	O	AB	72	
Et in terra	₵	₵	AB	198	
Qui tollis	O2	O	AB	81	339
Cum sancto	C2	C3	AB	60	
Patrem	O	☉	AB	225	
Crucifixus	O2	O	AB	99	406
Et in Spiritum	C2	C3	AB	82	
Sanctus	O	₵	A	99	
Pleni	O	—	—	60	359
Gloria tua–Osanna	O	₵	B	90	
Benedictus–Osanna	[₵]	C	AB	110	
Agnus I	O	O	AB	81	223
Agnus II	[₵]	—	—	61	
ut supra					

[a]Relative lengths are counted in semibreves in O, and in breves in O2 and C2/₵.

lengths of each tenor statement (counted in minims). After conversion to a common denominator, the semibreve beat in O, these lengths turn out to be as follows:

C3	54 semibreve beats in terms of O
C	58
O	63
₵ (augmentation)	162
☉ (augmentation)	171

Not surprisingly there is a rough 3:1 length ratio between the mensurations that call for augmentation and those that do not.[23] But, setting aside that division, the differences in length *within* the two groups are marginal. If large-scale length relationships had been Domarto's primary concern, two mensuration signs (possibly combined with proportion canons) would have sufficed to achieve them. Since he used five rather than two signs, the conclusion must be that rhythmic permutations were indeed his primary goal.

Other evidence tends to support that conclusion. Mensural transformation depends for its success entirely on the notational shape of the tenor. It is by no means easy to find or invent tenors that lend themselves well to the procedure. The problem is not how to achieve maximum rhythmic variety, but how to keep the tenor, metrically speaking, landing on its feet in every mensuration. For instance, the *L'homme armé* tune is by its nature unsuited to mensural transformation. Its innate *prolatio maior* rhythm and notation virtually preclude successful performance in O and C, and changes between ☉ and ₵ hardly affect its rhythm. Conversely, it is exceptional for song tenors in O or |₵ to allow of interpretation in major prolation without the occurrence of frequent across-the-bar rhythms and metric shifts.[24] In view of this it can hardly be coincidence that Domarto's mass tenor runs so naturally in every

---

[23] Although *prolatio maior* notation implied 2:1 augmentation, the length ratio found here is roughly 3:1 since the basis for comparison is the semibreve: one semibreve in major prolation is equivalent to three semibreves in minor prolation. Had the basis for comparison been the minim, then the length ratio would have been 2:1, since one minim in major prolation equals two in minor prolation.

[24] Among the few exceptions are the tenors of the songs *N'aray-je jamais* by Robert Morton and *De tous biens plaine* by Hayne van Ghizeghem. These tenors are mensurally transformed in the masses *N'aray-je jamais* by Jacob Obrecht and Johannes Ghiselin-Verbonnet, the *Missa De tous biens plaine* by Obrecht, and the motet *Omnium bonorum plena* by Compère. However, the procedure is not applied systematically in these pieces.

mensuration in which it is presented. This, no doubt, was the result of a deliberate attempt to make the melody suited to mensural transformation: from the moment Domarto turned the 'spiritus almus' melody into the notational archetype of the mass, he must have envisaged a cycle in which mensural transformation was to play the central role.

Mensural cantus firmus transformation is not found in any surviving mass predating *Spiritus almus*.[25] Did Domarto invent the technique, or do its origins lie elsewhere? The schematic nature of the technique would suggest origin in the Ars Nova motet.[26] This was the virtual cradle of such schematic devices as augmentation, diminution, transposition, retrograde and inversion.[27] In several later fifteenth-century masses we find the latter devices in combination with mensural transformation (see below), suggesting that composers did indeed perceive the procedures as related. Moreover, it was customary for motet composers in the late fourteenth and early fifteenth centuries to achieve different propor-

[25] A minor exception could perhaps be the anonymous, and presumably early, *Missa Te Deum* in TrentC 89, fols. 71ʳ–80ᵛ, based on the opening phrase 'Te Deum laudamus: te Dominum confitemur' of the hymn *Te Deum*, transposed up a fourth. The chant is rhythmicised in a highly schematic fashion: it is split up, by two groups of nine breve rests each, into three sections, each of which has a total duration of nine breves. The entry of the cantus firmus is invariably preceded by eighteen breve rests, so that the total durational layout of the tenor is 18:**9**:9:**9**:9:**9** (counted in breves; cantus firmus statements in bold type). The tenor appears in three different mensurations, ₵, O and O2 (the latter indicated by the uncommon signature ⊗). However, the changes of mensuration hardly affect the rhythmic shape of the tenor, since it is written almost entirely in maximas, longs and breves. There are only two (consecutive) semibreves on the same pitch (*d'*) whose rhythmic interpretation varies according to the mensuration signs, but in each case they still add up to one breve. Contrary to Domarto, who clearly tried to exploit the inherent possibilities of mensural transformation, the anonymous composer of *Te Deum* seems to have introduced the changes of mensuration only to create large-scale proportional structures. The durational proportions within the movements are either 1:1:1 (Kyrie and Agnus Dei) or 3:1:3 (Gloria, Credo and Sanctus). The overall durational relationships in the mass are 3:7:7:7:3. This mass is the exception that proves the rule: the mensural transformation in Domarto's mass betrays a unique attitude.

[26] The following paragraphs are strongly indebted to the work of Margaret Bent, who has kindly shared with me her thoughts on mensural transformation in the Ars Nova motet (private communication, 4 March 1990). In a forthcoming publication Professor Bent questions the twentieth-century concept of 'isorhythm' and proposes a definition based on sameness of notation rather than sameness of results: 'The starting point is an isomorphically notated tenor, subjected to one or more kinds of manipulation' ('The Late-Medieval Motet', *The Everyman Companion to Medieval and Renaissance Music*, ed. D. Fallows and T. Knighton). Bent's removal of the restrictions imposed by the concept of isorhythm clears the way for a better understanding of Domarto's compositional backgrounds.

[27] See R. L. Todd, 'Retrograde, Inversion, Retrograde-Inversion, and Related Techniques in the Masses of Obrecht', *The Musical Quarterly*, 64 (1978), pp. 52–4.

tions between successive tenor statements by means of mensural changes. This frequently results in rhythmic differences. However, in most cases these differences seem incidental rather than intentional (as with Domarto). The reason for this is that the tenors are mostly written in long note values, so that the rhythmic variations occur only on the level of modus. Moreover, the opportunities for alteration and imperfection are often limited, since only two different note values are used.[28] By contrast, Domarto operated on two mensural levels (tempus and prolation) and, by employing four different note values, exploited their potential for rhythmic transformation to the full.

But the *Missa Spiritus almus* does have a direct forerunner in the fourteenth-century motet repertory, in the shape of the 'mensural essay' *Inter densas/Imbribus/Admirabile* of c. 1380–90.[29] Analysis of this piece helps us to understand the significance of Domarto's contribution. The anonymous composer of *Inter densas* operated on four different mensural levels: major modus, minor modus, tempus and prolation (ruling the divisions of Mx, L, B and S, respectively). On each of these levels the division can be either duple or triple, and hence the number of possible mensurations (or 'species') is in theory $2\times2\times2\times2=16$ (see Table 2).[30] Only four of these were regularly employed in practice (i.e. species 11–12 and 15–16). The brief tenor of *Inter densas* has the rhythmic pattern M-M-S-B-L-Mx;

---

[28] A good example is *Portio nature / Ida capillorum / Ante thronum*, composed before 1376. The *talea* of this motet consists of repeated B-B-L patterns. During the first *color* statement the minor modus is perfect, and thus the second note of each pattern is altered. However, a verbal canon specifies that the subsequent *color* statements are to be performed in imperfect minor modus, so that alteration ceases. See the edition in U. Günther, ed., *The Motets of the Manuscripts Chantilly, Musée Condé, 564 (olim 1047) and Modena, Biblioteca estense, α.M.5, 24 (olim lat. 568)*, Corpus Mensurabilis Musicae 39 (n.p., 1965), pp. 57–65. For the date of the motet, see *ibid.*, pp. lvii–lviii.

[29] Edition in Günther, *op. cit.*, pp. 66–70; for the date, see *ibid.*, pp. lxii–lxiii. I am grateful to Margaret Bent for pointing out this motet to me.

[30] The system is fully explained in Tinctoris's *Tractatus de regulari valore notarum* of c. 1474–5 (*Opera theoretica*, I, pp. 121–38). For an important discussion of the mensural relationships and species see B. J. Blackburn, 'A Lost Guide to Tinctoris's Teachings Recovered', *Early Music History*, 1 (1981), pp. 29–116. The species are described in the present article according to the system of designation introduced by W. Apel, *The Notation of Polyphonic Music, 900–1600* (Cambridge, MA, 1953), pp. 97–100. In Apel's system, mensural relationships are indicated in square brackets as follows: major modus by Roman numerals II or III in italics; minor modus by Roman numerals in Roman type; tempus by Arabic numerals 2 or 3; prolation by Arabic numerals in italics. For instance, imperfect time in perfect minor modus (species 15) can be indicated as C [*II*, III, 2, *2*] or abbreviated to C [III] on the principle that divisions are binary unless otherwise indicated.

Table 2 *The sixteen species of the mensural notation system: (a) in numerical order and (b) in systematic order*[a]

(a)	1	*III*, ɪɪɪ, 3, *3*		9	*III*, ɪɪɪ, 3, 2
	2	*III*, ɪɪ, 3, *3*		10	*III*, ɪɪ, 3, 2
	3	*II*, ɪɪɪ, 3, *3*		11	*II*, ɪɪɪ, 3, 2
	4	*II*, ɪɪ, 3, *3*		12	*II*, ɪɪ, 3, 2
	5	*III*, ɪɪɪ, 2, *3*		13	*III*, ɪɪɪ, 2, 2
	6	*III*, ɪɪ, 2, *3*		14	*III*, ɪɪ, 2, 2
	7	*II*, ɪɪɪ, 2, *3*		15	*II*, ɪɪɪ, 2, 2
	8	*II*, ɪɪ, 2, *3*		16	*II*, ɪɪ, 2, 2

(b)		tempus and prolation			
		3, *3*	2, *3*	3, 2	2, 2
	III, ɪɪɪ	1	5	9	13
major and minor mode	*III*, ɪɪ	2	6	10	14
	II, ɪɪɪ	3	7	11	15
	II, ɪɪ	4	8	12	16

[a]See Johannes Tinctoris, *Tractatus de reguli valore notarum*, ed. A. Seay, *Johannis Tinctoris opera theoretica*, Corpus Scriptorum de Musica 22/ɪ (n.p., 1975), pp. 121–38. Mensural divisions are indicated according to the system of W. Apel, *The Notation of Polyphonic Music, 900–1600* (Cambridge, MA, 1953), pp. 97–100 (see note 30).

a verbal canon specifies that it is to be stated in eight different species.[31] Whenever either of the two modi is perfect, the final maxima of the tenor is to be silent for the last third of its duration.[32] In transcription, this results in the rhythmic shapes shown in Example 3.

Inter densas shows that Domarto's technique of mensural transformation was not a new invention: the principle was known by the end of the fourteenth century. But there are important differences. *Inter densas* is more extreme in its economy than the *Missa Spiritus almus*. The six-note tenor is presented in eight different rhythmic shapes; Domarto's tenor has nearly ten times as many notes, but

[31] See Günther, *op. cit.*, p. lxiv. The canon defines the various mensural relationships in abbreviated manner, and does not match the transcription in tenor statements 3, 5, 7 and 8.

[32] 'cludendo pausam ut modus sit perfectus' (Günther, *op. cit.*, p. lxiv). Günther states that this applies only to major modus, but her transcription shows that not to be the case. In statements 2 and 6 not the major modus but the minor modus is perfect; the dissonant clashes between the tenor and the other voices in bars 37–8 and 83–4 confirm that the tenor is to be silent here.

Example 3. Anonymous, *Inter densas/Imbribus/Admirabile* (*c.* 1380–90): Notation of tenor, and relative durations of cantus firmus notes (counted in multiples of minims) in eight different species. The 'silent' parts of the final maximas (in species with perfect minor or major modus) are printed between square brackets (cf. note 32). Based on U. Günther, ed., *The Motets of the Manuscripts Chantilly, Musée Condé, 564 (olim 1047) and Modena, Biblioteca estense, α.M.5, 24 (olim lat. 568)*, Corpus Mensurabilis Musicae 39 (n.p., 1965), pp. lxii–lxv and 66–70.

tenor statement	species (see Table 2)	relative durations

tenor statement	species (see Table 2)		relative durations					
1	1	[*III*, III, 3, *3*]	1	2	6	18	54	54 + [27]
2	7	[*II*, III, 2, *3*]	1	2	3	12	18	24 + [12]
3	10	[*III*, II, 3, *2*]	1	1	4	6	24	24 + [12]
4	16	[*II*, II, 2, *2*]	1	1	2	4	8	16
5	9	[*III*, III, 3, *2*]	1	1	4	12	36	36 + [18]
6	15	[*II*, III, 2, *2*]	1	1	2	8	12	16 + [8]
7	2	[*III*, II, 3, *3*]	1	2	6	9	36	36 + [18]
8	4*	[*II*, II, 3, *3*]	1	2	6	9	18	24 + [12]

* The eighth tenor statement falls outside the logical arrangement of the species: the species to be expected here is 8 [*II*, II, 2, *3*], not 4. However, the tenor produces awkward counterpoint if it is rhythmicised according to species 8.

appears in only four shapes. Domarto seems less concerned to make a theoretical point. He chose not to operate on such levels as major and minor modus, whose practical relevance was limited. And the technique of mensural transformation does not overshadow the identity and function of the cantus firmus itself. The 'spiritus almus' melisma is stated in full: it gives the mass its stamp precisely because it has retained its melodic integrity. By contrast, the brief motif in the tenor of *Inter densas* is of little melodic interest.[33]

These differences become all the more evident when we compare the *Missa Spiritus almus* with a cycle that seems to have been directly inspired by *Inter densas*: Eloy d'Amerval's five-voice *Missa Dixerunt*

[33] The role and nature of the tenor could be compared to that of bass grounds like the passacaglia or romanesca (cf. Günther, *op. cit.*, p. lxiv). Although texted 'admirabile est nomen tuum' (Psalm 8:1), the voice was probably freely composed (*ibid.*).

discipuli of *c.* 1470.[34] This mass is a didactic work, written to demonstrate the four mensural levels recognised in music theory. The tenor states the first seven notes of the antiphon *Dixerunt discipuli* from the Office of St Martin of Tours. Its notation closely resembles that of the tenor of *Inter densas*: Mx-M-M-S-B-L-Mx. In the course of Eloy's mass, the tenor runs through all sixteen species listed in Table 2, and assumes sixteen different rhythmic shapes (see Example 4). Comparison of Examples 3 and 4 shows that Eloy

Example 4. Eloy d'Amerval, *Missa Dixerunt discipuli*: notation of tenor, and relative durations of cantus firmus notes (counted in multiples of minims) in the sixteen species of the mensural notation system. The 'silent' parts of the first maximas are printed between square brackets (cf. note 35). Based on unique source, VatS 14, fols. 56^v–65^r.

species (see Table 2)	section of mass	relative durations						
1	Et in terra	[27] + 54	1	2	6	18	54	81
2	Qui tollis	[27] + 27	1	2	6	9	36	54
3	Qui tollis	[27] + 27	1	2	6	18	27	54
4	Patrem	[27] + 9	1	2	6	9	18	36
5	Patrem	[18] + 36	1	2	3	12	36	54
6	Et resurrexit	[18] + 18	1	2	3	6	24	36
7	Et resurrexit	[18] + 18	1	2	3	12	18	36
8	Et resurrexit	[18] + 6	1	2	3	6	12	24
9	Sanctus	[18] + 36	1	1	4	12	36	54
10	Osanna i	[18] + 18	1	1	4	6	24	36
11	Kyrie i	[18] + 18	1	1	4	12	18	36
12	Kyrie ii	[18] + 6	1	1	4	6	12	24
13	Agnus Dei i	[12] + 24	1	1	2	8	24	36
14	Agnus Dei iii	[12] + 12	1	1	2	4	16	24
15	Osanna ii	[12] + 12	1	1	2	8	12	24
16	Agnus Dei iii	[12] + 4	1	1	2	4	8	16

[34] Unique source: VatS 14, fols. 56^v–65^r; no modern edition. Eloy's mass existed by 1472–3, since Tinctoris mentioned it in his *Proportionale* (*Opera theoretica*, iia, pp. 55–6); it is unlikely that the cycle was much older than about 1470, since it contains many imitations for three and four voices, which often assume the character of points of imitation.

251

has simply copied and extended the principle of *Inter densas*: he subjects the same notation to sixteen species (rather than eight), and thus realises the potential already latent in the motet. That Eloy may well have known the motet is suggested by his verbal canon, which specifies that the first maxima of every statement is to be 'silenced' for the first three tempora of its duration.[35] This recalls *Inter densas*, where the final maxima is to be silent for the last third of its duration whenever the major or minor mode is perfect.

The different approaches of Domarto and Eloy tell us a lot about their attitudes. The cantus firmus treatment in Eloy's *Missa Dixerunt discipuli* seems to have been motivated primarily by didactic considerations. Although the mass aroused the interest of theorists as late as the 1530s,[36] it added nothing new to an idea that had already been worked out by the 1380s. If *Dixerunt discipuli* exerted any influence on later composers, it can be traced only in compositions exemplifying music theory, for instance by Hothby and Tinctoris.[37] With Domarto the picture is different. The application of mensural transformation in the *Missa Spiritus almus* never stood in the way of his practical concern with the nature and function of the mass tenor. He turned a mere mensural game into a viable practical technique, by fusing it successfully with the principle of the cantus firmus.

In hindsight that was a momentous step, and it is worth exploring its ramifications in some later masses. But first we must turn to another outstanding feature of Domarto's *Missa Spiritus almus*, its unusually colourful mensural usage. Three practices in particular need to be discussed (see Table 3):

(a) O and C with implicit 2:1 augmentation (the 'error Anglorum'),

(b) the use of C3 to indicate perfect prolation equating with O at the level of the semibreve, and

(c) the use of O2 to indicate perfect minor modus in ¢.

---

[35] VatS 14, fol. 56ᵛ: 'Canon tenoris pro tota missa: non faciens pausas sed signis capiens has tempora prima tria prime semper bene pausa sexdecies currens cunctaque signa videns' ('You must always pause well during the first three tempora, and not execute the rests [before the mensuration sign] but interpret them as signatures [see below], [thus] running sixteen times, and observing all signs').

[36] The mass was studied and discussed by Italian theorists as late as 1539. See Blackburn (*op. cit.*, pp. 29–30 and 90–1), who provides a theoretical context for the mass and discusses similar didactic compositions by Hothby and Tinctoris.

[37] Blackburn, *op. cit.*, pp. 90–1.

Table 3 *Mensural relationships in Domarto, 'Missa Spiritus almus'*

O/₵			
O			
O2			
₵/C2			
C			
C3			

As mentioned earlier, Tinctoris strongly criticised Domarto for all three of these practices in his *Proportionale*. Two other noteworthy practices are: perfect minor modus under O (indicated here as O [III]), and vertical juxtaposition of C and ₵.

The *Missa Spiritus almus* may well have been the earliest Continental mass cycle to adopt the 'English error'. This, at any rate, is what Tinctoris seemed to imply when he stated that Domarto was 'imitated in this error' by Regis, Caron, Boubert, Faugues, Courbet, Ockeghem and Busnoys.[38] In the eyes of Tinctoris, augmentation by means of major prolation was not just an isolated aberration. It was a contamination of the mensural notation system, which caused more confusion and error in its turn. Elsewhere in his treatise the theorist had listed three different (and incompatible) meanings of major prolation signs, in compositions by Le Rouge, Pullois and Dufay. Who of these dissenting composers should be believed? Tinctoris left no doubt about that, and attributed the confusion to the fourth meaning, the one adopted by Domarto:[39]

Regarding this signature [$\mathbb{C}$], since these three most distinguished composers disagree, put your trust in Dufay rather than the others. For the first of them [Le Rouge] is the most presumptuous of all users of proportions, since he falls into the English error of knowing no proportions and teaching them all. The second [Pullois], however, is entirely guileless.

Tinctoris may give the impression of a nagging old pedant, but it is not difficult to sympathise with his position. He was one of the few men to have a truly intellectual interest in the mensural notation system;[40] the confusion created by those 'but slightly read' dragged down music as a science and impaired its practical potential. This, if we are to believe Tinctoris, had started with the 'English error'. The root problem here was that the sign $\mathbb{C}$ had been made to denote both a mensuration and, implicitly, a proportion. According to music theory these two elements ought to have been specified separately, for instance as follows: $\mathbb{C}^1_2$, or $^1\mathbb{C}$-*crescit in duplo*. Failure to indicate the proportion could have only one result: the sign itself became unavailable to express what it had originally meant.[41]

---

[38] *Opera theoretica*, IIa, pp. 48–9.

[39] 'In quoquidem signo, quoniam isti tres famosissimi compositores dissentiant, Dufay potius quam aliis crede, quorum primus omnium proportionantium arrogantissimus, nam Anglorum errore labefactus nullas proportiones sciens, omnes praecipit. Secundus autem simplicissimus est' (after Seay, *Tinctoris opera theoretica*, IIa, pp. 47–8). The translation given here is from R. Woodley, 'The *Proportionale musices* of Iohannes Tinctoris: A Critical Edition, Translation and Study' (D.Phil. dissertation, University of Oxford, 1982), p. 361.

[40] As is illustrated by the precision and method of Tinctoris's definitions in his *Terminorum musicae diffinitorium* (Treviso, 1494; facs. New York, 1966), a compilation of statements made in his treatises. This is an indispensable reference book to anyone writing on the fundamentals of fifteenth-century music as perceived by those who had fully mastered the art. The notion that Tinctoris was a rigid conservative is contradicted by the enthusiasm with which he welcomed new stylistic trends, and his quickness to acknowledge the talents of young composers.

[41] This is true in any case of tenors, although there is one exception: if major prolation signs are used in all voices, augmentation is probably not implied. See for this Taruskin,

Remedies compounded the error. By the time Tinctoris wrote his treatise, other signs were already in use to denote what could be expressed unequivocally only by a perfect prolation sign in some proportion.

Domarto, for instance, used the signature C3 to denote perfect prolation equating with O at the level of the semibreve (cf. Table 3). By using that sign he was able to write sections of roughly the same length as those without augmentation, while retaining perfect prolation in the tenor (see the relative lengths in Table 1). This earned him even more criticism from Tinctoris:[42]

Moreover, this same De Domarto has erred on more than one occasion in this regard, in his aforementioned *Missa Spiritus almus*, for he wished for notes in sesquialtera [$\frac{3}{2}$] set under the sign of *prolatio minor* [C] to be reckoned as though they were in *prolatio maior*, as follows:

The reasoning behind Tinctoris's criticism is simple, and water-tight in its logic: so long as there is no dot in the sign C, the division of the semibreve cannot be other than duple (i.e., the prolation is minor). That is what the absence of the dot means. The addition of the figure 3 (meaning sesquialtera proportion: $\frac{3}{2}$) cannot possibly alter that meaning, for a sign of proportion must not contradict (let alone overrule) a sign of mensuration.[43] Indeed, to Tinctoris the addition of the figure 3 to C was a downright absurdity, for it leads to a contradiction in terms: the sign C says that both tempus and prolation are duple, but the figure 3 dictates that either of these levels be triple.[44] This defies mensural logic.

'Busnoys and the *L'homme armé* Tradition', p. 261, n. 15; R. C. Wegman, Communication, *Journal of the American Musicological Society*, 42 (1989), p. 438. Nor was it implied when voices other than the tenor made brief excursions to major prolation mensurations.

[42] *Opera theoretica*, IIa, p. 56; translation from Woodley, 'The *Proportionale musices*', p. 371.

[43] This is the very point Tinctoris makes in book 3, chapter 5, of his *Proportionale*, where he criticises Domarto's use of C3: when a composer introduces a proportion in the course of a musical composition, he must always observe the nature of the modus, tempus and prolation that are in force, for '[proportions] cannot alter the essential nature of the mensurations in which they occur' (*Opera theoretica*, IIa, pp. 53–6; Woodley, *op. cit.*, p. 368).

[44] Triple division of the *breve* under C3 was by far the most common practice in the

Tinctoris's impatience with the inconsistency is understandable, particularly since the mensural notation system offered a correct and unequivocal alternative for the proportion Domarto sought to notate. According to the theorist, he ought to have used the signature C$\frac{3}{2}$, in short C3 (in which C proper is seen as equating with O at the level of the minim).[45] Curiously, it is this particular sign which we actually find as a variant for C|3 in one of the sources for Domarto's mass, LucAS 238 (fol. 14ᵛ). Was this Domarto's original notation, or was Waghes, the main scribe of LucAS 238, made aware of the inconsistency, perhaps even by Tinctoris himself? Only a filiation of the sources can throw light upon this question; that matter will be dealt with below.

Domarto's use of O2 provides a comparable case of confusing mensurations with proportions. Strictly speaking, the sign is synonymous with ₵. But Domarto used it, in his Qui tollis and Crucifixus, to denote ₵ with triple division of the longa, or perfect minor modus:[46]

Domarto has failed many times in his mass *Spiritus almus*; for, having written *dupla* under the sign of *tempus perfectum*, he then allows the notes to be reckoned in *tempus imperfectum*, thus:

Contratenor

And notwithstanding Busnois and Regis, who follow his example both in their *L'Homme armé* masses[47] and in all their works, the excuse cannot be

---

fifteenth century. Tinctoris objected to this practice as well, citing as an example the lost *Missa Nigra sum* by Jean Escatefer *dit* Cousin (*Opera theoretica*, iia, p. 56). Other examples are cited in Wegman, Communication (*JAMS*), p. 439.

45 This confirms Leeman Perkins's assumption that in Robert Morton's [?] song *Il sera pour vous/L'homme armé*, in which all parts are cast in C3, 'the implicit proportion is probably sesquialteral, indicating that three minims are to be sung to the same time as two under the integral mensuration of imperfect tempus' (L. Perkins and H. Garey, eds., *The Mellon Chansonnier* (New Haven, 1979), ii, p. 331). Perkins's assumption was questioned by Richard Taruskin, who argued that the setting was originally written in C ('Busnoys and the *L'homme armé* Tradition', pp. 290–2; other objections that could be raised against Taruskin's hypothesis are given in note 52 below).

46 Tinctoris, *Opera theoretica*, iia, p. 55; translation from Woodley, 'The *Proportionale musices*', pp. 370–1. See also Wegman, 'Another Mass by Busnoys?', pp. 2–3.

47 Curiously, Johannes Regis's surviving *Missa L'homme armé* employs neither O2 nor perfect minor modus in any other mensuration. Regis was not unfamiliar with the sign, though:

made that in sections of the mass written in this way the *modus minor* is perfect, indicated as such by the circle of perfection with the figure 2, since this very circle of perfection (as is shown in countless works even of their own composition) is a sign not of *modus*, but rather of *tempus perfectum*. The figure 2, however, although deficient in the way they have indicated it, is in fact a sign of *dupla*.

Again, Tinctoris's objection is understandable: how can the circle denote tempus in one case and modus in another, and how can a cipher denote a proportion in one case and tempus in another? The correct alternative was to write ₵, and to indicate perfect minor modus by grouping breve rests in threes, either before the mensuration sign (in which case they are not counted) or after. That is what Eloy d'Amerval (whom Tinctoris regarded as 'most learned in the matter of modus')[48] had done in his *Missa Dixerunt discipuli* (see note 35 above). And, curiously, this is what Domarto himself had done to indicate perfect minor modus under O, in the Patrem. The latter practice, O [ɪɪɪ], is extremely rare in fifteenth-century masses, but it was to become characteristic of Busnoys's mensural usage in sacred music.[49]

Another mensural peculiarity to which Tinctoris drew attention was the superimposition of ₵ and C, in the Christe and Benedictus.[50] This time the theorist did not object, 'because of a certain equivalence of the former proportion and the latter prolation'; in other words, because the relationship ₵=C⌣ is logical and unambiguous. The purpose of the superimposition was to achieve a 2:1 proportion between the tenor and the contrapuntal voices: what Domarto had done was simply to write out 'augmentation' of the tenor by means of contrasting mensuration signs.[51] Interestingly, Domarto also obtained 2:1 proportions between the tenor and its surrounding voices by vertically combining the 'erroneous' proportional signatures C and O2 with *ut iacet* mensurations (cf. Table 1). It would appear that the composer had a reluctance to specify augmentation by means of verbal canons.

he used it in his motet *O admirabile commercium*. Possibly he composed two *L'homme armé* masses.

[48]   *Opera theoretica*, ɪɪa, p. 55.
[49]   See Wegman, 'Another Mass by Busnoys?', p. 3; and note 60 below.
[50]   *Opera theoretica*, ɪɪa, pp. 45–6.
[51]   Tenor augmentation by means of juxtaposition of C and ₵ is extremely rare, but it is also found in the Qui tollis and Crucifixus of the anonymous *Missa Rex dabit mercedem* (VerBC 755, fols. 54ʳ–63ʳ), and in three other masses to be discussed below.

None of the practices discussed here was unique to Domarto, and he was certainly not the first to employ them (as Tinctoris seemed to imply).[52] But three points need to be emphasised. First, it is most unusual to find all these practices together in one cycle. Secondly, there are not very many mid-fifteenth-century masses that employ, like *Spiritus almus*, as many as eight different mensurations: O, O [III], O2, C, ₵/C2, C3, O, and ₵. The overwhelmingly predominant practice was to alternate simply O and ₵. Thirdly, it may well be that the *Missa Spiritus almus* was instrumental in making the practices more widespread, and that it was for that reason that Tinctoris singled out this work for criticism.

In this context it seems of more than passing interest that a few masses from the 1460s and 70s adopt nearly all of the mensural practices that characterise *Spiritus almus*. While it would be rash to attribute these correspondences to any influence on Domarto's part, the situation becomes different when we find, in the very same masses, the extremely rare technique of mensural cantus firmus

[52]   The use of C with implied augmentation had been a regular practice in England from at least the second decade of the fifteenth century onwards. The practice seems to have been adopted on the Continent in the 1440s.
   C3 with triple division of the semibreve was a uniquely Continental manifestation. Among the first sacred works to use the sign in this sense are the anonymous Gloria in TrentC 92, fols. 116ᵛ–118ʳ and 147ʳ–149ʳ, and Johannes Pullois's *Victimae paschali laudes* in TrentC 90, fols. 286ᵛ–287ʳ (see J. A. Bank, *Tactus, Tempo and Notation in Mensural Music from the 13th to the 17th Century* (Amsterdam, 1972), pp. 136 and 145). Significantly, Pullois was active at the church of Our Lady at Antwerp until 1447, that is, two years before Domarto came to work there.
   The mensuration is also used prominently in several French combinative songs from the 1450s and 60s, e.g. *O rosa bella/Hé Robinet, Je soloie/Héz bergères, L'aire bien frique/J'ayme/Galoise, Je vous pri/Tant que/Ma très douce*; see the recent edition by M. R. Maniates, *The Combinative Chanson*, Recent Researches in the Music of the Renaissance 77 (Madison, 1989). These chansons provide a context for the best-known combinative song that employs the mensuration, Robert Morton's [?] *Il sera pour vous/L'homme armé*. The vertical juxtapositions with other mensurations in *O rosa bella/Hé Robinet* and *Je vous pri/Tant que/Ma très douce* are in agreement with those in Domarto's *Missa Spiritus almus*, and confirm that Richard Taruskin's interpretation of the sign C3, on which his tentative ascription to Busnoys hinges, is incorrect ('Busnoys and the *L'homme armé* Tradition', pp. 290–2; see also note 45 above).
   Among the few sacred works after the *Spiritus almus* Mass to employ C3 are Busnoys's *Missa L'homme armé*, and the Naples *L'homme armé* Mass III (see Taruskin, 'Busnoys and the *L'homme armé* Tradition', pp. 286–9; Wegman, Communication (*JAMS*), pp. 441–2; R. Taruskin, Communication, *Journal of the American Musicological Society*, 42 (1989), pp. 450–1).
   The use of O2 meaning perfect minor modus in imperfect cut-time occurs in Dufay's proper cycles in TrentC 88, which must date from the late 1440s (see A. E. Planchart, 'Guillaume Du Fay's Benefices and his Relationship to the Court of Burgundy', *Early Music History*, 8 (1988), pp. 117–71).

transformation. Three pieces in particular merit discussion: the anonymous cycle *Gross senen*, Busnoys's *Missa O crux lignum* and the anonymous *Missa L'ardant desir*.

The first, *Gross senen*, survives uniquely in TrentC 89, where it was copied around 1462.[53] Its cantus firmus is the tenor of the German lied *Gross senen ich im herczen trag* (MunBS Germ. 810, fols. 57^v–58^r); it seems likely that the mass itself is German as well.[54] The lied tenor is used in its original form as the notational archetype for the entire cycle. In most movements of the mass, the tenor statements are presented in two alternative notations: first, the unchanging archetype itself, with mensuration signs and canons, and second, the resolution, 'translated' into the mensuration of the other voices. It seems likely that the composer himself provided only the archetype and some of the canons, and that the resolutions and most of the signatures and canons in the archetype were added by a later scribe.[55] If that was the case, the mass might originally have looked like the anonymous *Missa Quant ce viendra* (TrentC 89, fols. 318^v–330^r), where the unchanging archetype is given without mensuration signs, its various proportions being left to the singers

---

[53] TrentC 89, fols. 26^v–41^r. For the date of this source, see Saunders, 'The Dating of the Trent Codices', pp. 87–91. The mass is discussed in L. E. Gottlieb, 'The Cyclic Masses of Trent Codex 89' (Ph.D. dissertation, University of California at Los Angeles, 1958), R. Schmalz, 'Selected Fifteenth-Century Polyphonic Mass Ordinaries Based upon Pre-existent German Material' (Ph.D. dissertation, University of Pittsburgh, 1971), and R. Strohm, 'Meßzyklen über deutsche Lieder in den Trienter Codices', *Liedstudien Wolfgang Osthoff zum 60. Geburtstag*, ed. M. Just and R. Wiesend (Tutzing, 1989), pp. 77–106.

[54] Some doubts could be raised as to whether this lied has always carried the text *Gross senen ich im herczen trag*. Although the tenor incipit occurs with this same text in a quodlibet in the Glogauer Liederbuch (I thank David Fallows for pointing this out to me) and the poem fits the music convincingly (as shown by Strohm, 'Meßzyklen über deutsche Lieder', p. 91), there is a marked disparity between the quality of transmission of the text and that of the music in the Schedelsches Liederbuch. The musical text is extremely corrupt: as so often happens in Schedel, there are no mensuration signs and accidentals, the clefs in the superius and tenor are incorrect, and the contratenor is incomplete. Moreover, numerous errors and missing notes and rests render performance from the source virtually impossible. In contrast with this, the five stanzas of the text appear to be quite accurate. And, significantly, there is no attempt at text underlay: the stanzas are just crammed in the space between the staves, with complete disregard for the music. Moreover, some arrangements of the anonymous rondeau *J'ay pris amours* have also been underlaid with the *Gross senen* poem in German sources. That the *Gross senen* lied in the Schedelsches Liederbuch is a contrafact of a Franco-Flemish song seems unlikely, however, on both formal and stylistic grounds. Whatever its original text may have been, *Gross senen* was very probably a German lied.

[55] Something similar seems to have happened in the anonymous *Missa L'ardant desir* (see below) and Jacob Obrecht's *Missa Petrus apostolus*. In these two cases, only the scribal resolutions of the tenors have survived; the archetypes themselves are lost (see Wegman, 'Another Mass by Busnoys?', p. 7).

to work out.[56] The scribe of *Gross senen* apparently attempted to clarify the interpretation of the archetype, by providing clues such as mensuration signs and augmentation canons. It is unlikely that he had the mass in score, for transcription reveals that most of these clues are incorrect. The resolutions, however, do fit the music.

Example 5 shows phrase A of the archetype, and its rhythmic shapes under the mensuration signs O, C, Ⓞ and Ȼ. The composer uses essentially the same signs as Domarto, and yet he achieves less rhythmic variety. The reason for this is simple: the *Gross senen* tenor was taken over in its original form, and in that form the melody offered no more scope for rhythmic transformation. There are no statements of phrase B in perfect prolation, probably because the augmentation implied by Ⓞ and Ȼ would render the sections based on that phrase too long (the cycle is unusually long as it stands).

Example 5. Anonymous, *Missa Gross senen*: (a) mass tenor (phrase A); (b) relative durations of cantus firmus notes in the mensurations O, C, Ⓞ, and Ȼ (counted in multiples of minims)

Apart from mensural transformation, the *Gross senen* tenor is also subjected to three further procedures, indicated by canons in the source. The first is straightforward tenor augmentation. The second procedure initially involves 4:1 or 3:1 augmentation, but the singer is required to reduce the notes by half or a third after each cadence, until they are sung *ut iacent*: 'In quadruplum/triplum crescit, sed clausulando decrescit'. In the Qui tollis, this procedure leads to the successive proportions 4:2:1, in the Osanna to 3:1. In the Crucifixus the second procedure is to be combined with a third, in which the singer is required to double every first of two consecutive minims: 'Inter binas minimas, prima alteratur'. Transcription

---

[56] The *Missa Quant ce viendra* applies proportional cantus firmus transformation, like Dufay's *Missa Se la face ay pale* and the anonymous *Missa Gentil madona mia* (TrentC 91, fols. 247ᵛ–256ᵛ). It was attributed to Antoine Busnoys by Richard Taruskin (cf. Taruskin, 'Busnoys and the *L'homme armé* Tradition', pp. 292–3).

reveals that this canon is to be applied even to consecutive minim rests.

The composer's intentions are on the whole clear and consistent, and can be easily reconstructed, even though in the manuscript they have become confused in a muddle of erroneous mensuration signs and canons. The *Missa Gross senen* employs all eight mensurations that had been used in Domarto's *Missa Spiritus almus*, with the possible exception of C3.[57] With regard to the 'erroneous' signs ₵ and O2, it is worth adding that the anonymous composer compounds Domarto's 'errors' by vertically combining the signs *with one another*. Thus he achieves a 4:1 proportion between the tenor and its surrounding voices. Busnoys was to take over the same practice in his *O crux lignum* and *L'homme armé* masses.[58] Two additional correspondences strengthen the relationship between *Spiritus almus* and *Gross senen*. First, the two signs Ⓞ and O [ɪɪɪ] occur only once in each mass, and in both cycles in the same section, the Patrem. Secondly, the *Missa Gross senen* presents, like *Spiritus almus*, the signs ₵ and ₵ in vertical juxtaposition (in Kyrie ɪɪ and Qui tollis).

Each of the mensural practices in the *Missa Gross senen*, taken by itself, is rare enough for a mid-fifteenth-century mass. But their combination, both in Domarto's *Missa Spiritus almus* and in this cycle, seems more than coincidental. Since the *Gross senen* Mass moreover employs mensural cantus firmus transformation, it is difficult to resist the conclusion that one of the two composers was influenced by the other. The question is: which? Both cycles must have been copied in Trent around 1462. But the style of *Gross senen* is definitely more advanced than that of *Spiritus almus*, for reasons to be presented below. While the *Spiritus almus* Mass could well date from around 1450, *Gross senen* is unlikely to have been more than a few years old when it was copied in TrentC 89. Domarto's mass was probably the model, *Gross senen* the emulation. From the viewpoint of transmission that conclusion is not surprising: if *Spiritus almus* reached Poland (in PozU 7022), there is no reason to assume that it would not have been distributed in Germany as well. But one question remains: what could have induced a German com-

---

[57] The anonymous composer introduces sesquialtera proportion at the end of the first Agnus Dei (which is in C|), but the passage in which this happens is too short to determine whether the composer intended triple division of the semibreve or the breve.

[58] Cf. Taruskin, 'Busnoys and the *L'homme armé* Tradition', pp. 284–5, who credits Busnoys with this innovation.

Rob C. Wegman

poser working around 1460 to adopt some of the typical structural and notational features of the *Missa Spiritus almus?* To address that question we will have to turn to the other masses that seem to show Domarto's influence.

The second relevant mass is Busnoys's *Missa O crux lignum*.[59] The tenor of this cycle is the twelfth verse of the Holy Cross sequence *Laudes crucis attollamus*. As in Domarto's mass, the chant melody is slightly ornamented and freely rhythmicised into a fixed notational archetype for the whole work (numbers of breve rests do vary, however). In the course of the mass, Busnoys presents the archetype in the same mensurations that Domarto had used for his tenor, with the exception of C3. But unlike *Spiritus almus*, this yields two different rhythmic shapes, not four: the notation of the tenor is such that only changes of prolation affect its rhythm, not changes of tempus. But the relationship with Domarto is evident: in fact, there is no other fifteenth-century cycle which so closely resembles *Spiritus almus* in its approach to the cantus firmus as *O crux lignum*.

To confirm the relationship, Busnoys's mass shares with *Spiritus almus* the very same mensurations as the *Missa Gross senen*, while adding two more signs, O3 and Φ. Again, the signatures O and O [III] occur together in the Patrem (though this time also in the Sanctus). The vertical juxtaposition of C with O2 in Busnoys's mass strongly recalls Domarto's combination of C and ₵, since O2 is an alternative sign for ₵ [III]. Finally, *O crux lignum* shares with *Gross senen* the vertical combination of C and O2 (the latter mensuration indicated in the unique source, VatS 51, as ₵ with triple groupings of breve rests, as recommended by Tinctoris).[60]

The Domarto–Busnoys relationship has important historical implications. These concern first of all the younger composer's

[59] Edition in D. W. Shipley, ed., *Antoine Busnois: Missa O crux lignum triumphale*, Das Chorwerk 123 (Wolfenbüttel, 1978); cantus firmus treatment discussed in E. H. Sparks, *Cantus Firmus in Mass and Motet 1420–1520* (Berkeley and Los Angeles, 1963), pp. 172 and 458–9, and Wegman, 'Another Mass by Busnoys?', pp. 5–6.

[60] The mensural usage in Busnoys's sacred music is a vast and complex subject, which fully deserves detailed study. It would therefore seem unwise to restrict the comparison with Domarto's *Missa Spiritus almus* to *O crux lignum*, and to pass over the evidence that is provided by Busnoys's other sacred compositions. Table 4 presents an inventory of Busnoys's mensural usage and provides a context for the relationship between the two composers. In this inventory, the mensural divisions are indicated, where necessary, as in Apel, *The Notation of Polyphonic Music* (see note 30 above). Of the eighteen mensurations employed by Busnoys, nine are found in Domarto's *Missa Spiritus almus* (i.e. 1, 2, 5, 6, 8, 11, 12, 13, 14). Two others, 7 and 9, are found in Domarto's three-voice *Missa quinti toni irregularis*.

Table 4 *Mensural usage in the Latin-texted works by Antoine Busnoys*

	Sign	Mensural divisions	Note value(s) equivalent to perfect breve in O	Works employing the mensuration (see list below)
(1)	⊙	III, 3, 3	1 S	1, 2 [implied augmentation]
(2)	₵	III, 2, 3	1 S	1, 2 [implied augmentation]
(3)	₵	III, 2, 3	4 S	1
(4)	Ɔ̇	III, 2, 3	3 Bᵃ	14
(5)	O	III, 3, 2	—	1, 2, 7, 14
(6)		II, 3, 2	—	6, 9, 10, 12
(7)	Φ	III, 3, 2	2 B	2, 10
(8)	O2	III, 2, 2	3 B	1, 2, 4, 5, 7, 10, 11, 14
(9)	O3	III, 3, 2	3 B	2, 7, 8, 9, 12, 13, 14
(10)	C	III, 2, 2	3 S	2
(11)		II, 2, 2	3 S	6, 10
(12)	₵	2, 2	3 B	2, 3, 6, 8, 13
(13)	C2	2, 2	3 B	8, 12
(14)	C3	2, 3	3 S	1
(15)		3, 2	9 M	2, 8
(16)	₵3	3, 2	3 B	8, 12
(17)	Ɔ	2, 2	4 S	6, 12
(18)	Ɔ̇	2, 2	4 B	1

Compositions: [1] *Missa L'homme armé*; [2] *Missa O crux lignum*; [3] *Patrem de village*; [4] *Ad cenam agni*; [5] *Alleluia verbum caro*; [6] *Anima mea liquefacta est*; [7] *Anthoni usque limina*; [8] *Conditor alme siderum*; [9] *In hydraulis*; [10] *Magnificat sexti toni*; [11] *Noel, noel*; [12] *Regina celi* I; [13] *Regina celi* II; [14] *Victime paschali*. Mensural divisions are indicated according to the system of W. Apel (see note 30).

ᵃThe sign Ɔ probably denotes sesquialtera proportion, carried out on the level of the minim (A. Seay, ed., *Johannis Tinctoris opera theoretica*, Corpus Scriptorum de Musica 22/IIa (n.p., 1978), p. 48). It is thus identical with the above mensuration 14 (C3).

musical development. Busnoys was active in Tours in 1460 and 1465 (and almost certainly in the intervening years) and began to work irregularly for the Burgundian chapel in 1465–7.[61] There are two indications that the *Missa O crux lignum*, copied in VatS 51 around 1474,[62] was probably written after his move to the north. First, the somewhat unobvious choice of the twelfth verse of *Laudes crucis* was probably determined by local liturgical usage in the Netherlands. Reinhard Strohm has pointed out that in Bruges and

[61] P. Higgins, '*In hydraulis* Revisited: New Light on the Career of Antoine Busnois', *Journal of the American Musicological Society*, 39 (1986), pp. 69–75.
[62] Roth, *op. cit.*, pp. 237–40.

Utrecht (and probably elsewhere in the Low Countries), the verse 'O crux lignum' alone was sung on the Exaltation of the Cross (14 September), whereas the sequence *Laudes crucis* itself belonged to the liturgy of 3 May.[63] Secondly, Jacob Obrecht also singled out the verse 'O crux lignum' in his motet *Salve crux arbor vite*.[64] Comparison of Obrecht's and Busnoys's elaborations of the melody shows that the two composers must have used identical versions of the chant (see Example 6).[65] Identical versions of chants in different polyphonic compositions are exceptional. The correspondence becomes all the more significant if one considers that the only place of activity common to both men's careers was Bruges, and that this was one of the places where the 'O crux lignum' verse had a separate liturgical significance.[66] Evidently Busnoys's *Missa O crux lignum* was written in the Burgundian Netherlands, between about 1465 and 1474.

In the context of other Flemish-Burgundian masses from the 1450s to 70s,[67] Busnoys's debt to Domarto becomes all the more striking. None of Busnoys's contemporaries in the Southern Netherlands (e.g. Wreede, Tick, Heyns, de Clibano) is known to have had any interest in mensural transformation, even though Domarto's mass was well known there (it was copied in the Bruges choirbook LucAS 238 in *c.* 1467–9; see note 4 above). So, whatever his musical backgrounds had been in Tours, Busnoys must have become strongly influenced by Domarto's *Missa Spiritus almus* after about 1465.

It would be speculative to suggest that Busnoys and Domarto came to know each other personally after the mid-1460s. Domarto's whereabouts after 1449 are unclear, and he might well have died by the time Busnoys came to the north. Moreover, it is doubtful whether Busnoys's travels with the Burgundian chapel would have left him much time to receive personal tuition from a master work-

---

[63] Strohm, *Music in Late Medieval Bruges*, pp. 145 and 177.
[64] Edition in A. Smijers, ed., *Jacob Obrecht opera omnia editio altera*, II/1 (Amsterdam, 1956), pp. 17–35.
[65] This is all the more significant since, as Donald W. Shipley has pointed out, the third line of 'O crux lignum' in Busnoys's mass (and Obrecht's motet) is completely different from that line in the original sequence by Adam de Saint-Victor (*Missa O crux lignum triumphale*, p. iii).
[66] Strohm, *Music in Late Medieval Bruges*, pp. 38–41, 54–5 and 145.
[67] Discussed in Strohm, *ibid.*, pp. 120–44.

Example 6. Comparison of cantus firmus statements of the verse 'O crux lignum' from the sequence *Laudes crucis attollamus*: (a) Jacob Obrecht, *Salve crux* (four tenor statements); based on unique source, *Liber selectarum cantionum quas vulgo mutetas appellant, sex, quinque et quatuor vocum* (Augsburg, 1520; RISM 1520[4]), fols. 128[v]– 143[r]; (b) reconstruction of Obrecht's cantus firmus (four phrases); (c) Antoine Busnoys, *Missa O crux lignum*; based on unique source, VatS 51, fols. 104[v]–113[r]

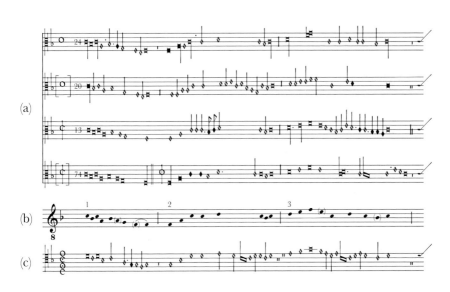

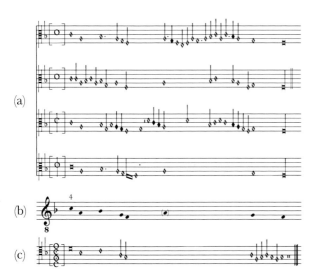

ing in the Netherlands.[68] The conditions under which Ockeghem might have influenced him in 1460–5 had surely been more favourable than those under which Domarto could have done so after that period. And yet there is surprisingly little trace of any influence of Ockeghem in Busnoys's surviving sacred works.[69] The problem that faces us here is not very different from the one that arose in our discussion of the *Gross senen* Mass. In both cases there is a clear and (in the context) unusual relationship with Domarto's *Missa Spiritus almus*, and yet the assumption of direct contact raises more questions than it provides answers.

A possible solution is provided by the third cycle, the anonymous *Missa L'ardant desir*. I have described and analysed this remarkable work elsewhere, arguing that it was probably written by Busnoys, so its relevant features need be only briefly summarised here.[70] The cantus firmus of the mass is the tenor of the song *L'ardant desir*, of around 1400.[71] This tenor serves, in its presumably original form, as the notational archetype for the whole mass, down to scribal details such as ligaturing and ligature shapes. In most of the sections the cantus firmus is subjected to mensural transformation, by presentation in the signatures O, C, ₵ and Ɔ. Indeed, this is the dominating type of cantus firmus treatment in the mass. But in several sections the mensural transformations are preceded by sophisticated manipulations such as omission of the stems, turning the notation upside down, exchanges of note values, and combinations of all three. In these and other respects, as I have argued, the *Missa L'ardant desir* forms the 'missing link' between the masses of Busnoys and Obrecht. At the same time there is a strong debt to

---

[68] On the other hand, Busnoys was not permanently associated with the chapel until 1470; before that date, his services were on a freelance basis (Higgins, *op. cit.*, pp. 41–53). During the irregular periods of Busnoys's activity in 1467–70, Charles the Bold was mostly in Flanders and Brabant; this may suggest that the composer was living somewhere in this area. From 1471 onwards, he is found travelling in the retinue of the duke through the entire Burgundian state (*ibid.*, pp. 53–61). If Domarto and Busnoys ever met, it was most probably in the period 1465–70.

[69] Some typical central French tendencies that occur in Busnoys's secular motet *In hydraulis* of 1465–7 are discussed in R. C. Wegman, 'Guillaume Faugues and the Anonymous Masses *Au chant de l'alouete* and *Vinnus vina*', *Tijdschrift van de Vereniging voor Nederlandse Muziekgeschiedenis*, 41 (1991), pp. 27–64.

[70] See Wegman, 'Another Mass by Busnoys?'; and Wegman, Communication, *Music & Letters*, 71 (1990), pp. 633–5.

[71] See D. Fallows, 'Busnoys and the Early Fifteenth Century: A Note on "L'ardant desir" and "Faictes de moy"', *Music & Letters*, 71 (1990), pp. 20–4.

Domarto, which is confirmed by the mensural usage of the mass.[72]

The most remarkable aspect of the cantus firmus treatment of the *L'ardant desir* composer is that he regarded and treated the mensurally notated tenor as an indivisible entity. More widely employed types of treatment, such as isomelism and embellishment, reduced tenors to sets of intervals, and would play on their melodic aspect only. The *L'ardant desir* composer played on much more than that: his procedures worked on note values as conceptual symbols, on notes and ligatures as graphic shapes, and on their behaviour under different visual and mensural conditions. His mentality was that of an experimenter; the *L'ardant desir* tenor served as a guinea pig. But what did the procedures have in common, and what did the 'experiments' reveal? And why was mensural transformation the dominant technique in the mass?

It is my contention that the key to these questions, and to the ones raised earlier, lies in the specific nature of the mensural notation system. Although it would go beyond the scope of the present article to explore fully the depths of that system – one of the great intellectual achievements of the late Middle Ages – it is nevertheless vital to our discussion to outline briefly some of its essential features.

The aim of mensural notation was not primarily to describe, as accurately and efficiently as possible, music as sound, but to represent it abstractly, according to what was perceived as its true nature. Mensural notation offered the information necessary to realise music in space and time, but a composition was seen as more than just its realisation: it had an independent existence on paper. Here it was shaped according to a conceptual logic, a logic that no performance (or modern transcription) could fully bring out. That logic was seen as essential to the piece. And it is that logic which the mensural notation system embodied.

Most relevant to the present discussion is the mensural understanding of concepts such as note and note value. Although we tend to speak of longs, breves, semibreves etc. as note values, in the

---

[72] The *Missa L'ardant desir* shares fewer signs with Domarto's *Missa Spiritus almus* than do the anonymous *Missa Gross senen* and Busnoys's *Missa O crux lignum*. A direct context for *L'ardant desir*'s mensural usage is provided by the sacred works of Busnoys (see note 60 above): the mass employs all but four of the mensurations listed in Table 4 above (i.e. mensurations 1–2, 5–13, 15 and 17–18). Other correspondences with Busnoys's mensural usage are discussed in Wegman, 'Another Mass by Busnoys?', pp. 2–5.

mensural notation system these were simply called notes. By the *value* of a note was understood the number of next-smaller notes to which it was equivalent. The value was not an intrinsic quality of the note (as it is now), but a variable property: any note could assume several different values. Therefore, a given series of notes signified nothing if that property was not defined in advance (i.e. by a mensuration sign). It is important to stress that mensural theory avoided speaking of relative duration; this was an irrelevant pragmatic concept, not synonymous with either note or note value.

A brief example may illustrate this. In ☉ a semibreve can, depending on the context, assume several different values (expressed in numbers of minims): 2 (imperfection), 3 (perfect), 4 and 5 (alteration plus imperfection), and 6 (alteration). Although the values are different, conceptually there is only one note, a semibreve. It may seem that *value* here is synonymous with relative duration, but that is not in fact the case. For different values can express the same durations: in ☉ an imperfect semibreve (value: 2 minims) has the same duration as an altered minim (indivisible), and an altered semibreve (value: 6 minims) has the same duration as an imperfect breve (value: 2 semibreves). The durations are the same, but the notes and values are different. To modern eyes this seems needlessly inefficient and confusing: present-day transcriptions of fifteenth-century music simply equate the concepts of note, value and relative duration. Yet despite the evident gains in explicitness, this inevitably involves straitjacketing the extreme flexibility that is one of the strengths of the mensural system. To treat essentially different concepts as synonymous is to lose a wealth of inherent meaning.

This is most clearly seen in works whose complex structures present-day notation is unable to represent adequately, for example, Ockeghem's *Missa prolationum*. It may be perfectly defensible from our point of view to edit this mass, for instance, with barlines drawn through all staves, since 'the mensurations of the individual voice-parts may be thought to conceal a basic pulse which in an edition ought to take precedence over their metrical peculiarities'.[73] Such an edition would grasp the music as a listener attempts to

---

[73]   J. Caldwell, *Editing Early Music*, Early Music Series 5 (Oxford, 1985), p. 28.

grasp it, namely, with reference to an intuitively postulated basic pulse. It would convert all notes to their durational equivalents in the uniform time signature which represents that hypothetical pulse. But mensural theory did not recognise such a concept as a 'basic pulse' (at least not before the sixteenth century), and its proponents would argue that the edition states untruths. It negates the underlying mensural processes, by turning strings of notes which interact under the influence of mensurations into merely additive sequences of rigid symbols. It replaces the inherent mensural order with an extraneous one, by drawing barlines for convenience. It represents as different what is intrinsically identical (e.g. different resolutions of the same canonic melody), and equates what is distinct. It is, moreover, inefficient, since it frequently represents long notes as successions of several tied notes. In a word, it is, as Tinctoris would have put it, an edition for the 'unlearned'.

Because of the distinction between what music is conceptually and what it is aurally, the notation of a melody was often seen *as part of its identity*. To rhythmicise a non-mensural tune was to give it such an identity. For that reason composers often respected the notational shapes of borrowed melodies with meticulous care. For instance, when Ockeghem took over the tenor of the anonymous *Caput* Mass for his own cycle, he '[left] the ligatures as well as the clef of the borrowed voice essentially unchanged', for he wanted to keep the melody 'untouched *in its external appearance*, although it is actually transposed to the bass register [by a verbal canon]'.[74] Indeed, the Sanctus of Ockeghem's mass 'retains even the trifling irregularities of [the *Caput* Master's] Sanctus, the omission of [bars] A43 and A55'.[75] Many more such instances could be given. There is even one case in which a composer took over only the rhythmic shape of his model, not the actual melody itself, the anonymous *Missa de Sancto Johanne Baptista*.[76] Here, notation takes precedence over every other aspect of the pre-existent melody. A direct consequence of the attitude described here is that composers who held the attitude were not able to change their pre-existent

---

[74] Bukofzer, *op. cit.*, pp. 266–7.
[75] *Ibid.*, p. 267.
[76] R. C. Wegman, 'Another "Imitation" of Busnoys's *Missa L'homme armé* – and Some Observations on *Imitatio* in Renaissance Music', *Journal of the Royal Musical Association*, 114 (1989), pp. 189–202.

tenors by anything but *external* (and hence schematic) means: mensural changes or verbal canons.

It is in this context that the procedures of the *Missa L'ardant desir* are to be understood. What these procedures (including mensural transformation) have in common is that they work on the *notation* of the original tenor, affecting both its graphic and conceptual nature. What the 'experiments' reveal is, ultimately, the nature and workings of the mensural notation system. This is the crucial difference from more traditional schematic techniques such as augmentation, diminution, transposition, retrograde and inversion. The latter techniques can conceivably remain effective even if the tenor is renotated (e.g. in different note values or in present-day notation). The most that is needed, if anything, is minor readjustments in the verbal canons, to change the actual ratios or intervals. In contrast, the *L'ardant desir* Mass is all *about* notation; the slightest change in the shape of its tenor would destroy the mass's very structure. To find mensural transformation as the dominant procedure in this context is surely significant. It indicates how the anonymous composer perceived Domarto's technique, and why he was fascinated by it. Mensural transformation, it is now apparent, was not just another trick in the vast stock of *Kanonkünste* of the Netherlands composers. It was a procedure motivated by an essentially different philosophy: the exploration of the possibilities inherent in the notation of a tenor. That philosophy had been the main innovation in Domarto's *Missa Spiritus almus*.

We may now draw some broader conclusions. The masses discussed here, *Gross senen*, *O crux lignum* and *L'ardant desir*, seem to be the only surviving products of a 'school' of mass composers who, following Domarto, were fascinated by mensural notation and its inherent possibilities. If they borrowed tunes from existing compositions, they adopted them as they found them, leaving their notational shapes intact. If they borrowed non-mensural tunes, as in the case of *O crux lignum* (and *Spiritus almus* itself), they provided them with fixed notational shapes. The range of cantus firmus procedures was limited by the desire to respect the notational shape of the tenor; hence composers had no option but to apply schematic procedures. The actual choice of procedure depended on the possibilities inherent in the tenor. Thus Busnoys, in his *L'homme armé* Mass, had to restrict himself to a· gmentation, inversion and transposition, since the notational shape of the *L'homme armé* tune rules out mensural transformation (see above). The *L'ardant desir* tenor, on the other hand, offered a wide range of possibilities, and the anonymous composer of the mass fully exploited those as he transplanted the tenor in the new context. In this latter mass, the cantus firmus treatment assumes almost the character of 'variations on a theme'. The crucial underlying philosophy is that notation is an inalienable part of the 'theme', and a potentially rich source of 'thematic' transformations. This philosophy – and probably Domarto's example – rather than direct contact with the older master himself, was the binding element of the 'school'.

Additional support for that conclusion comes from the fact that the philosophy remained a source of inspiration even to a composer of the Josquin generation, Jacob Obrecht. The procedures that are unique to Domarto's 'school' were to become the virtual hallmark of Obrecht's masses. Although it would exceed our terms of reference to give a full account of Obrecht's cantus firmus treatment, it is worth outlining the most relevant features. It has often been remarked that Obrecht had a consistent tendency to respect the original notation of voices quoted from polyphonic works. Mensural transformation was among his stock procedures. We find it particularly in the masses with segmented cantus firmi (e.g. *Je ne demande*, *Malheur me bat*, *Rose playsante*). Here the individual segments, in their original notation, are usually repeated in different mensurations. This results in a 'degree of rhythmic dissimilarity between statements that is not characteristic of framework tenors as a class'.[77] In a number of masses based on non-mensural tunes, Obrecht gave the tenors fixed notational shapes, and then transformed them mensurally. This was the case in *Maria zart* and *O lumen ecclesie*, and almost certainly in *Petrus apostolus*; another mass in which this may have happened is *Grecorum*. Some of Obrecht's more arbitrary procedures recall the *Missa L'ardant desir*: in the *Missa De tous biens plaine*, for instance, the tenor notes are to be sung in order according to their value, following the canonic instruction 'digniora sunt priora'. Elsewhere in the same mass Obrecht repeated this procedure in retrograde. Notationally, his masses

[77] Sparks, *op. cit.*, pp. 266–7.

have little in common with the *Missa Spiritus almus*.[78] This need not be surprising, since Domarto's mass must have been composed at least thirty years earlier than any of Obrecht's works. Nevertheless, it seems clear that Obrecht was a late follower of the philosophy of which Domarto had been the most important, and probably the earliest, exponent.

We shall never know whether Domarto was actually the founder of the 'school' (if we may call it that), since it is always possible that he adopted his procedures from earlier masses that are now lost. On the other hand, the unusually wide distribution of his mass, and Tinctoris's grudging admission that he was 'non parvae auctoritatis', would suggest that he was at least its chief missionary.

While the distribution and fame of Domarto's mass explain its apparent influence, they raise new questions in turn. It is extremely rare for a mid-fifteenth-century mass to have survived in five sources – one of which may have been copied as late as thirty years after the mass was composed (ModE M.1.13, of 1481). Two better-known contemporary masses, Dufay's *Se la face ay pale* and Ockeghem's *Caput*, are both found in fewer manuscripts, and neither of these cycles received anything like the attention Tinctoris gave to *Spiritus almus*. It may be, of course, that the chances of survival have favoured Domarto's mass more than any other contemporary cycle, and that the original patterns of transmission were quite different. On the other hand, the assumption that Domarto was a mere *Kleinmeister* compared to great names like Dufay and Ockeghem could well be a twentieth-century prejudice, stemming from our tendency to conceive music history in terms of great names. Only a critical examination of the transmission and style of the *Missa Spiritus almus* can throw light upon these questions.

Comparison of the five sources for the mass reveals that three, LucAS 238, TrentC 88, and VatS 14, form a closely knit group, and must be closest to the composer's original. The last two of these sources can even be shown to go back to a common exemplar. They alone share a scribal peculiarity in the notation of the tenor of the

---

[78] The mass that comes closest to Domarto's mensural usage is *Ave regina celorum*, which contains, like *Spiritus almus*, the vertical juxtapositions O2/O, C/ ¢, and ¢/ O. It may be significant that there are some elements of mensural transformation in this mass, but the procedure is not applied systematically. Reinhard Strohm has argued that Obrecht's *Missa Ave regina celorum* was composed in Bruges, *c.* 1485–90 (*Music in Late Medieval Bruges*, p. 147).

Example 7. Variant in notation of tenor notes 1–7 of Petrus de Domarto, *Missa Spiritus almus*: (a) TrentC 88 and VatS 14: Agnus Dei; (b) TrentC 88 and VatS 14: other movements, and all surviving movements in LucAS 238, PozU 7022, and ModE M.1.13

Agnus Dei (see Example 7): instead of combining notes 6 and 7 into one ligature – as all other manuscripts do, and as these sources do elsewhere – they ligate notes 5 and 6. Musically this makes no difference, of course, but since it is the point of Domarto's mass that the notation of the tenor remain unchanged, and since the two sources have this peculiarity at the very same place, it is unlikely that the variant cropped up in TrentC 88 and VatS 14 independently.[79] PozU 7022 and ModE M.1.13 must be separated from Domarto's original by longer lines of transmission: each in its own way introduces various changes in the musical text.[80] In ModE M.1.13 these changes almost assume the character of editorial reworkings; the scribe seems to have attempted to bring the mass in line with practices current in the 1470s. Tinctoris's four musical examples (all taken from the Gloria) provide too little information to relate them to any of the surviving sources.

A few peculiar features in the transmission of the *Missa Spiritus almus* deserve comment. Text placement is most carefully worked out in the Bruges manuscript LucAS 238, but the three southern sources follow basically the same underlay. LucAS 238, TrentC 88 and VatS 14 tend not to write Mass Ordinary text in the tenor; instead they provide the text of the original chant. In LucAS 238 this is done with the same careful text placement that characterises the underlay of the other voices, namely, with a long melisma separating the syllables 'al' and 'mus'. TrentC 88 retains this feature only in the Cum sancto but otherwise gives 'spiritus almus' as a mere incipit, as does VatS 14. In the Gloria tua both these latter sources omit the incipit and provide the appropriate Mass text instead. ModE M.1.13 consistently places Mass text in all

---

[79] According to Strohm, 'a filiation of the . . . sources based on the variant readings suggests that [VatS 14] itself depends directly or indirectly on [LucAS 238]' (*Music in Late Medieval Bruges*, p. 142). I have found no conclusive evidence to support this suggestion, and the common ancestry of TrentC 88 and VatS 14 seems to me to contradict it.

[80] Cf. Perz, *op. cit.*, p. 34.

tenor statements. It would appear from this that Domarto meant his tenor to be sung to its original words, and that the substitution of Mass Ordinary text was a later, southern tendency.[81]

Throughout the three most reliable sources there is a tendency not to provide the mensuration sign O in the contrapuntal voices when perfect tempus is intended. None of these manuscripts, indeed, gives that signature in the Sanctus and Agnus Dei. In the Patrem, neither TrentC 88 nor VatS 14 indicates perfect tempus, while the movement has not survived in LucAS 238. In the remaining movements, the sign O tends to be given in only one or two of the contrapuntal voices, never in all three. This would seem to suggest that Domarto never provided any sign in the first place, as is frequently seen in mid-fifteenth-century masses.

The three sources also show some confusion with regard to the indication of imperfect tempus in the contrapuntal voices. In the Christe, Benedictus, and Agnus II, the implied signature was almost certainly ₵. But in the Agnus II (a duo) only VatS 14 gives that sign; the other two sources write C. In the Christe and Benedictus there is more disagreement with regard to imperfect tempus. In both sections it is imperative that the mensuration be diminished, since the intended proportion with the tenor (which is in C) is 2:1. Nevertheless, TrentC 88 and (the top voice excepted) LucAS 238 erroneously write C in the Christe; LucAS 238 repeats this error in the Benedictus. In this latter section, VatS 14 gives ₵ and TrentC 88 C2. Again it would seem that Domarto's autograph looked different from the versions as we have them. If he provided a mensuration sign at all, it was most likely C with implied diminution.[82] This was an English practice,[83] but it was sometimes adopted on the Continent: we find it, for instance, in a northern copy of Dufay's *Missa Ave regina caelorum.* ModE M.1.13, predictably, has resolved all mensural ambiguities.

There is no ready explanation for the unique occurrence of the (correct) variant C3, for C3, in LucAS 238 (see above). Geographi-

---

[81] The same conclusion is reached in A. E. Planchart, 'Parts With Words and Without Words: The Evidence for Multiple Texts in Fifteenth-Century Masses', *Studies in the Performance of Late Mediaeval Music*, ed. S. Boorman (Cambridge, 1983), pp. 227–51.

[82] Precedent for the use of C in all voices with implied 2:1 proportion between tenor and contrapuntal voices is found in Leonel Power's *Missa Alma redemptoris mater.*

[83] See R. C. Wegman, 'Concerning Tempo in the English Polyphonic Mass, C. 1420–70', *Acta Musicologica*, 61 (1989), pp. 47–8.

cally this source, copied in the north, is closest to Domarto, and a critical comparison of the various versions of *Spiritus almus* confirms its authority. On the other hand, it seems unlikely that all the other sources (including Tinctoris) would have independently converted Lucca's sign to C3. Moreover, we have already observed that the use of C3 with triple division of the semibreve was an established practice, both before and after *Spiritus almus* was composed.[84] The Lucca sign, on the other hand, is an anomaly. In view of this, it seems most likely that the addition of the dot in LucAS 238 was the result of Tinctoris's influence, either when the source was copied, or when the *Proportionale* reached its users.[85]

The final feature relevant to our discussion of transmission is the use of ficta in *Spiritus almus*. Sharps figure prominently in every copy of the mass except ModE M.1.13. Their actual number and placement, however, differ in each source. Altogether, there are thirty-six sharps, whose distribution is as follows: 24 C♯, 5 G♯, and 7 F♯ (in D Dorian). The closely related versions VatS 14 and TrentC 88 together contain twenty-nine of these sharps, of which seventeen are identically placed. The Lucca fragment shares seven sharps with these manuscripts, and adds another six of its own; the Poznań fragment shares two sharps with VatS 14 and TrentC 88, and adds one. ModE M.1.13, significantly, has removed all sharps. It would seem from these figures that accidentals were among the notational symbols most likely to get lost in transmission; but that is not necessarily the case, for the three *flats* in Domarto's mass are faithfully transmitted in every copy. Even the Modena scribe, who had consistently purged the music of sharps, did not fail to copy any of the flats. It would appear that scribes tended to omit sharps rather than insert them, otherwise we should find similar variation with regard to ficta in many other masses. If that impression is correct, the conclusion must be that all thirty-six sharps in

---

[84] See notes 45, 52 and 60 above.

[85] The addition of the dot could perhaps be attributed to the theorist John Hothby, who was choirmaster and chaplain of Lucca Cathedral from 1467 to 1486. He had access to LucAS 238 by 1472, when the manuscript had been donated to the cathedral by Giovanni Arnolfini (Strohm, *Music in Late Medieval Bruges*, p. 122; suggestion made to me by Reinhard Strohm in a private communication, 20 February 1990). A similar addition of a dot to the signature C3 is found in ParisBNN 4379, fol. 11ᵛ, in the top voice of *Hé Robinet / Trigalore / Par ung vert pré* (the other two voices remain undotted). This is another combinative chanson to use the signature C3 (cf. note 52 above).

Domarto's mass may be original, and that the composer's auto-graph could well have contained more sharps.

The transmission of the *Missa Spiritus almus* sheds little light on the question of its date. The earliest *terminus ante quem* is provided by the TrentC 88 copy, which must have existed by about 1462 (see note 4 above). A more precise date must be established on the basis of stylistic evidence, but here we face an almost insurmountable problem: there is no uncontestably Continental four-voice mass (i.e. with a low contratenor)[86] which we know to have been copied before 1460.[87] Nor, indeed, is there any four-voice English mass which we know to have been copied before 1450.[88] The net result of these facts is that there are no criteria by which to establish a chronology of four-voice mass composition on the Continent before 1460. Consequently, any attempt to propose a precise date for Domarto's *Missa Spiritus almus* must be extremely tentative.

On the face of it, the source situation would seem to suggest that the Continental four-voice mass had taken off very rapidly, perhaps within about five or ten years. This would be in line with the dazzling style changes that evolved after about 1460,[89] and it would, moreover, explain the surprising absence of any Continental four-voice masses in such sources as TrentM 93 (*c.* 1450–6), TrentC 90 (*c.* 1452–8), and the early layer of TrentC 88 (fols. 1–24; *c.* 1456).[90] On the other hand, the Trent codices are obviously peripheral manuscripts for music from the north, and their value in this regard would seem at best dubious. Ultimately, it must be by a

---

[86] Four-part writing was, of course, hardly a novelty in the fifteenth century, but the four-part texture with low contratenor must have been a late invention (presumably in the 1440s). The significance of this invention is explored below.

[87] If the anonymous four-voice *Missa Thomas cesus* in the '1458' layer of VatSP B80 is Continental (despite the English origin of its tenor, see Reynolds, *op. cit.*, p. 285), it would push back the *terminus ante quem* for four-part mass writing on the Continent to 1458. Apart from this possible exception, the earliest copies of Continental four-voice masses are found in TrentC 88, TrentC 89, and the second layer of VatSP B80, all of which must date from the early 1460s.

[88] The earliest surviving copy of an English four-voice mass dates from *c.* 1451–2 (*Missa Caput*, in TrentM 93; for the date, see S. E. Saunders, 'The Dating of Trent 93 and Trent 90', *I codici musicali Trentini a cento anni dalla loro riscoperta*, ed. N. Pirrotta and D. Curti (Trent, 1986), pp. 60–83). The anonymous *Missa Salve sancta parens*, in the same source, also has four voices but does not include a low contratenor (see below); Margaret Bent has argued that the fourth voice may have been a later addition (M. Bent, ed., *Four Anonymous Masses*, Early English Church Music 22 (London, 1979), p. 181).

[89] See Wegman, 'The Anonymous Mass *D'ung aultre amer*'.

[90] For the dates, see Saunders, 'The Dating of the Trent Codices', pp. 87–91, and 'The Dating of Trent 93 and Trent 90'.

comparative analysis of the earliest surviving four-voice masses that we can attempt to establish a relative chronology – perhaps even a tentative time scale. This article is not the place to carry out such an investigation. I will merely attempt to show that there is a huge stylistic gap separating Domarto's *Missa Spiritus almus* from the most advanced masses that existed by the early 1460s. The question whether this gap corresponds to a span of five, ten or perhaps even fifteen years cannot be answered. But whatever the actual duration of that span, one conclusion will become increasingly clear: Domarto's mass must have been among the very first four-voice cycles to be written on the Continent.

As a point of reference the ideal cycle seems to be the anonymous *Missa Gross senen*, which we have already discussed above. First, like *Spiritus almus* this mass has a *terminus ante quem* of *c.* 1462. Secondly, the *Gross senen* Mass was very probably influenced by the structure and mensural usage of Domarto's mass, so if the anonymous composer decided *not* to imitate its style – the aspect most likely to become obsolete as the years went on – this indicates that fashions had significantly moved away from the styles that were current when *Spiritus almus* was composed. Thirdly, it is important not to select a mass by a composer who might be 'ahead of his time' and which may therefore give a distorted picture of current fashions. A work like the *Missa Gross senen* exactly satisfies this demand: composed probably in Germany, it is more likely to have followed fashions than to have led them. But fourthly, and most important, this mass is arguably among the most advanced pieces that existed by the early 1460s. Indeed, on its own terms it is an outstanding composition.

One could underpin these latter claims by pointing to readily identifiable features that are known to have been 'modern' in the 1460s and 70s.[91] Both contratenor and bass have assumed contrapuntal independence, and are written with pronounced rhythmic and melodic fluency. The handling of harmonic progressions is remarkably assured. There is a tendency to organise melodic lines

---

[91] A brief but important description of the style of the *Missa Gross senen* is in Strohm, 'Meßzyklen über deutsche Lieder', pp. 92–3. Strohm concludes: 'Der Komponist der *Missa Gross senen* ist ein Pionier der franko-niederländischen Messenkunst in der unmittelbaren Nachfolge Dufays ... Seine Identität oder wenigstens sein Tätigkeitsbereich wären der Erforschung wert!' (p. 93).

by means of repeated motifs, although this does not as yet result in actual sequences. The counterpoint is at times infused with imitation. Phrases of the cantus firmus are frequently imitated in the contrapuntal voices, particularly when the tenor is to be sung *ut iacet* (Agnus Dei III, Confiteor). Otherwise, most imitation in the four-voice sections tends to be between the top two voices only. In the tenorless sections there are frequent imitations of extended phrases between pairs of voices; in a number of cases the imitations even involve three parts (Pleni, Osanna II). The presence of such progressive elements, which were to be developed in the masses of Ockeghem, Dufay and Busnoys, indicates that the *Gross senen* composer was well aware of current stylistic trends. And, significantly, these same elements are virtually absent in the *Missa Spiritus almus*, as will be seen below.

But the progressiveness of the *Missa Gross senen* is evident from more than just these isolated elements. Example 8 shows how

Example 8. Anonymous, *Missa Gross senen*: bars 1–20 of Et in terra. Based on unique source, TrentC 89, fols. 28ᵛ–29ʳ.

Example 8 *continued*

Bass 15₁₋₂: semibreve rests separated by *punctus divisionis*; bass 16₃: breve dotted. The two dots cause the passage 15₁–16₃ to be shifted by one semibreve, but the contrapuntal context indicates that this must be incorrect.

radically innovatory Continental approaches to four-voice mass composition had become by the early 1460s. The example gives the first twenty bars of the Et in terra. The tenor carries the sign ☉, but the actual ratio of augmentation is not 2:1 but 4:1 (the source states 'in triplo crescere debet'). Thus the quick upward move of a fifth which opens the *Gross senen* melody (see Example 5) is turned into a prolonged arsis lasting seven bars. The composer seized on this opportunity to write a most impressive musical build-up.

The section starts with a self-contained, introductory duo in which the top two voices explore their modal ranges (bars 1–10). The duo stops three bars short of the tenor entry, with both voices cadencing on the same pitch, *g*. This cadence was traditionally the signal for all voices to enter simultaneously, and to surge forward in a thick, dynamic layer of sound (as in English masses such as *Caput* and *Veterem hominem*). But the *Gross senen* composer knew how to play his cards, and he played them in masterly fashion. The entry of contratenor and bass, in bar 11, is kept as unobtrusive as possible: both voices simply state, in unison, the note on which the introductory duo had ended. While the bass holds this note for two bars, the contratenor expands the combined range from unison to third, and – after the top voice has entered – to the fifth. Thus what happens in bars 11–12 is simply the gradual unfolding of a minor triad, out of a single note. When the tenor enters, in bar 13, the composer further expands the chord, by having the bass leap down an octave. So while the passage is kept static in harmonic terms, there is a progressive development of sonority and 'orchestration'. That development is reinforced by other means. The imitations between the top two voices give a sense of increasing momentum. The motifs are moreover shaped in such a way as to produce a gradual rhythmic intensification: from bars 11 to 16, the basic semibreve beat becomes increasingly filled in with minim and fusa patterns. Then the harmonic stasis is finally lifted (bar 16): the bass moves briefly in parallel tenths with the top voice – a major musical event after the prolonged G minor chord in bars 11–16. Bars 17–19 carry all these developments to their natural conclusion. Both top voice and bass leap up an octave (bars 16–17) and, while the tenor rises to the fifth, expand their combined range to two octaves (bar 18). The three contrapuntal voices now assume full melodic and rhythmic equality. By the time the cadence in bar 19 is reached, the music is in full motion.

This is an opening worthy of a Josquin. Although seemingly very simple, the passage shows a superb handling and coordination of musical parameters such as tone colour, pitch, rhythm and harmony. The composer uses these elements with refinement and a keen sense of drama: each new bar witnesses a further step in the gradual unfolding of sonority, the intensification of rhythm, and, finally, the unloosening of harmonic stillness. Rather than taking the standard four-part counterpoint for granted by simply stating it at the outset, the composer builds it up in an impressive, written-out crescendo.

The opening of the Et in terra is not an isolated example, but illustrates a broader trend. Throughout the 1460s we see Continental composers breaking away from the rigid patterns of their English exemplars, experimenting with new styles and approaches, and exploring the musical language in search of eloquent musical effects.[92] Increasingly they abandoned the evenness and balance that had characterised earlier mass styles and began to infuse their music with dramatic elements: sudden contrasts in scoring and rhythmic intensity, dazzling melodic rises and descents, and the use of imitations as rhythmic propellants.[93] The opening of the Et

[92] See Wegman, 'The Anonymous Mass *D'ung aultre amer*'.

[93] The best illustration of these trends is provided by Ockeghem's *Missa L'homme armé*, which must have existed by 1467–8 (Strohm, *Music in Late Medieval Bruges*, p. 30; all following references to D. Plamenac, ed., *Johannes Ockeghem: Collected Works*, I (2nd, corrected edn, American Musicological Society: Studies and Documents 3 (n.p., 1959), pp. 99–116). This mass is a virtual study in musical contrast. Particularly striking are the contrasts in rhythmic density. Most sections open in breve–semibreve movement, and end in minim–semiminim movement; Ockeghem alternates the two types of movement in between (compare, for instance, Et in terra bars 1–6 and 15–19 with bars 10–13 and 42–5). The maximum feasible speed depends on the rhythmic movement in the closing bars: if a section starts too fast, the music will sound increasingly huddled towards the end. On empirical grounds, the optimum tempo for the semibreve in O is unlikely to be much in excess of 60 M.M. At that speed, which seems right for the rhythmically most active passages, the opening bars sound extraordinarily 'slow': Ockeghem seems to have consciously 'written out' majestic, chordal openings. These contrast sharply with the floridity displayed elsewhere, especially in the tenorless sections (see particularly the Benedictus and Agnus Dei II).

The Other contrasts exploited by Ockeghem are those of scoring and tone colour. These occur first of all on a structural level. In the Agnus Dei the cantus firmus is transposed down an octave, and the voice ranges in this movement are approximately a fourth lower than in the remainder of the mass. There is thus a clear shift to a darker and denser sound – the sound we know so well from Ockeghem's later 'low' works (see particularly the Agnus Dei, bars 85–103). The suspicion that the composer was concerned to create a special effect at the end of his mass is confirmed by the expressive Agnus Dei III, which opens with remarkable (and unprecedented) 'soloistic' flourishes above the drawn-out notes of the cantus firmus. In the Credo, the cantus firmus has been transposed, too, from *G* down to *C*. This time, however, the transposition hardly affects the overall ranges, although it does affect the modality (this procedure was to be repeated in the Credo of Ockeghem's *Missa Ecce ancilla Domini*).

Ockeghem employs several means to heighten the variety of tone colour in his mass, the most simple being that of scoring. In the Gloria and Credo, full scoring is employed with considerable restraint: most of the time, either two or three voices are sounding. The ways in which these are combined, and in which the various voice groupings flow into one another, are so irregular that this gives the style an almost impressionistic quality. In all sections, the combined range of the voices continuously contracts and expands, from as little as a fifth to two octaves plus third (compare Credo bar 39 with 43, bar 83 with 93, and Sanctus bar 22 with 24). If the combined range is contracted, all voices can together easily remain below or above *c'* (compare Gloria bars 17–19 with Credo bars 122–3). Such collective shifts to either side of *c'* occur frequently in Ockeghem's mass and constitute one of its most distinctive features.

Other noteworthy special effects in Ockeghem's *L'homme armé* Mass are: the entry of a cantus firmus phrase on a musical culmination point (Credo bars 13–14; the entry is

in terra of the *Missa Gross senen* should be seen in that context. In terms of the handling of musical momentum it is a virtual counterpart of the well-known Continental device of the 'drive to the cadence'. If it were not for its copying date of *c.* 1462, and the German origin of its model, one could easily mistake the *Missa Gross senen* for a Franco-Flemish cycle from the late 1460s. Without doubt the cycle was a recent composition when it was copied in the Trent manuscript.

When we turn now to Domarto's *Missa Spiritus almus* we seem to be entering a different world, a world that must already have sounded archaic by the time TrentC 88 was copied. We are struck immediately by the dark, vibrant sonorities; the frequent modally incongruous progressions, dissonant combinations, and closely spaced cross-relations; the slow harmonic rhythm; the sparseness of imitations and cadences; and the undistinctive melodic style. Compared to *Gross senen* and other masses from the early 1460s this is a crude work, going back, it seems, to the very prehistory of the four-voice mass cycle. Yet, whatever its apparent position in long-term stylistic developments, Domarto's mass must be judged on its own terms and compared with closely related works. A closer inspection of its style seems therefore in order.

Although the *Missa Spiritus almus* is scored with a low contratenor (called 'tenor secundus' in all sources except ModE M.1.13 and PozU 7022), only eight of the ninety-nine cadential progressions are of the 'dominant–tonic' type; the remainder (including all final cadences) are of the vii_6–i type. In the final cadences Domarto invariably lets the contratenor state the third of the final chord (in four cases a major third), which note he then resolves into the fifth.

The rhythmic movement of the bass closely follows that of the tenor: it moves mainly in longs, breves and semibreves when the tenor is in augmentation, and in semibreves and minims when the tenor is stated *ut iacet*. As a consequence, the augmented-tenor sections are characterised by slow harmonic rhythm and show a sharply delineated stratification in two layers of rhythmic activity: the two active upper parts move above a harmonically solid layer of

accidentally misplaced by one bar in Plamenac's edition, p. 104); the dazzling melodic rise in the top voice and bass in Credo bars 110–13; the introduction of ficta in Credo bars 122 and 176–7; and the opening of the third Agnus Dei, mentioned above.

long, drawn-out notes. Apart from the duos, it is only in sections such as these that Domarto ventures to introduce occasional imitations between the upper voices. In the sections with the tenor *ut iacet*, the stratified texture gives way to a more integrated contrapuntal fabric, and imitation is almost totally absent. In either type of section the tenor and bass are hardly ever involved in the imitations. Even in sections or passages without cantus firmus, Domarto shows no great inclination to imitation.

There is also a tendency to couple the rhythmic movement of tenor and bass *within* sections. The preconceived tenor is structured in such a way that it has longer notes at the beginning and after about two-thirds of the melody, and smaller notes in the middle and towards the end (see Example 2). Thus every section has two 'built-in' drives, which the bass underscores by following the tenor's rhythmic movement. But, significantly, Domarto nearly always plays down the middle drive, by reductions of scoring. This can be seen, for instance, in the Christe (Example 9). The bass is clearly linked to the tenor in its rhythmic movement, stating longs and breves in bars 4–15, and breves and semibreves in bars 17–22. But while the former passage is in full scoring, thus exemplifying Domarto's typical dense and placid sonorities, the latter is merely a duo providing relief from those sonorities – the very place where one would expect an increase in rhythmic activity. It is noteworthy that the cantus firmus is 'laid bare' as the leading voice in this duo. A nearly identical passage is in the Crucifixus (cf. Example 11c below); here the tenor–bass duo is preceded by an extended, dovetailing duo for top voice and contratenor. Similar dovetailed duos involving the tenor are found in early English masses such as *Caput* and *Veterem hominem*, but English composers generally tended to couple the tenor with the top voice or contratenor and thus avoided giving it the prominence that it received in Domarto's mass. Dufay, in the Confiteor of his *Missa Se la face ay pale*, also 'exposed' the cantus firmus in a duo. Duos involving a scaffold tenor are a typical feature of early Continental four-voice masses (Dufay, *Se la face ay pale*; Ockeghem, *Missa Caput*); they are not found in isorhythmic motets. This English-inspired habit was to disappear in the 1460s: by then composers tended to regard the presence of the cantus firmus as something to be articulated musically, by means of full scoring.

Example 9. Petrus de Domarto, *Missa Spiritus almus*: bars 1–22 of Christe. Based on TrentC 88, fols. 401ᵛ–402ʳ (variant readings in the other sources not listed except when preferred to those of TrentC 88).

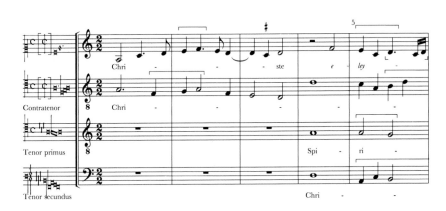

Example 9 *continued*

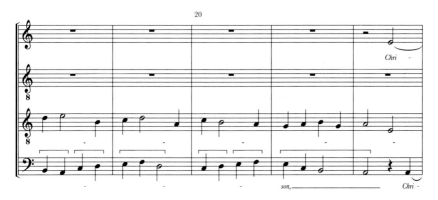

Top voice 2₃: MS reads *d'*; emended after all other sources except PozU 7022, which does not transmit this section.

Unlike the bass, the top voices are not linked to the tenor in their rhythmic activity, but rather tend to move independently. This is particularly obvious in sections with augmented tenor, for instance the Patrem (Example 10). After a brief, introductory duo for top voice and contratenor, the cantus firmus enters, accompanied by the bass in long note values. Above this slow-moving layer the top voices deliver the text, typically in brief melodic patches, with occasional hints of imitation. The origins of this stratified style evidently lie in the Ars Nova motet. We find the same style in such early cycles as Dufay's *Se la face ay pale* and Ockeghem's *Caput*,[94] but

---

[94] For the approximate date of Ockeghem's *Caput*, see below. Dufay's *Missa Se la face ay pale* was copied in TrentC 88 before *c.* 1462. The internal evidence of this mass is difficult to evaluate. Close parallels to its cantus firmus treatment are found in the (presumably later) anonymous Masses *Quant ce viendra* and *Gentil madona* (see note 56 above). As regards mensural usage, the Mass alternates O [ɪɪɪ] and C [ɪɪɪ]; this seems to relate it to the masses of Busnoys (cf. Wegman, 'Another Mass by Busnoys?', pp. 2–5). Since *Se la face ay pale* is written entirely in perfect minor modus, it is not a notational twin of the anonymous English *Missa Caput*, as claimed by Charles Hamm (*A Chronology of the Works of Guillaume Dufay Based on a Study of Mensural Practice* (Princeton, 1964), p. 129). The *Missa Se la face ay pale* is stylistically far removed from Domarto's *Missa Spiritus almus*; direct comparisons reveal little about the historical position of either cycle. Although the two masses could well have been composed around the same time, they seem to belong to different compositional traditions. After this article had gone to press I found a third source for Dufay's *Missa Se la face ay pale*: Siena, Biblioteca Comunale degli Intronati, MS K.ɪ.2, fols. 222ʳ–223ᵛ (portions of Credo and Sanctus).

Example 10. Petrus de Domarto, *Missa Spiritus almus*: bars 1–22 of Patrem. Based on TrentC 88, fols. 404ᵛ–405ʳ (variant readings in the other sources not listed except when preferred to those of TrentC 88).

Example 10 *continued*

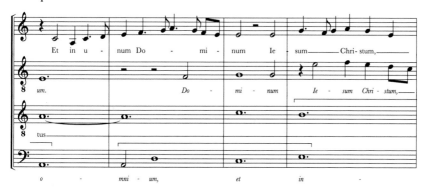

Top voice 21₃₋₆: MS gives rhythm F-F-M-M; emended after VatS 14 and ModE M.1.13 (passage does not survive in PozU 7022 and LucAS 238). Text placement in contratenor, bars 7–22, and second tenor, bars 16–22, based on the fundamentally identical underlays of ModE M.1.13 and VatS 14.

it was to disappear in masses from the 1460s (*Gross senen* provides an example). Noteworthy in Example 10 is the simultaneous rest in bar 6; a similar break in a duo occurs in the middle of the Pleni (edited out in ModE M.1.13 and PozU 7022). This was a typical English practice, which was rarely adopted on the Continent; it does figure prominently, however, in Ockeghem's *Missa Caput*.

The melodic style in the top voices is undistinctive. Sharply profiled motifs, and phrases of great melodic individuality, are absent. Instead, brief clichés that recur elsewhere in the mass are repeatedly encountered (one such cliché appears in bars 15–16 of Example 9 and bars 16–17 of Example 10). The overall impression is that Domarto wrote more or less *ad hoc* counterpoint to see the predetermined tenor through each statement. Cadences are comparatively rare in this counterpoint, again a feature which recalls the Ars Nova motet. In fact, the *Missa Spiritus almus* employs hardly any means of structuring the musical flow. Although the internal duos are sometimes clearly set off against the full passages, the general impression remains one of inarticulate counterpoint pushing steadily forward, with voices irregularly dropping in and out.

Yet the *Missa Spiritus almus* is a work of considerable individuality. The piece derives this quality from its stylistic homogeneity, the characteristic D Dorian flavour (to which the frequently prescribed ficta adds spice), and the typically low, dense sonorities. Domarto is particularly fond of writing sixth chords in the lowest three voices, often in parallel motion. Since the ranges as such are comparatively low, the frequent parallel thirds between the tenor and bass give the sound a dark, vibrant quality.

Domarto's use of ficta consists basically of two types: (a) harmonic ficta, to create major triads on D, E and A; (b) melodic ficta, to write melodic lines structured on diminished fourths (G♯–C, F♯–B♭, C♯–F). Sometimes the use of ficta leads to problematic situations which are difficult for the editor to resolve. For instance, in bar 9 of the second Kyrie (Example 11a), the *g♯′* prescribed in the top voice in TrentC 88 and VatS 14 belongs to the second type of ficta (the sharp is not transmitted in ModE M.1.13 and LucAS 238). It requires a simultaneous sharpening of the *g* in the bass, leading to a first-inversion chord of E major, which is then resolved into an F major triad – a most unusual progression, since the bass has to sing the interval of an augmented second (*g♯–f*). It is interesting to note that the top voice quotes notes 3–12 of the cantus firmus in this passage (indicated by asterisks in the example). Further on in the same movement, there is a closely spaced cross-relation: an A major triad (*c♯′* prescribed by TrentC 88 and VatS 14) is directly followed by one on C major (Example 11b). One could argue that these two problematic situations might have been caused by scribal corruption, since the ficta occurs only in the interdependent sources TrentC 88 and VatS 14. However, there are similar passages where PozU 7022 or LucAS 238 supports the readings of these manuscripts, for instance, the Crucifixus, bars 26–8 (Example 11c), and Et in terra, bars 9–10 (Example 11d). It would seem, therefore, that the 'strange' progressions and cross-relations were an integral part of the style of *Spiritus almus*.

A companion piece to Domarto's *Missa Spiritus almus* is the *Missa Caput* by Johannes Ockeghem. Although well known from Manfred Bukofzer's brilliant descriptive analysis,[95] this mass remains a little-understood work, mainly because no context for its apparently anomalous features has been found – even among Ockeghem's other masses. Thus the cycle has tended to portray Ockeghem as a man determined to assert his independence at the very beginning of his career. And by extrapolation, it has led to the view that the composer remained an individualist throughout his creative life, whereas it is now becoming increasingly clear that stylistic individualism was a general tendency for mass composers in the 1460s and 70s.[96] The root problem may lie in Bukofzer's point of departure: he compared Ockeghem's *Caput* Mass with an English cycle from the 1440s (the anonymous *Missa Caput*) and a Continental cycle from after about 1480 (Obrecht's *Missa Caput*) in order to illustrate different approaches to the same mass tenor. Although the comparison was most illuminating, it was perhaps inevitable that Ockeghem's mass would emerge as a highly individual work, and its composer as virtually an extremist.

If the *Missa Caput* is compared with Domarto's *Missa Spiritus almus* it becomes apparent that Ockeghem may have been neither an extremist nor an individualist. Bukofzer's verdict[97] that Ockeghem 'renounces with amazing consistency all customary means of articulating a composition: cadences, profiled motives, symmetrical phrase structure, lucid interrelation of parts, imitation, sequences, prominence of one voice over the others, and so forth' is valid, but leaves room for qualification. One of the features to which Bukofzer drew attention was the marked 'avoidance of cadences'.[98] However, at least 104 cadential progressions can be detected in Ockeghem's mass, and although this is a relatively

---

[95] Bukofzer, *op. cit.*, pp. 278–92.
[96] Wegman, 'The Anonymous Mass *D'ung aultre amer*'.
[97] Bukofzer, *op. cit.*, p. 291.
[98] *Ibid.*, p. 284.

Example 11. Ficta in Petrus de Domarto, *Missa Spiritus almus*: (a) Kyrie II, bars 8–11 (top voice 9_1: sharp in TrentC 88 and VatS 14; passage does not survive in PozU 7022); (b) Kyrie II, bars 19–21 (top voice 20_1: sharp in TrentC 88 and VatS 14; passage does not survive in PozU 7022); (c) Crucifixus, bars 22–9 (top voice 26_3 and contratenor 26_1: sharps in TrentC 88, VatS 14, and PozU 7022; passage does not survive in LucAS 238); (d) Et in terra, bars 8–11 (contratenor 9_1: sharp in LucAS 238 and TrentC 88; passage does not survive in PozU 7022).

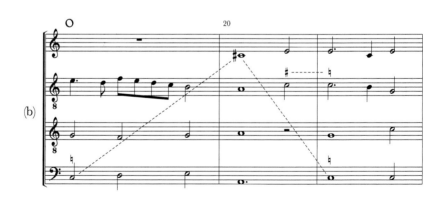

Example 11 *continued*

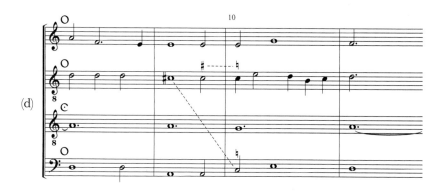

291

small number, it compares well with Domarto's ninety-nine cadential progressions. The ratio between 'v–i' and 'vii$_6$–i' cadences is also very similar: 5:99 in Ockeghem, and 8:91 in Domarto (this relationship was to be reversed dramatically in the early 1460s). Of course, these figures should be related to the lengths of the masses, since substantial differences in length could render these comparisons meaningless. However, the two cycles are of approximately the same length: *Spiritus almus* has a length of 1535 tempo units (i.e. semibreves in O; breves in ₵ and O2), whereas this figure is 1679 in *Caput*. On average, then, Ockeghem has one cadential progression in every 1679/104=*c*. 16 tempo units, while Domarto has one in every 1535/99=*c*. 15.4 tempo units.

One could argue that Ockeghem may have conceived his mass at a completely different speed from Domarto's, and that tempo units may not therefore represent a reliable standard. The only objective means of deciding on this is to measure the relative rhythmic densities in the two upper voices, and to express them in terms of average note values.[99] Application of this method leads to the surprising discovery that Ockeghem and Domarto appear to have conceived their masses at virtually the same speeds: the average note values under O are 0.897 semibreve in *Spiritus almus* and 0.891 semibreve in *Caput*, while those under ₵ are 1.251 and 1.222, respectively. It is quite rare for fifteenth-century compositions to approach one another so closely in terms of rhythmic density.[100] The relationship observed here may well indicate that the two masses are of approximately the same date.[101]

Bukofzer's remarks on the use of imitation in the *Missa Caput* also need to be qualified.[102] Although imitation does not occur particularly often in Ockeghem's mass, there are some interesting attempts to introduce imitation involving three voices (Credo bars 49–51; Agnus I bars 27–9), imitation of relatively long phrases (Credo bars 49–51; last three bars of Agnus III) and even a short

---

[99] See Wegman, 'Concerning Tempo in the English Polyphonic Mass'.
[100] See, for example, the tables in Wegman, 'Concerning Tempo in the English Polyphonic Mass', pp. 49 and 55.
[101] *Ibid.*, pp. 54–8.
[102] Bukofzer, *op. cit.*, pp. 281–2.

sequential repetition (Sanctus bars 72–4).[103] These do not affect the general picture outlined by Bukofzer – which is remarkably similar to that in *Spiritus almus* – but they may indicate that Ockeghem's mass was slightly more advanced than Domarto's.

Other parts of Bukofzer's analysis read like a description of the *Missa Spiritus almus*: the D Dorian modality, with frequently pre-scribed ficta; the undistinctive melodic writing; the low ranges, dark sonorities, and the frequent sixth chords in the lowest voices; the sometimes unorthodox dissonance treatment; and the closely spaced cross-relations.[104] Additional correspondences have been mentioned above. Ockeghem's mass seems somewhat more advanced, though, particularly in that the 'bass' (i.e. not the transposed tenor) is at times more equal, contrapuntally speaking, to the upper voices, and that the build-ups towards the final cadences are more energetic and less tentative than those in *Spiritus almus*.[105] Even so, placing the two cycles side by side, one cannot help being struck by their close stylistic similarities.

It may be significant that both Domarto and Ockeghem were associated with the church of Our Lady at Antwerp in the 1440s. However, the documentary evidence does not support the hypo-thesis of a possible 'Antwerp connection'. Ockeghem worked at Antwerp for only about half a year (1443–4) and he had already moved to Moulins by the time Domarto came to work there (Ock-eghem has been traced in Moulins in 1448).[106] Domarto himself seems to have worked at Antwerp for only about three or four weeks (see note 1 above). If, as I suggest, Ockeghem's mass is somewhat more advanced than Domarto's, it becomes impossible to attribute the strong similarities in style to both composers' association with Antwerp. The most one can say is that the two

---

[103] All references to Plamenac, ed., *Johannes Ockeghem: Collected Works*, II (2nd, corrected edn), American Musicological Society: Studies and Documents 1 (n.p., 1966), pp. 37–58.

[104] Bukofzer, *op. cit.*, pp. 279–89.

[105] *Ibid.*, pp. 283–6.

[106] For Ockeghem's activity at Antwerp, see the transcriptions of the relevant documents in M. Bovyn, '(Van) Ockeghem's te Dendermonde', *Johannes Ockeghem en zijn tijd* [exhibi-tion catalogue] (Dendermonde, 1970), p. 58. Ockeghem earned 145 *loten* between 24 June and 24 December 1443; these would have covered at least twenty weeks (cf. note 1 above). Between 25 December 1443 and 23 June 1444 he earned 67 *loten*, which would have covered at least nine weeks.

Rob C. Wegman

pieces seem to have been written in a common stylistic idiom. That idiom may well have been widespread outside Antwerp.[107]

On the other hand, the evidence collected here does add up to a suggestive pattern, converging with amazing consistency on the Low Countries. The *Missa Caput* is the only mass by Ockeghem to respect and maintain the notational shape of the pre-existent tenor. Ockeghem built his mass on a borrowed structural plan, a procedure which was to be repeated in three masses from the 1480s or 90s, all three probably associated with the Southern Netherlands: Obrecht's *Missae Caput* and *L'homme armé*, and the anonymous *Missa de Sancto Johanne Baptista*.[108] The relationship between Ockeghem and Obrecht is strengthened by several allusions to the former's *Caput* Mass in the latter's 'imitation'.[109] Obrecht's other cycles show him to have been a late follower of the 'school of Domarto'. Busnoys had joined that 'school' earlier, very probably after his move to the Low Countries. The latter's *Missa O crux lignum* faithfully adopts the techniques that Domarto had applied in his *Missa Spiritus almus*. The choice of the *O crux lignum* melody indicates that Busnoys's mass was most probably written in the Southern Netherlands, like Obrecht's motet *Salve crux* which uses the same tenor. Domarto's mass, in turn, can be associated with the Southern Netherlands on the basis of its relationship with Busnoys's motet *Anima mea liquefacta est*. Finally, Ockeghem's *Missa*

[107] It should be pointed out, however, that the later careers of some of the musicians employed at the church of Our Lady in the 1440s (cf. Van den Nieuwenhuizen, *op. cit.*, pp. 38–40) suggest that it was one of the major musical centres in the Low Countries. Johannes Pullois was not the only Antwerp singer to move to the Papal Chapel. *Heer* Lucas Wernerii (1430–4) is almost certainly the Lucas Warner / Varnery who has been traced in the Papal Chapel in 1443–50 (F. X. Haberl, 'Die römische "schola cantorum" und die päpstlichen Kapellsänger bis zur Mitte des 16. Jahrhunderts', *Vierteljahrsschrift für Musikwissenschaft*, 3 (1887), pp. 223–5). *Heer* Jan Philiberti (1441–2) worked at the Ducal Chapel in Ferrara in 1445–50 and from 1450 to 1482 at the Papal Chapel (Lockwood, *op. cit.*, pp. 48–52 and 316–17; Haberl, *op. cit.*, pp. 226–31). *Heer* Claus Philippi (1441–2) is presumably identical with the Ferrarese singer Niccolò Philippo di Olanda, who worked in the Ducal Chapel in 1446–81 (Lockwood, *op. cit.*, pp. 47–50 and 316–22). Leonard Bruynbaert (1444–6) has been traced at Ste Gudule, Brussels, in 1464–5 (Haggh, *op. cit.*, p. 561). Jan Kijc (1441–3) worked at 's-Hertogenbosch from 1443 until his death in 1467–8 (A. Smijers, *De Illustre Lieve Vrouwe Broederschap te 's-Hertogenbosch* (Amsterdam, 1932), pp. 87–133). Pieter Laurentii (1449; cf. Figure 1) also worked at 's-Hertogenbosch, in 1469–71 (Smijers, *De Illustre Lieve Vrouwe Broederschap*, pp. 142–4).

[108] See Wegman, 'Another "Imitation" of Busnoys's *Missa L'homme armé*'.

[109] Bukofzer, *op. cit.*, pp. 270–1.

Caput is in terms of style a virtual twin of Domarto's *Missa Spiritus almus*. To summarise: with the exception of the anonymous *Missa Gross senen*, all the evidence – both direct and circumstantial – points to the Low Countries as the area where a small group of composers shared the same compositional ideals and habits. Their combined output abounds with cross-references, interrelationships, and identical approaches to compositional problems.

So there are good grounds for believing that Ockeghem's *Missa Caput*, if perhaps not composed in Antwerp, was at least written in the north. Although the mass stands alone in the composer's output, its anomalous features fit remarkably well into the pattern outlined above. The stylistic divide between the *Caput* Mass and Ockeghem's later cycles could be explained by the composer's move to central France, which was permanent by 1451 at the latest (his whereabouts in the periods 1444–8 and 1448–51 are unknown).[110] The use of a canon 'per totam missam' could be seen as the direct consequence of Ockeghem's decision to respect the notational shape of the tenor, something for which a context can be found in the north. Admittedly we are entering the realm of speculation, and it would be rash to propose a date in the 1440s (when Ockeghem was not yet permanently in France) purely on these circumstantial grounds. Yet there is additional evidence that seems to point to the same conclusion.

To present that evidence, however, we need to shift our angle radically and examine Domarto's and Ockeghem's masses from an entirely different standpoint: the early history of the four-voice mass. If the two cycles are as archaic as their style seems to indicate, there is a strong probability that they were among the first to be written for four voices, at least on the Continent. But was that really a momentous event? If it was, where and when did four-voice writing in the mass start? And what could this tell us about the possible date and origin of the cycles by Domarto and Ockeghem?

Although four-voice writing as such had been widespread throughout the first decades of the fifteenth century, the four-part

---

[110] For Ockeghem's appointment in 1451, see L. Perkins, 'Musical Patronage at the Royal Court of France under Charles VII and Louis XI (1422–83)', *Journal of the American Musicological Society*, 37 (1984), p. 522.

texture with a low contratenor (that is, a contratenor moving beneath the borrowed tenor) was a relatively late invention, probably from the 1440s.[111] This new type of scoring took Europe by storm, rapidly superseded all other textures in sacred music, and was to remain the dominant texture until well into the sixteenth century. The key to its success lay not in the fact of its four voices, but in the invention of a new contrapuntal *function*, the low contratenor. This voice added more to the three-part texture than just an element of sonority: it was free to assume total control over the harmonic progressions, a task that had not previously been associated with any single, freely composed voice. Whether contemporary composers perceived the innovation in these harmonic terms is unknown, but the distinctive nature of the new voice part was soon recognised in terminology: scribes began to specify the voice as '*low* contratenor' from the 1460s onwards. That seems but a trivial change. But its significance is apparent from the huge semantic development that the mere adjective *bassus* (and its modern derivative 'bass') have since undergone. This word rapidly assumed overtones beyond its literal meaning: rather than denoting a relative range, *bassus* came to signify the *identity* of the new voice part as a functional component in polyphonic textures.

The new four-voice texture is not yet found in such early sources as AostaS D19, TrentC 87 and 92 (all of which must have been finished by about 1445). Among the first works to employ it (albeit somewhat tentatively) are Dufay's late isorhythmic motets *Fulgens iubar* and *Moribus et genere*, both believed to date from the late 1440s.[112] But the first work to handle the texture with truly 'modern' confidence and assurance is the anonymous English *Missa Caput*, whose earliest copying date, in TrentM 93, is *c.* 1451–2 (see note 88 above). This is an extraordinarily bright and lively work, characterised by energetic harmonic rhythm, triadic sonorities and almost obsessive repetitions of melodic and harmonic progressions. The mass derives these qualities mainly from the new role of the low contratenor (labelled 'tenor secundus' in the most authentic

---

[111] The early development of this voice in three-part music is described in H. Besseler, *Bourdon und Fauxbourdon: Studien zum Ursprung der niederländischen Musik* (2nd edn, Leipzig, 1972), pp. 45–65.

[112] D. Fallows, *Dufay* (paperback edn, with revisions, London, 1987), pp. 60–1 and 309.

sources, but rechristened 'contratenor secundus' and 'bassus' in less authentic ones).

The *Caput* Mass must have made an enormous impact on the Continent.[113] Perhaps the invention of the low contratenor was chiefly responsible for this, in which case Ockeghem's decision to let the tenor overtake the upstart contratenor in its search for the depths seems like a comment on the novelty. As we have seen, Domarto's *Missa Spiritus almus* shows several signs of English influence: dovetailed duos involving a scaffold tenor, simultaneous rests, and the use of *prolatio maior* augmentation. The first of these English-inspired habits implies a four-part texture, so it seems likely that Domarto was acquainted with English four-voice mass music. Ockeghem's *Missa Caput* shows the same signs (with the exception of ₵ augmentation)[114] and is, moreover, an early witness to the anonymous *Caput* Mass's popularity on the Continent. Since the patterns of transmission were almost certainly unilateral (English music being distributed on the Continent, but not the other way round), it seems reasonable to assume that the new four-part mass texture was an English invention.

Continentals probably first came to know that texture in the anonymous *Missa Caput*. In Trent this was the only four-voice mass available until the copying of the likewise English *Missa Veterem hominem* in TrentC 88, around 1456.[115] I will shortly present evidence that the Trent repertory of the early 1450s may reflect the repertory available elsewhere more closely than its peripheral nature would suggest. In its earliest Continental source (TrentM 93), the *Caput* Mass appears as the first of a unified group of six cycles, whose movements (Kyries excepted) are distributed over three separate sections of the manuscript (Gloria, Credo, Sanctus–Agnus Dei). Of these six cycles it is the only one to employ a low contratenor. The remainders of the three manuscript sections were filled with miscellaneous mass movements and other compositions, all in three voices. So the *Caput* Mass stands out in this anthology, not only because of its prominent position, but also because of its unique scoring.

---

[113] Wegman, 'Another "Imitation" of Busnoys's *Missa L'homme armé*', pp. 189–90.

[114] The reason for this, of course, is that the tenor of the anonymous English *Missa Caput* was not written in major prolation in the first place.

[115] For the date, see Saunders, 'The Dating of the Trent Codices', p. 91.

Reinhard Strohm has pointed out that the early TrentM 93 version of the *Caput* Mass contains several Continental corruptions and adaptations,[116] so the cycle must have been in circulation for some time by the early 1450s. The early version lacked the Kyrie and contained an adapted version of the cantus firmus. It was this version on which Ockeghem modelled his own *Caput* Mass. A second, more authentic (and complete) version would reach the Continent later, probably before 1463.[117] So it is the TrentM 93 version that is relevant to Ockeghem and Domarto, and on which we must focus our attention. It need hardly be repeated that TrentM 93 is a peripheral manuscript for English music, and that it could be dangerous to rely on it too much. On the other hand, since the *Caput* version in this source was related to the one available to Ockeghem, it is extremely important to disentangle the little evidence this manuscript provides. In this context three points need to be made.

First, the original nucleus of TrentM 93 (gatherings 1–30) was organised into various sections according to a logical, preconceived plan, roughly as follows: *Asperges/Vidi aquam* (gathering 1), Introit settings (gatherings 2–8), Kyries (gatherings 9–11), other Mass settings, organised according to movement (Gloria, Credo, Sanctus–Agnus; gatherings 12–30).[118] Although several copying stages can be discerned in the original nucleus, the copying process as a whole must have taken place within a relatively short time span. This indicates that the Trent scribe had before him a sizable collection of exemplars, which he wished to copy systematically in a rationally structured anthology. Other evidence tends to support that assumption. Throughout the original nucleus, the scribe left pages blank, apparently in the expectation that other relevant pieces would reach him in years to come. However, by the time the entire original nucleus of TrentM 93 was copied into another

---

[116] R. Strohm, 'Quellenkritische Untersuchungen an der Missa "Caput"', *Quellenstudien zur Musik der Renaissance*, II: *Datierung und Filiation von Musikhandschriften der Josquin-Zeit*, ed. L. Finscher, Wolfenbütteler Forschungen 26 (Wiesbaden, 1983), pp. 155–65.

[117] *Ibid.*, pp. 165–9.

[118] For this and what follows, see in particular: M. Bent, 'Trent 93 and Trent 90: Johannes Wiser at Work', *I codici musicali Trentini*, ed. Pirrotta and Curti, pp. 84–111, and R. Strohm, 'Zur Rezeption der frühen Cantus-firmus-Messe im deutschsprachigen Bereich', *Deutsch-englische Musikbeziehungen: Referate des wissenschaftlichen Symposiums im Rahmen der Internationalen Orgelwoche 1980 'Musica Britannica'*, ed. W. Konold (Munich and Salzburg, 1985), pp. 9–38.

manuscript (TrentC 90, of *c.* 1452–8),[119] the only relevant pieces that could be added were six Kyries.[120] So the arrival of the TrentM 93 exemplars seems to have been a singular event, or at least a series of such events within a relatively short time span.

Secondly, Margaret Bent has shown that the Trent scribe worked from various exemplars, whose repertory he rearranged, at least in part, in his own manuscript.[121] One of these exemplars must have been a collection of six masses, arranged by complete cycles (though lacking the Kyries), of which *Caput* was one. The preconceived size and layout of TrentM 93 suggests that when the scribe started to distribute the movements of these masses over the various sections, the other movements that he would use to complete those sections were already available. These latter movements may well have been selected from various exemplars, but those exemplars, again, seem to have arrived in Trent as a group.

Thirdly, the Ordinary movements copied in TrentM 93 (including the Kyries, but excluding blank pages and miscellaneous motets) fill a total of 221 folios (or 442 pages). This was an enormous quantity of Mass music to be circulating in southern Germany around 1451–2, and it is well worth asking where that repertory might have come from. Altogether there are thirty-eight Kyrie settings, and sixty-three compositions comprising Gloria, Credo, Sanctus and/or Agnus Dei (individual movements, pairs, or cycles). Attributions are known of only twenty-seven of the 101 compositions. Dufay is the best-represented composer (with eight compositions), followed by Binchois and Power (each with three). A considerable portion of the repertory must be English, either because of ascriptions or on the grounds of style. If, as I suggest, the repertory copied by the Trent scribe came from a more or less unified collection of exemplars, that collection was most likely compiled in the north.

There is a possibility that the collection had been available in Cambrai only two years before TrentM 93 was copied. In 1449–50, the Cambrai scribe Simon Mellet was paid for copying, among other things, two (duplicate) books of *cantus modernorum*, each containing 228 folios, 'in quibus sunt Kirieleison, Et in terra, Patrem,

[119] Saunders, 'The Dating of Trent 93 and Trent 90', pp. 69–70.
[120] Bent, 'Trent 93 and Trent 90: Johannes Wiser at Work', pp. 92–7.
[121] *Ibid.*, pp. 85–8.

Sanctus, Agnus, et cetera talia'.[122] The presence of two similarly arranged repertories of Mass music within a span of about two years – one comprising 228 folios, the other 221 – is suggestive. It opens the possibility that an enormous quantity of recent Mass music, comprising about twenty gatherings, began to circulate as a unit in the north during the late 1440s, reaching Cambrai around 1449–50, and moving south to Trent around 1451–2. In both centres the repertory (if indeed it was the same repertory) was rearranged according to movement. The predominance of English music in TrentM 93 would suggest that the assembly of the collection had started after a body of previously unknown Mass music was released from England. Rearranged, and enriched with Continental products, it became a collection that any musical centre (or musician) would have been eager to copy in its entirety. In fact this is precisely what happened in Trent: only a few years after TrentM 93 had been completed, Johannes Wiser copied the entire original nucleus straight into the manuscript that has survived as TrentC 90. Even then the anonymous English *Missa Caput* was the only cycle to contain the novelty of a low contratenor.

If this hypothesis is correct, it becomes easy to see Domarto's *Missa Spiritus almus* and Ockeghem's *Missa Caput* as early Continental responses to the English *Caput* Mass. For the enormous collection of new Mass music, in which this latter cycle figures so prominently, is likely to have stimulated and inspired composers wherever it arrived. The crucial question, of course, is where that collection might have been assembled. It would be unwise to indulge too much in speculation here, since the existence of the collection is hypothetical to begin with. But two possibilities need to be examined.

First, the dominance of compositions by Dufay in the attributed part of TrentM 93 may suggest that the assembly had taken place at Cambrai. A strong counter-argument to that possibility is the fact that the Proper cycles that were copied at Cambrai in 1449–50 did not reach Trent until about 1456–62.[123] If, as I suggest, the TrentM 93 repertory represents a distinct wave of transmission

---

[122] C. Wright, 'Dufay at Cambrai: Discoveries and Revisions', *Journal of the American Musicological Society*, 28 (1975), pp. 225–6.
[123] They were copied in TrentC 88; see Planchart, 'Guillaume Du Fay's Benefices', pp 140–69.

from the north, the second such wave must have swept to southern Germany around 1460. This latter wave must have contained compositions that had been copied alongside the 'first wave' repertory in some centres (the TrentC 88 Proper cycles), Continental masses written in response to that repertory (Ockeghem's *Missa Caput*, Domarto's *Missa Spiritus almus*, Simon de Insula's *Missa O admirabile commercium*) and new English music (the second, more authentic version of the anonymous *Caput* Mass). So if we are correct in assuming that the TrentM 93 repertory was largely identical with the mass repertory copied at Cambrai in 1449–50, both repertories must ultimately go back to a third one; otherwise the Cambrai Proper cycles of 1449–50 ought to have been transmitted in the first 'wave'.

Secondly, the presence of a cycle attributed to the Antwerp composer Pullois, in the same set of six masses as *Caput*, may indicate that the TrentM 93 repertory had been assembled at Antwerp. But again, the case is extremely tenuous. The cycle in question was already widely distributed by about 1445 (since it appears in TrentC 87) so its inclusion in the set of six masses need not necessarily have taken place at Antwerp. Moreover, the ascription to Pullois has been questioned on good grounds by Gareth Curtis, who argued that the mass is more likely to be an English work.[124]

But whatever the origins of the 'Pullois' mass may have been, it seems at least significant that an Antwerp composer either wrote, or was widely held capable of writing, a cycle in the English style. It gives a hint of the climate in which English Mass settings were received in the Southern Netherlands: not as any old music, to be transmitted and performed passively, but as a source of exciting compositional ideas. Confirmation for that climate is provided by Simon de Insula's four-voice *Missa O admirabile commercium* (TrentC 88, fols. 304ᵛ–311ʳ). Although stylistically quite distinct from Domarto's *Missa Spiritus almus* and Ockeghem's *Missa Caput*, it contains so many English-inspired features, and so resembles the English *Caput* Mass in its style, that it was once believed to be an English work.[125] It is in this climate that the *Caput* Mass must have

---

[124] G. R. K. Curtis, 'Jean Pullois and the Cyclic Mass – or a Case of Mistaken Identity?', *Music & Letters*, 62 (1981), pp. 41–59.

[125] See C. Hamm, 'A Catalogue of Anonymous English Music in Fifteenth-Century Continental Manuscripts', *Musica Disciplina*, 22 (1968), p. 72. Reinhard Strohm has identi-

been received in the Low Countries, and it is in this same climate, I suggest, that Domarto's *Missa Spiritus almus* and Ockeghem's *Missa Caput* were written.

We may now attempt to draw our conclusions. The evidence as it now stands suggests that four-voice mass writing on the Continent started in the Southern Netherlands in the late 1440s, in response to the recent transmission of the anonymous English *Missa Caput*. Ockeghem and Domarto may have been among the first Continental composers to imitate the novel features of that cycle. They did so in a common stylistic idiom, which, although it contains some English features, is remarkably dissimilar from that of their model. By the 1460s, when a younger generation of composers had entered the stage (Busnoys, the *Gross senen* composer), that stylistic idiom had become obsolete. Ockeghem himself would also abandon it in his later masses. However, the novel and unique philosophy underlying Domarto's cantus firmus usage was to remain a source of inspiration, until about 1500, to a small number of composers working in the Netherlands, particularly Busnoys and Obrecht.

Whether by virtue of its age, its later influence, or its musical qualities, the *Missa Spiritus almus* remained a cycle that carried special *auctoritas*. It was a work considered worth having, in Trent, Bruges, Naples, Poznań and Ferrara alike. The cycle remained important enough to be criticised by a leading theorist in the 1470s, and to remain in circulation until the 1480s, when its style must have seemed hopelessly out of date.

Now, five centuries later, outdatedness is no longer a relevant criterion. To us the historical continuum of the fifteenth century has become one-dimensional, a flat surface in which consecutive events are simultaneously present. We are able to see Domarto's mass as a work conditioned by its own past, while breaking away from it in many ways, and at the same time in terms of the future that it helped shape. From both vantage points, the *Missa Spiritus almus* emerges as a key work in the history of the fifteenth-century mass.

University of Amsterdam

fied Simon 'de Insula' with Simon de Vromont, who was master of the children at St Pierre, Lille, in 1450–1 and 1460–1 (Strohm, 'Insular Music on a Continental Island').

POSTSCRIPT

After this article had gone to press I learned that David Kidger had just completed a study entitled 'The Music and Biography of Petrus de Domarto' (M.A. thesis, University of California at Santa Barbara, 1990). His thesis unfortunately arrived too late to be taken into account here, but I would like to express my gratitude for his generosity in sending it to me. Mr Kidger is currently preparing an edition of Domarto's complete works (Newton Abbot, forthcoming).

REVIEW

CRAIG WRIGHT, *Music and Ceremony at Notre Dame of Paris, 500–1550.*
Cambridge, Cambridge University Press, 1989, xviii+400 pp.

The earliest Christian shrine at Paris, as at Rome, was built on the
ruins of the pagan edifice and its observances. An eighth-century
oratory dedicated to the Virgin Mary spawned a new church,
c. 860, that rapidly became established under royal protection as
the foremost ecclesiastical foundation of the settlement. The construction of the present cathedral was begun in 1160, and with it
the building of one of the most enduring symbols of the high
medieval renaissance, whose physical structure was reinterpreted
in every century until the eighteenth. Thus it may be that 'institutions preserve their name, but they change their qualities, or, main-
taining the type of their original structure, they exercise new
powers altogether', and that 'under such conditions alone are they
truly, actively and healthily permanent'.[1] The cathedral of Notre-
Dame was more than the physical edifice, and more than the sum
of its members' concerns, for – as is well known – institutions have
a habit of developing a momentum of their own. But they are also
in part the creation of their historians, and nowhere is this clearer
than in the interpretation placed on their traditions.

Craig Wright is no stranger to the history of institutions and the
musical cultures they supported, and indeed his new study of
Notre-Dame shares much with his earlier *Music at the Court of
Burgundy*.[2] Both books draw heavily on a large and voluminous
archive (in this case the long series of cartularies and chapter

---

[1] H. H. Vaughan (Inaugural Lecture; University of Oxford, 1848); quoted in L. Stone,
The Past and the Present (London, 1981), pp. 4–5.
[2] *Music at the Court of Burgundy, 1364–1419: A Documentary History*, Musicological Studies 28
(Henryville, Ottawa and Binningen, 1979).

registers now in series LL at the Archives Nationales, Paris), and in both Wright has chosen to anatomise his subject under a series of musical subject-headings. There are, however, also some differences. Wright's study of Notre-Dame is a much more sophisticated account of its subject, and a greater sense of the 'institution' emerges from its pages. But this book is not the continuous history of music at the cathedral over more than a millennium that its title might seem to imply. For its centre of gravity is firmly located in the late twelfth and early thirteenth centuries, with the polyphony of what has become known as the Notre-Dame school, and to a certain extent this subject forms the mirror to which both earlier and later manifestations of musical activity are held up for comparison. Broadly stated, Wright's thesis is that the period between c. 1150 and 1250 saw a remarkable efflorescence of musical culture centred on Notre-Dame, supported in general by the rising political fortunes of the Capetians, but more particularly by links with the internationally famed intellectual culture of the Parisian Schools. In later centuries, Wright argues, the cultivation of polyphony was less actively encouraged, as the bias in the composition of the cathedral chapter shifted away from the university in favour of royal secretaries and lawyers. Only in the early sixteenth century did polyphony fully revive under the stimulus of an imperialising state ceremonial and the French crown's policy of enlisting the major civil and ecclesiastical institutions of the metropolis in its service. A similar pattern is cast here for the careers of individuals: while late twelfth-century musicians – and particularly composers – at Notre-Dame were fundamentally schoolmen destined for brilliant clerical careers, it was only much later that singers and organists came to the fore as the leading exponents of polyphonic composition. In much of this, according to Wright, the guiding principle was fidelity to local tradition. This, as elsewhere, formed a part of the institution's self-image, but it served also to suppress further liturgical change and elaboration in an establishment where, it is argued, the restrictive content of ecclesiastical dogma and decree were taken more than usually seriously.

This is an unexpected picture, at least in so far as it defies the conventional expectation of growth, reflected at every turn in the historiography of late medieval and early modern music. But Wright's approach to the institution and his taxonomy of its constituent parts are in fact highly traditional. A series of subdivided studies is used to define the roots and character of positions within the cathedral, and the duties and rewards of its musical personnel, and to chronicle the emergence of the organ. A similar approach is taken in the two much larger essays, concerned with liturgy and ceremonial, that form the opening chapters of the book, and in the final chapter devoted to performance practice. Here the emphasis once again lies with definitions: with the origins of individual practices, and with tracing the shape of the ritual complex as a whole. There are important gains here, particularly for the study of performance practice. The carefully documented thesis, advanced in the introduction, that the acoustic character of medieval buildings changed over the medieval centuries, as they acquired more hangings and internal walls, affords an important new perspective on the physical context for the performance of polyphony. There are clear and authoritative statements on the use of the organ. And the account provided here of the choirboys' contribution to the musical life of the church prompts some invaluable observations on the genesis of a group of pieces, by Brumel and others, seemingly written for boys' voices alone.

But there are also problems. Wright's approach owes much to a nineteenth-century positivist tradition in institutional historiography, heavily legal and constitutional in emphasis, and this has consequences for his view of Notre-Dame and its musical and ceremonial traditions as well as for the study's wider historical perspectives. In particular, the author has a tendency to organise his materials into a seamless, centralised development, often with the effect that chronologically remote musical cultures are assimilated to the more familiar and accessible patterns found in later periods. At a more subtle level this pattern of explanation also encourages the reader to view the music history of the cathedral as a sealed unit, immune from external change. The chapter dealing with the liturgies of the early medieval cathedral provides a case in point; here a continuous – and by implication complete – narrative is built exclusively from the surviving remains. In this period alone, for example, Paris was variously an important town in the Merovingian kingdom, a royal appanage where the king's powers were secondary to those wielded by the Duke of the Franks (923–87), and only much later truly a royal capital. Chance survivals alone do not reveal how the cathedral and its musical cultures fared against this shifting background.

Indeed the question of quite how widely the contextual net should be cast remains one of this book's main unresolved dilemmas. Wright is fully aware of the dangers of writing the history of a fictitious 'musical institution', and frequently comments that the musical tradition of Notre-Dame was neither autonomous nor the main motivating concern in the life of the cathedral. But he nonetheless fails at a number of points to establish an adequate context for the musical events and practices described. This is perhaps most noticeable, and most understandable, in the self-contained histories of the organ, organists and choirboys. It is also a problem in the use made by Wright of political narrative, where frequently the characterisations of personages and gestures are too idealised or theatrical to carry force. The account of events surrounding the coronation of Henry vi, King of England, as King of France provides a case in point: 'With the illustrious King Henry v of England, the mad Charles vi of France, the brilliant but sybaritic Duke Philip the Good of Burgundy, the saintly Joan of Arc, and minor players such as Sir John Fastolf among the *dramatis personae*, the stage was full of vivid, forceful personalities against a general background of misery and suffering caused by decades of warfare and economic decline' (p. 206). The background to the coronation in the politics of English rule in France is here largely ignored ('It is not necessary to recount the events that led to the English domination of France and its capital'); the account of the ceremony thus becomes an annalistic pageant, in which musical details make star appearances. It may be that this is an extreme case, but there are numerous other instances in which context seems to be supplanted with mere *Zeitgeist*. A further manifestation of this problem is the lack of a wider urban and ecclesiastical backdrop for the cathedral and its musical cultures. The chapters devoted to the Notre-Dame school inevitably draw in the university, but the impact of relations between the cathedral and, for example, St-Denis, the Ste-Chapelle or its own dependent churches are not systematically covered. Nor is there an account of relations with the metropolis, although, as Wright points out, confraternities and other objects for the devotions of the urban bourgeoisie appear to be less in evidence here than at other cathedral churches in northern France. But even if

Notre-Dame was 'introspective, defensive, protective' (p. 359), it is not always clear to what extent this facet of the character of the institution is the author's own creation. Indeed the whole issue of causation is taken somewhat for granted: *a priori* goals – the inevitability of musical developments and the complicity of surrounding circumstances – tend to emerge as the most important factors.

In the end much of this comes down to the use of sources. A large archive is an asset, but it also presents special problems of its own. The sheer coherence and consistency of the materials can give a false sense of continuity; similarly, the wealth of archival detail can convey the impression that records will speak for themselves and thus need no further interpretation, particularly where these records are descriptive in character. At a number of points there is a tendency for Wright's text to become simply a narrative of entries from the registers of the chapter's deliberations, and to a certain extent he emerges from these passages as the prisoner of his materials. But there is also a more fundamental commitment in Wright's work to the use of documents, a credo even. It is not just that documents contain what the historian seeks and are thus held to be unimpeachable witnesses to his conclusions; administrative records are somehow made to form part of the exposition of the subject, and their discovery and presentation becomes almost an end in itself. There is a sense here in which the patterns of archival work have been translated into a rationale, a structure for Wright's narratives and explanations. There is seldom a recognition that documents reflect the preoccupations of the administrative institutions from which they emanate, rather than the expectations of posterity. One might wonder too how the ritual practices and traditions of the cathedral were reflected in the records of other bodies, for example the Parlement of Paris, where the chapter frequently brought cases concerning precedence and ceremonial. Admittedly there are numerous musicological studies in which administrative records are treated in this way, and no doubt nuance in such sources is easily missed. Even so, I am inclined to think that the problem manifests itself in a more extreme and systematic form here than elsewhere.

The main and undeniable contribution of this book lies in its account of polyphony at Notre-Dame in the twelfth and thirteenth centuries, where Wright conclusively links the repertories of organa preserved in F with the liturgical usage of the cathedral.[3] Other attempts have of course been made to connect the contents of this manuscript, and of the two other major Notre-Dame sources, W_1 and W_2, with Paris, most notably by Heinrich Husmann.[4] He argued for the division of the repertory into two layers: the first of these he associated with the work of Leoninus and the church of Notre-Dame; the second and later layer was, in his view, the work of Perotinus and could be linked with a number of churches and abbeys in Paris, in particular St-Germain-l'Auxerrois. Wright substantially revises this picture, demonstrating convincingly that these repertories were created solely for the metropolitan church and rejecting the notion of a broad chronological enlargement in the contents of the *Magnus liber organi*. Building on the work of Baltzer, Roesner and others,[5] he also shows that the three principal surviving sources of this repertory were not related in a single tradition, in which W_1 represented the original form of the collection, and W_2 and F its successors. Instead, F emerges as the earliest source and the most closely linked with the cathedral; W_1 and W_2 present localised versions of the same tradition, whose contents reflect the deletion of material to agree with the liturgical customs of other churches. This marks an important historiographic shift, and it also gives new meaning to the comment made by the Bury monk ('Anonymous IV'), writing *c.* 1285, that the organa of the *Magnus liber* were later 'abbreviated'. The main strength of this work lies in its grasp of the Parisian liturgy and here the detailed comparative scholarship of the earlier chapters pays off in full. Wright's theory that the dissemination of this repertory was effected by Parisian *magistri* returning to their native lands is less fully supported; nonetheless, the close involvement of this group with organum has recently been amply demonstrated by Christopher

---

[3]   In what follows F denotes Florence, Biblioteca Medicea-Laurenziana, Pluteus 29.1; W_1 and W_2 denote respectively Wolfenbüttel, Herzog-August-Bibliothek, MSS 628 and 1099.

[4]   'The Enlargement of the *Magnus liber organi* and the Paris Churches St. Germain l'Auxerrois and Ste. Geneviève-du-Mont', *Journal of the American Musicological Society* [hereafter *JAMS*], 16 (1963), pp. 176–203.

[5]   R. A. Baltzer, 'Thirteenth-Century Illuminated Miniatures and the Date of the Florence Manuscript', *JAMS*, 25 (1972), pp. 1–18; E. H. Roesner, 'The Origins of W_1', *JAMS*, 29 (1976), pp. 337–80, and 'The Problem of Chronology in the Transmission of Organum Duplum', *Music in Medieval and Early Modern Europe: Patronage, Sources and Texts*, ed. I. Fenlon (Cambridge, 1981), pp. 365–99.

Page using a completely different set of materials.[6] In addition, Wright develops further his views on the individual authors of this repertory, first exposed in a study that identified Leoninus with the Leonius who was a canon of Notre-Dame, a master in the university, and the author of a biblical commentary and Latin poetry.[7] A comparable picture is drawn for Perotinus, here identified (following Gastoué[8]) with the succentor of the cathedral between 1207 and 1238, who was a canon from 1198, and before that possibly chaplain to Maurice de Sully (d. 1196). For all their attraction, however, a question mark still hangs over these identifications.[9]

The strengths and shortcomings in Wright's treatment of the Notre-Dame school broadly reflect those found elsewhere in the book. In particular his narrative is too much orientated towards confirming prevailing orthodoxies, and in pursuit of this end the uncertainties and qualifications underlying the arguments presented here are often lost. Thus Wright frequently refers to the *Magnus liber organi* (the phrase appears only in Anonymous IV's famous description) as though it were synonymous with F ('F, W¹ and W²

---

[6] C. Page, *The Owl and the Nightingale: Musical Life and Ideas in France, 1100–1300* (London, 1989), pp. 134–54.

[7] 'Leoninus, Poet and Musician', *JAMS*, 39 (1986), pp. 1–35.

[8] A. Gastoué, *Les primitifs de la musique française* (Paris, 1922).

[9] A wider range of administrative sources than those used by Wright (confined mainly to the Notre-Dame chapter registers and the published registers of papal letters) may prove more informative, particularly in the case of Petrus succentor. One such source, which came to light only after this review went to press, is a dossier of legal records produced by an excommunication case between the Bishop and municipality of Laon in 1235–6 in which Petrus succentor was appointed one of the judges, now Laon, Archives Communales, FF1, nos. 1–10. These documents deal not only with the formal hearing, but also a wide range of judicial business related to the case: the procurement of witnesses, correspondence with the papacy (by whom the judges were appointed), adjournments and appeals against individual procurators and witnesses whom the plaintiffs or defendants wished to have struck off. Four documents issued under the judges' own seals survive: a mandate to the priest of the church of St-Jean, Laon, to take the deposition of one Jean Piot, clerk (FF1, no. 3; 27 January 1235); a summons to the *curé* of the church of Ste-Geneviève, Paris, to appear as a witness before Jacques, Archdeacon of Thérouanne, and André, canon of Laon (no. 4; Thursday after Passion Sunday, 1235); a signification to the prior of Issy of a papal rescript summarising the case, sent to the judges at the request of the town (no. 5; 11 July 1235); a record of an objection heard by the judges concerning one of the witnesses produced by the town against the bishop, and an adjournment for pleading and judgement (no. 10; 29 July 1236). No. 4 bears a fragment of the judges' seal. For a brief abstract of the contents of this dossier, see A. Matton and V. Dessein, *Inventaire sommaire des Archives communales antérieures à 1790 . . . Ville de Laon* (Laon, 1885), fasc. F, pp. 1–2. For a further case, not noted by Wright, in which Petrus was appointed judge by the Holy See in 1221, see A. Teulet *et al.*, *Layettes du Trésor des Chartes*, 4 vols. (Paris, 1863–1902), I, p. 515 (no. 1443) (from Archives Nationales, J 198B, no. 137).

... preserve the *Magnus liber organi*' (p. 237); 'the ninety-two compositions of the *Magnus liber organi*' (p. 257)). Similarly, its ascription to Leoninus, again known only from Anonymous IV, and that of its contents, are often taken for granted ('the one hundred or so organa in the *Magnus liber organi* of Leoninus', or the reproduction of F, fol. 99, described as 'the *Magnus liber organi* of Magister Leoninus' (p. 245)). Anonymous IV, looking back to the time of Leoninus, is said to 'chronicle the evolution of musical style and genres for nearly a century' (p. 236), but this is a modernistic reading of the monk's text; there is no close analysis of this passage, or appreciation that this description may have rationalised parts of its subject in terms of the musical thought of the late thirteenth century. Other points of details arise elsewhere in the book. Were the *pueri/pauperes pueri* who 'signed' important charters of the church in the late eleventh century really 'choirboys' (p. 166), or did this term denote – as it did in a number of contemporary sources including the Bayeux Tapestry[10] – adult servants, or others of inferior standing? The 'Normans' who laid siege to Paris in the 880s (pp. 68–9) are 'Les Normands' in the source cited by Wright, i.e. Vikings. And it seems odd to conclude that polyphonic settings of the Ordinary of the Mass and motets were not part of the musical culture of the fourteenth-century cathedral simply because they are not mentioned in its statutes (p. 344). Finally, it is doubtful that Gilles Binchois was in the service of William de la Pole, Earl of Suffolk, in 1424 (pp. 207, 302). The source for this claim, a deposition by Guillaume Benoît (on which a venerable, but still valuable, study has been missed[11]), states merely that Binchois made a rondeau *Ainsy que a la foiz m'y souvient* and was rewarded with a gift of cloth; the nature and context of this gift suggest that it was a one-off recompense, and do not demonstrate the existence of a formal attachment. There is some evidence also that by this time Binchois was already in the employ of the Duke of Burgundy.

The true commitment of the nine studies that make up this book is ultimately to an established tradition in music historiography, rather than to the history of the institution, or to its wider social

[10] See for example K. Leyser, 'Early-Medieval Canon Law and the Beginnings of Knighthood', *Institutionen, Kultur und Gesellschaft im Mittelalter: Festschrift für Josef Fleckenstein*, ed. L. Fenske *et al.* (Sigmaringen, 1984), p. 550.

[11] C. Rutherford, 'The Forgeries of Guillaume Benoit', *The English Historical Review*, 30 (1915), pp. 216–33.

and cultural aspects. The traditional concerns of musicology in this period – in particular composer biography, the location and dating of compositions and the exploration of liturgico-musical issues – are well and often admirably served. There is much here to be welcomed and much for which the book will be regularly, indeed copiously, cited. The low priority accorded to the broader historical perspective, or to historical explanation, is in places something of a disappointment. But this is perhaps a pointer to the direction that future research, and more detailed studies of the musical cultures of Notre-Dame, might now take. That this book, in consequence, opens up rather than seals off its field of inquiry is an important strength.

Andrew Wathey
Royal Holloway and Bedford New College,
University of London

Early Music History
Back Volumes – Special Offer!

Back Volumes of *Early Music History* are now available for only £25 each (airmail £8 per volume extra) – normal price £34.

Contents of Volume 1 include:
Bent & Bowers The Saxilby fragment · **Blackburn** A lost guide to Tinctoris' teachings recovered · **Bryant** The *cori spezzati* of St Mark's: myth and reality · **Irwin** The mystical music of Jean Gerson

Contents of Volume 2 include:
Conomos Experimental polyphony, 'according to the...Latins', in late Byzantine psalmody' · **Roesner** Johannes de Garlandia on *organum in speciali* · **Rumbold** The compilation and ownership of the 'St Emmeram'codex (Munich, Bayerische Staatsbibliothek, Clm 14274)

Contents of Volume 3 include:
Agee The Venetian privilege and music-printing in the sixteenth century · **Fabbri & Nádas** A newly discovered Trecento fragment: scribal concordances in late-medieval Florentine manuscripts · **Morell** New evidence for the biographies of Andrea and Giovanni Gabrieli

Contents of Volume 4 include:
Murata Classical tragedy in the history of early opera in Rome · **Bianconi & Walker** Production, consumption and political function of seventeenth-century Italian opera

Contents of Volume 5 include:
Berger The relationship of perfect and imperfect time in Italian theory of the Renaissance · **Lockwood** Adrian Willaert and the Cardinal Ippolito I d'Este: new light on Willaert's early career in Italy, 1515-21

Contents of Volume 6 include:
Bernstein A Florentine chansonnier of the early sixteenth century: Florence, Biblioteca Nazionale Centrale, MS Magliabechi xix 117 · **Boorman** Some non-conflicting attributions, and some newly anonymous compositions, from the early sixteenth century

Contents of Volume 7 include:
Forney Music, ritual and patronage at the Church of Our Lady, Antwerp · **Levy** On the origin of the gradual · **Welker** New light on Oswald von Wolkenstein

Contents of Volume 8 include:
Guidobaldi Music publishing in sixteenth- and seventeenth-century Umbria · **Haar** Cosimo Bartoli on music · **Woodley** Tinctoris's Italian translation of the Golden Fleece statutes: a text and a (possible) context

Contents of Volume 9 include:
Atkinson Franco Cologne on the rhythm of organum purum · **Monson** Elena Malvezzi's keyboard manuscript: a new sixteenth century source · **Wathey** The Peace of 1360-1369 and Anglo-French musical relations

For details contact:

Cambridge University Press
The Edinburgh Building, Cambridge
CB2 2RU, UK
40 West 20th St, New York, NY
10011-4211, USA